walkbritain

Great Views

The Ramblers' top 50 walking routes
to Britain's finest views

ramblers
at the heart of walking

Credits

Managing Editor: Dan French.
Text: David Abram, Dan French.
Editorial: Helena Smith,
David Abram, Dan French.
Design: Phil Tristram, Tim Harrison.

Front cover photo: Old Harry Rocks/
Guy Edwardes.
Back cover photos: Kestrel/John
Gardner. Clifton Bridge; Golden Cap;
Giant's Chair/Guy Edwardes.

All photos © Ramblers except:

Iain Brownlie Roy: pp178-179; p181;
p183; pp255-259.

Peter Cairns: p121; p127.

Ian Cameron: p221; p223; p261; p263.

Guy Edwardes: p5; p9; p11; p22; p23;
pp24-25; p33; pp40-41; p43; p45;
p47; p61; p62; p63; p67; p75; p87;
p92; p129; pp136-137; p145; p147;
p153; p159; p160; p193; p195; p201;
p204; p215; p217; pp241-245; pp247-
253; pp267-272; pp296-299; pp319-
325; pp335-338; pp342-345.

John Gardner: p21; p55; p56; p57;
p69; p73; pp94-95; p97; p99; p101;
p106; pp108-109; p111; p115; p165;
p166; pp185-191; pp209-211; p227;
p229; pp234-235; p283; p285;
pp289-294; pp303-309; pp327-330;
pp366-372.

Mark Hamblin: p14; p81; pp312-315;
pp350-351.

Simon Kitchin: p275.

Colin Prior: pp374-375.

With special thanks to the following Ramblers volunteers who provided
invaluable assistance in suggesting and checking the routes:

Vic Royce
Edwina Moore
Sheila Smith
Peter Butterworth
Allan Thomas
Dawn Davies
David Dixon
Des Garrahan
John Esslemont
Margaret Norwood
Jinney Kucera
Ginnie Hall
Tony Law
Margaret Kettlewell
Zetta Flew
Andrew Morgan
Ros Blaylock
Felicity Leenders
Bridget Read
Mike Garner
Bernard Smith
Annie Clement
Canon Edmund Plaxton
Keith Wadd
Ray Curtis-Clarke
Seonaid Miller
Alan Bowley
Roy Howells

Jacqueline Stow
Paul Brown
David Chapman
Ann Marks
Henry Mason
Bill Millar
Sue Shewan
Shirley Lunt
Angie Guest
Jack Greer
Louise Moore
David Gibson
John Biggins
Robert & Carole Woolcott
Myra Clark
Neil Schofield
Terry Howard
Geoffrey Williams
David Murfin
Bernardette McDougall
Andrew Richards
David Oldfield
Mike Murgatroyd
Ann Dodd
Ivan Smith
Lisa Gibson
Robert Powell

Foreword

Mark Horton,
BBC Coast presenter
and archaeologist

The landscape of Britain is utterly amazing and the only way to see it properly is on foot. This guide will take you to fifty of the most spectacular places on our islands, where you can breathe in the views and feel the shape of the land under your feet. It will take you to some of the rocks that are as old as you can find anywhere in the world, to where the landscape seems to have remained unchanged for millennia or where the scars of man's industry have been healed by nature to create their own very special place.

As an archaeologist, I have traced many of these walks myself looking for ancient remains. With Ordnance Survey map and compass in hand, I have peered through the heather to find some stone, or tried to make out the shape of earthworks through the bracken. In these walks you can find it all – Palaeolithic caves, prehistoric settlements, Roman forts, or medieval castles and the work of Victorian engineers. But to me, it's the thrill of the unexpected discovery, or some new idea about how our ancestors once lived, that makes walking in the British landscape so wonderful.

Our coast is of course the very best bit. It's where land and sea join together creating a unique environment, and somehow defines our special island identity. It is no coincidence that many of the walks in this guide lead you to the seashore, where you can experience some of the strangest shapes that nature can produce and enjoy those extraordinary views. Much our coast is now becoming accessible for the first time, and we are beginning to appreciate how important it is to save and conserve.

Put on those walking boots, take out map and compass, and explore. There is nowhere else in the whole world quite like it!

Contents

The view south from the top of Leith Hill tower, the Surrey Hills. Walk 26

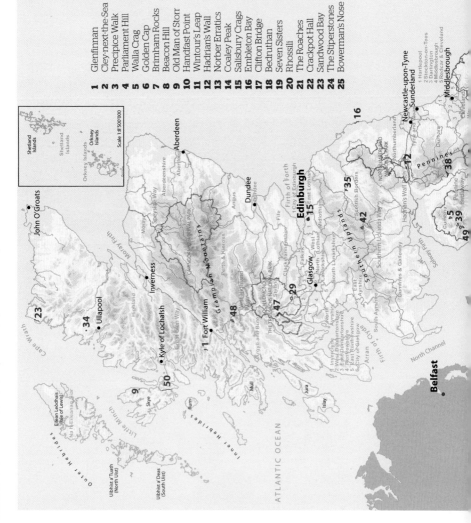

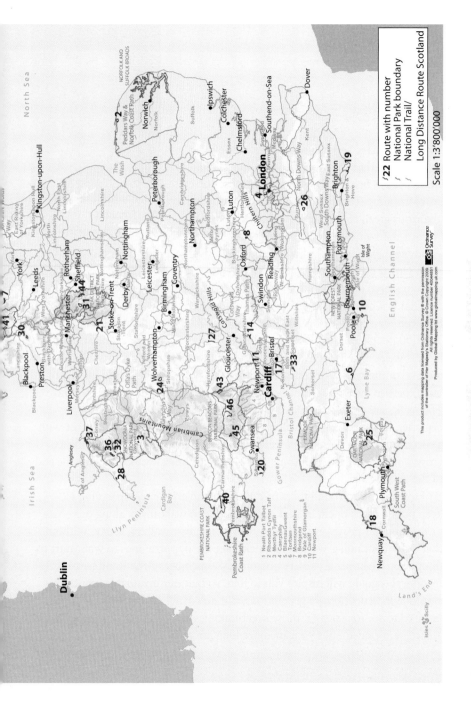

Route with number `22`
National Park boundary
National Trail/
Long Distance Route Scotland

Scale 1:3'800'000

1 Neath Port Talbot
2 Rhondda Cynon Taff
3 Merthyr Tydfil
4 Caerphilly
5 Blaenau Gwent
6 Torfaen
7 Monmouthshire
8 Bridgend
9 Vale of Glamorgan
10 Cardiff
11 Newport

Preface

Tom Franklin,
Chief Executive of the
Ramblers

Many of us have seen those wonderful television programmes that show off the most spectacular landscapes in Britain. They give us glimpses of heart-stopping scenery – the dramatic coastlines, luxurious green forests and riverbanks, and that "top-of-the-world feeling" on our mountains – and we think, "wow, that's so beautiful!" I've often settled down on my sofa to watch them and wondered how I could get to see those views for myself.

That is where this Ramblers guide comes in. For 75 years, the Ramblers has been *the* expert on walking, leading over 28,000 walks involving over 300,000 people each year. It's a privileged position for any organization to be in, and we're especially grateful to the many Ramblers volunteers who shared their favourite walks, or tested routes for this guide. We've made full use of our expertise throughout this book, but written it with the novice in mind. The walks are graded from easy to challenging, so whether you're an absolute beginner, or have been walking all of your life, there's a route – together with a spectacular view – that will suit you. As your experience and confidence grow, you may want to try some of the more technical walks towards the end of the book.

However, it's through the work of the Ramblers – in campaigning to keep public paths open, or making it possible to walk freely along our coast or through our heathland – that so many can enjoy walking today. Without that work continuing we would quickly see the opportunities to walk start to disappear. We hope, if you are not already a member of the Ramblers, that reading this guide will inspire you to join, so that our invaluable work can continue to benefit future generations. But above all, we hope you will be inspired to see for yourself those breathtaking views, and that the experiences will remain etched onto your memory long after the walk ends.

Approaching Yr Eifl, the Lleyn peninsula. Walk 28

Introduction

Great views, like great walks, come in all shapes and sizes. Some derive their power from extraordinary landforms; others from the sense of distance and space they inspire, or from a new perspective they may yield on familiar terrain.

A great view can hinge on something elemental – such as the sea, a spectacular waterfall or rock formation. Or it can be defined by something artificial: a bridge, roofscape or ancient fortress.

This book features walks based on fifty of the very finest views across Britain, encompassing sights as diverse as you'd expect from an island as multi-faceted as ours. The one thing they all have in common is that none of them can be seen from any road. To experience their special atmosphere you have to press beyond the limits of the internal combustion engine and, simply, walk.

The physical exertion that may be required in each case varies considerably. At one end of the scale are leisurely, flat ambles of less than an hour; at the other, full-day yomps through some of the roughest, wildest corners of the Scottish Highlands. You can, however, be sure that the effort involved, whether minor or major, will only serve to enhance your experience of the panoramas themselves.

A view is never so impressive as when you've had to walk for it. Why? Because a little effort can pay huge dividends. It's a scientifically proven fact: as little as thirty minutes of gentle walking each day can have a significant impact on one's health, inducing a sense of wellbeing, reducing stress and anxiety, and reviving the mind and body.

The French have a neat expression for the phenomenon: *"un jour a pied vaut quatre de santé,"* which roughly translated means "one day on the trail equals four of health." By that reckoning, you have in your hands a recipe for seven months of top form, with some of the most wonderful spectacles in Britain as incentives.

You probably won't manage all fifty in a year, but hopefully should find plenty of inspiration for the future in the routes we've devised, and the photographs, writing and maps that accompany them.

When it comes to picking views and walks, the Ramblers has a distinct advantage. Leading over 28,000 walks across Britain each year, the charity's membership has been working out the best places to

ABOVE: Rhossili, the Gower peninsula. Walk 20

walk on a massive scale for decades, co-ordinating a wealth of local knowledge and experience.

Ramblers volunteers were not only happy to spill the beans on their favourite viewpoints, but also agreed to test the routes after they'd been written up and walked by our researchers – a "belt-and-braces" approach unique to this guide.

As you'd expect, we were inundated with suggestions. To make it onto the short-list, however, a walk had to tick a few important boxes first. The Ramblers promotes walking for health and as green mode of transport. So our vistas had to be not only potent inducements to get walking, but also worth leaving the car behind to see.

The routes had to cover a broad ability range, including some that could be tackled by children and older walkers. So an upper limit of 16km/10miles was set. Only one

walk – the last – pushes well beyond this ceiling, and when you see the view it leads to you'll understand why we felt this exception worthwhile.

We also wanted to reflect Britain's great potential as a walking destination, showcasing this island's magnificent scenic variety and cultural landscapes, which meant including both urban and rural walks

Above all, however, the view the walks led to had to be inspirational. To illustrate this, all the photos in the guide were commissioned and shot from points along the route – and we think you'll agree, they're fantastic. The photographers responsible for them won't mind us saying, that, alluring though their images may be, they only approximate the first glimpse of a truly great view. To understand just how wonderful these scenes are in real life, the only way is to get walking...

How to use this guide

The walks are arranged throughout the book in order of difficulty, beginning with the easiest and progressing through colour-coded gradations to the more challenging. Walk ratings are featured at the top right of the page along with a general location map. A key map featuring the location of all the walks appears on pages 6-7. Each walk starts with a short introduction sketching out the route's main selling points, followed by an **AT A GLANCE** box summarizing essential information; **ON YOUR WAY** providing interesting context; and **WALK IT** delineating the route.

Difficulty
Indicates the level of fitness recommended before undertaking the walk, as dictated by route terrain and overall ascent/descent. You should also bear in mind the duration/distance and specific terrain information in At a Glance.

Navigation
Deals with the general difficulty in navigating on the ground, and level of outdoors experience and equipment required before attempting the walk.

Route Status
Indicates how open and usable the path is; the condition of signs, stiles, gates etc, or whether you can expect to encounter any obstructions en route.

For an explanation of the ratings see page 17.

At a glance

Where The general location of the walk.
Why A few reasons to pull on your boots.
When A recommended time of year to make the journey.
Downsides Small disadvantages worth knowing about in advance.
Start/Finish The specific location of the beginning and end points of the route, including grid references.
Duration Timespan based on stopwatch recordings of the walk at a steady pace of between 2 and 3mph, depending on the terrain. Does not include rest breaks.
Distance This is worked out using GPS data, or mapping software.
Cut It Short For some of the longer walks, we've suggested a point en route, linked to public transport, where you can curtail the walk if you wish.
Terrain Indicates the type of ground you can expect to encounter.
Maps We recommend you obtain these maps before undertaking the walk. Ramblers members can hire OS maps from our central office (see inside front cover) for a small fee.

ON YOUR WAY

Here we set out interesting background to the route and its landmarks. This might comprise historical anecdote,

46 Pen-y-Fan

On your way

The distinctive appearance of t
Beacon range, with its text-boo
dip slope profiles and table-top

some layman's geology, perhaps a few snippets on unusual flora, fauna or folklore – basically anything likely to deepen your appreciation of the ground you'll be covering. Rather than dipping into it during the walk, it's the kind of thing you might want to read as a primer, or while relaxing in the pub afterwards. **EMBOLDENED** text relates to the Walk It instructions.

WALK IT

This is the section you'll probably find yourself referring to most while actually

walk it 46

on the trail. It comprises a step-by-step set of instructions designed to help you navigate your way around the course. As far as possible we have avoided using technical language, though you'll find useful grid references creeping in from time to time (see p16 to learn more about grid references). This description should, however, not be used as a stand-alone guide, but in conjunction with the map, on which we highlight the route and its various numbered stages.

Sprinkled throughout are **EMBOLDENED** place names. These correspond with similarly emboldened names in the On Your

Way section, enabling you to flick more easily between the two.

ROUTE MAP

The route of the walk is highlighted in red over an extract from the relevant Ordnance Survey Explorer series map, along with various numbered stages which relate back to the Walk It instructions. In most cases we've shrunk these maps to fit our pages. Although perfectly serviceable as reference aids, they're not nearly as useful as a hard copy of the map itself, which in all instances we recommend you obtain in advance, and use accordingly to the advice set out on page 16.

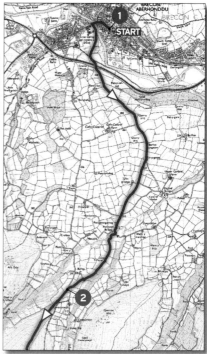

Route profile

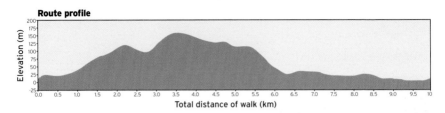

Total distance of walk (km)

ROUTE PROFILE (ABOVE)

Route profiles are graphic representations of the distances covered relative to the heights gained and lost along the route. They do not, however, show precisely the gradients included. In the majority of cases the lines run far more steeply than does the actual ground walked.

CHECKED BY

The Ramblers group that checked the route prior to publication. If you have comments about any of the routes in this guide please contact the Ramblers central office (see inside front cover).

 Getting There
Wherever possible, the start and finish of each walk lie within easy distance of public transport, details of which are posted here. In a few instances we've had to suggest an alternative method to reach the trailhead.

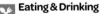 **Visitor Information**
Usually the local Tourist Information Centre, but occasionally other useful sources for visitors are identified.

Eating & Drinking
Commendable places close to the walk where you can revive and refuel.

 Sleeping
Recommended accommodation on or near the route. You can find many of these listings, and more, at www.ramblers.org.uk/accommodation.

More Info
Useful resources for those who want to find out more about the area. Includes books and websites used to research the walks.

More Walks
For anyone planning to spend longer in the area described, we've pinpointed relevant guide books published

by, or in conjunction with, the Ramblers. These guidebooks are all available to buy through the Ramblers website www.ramblers.org.uk.

Abbreviations

L = Left
R = Right
N, S, E & W = North, South, East & West
TIC/VIC = Tourist/Visitor Information Centre
NT = National Trust

BELOW: Loch Skeen, Dumfries & Galloway. Walk 42

Walk ratings

DIFFICULTY

1 = Easy
Gentle walks over mostly even gradients. Suitable for anyone who does not have a mobility difficulty, a specific health problem or is seriously unfit. Pushchairs may need to be lifted over occasional obstructions.

2 = Leisurely
Mainly on unsurfaced rural paths, and may involve some sustained ascents and descents. Requires a reasonable level of fitness.

3 = Moderate
May include rough terrain, with steep climbs and descents. Requires a good level of fitness.

4 = Challenging
Physically demanding route that includes sections over very steep ground, hills and rough country. This route is for people with an above average level of physical fitness.

NAVIGATION

1 = Novice
Navigation is easy, and the route is clearly identifiable on the ground, or follows linear features such as walls or a coastline. Requires no specialist skills. Comfortable shoes or trainers can be worn.

2 = Easy
Route over mountainsides, valleys, hilltops or exposed moorland, mostly following paths, but which might be more challenging in poor visibility. Basic map and compass skills required (see p16 for a quick start guide to navigation). Specialist footwear and warm, waterproof clothing are recommended.

3 = Moderate
Includes some pathless stretches across wild valleys, open moorland, mountain- or hill-tops with few distinctive features; fairly straightforward to navigate in fine weather but tricky if low cloud descends. Good map and compass skills essential; GPS recommended. Specialist footwear and warm, waterproof clothing are essential.

4 = Experienced
Route may involve high exposed ridges, and sections over open, featureless moorland, crags and/or exposed mountain ridges where route confusion is likely, even in clear visibility. Simple handholds may be required on steep rock. May involve walking in isolated areas away from traffic and/or assistance. Specialist equipment required, and advanced map and compass skills essential. GPS strongly recommended. Walking boots and warm, waterproof clothing are essential.

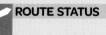

ROUTE STATUS

1 = Open
Clear, unobstructed paths throughout, with no access problems. Signs, stiles and gates are in good condition.

2 = Usable
Some sections of the route are partially obstructed or overgrown making progress difficult. Signs, gates and stiles are in an adequate condition.

3 = Obstructed
Sections of the route are severely overgrown, or obstructed making progress very difficult. Access rights are ambiguous and/or restricted by poor and misleading signs. Some damaged signs, stiles or gates.

4 = Closed
Sections of the route require immediate attention before the walk can be completed.

PROBLEMS

You shouldn't encounter any routes in this guide with a status of "Obstructed" or "Closed", but if you do come across a problem on a walk – whether it is overgrown vegetation, a blockage, a broken stile or misleading signage – please report it to the Public Rights of Way Officer at the local highway authority, detailing the location and nature of the problem with grid references and photos if possible. (Find a complete list of highway authorities at www.directgov.gov.uk.)

Make sure you send a copy of your correspondence to the Ramblers so it can follow up on the status of your claim. Post it to Ramblers central office (see inside front cover) or online at www.ramblers.org.uk/rights_of_way.

Quick start guide to navigation

If you've never used a map and compass before, the following tutorial should be all you require to complete walks in this guide with a Navigation rating of 1 or 2. For walks rated 3 or 4 we recommend further reading and practise: see www.ramblers.org.uk/info/practical for detailed information about navigation and maps, including a list of recommended books and course providers. Basic map and compass skills are useful for many walkers, and essential in hilly, heavily wooded or remote areas. Even if you are following a signed route or using a good guidebook, knowing how to find your way around with a map will give you more options for diversions and escape routes, and will help you if you get lost or encounter damaged or missing signs.

THE MAP

Maps are simply an accurate picture of the ground as seen from above, scaled down from life size and with symbols to show particular features and landmarks. The best and most comprehensive walkers' maps of Britain are the 1:25,000 scale Ordnance Survey (OS) Explorer series in orange covers. They include a range of geographical features and landmarks at a high level of detail, including field boundaries, heights shown as contours, and "spot heights". They also show rights of way (except in Scotland), permissive paths, many long-distance paths, off-road cycle paths, open access land (including new access land in England and Wales), locations of shorter circular walks and nature trails, information centres, visitor attractions and many other useful features.

On a 1:25,000 map such as an OS Explorer, one unit of length on the map represents 25,000 units on the ground, so 1cm on the map represents 0.25km on the ground.

A right of way marked on a map will often be visible as a distinct path or track on the ground but in less well-walked areas the path may not be visible. Footpaths and bridleways are marked as green dashes on Explorer maps.

Contours are lines connecting points of equal height above sea level. Together with spot heights, they are the means used by the map-maker to portray the shape of the land, its height, the form taken by hills and valleys, steepness of slopes, and so on. On Explorer maps, the interval between contours is five metres in lowland areas and ten metres where mountainous.

At random points along many of the contour lines a number is shown to indicate its height, always printed so that the top of the number points uphill. Every fifth contour line is printed more thickly than the others. The closer together contours are the steeper the ascent or descent for the walker. Spot

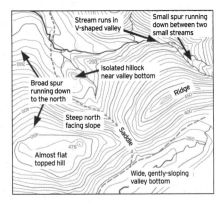

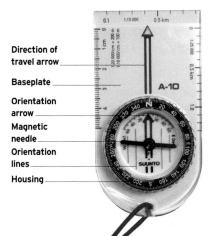

Direction of travel arrow

Baseplate

Orientation arrow

Magnetic needle

Orientation lines

Housing

A-10

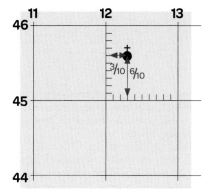

The grid reference of the church is: AB123456

heights – shown as a number beside a dot – appear at strategic points, often along roads where they level out at the top or foot of a hill. These can be a useful guide where contour height numbers are infrequent.

THE COMPASS

In lowland areas you could rely purely on map-reading skills, but using map and compass together will help you follow your route with much more accuracy, particularly in woods. In the hills a compass is essential, especially when visibility is poor. Choose an "orienteering" or "protractor" compass with a rectangular baseplate of reasonable size so you can turn it while wearing gloves, and with clearly-marked km/m scales that can be read in poor light.

OTHER USEFUL EQUIPMENT

For effective navigation in addition to the map and compass you should also carry: a reliable watch, to help judge speed and monitor progress; a torch, especially on short winter days; something to protect non-waterproof maps, such as a map case or polythene bag; and a GPS which provides an accurate check of position at any time, and can be programmed to provide directions for a complete route (they can of course lose their satellite signal in unfavourable conditions, or run out of batteries).

SIX FIGURE GRID REFERENCES

Grid references are a means of pinpointing specific locations on a map. You'll find them cropping up throughout this book, set out in the following way, with two letters preceding six numbers: AB123456.

The two letters at the start correspond to the overarching National Grid, which divides the UK into boxes of ten-square-kilometres. Because each of these squares is so large you generally only find one or two pairs of letters appearing on any 1:25,000 OS Explorer map.

The big grid is in turn sub-divided by much smaller squares of 1km, delineated by pale blue lines. Each line is numbered by bold blue figures running up the vertical and along the horizontal axes of the map.

To translate a grid reference into an actual point on the ground, look at the first two digits in the sequence (eg AB**12**3456). These correspond to the vertical blue lines – or "eastings", because they run in numerical order from west to east (left to right). Locate the relevant number on the edge of you map ('12'). Then do the same for the fourth and fifth digits (AB123**45**6) – known as the "northings", because they run from south to north from the bottom to the top of the map sheet.

Next trace these two easting and northing lines to the point they intersect. Finally, look at the third and sixth numbers AB12**3**45**6**. These represent further divisions of the one-kilometre square you're looking at into 100-metre parcels (which you'll have to visualize because they're not drawn).

So for our particular grid reference (AB123456), once you've identified easting line '12', and followed it to where it crosses northing line '45', count '3' tenths of the square east (to the right), and '6' tenths to the north (upwards), then look at the point these latter, invisible lines cross each other – this gives you your precise location.

You can practise locating grid references with any of the OS map recommended for the walks in this guide. Start by situating the reference for the start point, given under "Start/Finish" in "At a glance", then try your hand at others specified in the route description.

BASIC NAVIGATION

There are two basic techniques detailed here that should be mastered using a map and compass:

Setting the map – aligning the map in the direction you are facing so features on the map match those on the ground.

Travelling on a bearing – walking over open ground on a bearing taken from the map.

SETTING THE MAP

Setting the map (or orientating the map) helps relate the map to the countryside by turning the map so that your direction of travel is at the top. When done, all features on the map and on the ground are seen to lie in the same direction from your current position, and the north edge of the map points to north on the ground.

Travelling on a bearing

If you want to travel from your present position to a landmark you cannot see, or check the direction of a path in poor visibility, use the following procedure:

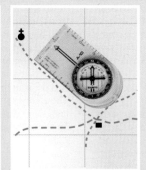

1 Place the edge of the compass so that you line up your destination and the starting point.

2 Holding the baseplate firmly, turn the circular housing so that the orientation lines are parallel with the north-pointing grid lines.

3 Take the compass off the map and hold it flat, as shown. Turn your body to align the red end of the compass needle to the red end of the orientating arrow ("red on red"). The direction of travel arrow now points along the path to take.

The map can be set by aligning it to prominent features in the landscape, or by compass. Place the compass on your map in any orientation (or even just drop it into your map case). Then rotate the map and compass together so the compass needle aligns with any north-pointing gridline, with the red end of the needle pointing to the top of the map (ignore all other parts of the compass).

Wherever you decide to walk in Britain please follow the Countryside Code or the Scottish Ourdoor Access Code.

The Countryside Code
- Be safe - plan ahead and follow any signs
- Leave gates and property as you find them
- Protect plants and animals, and take your litter home
- Keep dogs under close control
- Consider other people

For the full code,
visit www.countrysideaccess.gov.uk/ or www.countrysidecodewales.org.uk.

Scottish Outdoor Access Code
- Take personal responsibility for your own actions and act safely
- Respect people's privacy and peace of mind
- Help land managers and others to work safely and effectively
- Care for your environment and take your litter home
- Keep your dog under proper control
- take extra care if you're organizing an event or running a business

For the full code,
visit www.outdooraccess-scotland.com.

At the heart of walking

Britain is a nation of walkers. Nearly eight in ten of us walk regularly for pleasure. Although the extent of land available for public recreation is greater than ever before, it should not be taken for granted. For seventy-five years the Ramblers has played a key role in shaping Britain's landscapes and extending people's opportunities to walk in some the nation's most wild and magical places.

HOW IT ALL BEGAN

In the late nineteenth century a growing number of people turned to the countryside as a haven from increasing industrialization. The health benefits brought by escaping the towns and cities led to a strong desire to protect the right to walk on footpaths and enjoy open spaces. Organized rambling groups soon began to spring up all over the country.

London-based walking clubs such as the Sunday Tramps consisted largely of writers, philosophers and professional types; but from the earliest days it was men and women from working class backgrounds who took an active interest in safeguarding access to the hills and moors, particularly around the industrial cities in northern England.

Federations of rambling clubs developed in several northern cities: Manchester Ramblers' Council in 1919; Liverpool and District Federation in 1922; and Sheffield and District Federation in 1926. But by the early 1930s many in the outdoor movement were beginning to call for a national body to represent the interests of walkers, and so the National Council of Ramblers' Federations was established. In 1934 the decision was taken to change the council's name, and on 1 January 1935 the Ramblers' Association was officially founded.

POST WAR YEARS

The Ramblers soon proved itself to be an effective campaigning organisation. One of its earliest successes came with the passing of the National Parks and Access to the

Countryside Act 1949. The Act supplied the framework for the creation of official long-distance paths, and led to the establishment of national parks.

The Ramblers campaigned for the highest designation of landscape protection for all ten areas defined by the Act, and in 1951 Britain's first national park was inaugurated in the Peak District. The following decade saw the establishment of national parks in the Lake District, Snowdonia, Dartmoor, Pembrokeshire Coast, North York Moors, Yorkshire Dales, Exmoor, Northumberland and the Brecon Beacons.

Long-distance paths took a little longer. It was not until 1965, thirty years after the Ramblers' general secretary Tom Stephenson first proposed a 250-mile route along the 'backbone' of England, that the Pennine Way became the country's first official long-distance footpath. The success of the Pennine Way opened the door for the creation of more recreational trails, many of them based on routes proposed and surveyed in detail by the Ramblers.

In the following years the Ramblers worked hard to put other provisions in the 1949 Act into effect. Maps of footpaths were drawn up by county councils throughout England and Wales, and Ramblers volunteers collected every

Britain's first national trail was proposed by the Ramblers 75 years ago.

available scrap of evidence and submitted thousands of claims for footpaths to be included on these 'definitive maps' of rights of way. Many paths we walk today would probably have disappeared had it not been for the Ramblers' vigilance in those years.

Throughout the 1960s and 1970s the Ramblers grew in strength and secured many more benefits for walkers. They worked with Ordnance Survey to include rights of way on their maps – so that for the first time people knew precisely where they had a right to walk – and through the Countryside Act 1968 they managed to get footpaths signposted "on the ground". Ramblers Scotland was established in 1967, and Ramblers Wales in 1974, in recognition of the different campaigning needs of these countries.

THE NEW MILLENNIUM
The year 2000 saw one of the biggest milestones in walking history. After decades of campaigning by the Ramblers, the passing of the Countryside and Rights of Way Act 2000 finally granted everyone the "right to roam" in open countryside in England and Wales. The Ramblers again worked with Ordnance Survey to check areas of open access, and these are now shaded in orange on all Ordnance Survey 1:25,000 Explorer maps. This success was closely followed in 2003 by the Land Reform Act granting statutory access rights to almost all land in Scotland, making it one of the most walker-friendly countries in Europe.

THE PRESENT
Today, Britain boasts fourteen nationals parks (with one in development), fifteen national trails, four long-distance routes in Scotland, and hundreds more long-distance paths. An estimated £6.5billion is generated each year as a direct result of recreational walking. All this is underpinned and enhanced by 150,000 miles of public paths, which the Ramblers' work helps to keep open and usable for everyone.

A recent example of this work in action came in 2007, when the Ramblers won a historic victory in the House of Lords. The landmark judgment in what became known as the "Dorset case" means that actions to stop paths being recognized as public rights of way will have to be open and transparent. The ruling will greatly enhance the Ramblers' ability to protect paths in the future.

However, there is currently no general right of access on foot to beaches, cliffs and the foreshore in England or Wales. The Ramblers is campaigning to change this, and has proposed a continuous coastal path with "spreading room" on each side, so that future generations will be able to walk freely along Britain's shoreline. These proposals are included in the Marine and Coastal Access Bill, and look likely to become a reality.

While the Ramblers' influence in opening up the countryside for the public is well established, it was not until the twenty-first century that it began to actively promote the health and social benefits of walking. With a rise in preventable diseases such as obesity and diabetes, and an increasingly sedentary population, the Ramblers launched Get Walking Keep Walking in 2007. The aim of the project is to halt, and ultimately reverse, the overall decline in walking in Britain by helping people, especially in big cities, to improve their health and wellbeing by walking regularly and locally. The Ramblers' Get Walking project is funded by the National Lottery and runs 12-week walking programmes in five major cities across England. Along with the provision of special "DIY packs", it's estimated that by 2012 the

Contrary to popular belief, there is currently no right of access on foot to beaches, cliffs or the foreshore in England and Wales – the Ramblers is campaigning to change this.

project will have helped over 80,000 people kick-start a healthier lifestyle.

SUPPORT THE RAMBLERS

It's the founding principle that everyone, from whatever background, can benefit from greater access to the outdoors, which is still at the heart of the Ramblers' work today. The Ramblers' vision is for a "walking Britain", where walking for fun, transport, and wellbeing is a part of everyday life. It is the greenest, cheapest, most pleasurable activity around, and everyone from toddlers to grandparents, city strollers to seasoned hikers, can enjoy the benefits of walking.

The charity relies on the support of 137,000 members who share this vision, and thousands of volunteers who give up their spare time to achieve these goals.

If you've enjoyed the walks in this guide, and would like contribute to the Ramblers' work, please consider joining (see p384), donating to one of its campaigns, leaving a legacy, or finding a little time to carry out voluntary work in your area. You can find out more about how to get involved at www.ramblers.org.uk.

The Walks

In the Rebels' Footsteps
Glenfinnan

The reckless, active splendid Gaels
Will rise with silken banners.
In hundreds they'll encircle him
Keen to prepare for action...
Like the wild lion's fearful charge
When spurred by ravening hunger.
From the Gaelic by Alexander MacDonald
(translated by John Lorne Campbell in *Highland
Songs of the Forty-Five*)

This is almost sacred ground for Scots. It was at Glenfinnan in August 1745 that Charles Edward Stuart – Bonnie Prince Charlie – unfurled his standard to signal the start of the ill-fated '45 Uprising. Clansmen from across the Highlands had gathered on the shores of Loch Shiel in response to the Young Pretender's rallying call. However, less than eight months later, with the Jacobite army in tatters after the rout at Culloden, barely a handful would still be alive to hear news of the Prince's desperate flight past this same spot.

Ringed by Munros at a nexus of spectacular valleys, Glenfinnan is a site whose setting echoes the events that unfolded here two-and-a-half centuries ago.

A magnificent spread of lake, forest and snow-capped mountains forms an appropriately epic backdrop for the stone pillar erected on the lochside as a memorial to the men and women who died in the rebellion. Viewed from the little hill behind, where the Prince's standard was first raised, the column and its statue of a kilted Highlander appear dwarfed by the scenery – a perfect symbol for the hubris of the Jacobite cause.

Our route makes a pilgrimage to the supposed site of the flag-raising, just above the modern visitor centre on the main Fort William to Mallaig road. Even without its historic associations, this viewpoint – known in Gaelic as "Torr á Choit" ("Mound of the Small Boat") – would rank among the very finest in Scotland, offering as it does a superb panorama over Loch Shiel and across the West Highland Railway viaduct to the mountains of the Corryhully Horseshoe beyond.

From the opposite side of the river, an estate road delves northwards into the beautiful valley of Glen Finnan itself, providing easy access to some of the region's

At a glance

Where Glenfinnan, west of Fort William, Lochaber, Highlands.
Why Monument to the 1745 Uprising; spectacular railway viaduct; possible sightings of red deer, golden eagles and black-throated divers.

When August, to catch the best situated Highland Games in Scotland.
Start/Finish Glenfinnan Visitor Centre (NM908807).
Duration 2hrs 30mins.
Distance 10.5km/6.5miles.
Terrain Mostly level, easy

walking on tarmac or unsur-faced forest tracks, with one short ascent and descent. Wheelchair or pushchair users can follow the first leg to the bothy and then return by the same route.
Maps OS Explorer 398.

wildest, and most spellbinding landscapes – a boon for wheelchair and buggy users, and anyone who wants a break from having to watch their feet every step of the way. It was along this route that the Clan Cameron descended in 1745 to tip the scales of the Jacobite cause in favour of action. We follow their tracks in reverse, along the banks of the River Finnan to the Corryhully Bothy, a pretty stone walkers' hut where you can pause for lunch next to the burn. From there, a higher track leads through a spruce forest down the south side of the valley back to the viaduct and visitor centre.

On your way

Even if you count yourself as more of a "Stoneheart" than a "Braveheart", it's hard not to be moved by the **GLENFINNAN MONUMENT**. Seen in early morning light, rising from the mists of Loch Shiel against that awesome hinterland of crags and luminous water, the lone Highlander holds the equivalent patriotic power of a hundred woad-painted Mel Gibsons. Yet in truth, the rebellion against the English crown that began here in August 1745 was not the unequivocal, purely nationalist uprising it's often characterized as.

The roots of "the Forty-Five" date back to 1688, when King James VII of Scotland (and II of England) was deposed by William of Orange and Queen Mary – a coup mounted by Protestant nobles in fear of a Catholic monarchy. Supported by France and Spain, a series of botched attempts were mounted to restore James to the throne, before his grandson – Charles Edward Stuart – finally took up the "Jacobite" cause.

An effete, 25-year-old dilettante who'd grown up in high-society Italy, Bonnie Prince Charlie was convinced he could achieve what a Spanish army and French fleet had previously failed to, and in July 1745 set sail for Scotland. A bruising encounter with the Royal Navy en route ensured he arrived in the Western Isles deprived of funds, troops and munitions but, undeterred, the Young Pretender (his father, James, was the Old Pretender) pressed on with eight companions to the mainland to find out if letters he'd previously sent requesting support from the Highlands' clan chiefs had borne fruit.

After a tense couple of days sheltering in a barn at Glenfinnan, it seemed as if the uprising was dead in its cradle. But then the drone of pipes swirled down the glen from the north, announcing the arrival of a thousand Camerons, followed by three hundred MacDonnells who'd been delayed in a skirmish with government troops. Charles considered the show of force sufficient and, to cheers and pegs of brandy all round, raised his standard on **TORR Á CHOIT**.

The adventure started promisingly enough, with a string of victories at Perth, Edinburgh and Prestonpans. But as the Highlanders continued southwards towards London, the expected support from English Jacobites failed to materialize. With no word of the promised French invasion and government forces mustering in numbers around Lord Cumberland, the Bonnie Prince and his supporters felt themselves dangerously exposed and, at Derby, decided to turn tail.

Cumberland's well-drilled army caught up with them five months later at Culloden, near Inverness. The redcoats, with their muskets, canons and cavalry, took barely an hour to wipe out an exhausted, poorly armed, under-fed and grossly out-numbered Jacobite force. The defeat signalled the start of a merciless campaign of retribution that would all but wipe out the Highland way of life. Charles Edward Stuart, meanwhile, fled the scene, evading capture for five months by hiding out in remote corners of the Western Isles, despite the £30,000 price tag on this head. Having slipped back to France, he ended his days a disillusioned, drunk and penniless divorcee in Rome in 1788.

Whether Bonnie Prince Charlie was the messianic figure he's sometimes depicted as by Scottish patriots, or merely an opportunist who exploited religious affiliations and clan loyalties to further his family's self-interests, is a subject that will doubtless be debated for centuries. For generations of Scots, however, Glenfinnan and the '45 Uprising will always be remembered with a mixture of pride and regret. Each year, to mark its anniversary, clan members and chiefs gather on the lochside for a traditional Highland Games.

The pillar overlooking the site of the gathering was erected seventy years after the standard-raising by a wealthy descendent of one of the Jacobite leaders. It is crowned by a statue of a clansman that was supposed to be modelled on an accurate portrait of Bonnie Prince Charlie hanging in a Lanarkshire castle. However, whether by design or not, it seems the sculptor copied the wrong painting. When this was later pointed out to him, he commented, "well, be that as it may, I shall stand by my model, it is a thousand times more fitting than the Prince in tartan pantaloons".

Glenfinnan's other principal landmark, doubly famous since its cameo role in recent Harry Potter movies, is the 21-arch **VIADUCT** just up the valley from the monument. Running at a height of 30m/98ft, it was built between 1897 and 1901 by Robert MacAlpine for the West Highland Railway. Local stone was deemed too hard to dress and MacAlpine decided to deploy concrete as a cheaper alternative – allegedly the first large-scale use of the material in the world, earning for the viaduct's designer the nickname "Concrete Bob". Time your visit well and you can admire it in action, as a steam locomotive of the Jacobite Railway chuffs across – one of the great man-made spectacles of the Highlands. Harry Potter fans may recognize the engine as the Hogwarts Express from two of the recent movies.

Flanked by towering summits, the glen behind the viaduct falls within the 9000-acre Glenfinnan Estate, a privately owned deer-hunting reserve. Guests travel to a luxury lodge up the valley along a tarmac lane that follows the river as far as the **CORRYHULLY BOTHY**. Walkers

ABOVE: Glenfinnan's 21-arch viaduct, as featured in the recent Harry Potter movies

attempting the famous **CORRYHULLY HORSESHOE** – a high-level loop over the amphitheatre of Munros to the north – often spend the night in the little stone cottage. But day visitors are welcome to use it as a streamside lunch stop. Beyond, the track winds over Bealach á Chaorainn pass to Loch Arkaig – the route the Camerons followed to join the Jacobite rally in August 1745. Bonnie Prince Charlie and his associates had all but given up hope of marshalling enough men for the march on London when the skirl of the clan's bagpipes drifted down Glen Finnan – a scene enacted to memorable effect in the otherwise historically slapdash 1948 Hollywood rendition of the 1745 Uprising, starring David Niven as the Young Pretender.

It's doubtful this remote spot has seen much traffic since. Apart from the crack of a deer stalker's rifle or the odd blast of bagpipes during the annual Glenfinnan games, the only sound likely to disturb the peace and quiet here is the cry of an eagle soaring overhead or the yowl of an invisible wild cat prowling the larch forest.

CHECKED BY
✔ **Lochaber & Lorn Ramblers**

1 Turn R out of the **Glenfinnan** Visitors' Centre car park and follow the main road over the bridge to enter a second car park on your R, at the far side of the river. A gate marks the start of the private road running 2.5miles/4km up the glen. After following it for 8mins, you pass under the **viaduct**, with a sawmill to your R, and shortly after, two houses on your L.

Keep to the road as it continues to wind northeast, skirting bends in the River Finnan. As you progress, fine views begin to open up of the mountains of the **Corryhully Horseshoe** to the north, improving as the road swings decisively L, then around a big arc in the river. Look out for a series of waterfalls, reached via rough paths to your R. After around 45mins–1hr of walking you'll reach a bridge where the road crosses the Allt á Chaol-ghlinne stream to arrive at a T-junction. The tarmac continues L towards the Glenfinnan Lodge, now clearly visible on the mountainside above, but you should follow the public footpath running R along the river bank, signed to "Loch Arkaig 7 mls/Bothy". The hut lies 3-4mins further on your L.

2 In front of the **Corryhully Bothy** is a ford in the river. You should check the depth before attempting to cross (walking poles are recommended), and follow the rough, but obvious track which continues uphill along the side of a spruce and larch plantation. Should the ford be impassable, retrace your steps to a T-junction, and go back over the road bridge to a point about 150m/164yd down the road, where you'll see a new suspension bridge. Cross this, and immediately turn L back along the bank of the river to reach the far (east) side of the ford. After a 10-min climb from the ford, you'll see a wide wooden bridge across a gully to your R

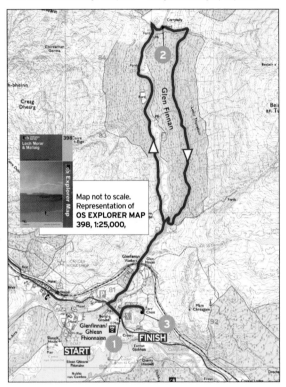

Map not to scale. Representation of **OS EXPLORER MAP 398, 1:25,000,**

Route profile

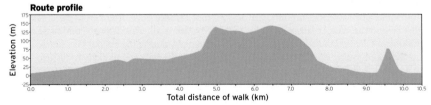

(at NM916843), where the track veers into the woods to begin a contouring descent of the glen. It's impossible to lose the trail, which keeps to around the 130–140m contour for half an hour, until NM916826, where it begins to drop in earnest. Ignore the tracks forking L at NM916822 and NM914818, and follow the main branch looping down to cross the river and re-join the road.

The remainder of the route retraces the outward leg back under the viaduct to Glenfinnan, but for our featured viewpoint, continue up the rocky path starting from the car park behind the visitor centre (signed "Viewpoint"). After a couple of minutes of steady ascent through the trees you'll reach a small clearing on an open spur with a bench. Most people stop here, but it's worth continuing along the fainter path cutting back up the hill to your R. This leads around the rear side of the low hill visible above – **Torr á Choit** – scaling it through thick bracken on its far side to avoid a more scrambly ascent of the southern face: look for a small brick structure marking the summit (NM910807).

3 It is thought this structure marks the exact spot where Bonnie Prince Charlie raised the Jacobite standard (though some think the unfurling may have taken place on the opposite side of the river). Either way, the view down to the monument and across Loch Shiel is magnificent. For an equally great panorama of the viaduct, improvise a path up the hill's northeastern top, just behind the main summit, which looks straight up the valley.

Getting There

Trains run year round to Glenfinnan on the West Highland Railway between Fort William and Mallaig, and in the summer months you can get there via the splendid Jacobite Steam Railway, ✎www. steamtrain.info. Regular buses also cover the route on the A830 "Road to the Isles". See ✎www. travelinescotland.com, ✆0871 200 2233.

Visitor Information

The National Trust Glenfinnan Visitors' Centre Open from April to October. It holds an exhibition on the 1745 Uprising, a small shop, café and toilets. ✆0844 4932221 ✎www.nts.org.uk/Property/26

Cruises on Loch Shiel are offered by the **MV Sileas**, an 52-ft, ex-admiralty harbour launch dating from the 1940s. For current prices and timetables, contact Jim Michie. ✆01687 470322 ✎www.highlandcruises.co.uk

Eating & Drinking

As well as the Station Dining Car reviewed below, the **National Trust Visitor Centre** has a small café serving hot and cold snacks, sandwiches, cakes and drinks.

The Station Dining Car

Glenfinnan Railway Station ✆01397 722300 This lovingly converted 1950s Pullman carriage is a great place for a pitstop, especially if your visit coincides with the arrival of the steam train – though it can get inundated as the train pauses here for an hour or so. For evening meals, you have to reserve in advance by telephone.

Sleeping

The Glenfinnan Sleeping Car Glenfinnan Railway Station, Station Rd, Glenfinnan, PH37 4LT ✆01397 722295 ✎www.road-to-the-isles.org.uk Centrally heated sleeper car in a siding at the museum. It's fitted with most mod cons, can accommodate up to ten people in its four compartments, and boasts a fully equipped kitchenette. A great novelty option for families and railway buffs.

Glenfinnan House Hotel

Glenfinnan, PH37 4LT ✆01397 722235 ✎www.glenfinnanhouse.com Smart country hotel in a stylishly converted mid-eighteenth-century manor, complete with rolling lawns, wood-panelled interiors and antique canvasses of Bonnie Prince Charlie and Loch Shiel. It's perfectly placed for our walk, but a pricy option.

More Info

✎www.road-to-the-isles.org.uk. Detailed online resource for travellers, including accommodation, events info and transport. ✎www.visitglenfinnan.co.uk. The village website, useful mainly for its links. ✎www.glenfinnanestate.co.uk. Introduction to the big estate which our route crosses, pitched mainly at trout fishermen and prospective punters of the shooting lodge, but worth a browse. ✎www.mountainbothies.org. uk. Website of the charity that looks after a hundred or more of Scotland's hidden bothies. ✎www.mwis.org.uk. Detailed weather forecast for the central Highlands, aimed at walkers, with windspeeds and freezing levels.

Surf 'n' Turf
Cley-next-the-Sea

The first half of this route is, strictly speaking, a coastal walk. All the ingredients are here: quays, jetties, boats and general maritime gear, but you will barely glimpse the sea. Instead this section of the Peddars Way and Norfolk Coast Path navigates a course through the wide saltmarshes and creeks left behind when the sea turned its back on this once prosperous port over a hundred years ago.

The remaining marshes have created a haven for salt-loving plants and migratory birds. Brent geese from Siberia and pink-foot geese from Iceland arrive here in the winter months. In summer, the explosive "teu-he-he" of redshank taking flight from the higher grassy areas blends with the "seep" of tiny reed buntings perched on the shrubby sea-blight bordering the path.

This is a Mecca for twitchers: thousands of bird-lovers from all over the world make the annual pilgrimage to the coast during the summer and winter migrations. The coast path winds through a network of nature reserves littered with the shells of abandoned fishing boats, and criss-crossed with boardwalks and birdwatching hides. On the approach to

Cley-next-the-Sea the broad landscape and wide open skies are neatly punctuated by the silhouette of the village's eighteenth-century windmill, one of Norfolk's defining landmarks.

The second half of this route retreats inland through the low-lying fens of the Glaven Valley, before climbing onto Blakeney Esker for panoramic views of north Norfolk from a rare vantage point high above sea level. The grand Glaven Churches at Blakeney, Wiveton and Cley decorate this tapestry of golden marshland stretching north to the shingle spit of Blakeney Point, and from the raised ridge of the esker you finally catch a glimpse of the elusive North Sea, as you descend on the final leg of your journey back to Blakeney harbour.

If you're attempting this walk in winter you are almost certain to experience a "snitern". It's not type of bird as you might expect, but means "biting wind". Blakeney's original name, Snitterley, is thought to derive from this archaic term, and, appropriately enough, sniterns regularly blow in from the North Sea, unopposed by the flat saltmarshes, to buffet the quay at Blakeney.

At a glance

Where Cley-next-the-Sea, west of Sheringham, on the North Norfolk Coast.
Why A twitchers' paradise; seals on Blakeney Point; the Glaven Ports.
When August, for Blakeney

Regatta and its famous "greasy pole" event.
Start/Finish Blakeney Quay, Blakeney (TG027441).
Duration 4hrs.
Distance 15.6km/9.7miles.
Cut it Short The Picnic

Fayre Deli, Cley-next-the-Sea, 4.4km/2.75miles.
Terrain The coast path can become very muddy; but mostly you'll be walking on good surfaced lanes and bridleways.
Maps OS Explorer 251.

On your way

The harbours at **BLAKENEY**, Cley and Wiveton were known collectively as the Glaven Ports, and together formed one of Britain's most important trade hubs from the thirteenth century until the sea finally abandoned them over six hundred years later. Gathered closely around the mouth of the River Glaven, they specialized in the export of wool, flour, corn and fish, and the importation of coal from Newcastle and stone quarried in Northamptonshire. They were also among the few English ports trusted to carry gold and silver, and had a special licence to "export" pilgrims during the fifteenth century.

Apart from the North Sea floods of 1953, the sea rarely troubles the Glaven estuary today. It was partly the greed and ignorance of the nineteenth-century landowner Lord Henry Calthorpe that hastened the sea's retreat. In an effort to prevent flooding in the valley and increase the amount of land for pasture he constructed a sea wall with sluice gates across the valley near Cley, despite bitter warnings from local fisherman. The new wall prevented the sea flowing inland and scouring the channel, and gradually the estuary began to silt. As the estuary dried up so did the prosperity and influence of the Glaven Ports. The last ship left Cley Mill Quay in 1876.

Today, the area's main source of trade is from the influx of twitchers and walkers drawn by the unique coastal habitat and rich history. But other visitors to take advantage of the ports' misfortune dwell out on Blakeney Point. The seal colony at the western tip of this shingle spit forms part of a larger population at the Wash: together they're home to forty percent of Europe's common seals. Grey seals have also used the spit to rear their young, and since the 1980s their population has been increasing steadily. The common seal (*Phoca vitulina*), also known as the "harbour seal", gives birth to a single pup between June and July, and the grey seal (*Halichoerus grypus*, or "sea pig with a hooked nose") to a single white pup between November and December. There are boat trips to view the seals from Blakeney and Morston quays.

Rounding Blakeney Eye, the village of **CLEY-NEXT-THE-SEA** (pronounced, and originally spelled "Cleye") looms into view fronted by the imposing eighteenth-century windmill. **CLEY WINDMILL** was a working flour mill until 1919, after which it passed into the family of the singer James Blunt. Today it operates as a top-end guesthouse.

A pilgrimage too far

A white sparrow caused something of a flutter among the bird-watching community in January 2008. When news of its sighting spread, an army of twitchers descended on Blakeney eager to catch a glimpse of this elegant North American songbird. It's not known how the sparrow ended up so far from its natural habitat: perhaps it was blown off course on the way to northern Canada, or hitched a ride on a ship bound for Europe. Alas the intrepid little fellow hadn't thought his journey through, and naturally would've failed to find a suitable mate among the native Norfolk bird population. It's possible he made the return trip to America, or perhaps even found himself a pied à terre among the reeds nearby. But we fear the worst. He's very small with a white stripe down the middle of his forehead. Do let us know if you spot him.

ABOVE: The saltmarshes are littered with the shells of abandoned fishing boats

This part of Cley-next-the-Sea originally served as the harbour, with the town centre sited half a mile south at **NEWGATE GREEN** (Cley Green on OS maps). But in 1612 a fire destroyed over a hundred buildings, and this, coupled with the gradually receding tide, provided an opportunity to move the town further upriver so that it could be more "next-the-sea".

As with all prosperous ports, smuggling was rife, and pirates were never far off shore. There were numerous tunnels used to smuggle contraband in and out of Cley, right under the noses of the Customs & Excise Men. Even today at least two local houses are said to have smugglers' tunnels connected to their basements.

But Cley's unsung jewel is magnificent **ST MARGARET'S CHURCH**. The local De Vaux family are responsible for its cathedral-like proportions. These wealthy merchants rebuilt the church in the fourteenth century to reflect Cley's growing importance. Unusually the three Glaven churches at Cley, Wiveton and Blakeney are all within sight of one another, their grandeur a reminder of how the wealthy merchant patrons competed for status.

WIVETON's jewel is the small bridge crossing the River Glaven. It was constructed over seven hundred years ago to provide a vital connection to the port at Cley, and is today one of the oldest working bridges in England. Wiveton specialized in ship-building and repair, and provided ships for the Hundred Years' War, and as many as 36 ships to combat the Spanish Armada. The harbour ran alongside the church of St Mary the Virgin, and the churchyard wall still bears the scars of ships anchored here.

The final stretch of our walk follows a 3-km/2-mile "esker" from **WIVETON DOWNS** across **BLAKENEY DOWNS** and back to the coast. An esker is formed by meltwater flowing through a tunnel beneath a glacier; when the glacier disappears a long ridge of sand and gravel is left in its place. **BLAKENEY ESKER** was formed during the last Ice Age, 15,000 years ago, and is one of the finest examples of this geological process anywhere in England, which has earned it SSSI status.

The height of the esker, in an otherwise flat Norfolk landscape, provides a perfect vantage point to survey the Glaven Valley. In fact the view here, with St Nicholas' Church on the bluff above Blakeney, rivals our classic great view at Cley.

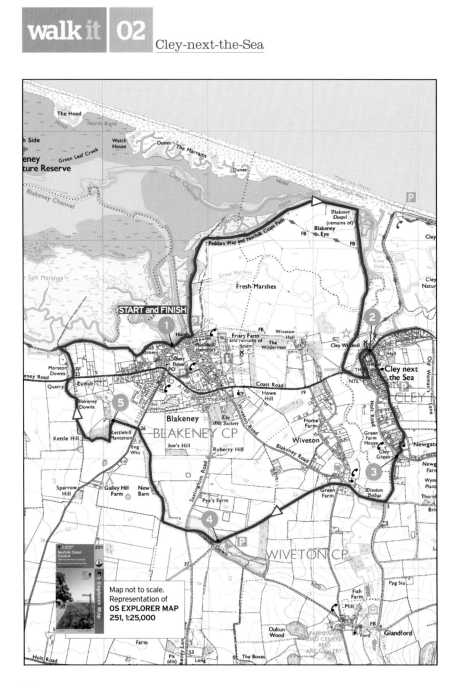

Map not to scale.
Representation of
OS EXPLORER MAP
251, 1:25,000

CHECKED BY
✔ **Sheringham & District Ramblers**

1 Facing out to sea from the old quay in **Blakeney**, turn R passing the Blakeney Hotel on your R to join the Peddars Way and Norfolk Coast Path (PW & NC Path) which heads out to into the saltmarshes towards Blakeney Point.
Follow the PW & NC Path for about an hour (5km/2.75miles). The path arcs back on itself to bring you towards **Cley-next-the-Sea**. When approaching the village bear R, keeping on the L side of the river with the unmistakable form of **Cley Windmill** on your L. You'll soon come to a small road bridge over the river which leads into Cley. (Cut it short: buses back to Blakeney or to Sheringham leave from outside Picnic Fayre Deli.) Walk L round the far corner from the Deli into the high street and turn L down an alley opposite the phone box.
Walk past the Old Town Hall and follow the path that takes you behind the houses on the main street, along an old jetty and straight to the windmill. Here you have to turn R through a small alley. Then walk up some steps to emerge on the main street outside Crabpot Books.

2 To continue, take the public footpath to the L of Crabpot Books which slips down the centre of the village behind the George pub to emerge on a surfaced lane (Church Lane). Continue along this lane in a southerly direction past the village hall, ignoring the road on your R, until you reach a long flint-cobbled wall and Knoll House. Turn R into **St Margaret's Church**. Go through the gate into the churchyard and round to the far side of the church where there is a large picnic area. Exit R onto **Newgate Green** (Cley Green on OS maps).

3 Cross over to the far (south) side of the large triangular green, ignoring the first road L (Three Swallows pub is back to your R), taking the road opposite, to the R of the houses. Follow this road south, with the river on your R, to a crossroads where you turn R across Wiveton Bridge up to **Wiveton**, with St Mary the Virgin Church and the Bell pub on the green. On the opposite side of the green from the church take the centre road marked with a picnic spot signpost (not the main Holt road L or R) and continue uphill to **Wiveton Downs** (approx 15mins).

4 Here you'll come to a fingerpost pointing L to Wiveton Common and R to Blakeney. It's worth a short detour L through the kissing gate onto the common to admire the views south, but retrace your steps and take the R path marked "Blakeney" onto Wiveton Downs/**Blakeney Esker** SSSI). Upon entering Wiveton Downs follow the path bearing L passing a small bump (which is irresistible to climb), and circle round L past a gate to exit on Saxlingham Road. Cross the road and walk up the bridleway marked signed towards Blakeney. Follow this bridleway through New Farm to the next road crossing (approx 15mins), where you cross over onto a surfaced path (through white gates) and up to some houses.

5 Turn L here following a well-worn path at the side of fields making your way across **Blakeney Downs**. When the path cuts through a gap in the trees bear R towards the house on the small hill (or bluff). The path skirts the L side of the bluff until you reach the main road. Turn R on the road, crossing carefully near the brow of the hill and then almost immediately L onto the bridleway which drops down to meet the PW & NC Path. Turn R to follow the coast path back to Blakeney.

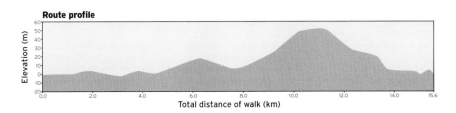

Route profile

Elevation (m)

Total distance of walk (km)

Getting There
Norfolk County Council's CoastHopper Bus (CHOP) provides an hourly service all year leaving from the Sheringham TIC, calling at Cley, Blakeney, Morston and Wells-next-the-Sea; contact Norfolk Green for details.

📞 01553 776980
🖊 www.norfolkgreen.co.uk

Sheringham is the nearest railhead with a frequent service from Norwich. Contact National Express for service details.

📞 0845 600 7245
🖊 www.nationalexpresseast anglia.com

Visitor Information
Sheringham TIC
Station Approach, Sheringham, NR26 8RA
📞 01263 824329

Eating & Drinking
Picnic Fayre Deli and the Cley Smokehouse in Cley-next-the-Sea are perfectly positioned to stock up with tasty morsels for the second leg of our route. For a more substantial meal try:

Three Swallows
Newgate Green, Cley-next-the-Sea
📞 01263 740526
Gorgeous pub off the old village green with open fires, pub games, and twitchers swapping stories. Serves Adnams, IPA and Abbott ales. Menu includes local Morston mussels and Holt ham. We'll leave you to guess the ingredients of their Grunt, Gobble and Zoom Coo Pie!

The Wiveton Bell
Wiveton
📞 01263 740101

🖊 www.wivetonbell.com
Recently revitalized village pub opposite the church in Wiveton, which has already caused a stir with locals. Expert menu using local produce, including from the Cley Smokehouse (above). Ales include the local Holy Trinity: Woodforde's Wherry, Yetman's and Adnams Broadside. They claim you can wander in wearing your walking boots – 'nuff said!

Sleeping
Cookes of Cley
Cley-next-the-Sea, NR25 7RX
📞 01263 740776
Great-value guest house and self-catering apartment in the centre of Cley, with a licensed bar and tea garden.

Scaldbeck Cottage
Morston, NR25 7BJ
📞 01263 740188
Small traditional flint-cobbled cottage near the quay at Morston, providing B&B at reasonable prices. Also has space for up to six two-man tents.

Cley Windmill
Cley-next-the-Sea, Holt, NR25 7RP
📞 01263 740209
🖊 www.cleywindmill.co.uk
Upmarket bed and breakfast or self-catering accommodation in Cley's eighteenth-century windmill, which has a fine circular sitting room and sweeping views of the marshes.

More Info
The Glaven Valley by Derek Mellor. Fascinating and meticulously researched collection of historical jottings in three volumes, complied by Marjorie Missen, from articles published in the local parish newsletter over the past twenty years. You can obtain copies from any of the churches that you come to en route.
🖊 www.ramblers.org.uk/info/paths/name/p/peddars.htm. For more about the Peddars Way and Norfolk Coast Path including accommodation, guidebooks and contacts.
🖊 www.norfolkcoastaonb.org.uk. Norfolk Coast Partnership's website aimed at promoting sustainable use of the Norfolk Coast AONB.

More Walks
Peddars Way and Norfolk Coast Path (Ramblers Norfolk Area). The 39th edition of this indispensable guide to Norfolk's National Trail.

West Norfolk Walkaway 2 and *West Norfolk Walkaway 3* (King's Lynn Ramblers). Two volumes each with sixteen circular walks devoted to the fresh air, sandy beaches and fenlands of Norfolk.

Nelson's Heritage Walks by Allan Jones (King's Lynn Ramblers). Nelson was a Norfolk man. This book features sixteen walks with connections to the great admiral's life, from where he went to school to where he learned the ropes.

Walks Around Norwich by Sue Walker (Ramblers Norfolk Area). Sixteen short circular walks in and around Norwich. Accessible by public transport.

Iceni Way Guide (Ramblers Norfolk Area). An 135-km/84-mile route from Knettishall, Suffolk to Hunstanton, Norfolk via the Little Ouse and Great Ouse valleys. Includes accommodation.

River of Gold
Precipice Walk

The Mawddach, how she trips!
Though throttled
If floodtide teeming thrills her full,
And mazy sands water-wattled
Waylay her at ebb . . .
From *Penmaen Pool* by Gerard Manley Hopkins

The Mawddach is the deepest of the estuaries delving into the mountainous heart of north Wales from the Cambrian coast, and unquestionably the most beautiful. From its meeting point with Cardigan Bay at Barmouth, the Afon Mawddach coils inland through a glorious vista of glistening sandflats and green hillsides towards Snowdonia. High, dark ridges recede endlessly to the north and east, but it's the long, pale-grey scarp of Cadair Idris rising sheer to the south that really steals the show. Wordsworth, a connoisseur of the Picturesque, classed the panorama as "sublime". And for once, the perfect viewpoint up the valley is one you'll barely have to break sweat to reach.

A gentle, family-friendly ramble over mostly level ground, the "Precipice Walk" just outside Dolgellau is – contrary to its name – decidedly un-precipitous, though

its does skirt some steep slopes in the course of its four-mile loop around Foel Cynwch. A natural platform on the north side of the hill provides an unrivalled view westwards down the estuary to the sea. Six main tributaries of the Mawddach flow together below it, looping in giant meanders over a narrow flood plain which has for centuries been the centre of lucrative industries, from boat construction to gold panning.

Nowadays it's a backwater, but one of considerable beauty, attracting streams of visitors in the summer. Many come to walk the famous eight-mile Mawddach Trail between Dolgellau and Morfa Mawddach, managed by Snowdonia National Park as part of the long-distance Cross Wales Cycling Route.

Early in the day, when soft morning sunlight picks out the contours of the mountains and brightens the yellow sandbar at the river mouth, is the best time to do this walk. But the views are equally beautiful in the hours around sunset, with the tangled water channels of the Mawddach shining red like molten gold as they approach the open sea.

At a glance

Where Precipice Walk, 4km/2.5miles north of Dolgellau, Gwynedd, Wales. **Why** Spectacular view of the Mawddach Estuary and the north face of Cadair Idris; minimal effort involved; enchanting Llyn Cynwch. **When** Last weekend of Sept for the Barmouth Walking Festival. **Start/Finish** National Park car park, Saith Groesffordd (SH745211). **Duration** 1hr 30mins-2hrs.

Distance 5.9km/3.6miles. **Terrain** A well-made footpath over mostly even ground, though it's muddy and rocky in places. **Maps** OS Explorer OL23 and OL18.

Evening light on the Mawddach
Estuary from the Precipice Walk

On your way

From its source high in the Aran mountains of Snowdonia, the Mawddach River (Afon Mawddach) flows south for 40km/25miles, joined along its course by six major tributaries and countless side streams that tumble down slopes patchworked by sheep farms and conifer plantations. Glaciers carved the sides of the spectacular valley cradling its estuary, and the tides added the finishing touches to the masterpiece, sweeping in the banks of soft sand through which the river now winds its unpredictable course from the open sea at Barmouth.

Leather-tanning, forestry, munitions storage and – most famously – gold-mining have at various points provided the mainstay for the only sizeable town along the Mawddach's banks: **DOLGELLAU**. Sitting astride a nexus of three Roman roads, the settlement has enjoyed greater historical prominence than its grey Victorian architecture would suggest. It was here that Owain Glyndwr convened his last Council of Chiefs in 1404, and where he later concluded a treaty with Charles IV of France to provide soldiers for his insurrection against Henry IV, King of England. Dolgellau later become an important centre for Welsh Quakers, many of whom fled to America in the late-seventeenth century before the 1689 Act of Toleration forbade persecution of their non-conformist, pacifist views.

A town in Pennsylvania called "Bryn Mawr" recalls the name of the farm belonging to the Quaker leader, Roland Ellis. Beginning 3km/2miles northeast of Dolgellau, the famous **PRECIPICE WALK** crosses the estate of another family of local grandee farmers, the Nannau or Vaughans, who can trace their lineage back to Cadwgan ap Bleddyn, Prince of Powys, in the 1100s. The dynasty's Georgian mansion on the floor of the Wnion Valley was the fifth to have been built on this site – the first was burned down by Glyndwr in 1404, the Nannau having remained loyal to the King.

Welsh Gold

The gilded appearance of the Mawddach at dusk may not be merely the result of light refraction, for its sandy banks remain a rare source of Welsh gold. People probably panned for nuggets along the river's course as far back as the Bronze Age, when finely worked gold torques graced the necks of Celtic princes. But it was the Romans who first mined the metal from the shale and compacted mudstone sediment beneath the Coed y Brenin Forest, upriver from Dolgellau. Although the discovery of some particularly rich lodes precipitated waves of full-blown gold rushes in the 1860s, major finds were too sporadic to stimulate investment by big firms and as a result the industry went into decline. It now verges on extinction: the last traces of viably extractable gold were removed from Gwynfynydd mine near Dolgellau in January 2007. As a consequence, Welsh gold is officially one of the rarest and most expensive metals in the world. It's also the material of choice for British royal wedding rings. George V and Princess Mary started the trend in 1893, followed by Elizabeth Bowes Lyon (the present Queen's mother), then her daughter, Queen Elizabeth II, and most recently Charles (for both his marriages to Diana Spencer and Camilla Parker-Bowles). Recent celebrity purchasers of pure Welsh wedding bands include Catherine Zeta-Jones and Michael Douglas, and weather presenter Siân Lloyd, who kept hers even after her former fiancé, Liberal Democrat MP Lembit Opik, ran off with one of the Cheeky Girls.

ABOVE: The ruins of Cymer Abbey, founded in 1198 by the Cistercians

Set amid forty acres of deer park, **NANNAU HALL** is overlooked in the east by the distinctive peak of Foel Offrwm ("Hill of Sacrifice"), from whose summit crags in ancient times criminals are said to have been hurled to their deaths. Following the demise of the last Vaughan incumbent in the 1990s, the house lapsed into disrepair before being renovated as a hotel and country club; it's now a private residence once again.

The Precipice path itself makes use of an old grazing trail which, after skirting the shores of beautiful **LLYN CYNWCH** (a renowned source of wild Welsh trout) contours at roughly 244m/800ft around a dramatic sequence of slopes draped in heather and whinberry bushes. In the north, these fall away to a particularly narrow stretch of the Mawddach Valley; in the west, they overlook the river's confluence with the Wnion. Next to it stand the ruins of Cymer Abbey, founded in 1198 by the Cistercians. Its monks chose the site for the fine views and proximity of a major medieval trade route, scraping a living from sheep farming and metallurgy (their original charter conferred rights, "in digging and carrying away metals and treasures free from all secular exaction"). Such income as they did derive from their excavations, however, was clearly not sufficient to complete work on the abbey's long, rectangular church, which never acquired transepts.

Poverty worsened during the wars of the thirteenth century, but despite this the community somehow gathered enough money to acquire two of Wales' great treasures – a silver gilt chalice and paten (bread plate) – which were hidden in the hills during the Dissolution of 1536 and seemingly forgotten. Rediscovered by a pair of local gold prospectors in 1890, they are now on display in the National Museum of Wales in Cardiff – much to the chagrin of the prospectors' descendents, who are campaigning to have them brought back to Dolgellau. Squashed between a farm and caravan park, the ruins of Cymer possess little of the tranquility that must have originally attracted the Cistercians, though out of season they're worth a visit.

1 From the car park at Saith Groesffordd, follow the lane running L in the direction of Tŷ'n y Groes bridge for 200m/220yds, where a signposted track rises sharply L through a conifer plantation. After a few minutes ascending this muddy forest track you emerge from the trees at a junction. Turn R here, following the unsurfaced road between the wood and an open field (from where **Nannau Hall** can be glimpsed to your L) as far as a small estate farm, Gwern-offeiriaid. The path bends L here, skirting the farm on its R to begin a short climb through some deciduous trees.

2 Shortly after emerging from the coppice (just before you reach the lake shore) look for another path peeling R along the side of a drystone wall. This marks the start of the **Precipice Walk** proper. From here, the route continues easily through the bracken to crest a rocky rise, after which it winds steadily southwest though patches of heather and whinberry, keeping to the 180-200 metre contour.
The views grow gradually more impressive as you progress, with the Mawddach River crashing

far below at the foot of the steep hillside. Having wound along the west flank of the hill, the trail then begins to bend L.

3 Just before you arrive at the drystone wall and ladder

stile, keep an eye out for a side path turning R to the finest viewpoint of the day, a little bluff at SH730204, which surveys the whole Mawddach Estuary and the northern crags of Cadair Idris. Beyond the stile, the path begins a

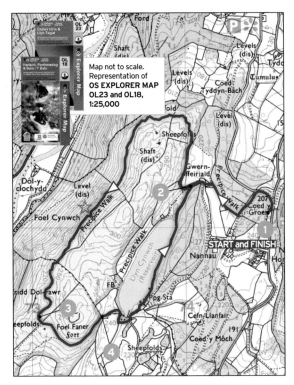

Map not to scale. Representation of OS EXPLORER MAP OL23 and OL18, 1:25,000

Route profile

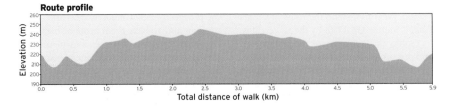

short descent to the lake, around the lower slopes of an Iron Age hill fort, Foel Faner.

4 Once over another wall, it reaches the shore of **Llyn Cynwch**, where you should turn R, passing through a gate and small car park to join a broad track heading through the oak trees along the eastern shore of the lake.
This eventually rejoins the path you branched off earlier. Return to the main National Park car park at Saith Groesffordd via the route described above, but in reverse..

Getting There
Bus 33 runs between Machynlleth and Dolgellau, stopping at the trailhead on Tuesdays and Fridays. See www.gynedd.gov.uk for a current timetable. The nearest train station is at Machynlleth.

Visitor Information
Dolgellau TIC/Snowdonia National Park IC
Eldon Square, Dolgellau
01341 42288

Eating & Drinking
Dylanwad Da
Smithfield St, Dolgellau
01341 422870
www.dylanwad.co.uk
Among the loveliest bistros in Wales, with down-to-earth specialties including rosemary and garlic roast leg of Welsh lamb, Thai style seafood stew and, for veggies, pecan and vegetable cakes. They also claim - with some justification - to serve "Dolgellau's best cappuccino", which you can enjoy with freshly baked pastries in their coffee shop.

ABOVE: Partially submerged tree, Llyn Cynwch

George III
Penmaenpool
www.georgethethird.co.uk
Historic pub, in a former station and ship's chandlers, superbly situated on the banks of the Mawddach Estuary overlooking Penmaenpool Bridge. The perfect spot to enjoy a pint or meal with a view; the menu features hearty pub standards, with locally sourced lamb and beef taking pride of place.

Sleeping
Cae Gwyn Farm
Bronaber, Trawsfynydd, LL41 4YE
01766 540245
www.caegwynfarm.co.uk
Characterful B&B, campsite and bunk barn, on an organic sheep farm 10miles north of Dolgellau via the A470. The site boasts superb views of the nearby Rhinogs and abuts a nature reserve.

Craig Wen
Arthog, LL39 1BQ
01341 250482
www.graigwen.co.uk
Converted Victorian slate-cutting mill on the banks of the Mawddach, 5miles down the A493 from Dolgellau (at SH654157). You can stay in their attractively furnished guest rooms, in domed yurt tents, or camp in a field overlooking the water - recently voted one of Wales' top five sites.

More Info
www.eryri-npa.co.uk. The Snowdonia National Park website features an engaging page on the Precipice Walk. Click on "Leisure Walks" then "Precipice, Dolgellau".

www.metoffice.gov.uk.outdoor/ mountainsafety/snowdonia.html. Detailed mountain weather forecast for north Wales.

Fleet on Foot

Parliament Hill

Sir, if you wish to have a just notion of the magnitude of this city, you must not be satisfied with seeing its great streets and squares, but must survey the innumerable little lanes and courts.
Dr Samuel Johnson

If you lean over the north bank of the Thames underneath Blackfriars Bridge you can just make out a small grill set into the wall. This inconspicuous drain is in fact the mouth of one of London's most historically important rivers – the Fleet.

The Fleet has been confined for over two hundred and fifty years beneath the concrete, traffic and bustle of London's streets, and our route loosely follows its subterranean course from the mouth, across Fleet Street, through Kings Cross and Camden Town to the source on Hampstead Heath, where shortly before reaching Hampstead Village we cross one of its last remaining overground sections.

Beloved of walkers and kite-flyers alike, the best spot to view the capital has to be from Hampstead Heath's Parliament Hill. St Paul's Cathedral, the Palace of Westminster,

Tower 42, and the "gherkin" are all laid at your feet, and from this vantage point – 98m/321ft above the city – you can trace the route you took across town.

This is an ambitious urban walk that seeks out the hidden corners of London. There are rich layers of Roman, Saxon, medieval and Victorian remains, piled one on top of the other. A perfect example of this archaeological "layer-cake" can be found in the crypt of St Bride's church, where the remnants of no fewer than eight churches dedicated to St Bride over the past 1500 years are now exposed, along with the original stretch of Roman pavement they were built on.

Although the going is mostly over level ground, this is not a simple walk in the park. Pounding the streets of London can take its toll, so it's advisable to wear a pair of well-fitting trainers with nice, thick soles. Also, because of the volume of historical interest en route, allow plenty of time to explore the "innumerable little lanes and courts" and to sample traditional London pleasures such as the Seven Stars pub, a feature of life in the City for over four centuries.

At a glance

Where Central London to Hampstead Heath, North London.
Why Rich layers of history; Victorian alleys and squares; grand cityscapes from Primrose and Parliament hills.
When October, to kick leaves on Hampstead Heath.

Downsides Weekday congestion in the city.
Start/Finish Blackfriars Bridge, Southwark/Flask Walk, Hampstead.
Duration 4hrs 30mins.
Distance 13km/8miles.
Cut it Short King's Cross,

4.8km/3miles.
Terrain Mostly level on pavements, with two easy hill climbs. A few steps at St Bride's Passage and to enter and exit the Grand Union Canal.
Maps The London A-Z or OS Explorer 173.

On your way

We begin where two rivers meet: at the confluence of London's "dirty old river" Thames, as the Kinks called it, and the even dirtier and almost forgotten Fleet. This once navigable river formed the natural western boundary of the city, and boasted five bridges and a harbour providing early Londoners with a vital artery for trade and industry. But by the thirteenth century its lower reaches had become so polluted by waste from the many tanneries, butchers and prisons lining its banks that the waters were often dyed a ghastly red, and "putrid exhalations" rose from the surface, earning it the nickname "the stinking river".

Despite many attempts to solve the problem, these unhygienic conditions worsened over the following centuries, and ultimately contributed to the rapid spread of the Great Plague of 1665. The Fleet was finally confined beneath the streets in 1766.

The Catholic Church also helped to shape this part of the city. In preparation for the Inquisition, a number of religious orders received papal approval, among them the Dominicans and the Carmelites, who settled along the Fleet Valley at Lincoln's Inn and Holborn respectively. These orders prospered under the reign of Edward I, and the Blackfriars (Dominicans) and White Friars (Carmelites) established priories further south at the confluence of the Fleet and the Thames, just east of the already well-established **TEMPLE**. (Temple grounds are well worth a short detour, but access is limited at weekends.)

ABOVE: The oldest boundary stones in London, dividing St Clement Danes and St Dunstan's

Literary Landmarks

There's a bewildering array of literary landmarks on our route – not least the heartland of the Bloomsbury Group – but here we've cherry-picked some sights you might otherwise miss.

On the corner of **Serle Street** and Carey Street is the memorial to Sir Thomas More, scholar, author, statesman, and member of Lincoln's Inn. He was executed for treason by Henry VIII in 1535. Look left to the Senate House on **Russell Square**, the inspiration for the Ministry of Truth in Orwell's *Nineteen Eighty Four*. Mary Shelley's mother Mary Wollstonecraft, author of *A Vindication of the Rights of Woman*, married William Godwin in **St Pancras** Church in 1796, a mere five months before her death. They were buried in the churchyard and their tombstone is near the exit to **Camley St**. Sylvia Plath and Ted Hughes rented the top flat of 23 **Fitzroy Road, Primrose Hill**, in the November of 1962. WB Yeats also resided here from 1867-73, and the couple took this as a sign of great literary things to come. Tragically it was not to be, and Plath ended her own life here, barely three months later.

At the bottom of **Pond Street** on the wall of the corner building is the death mask of George Orwell. He worked here at Booklover's Corner from 1934-5, and wrote *Keep the Aspidistra Flying* while living above the bookshop.

ABOVE: The Seven Stars survived the Great Fire, and is one of the oldest pubs in London

However, by the early fourteenth century the entire district had become a "thieves kitchen" occupied by ne'er-do-wells seeking a "right of sanctuary" (an obscure law that allowed criminals temporary refuge in religious institutions). The area became so notorious that even the King's men-at-arms would not roam the streets of **BOUVERIE** and **WHITEFRIARS** unaccompanied. The only remaining section of the White Friar's monastery is the crypt, which can be viewed at the bottom of a stairwell between **ASHENTREE COURT** and **MAGPIE ALLEY**.

The Blackfriars originally settled at Lincoln's Inn; **LINCOLN'S INN FIELDS** is today the largest and most pleasant of London's public squares. The fields became the property of Henry VIII after the Dissolution, but many early attempts to build over them were successfully opposed by the Society of Lincoln's Inn. Later, Inigo Jones was commissioned to lay out plans for the central square, which opened to the public in 1895 and has been a favourite spot for picnickers ever since. But the square also has a bloody history. The bandstand in the centre marks the spot where many executions took place, including the beheading of Lord William Russell in 1683 for his complicity in a plot to assassinate King Charles II.

Bloodier still, on the south side of the square stands the imposing Royal College of Surgeons of England, which today houses the Hunterian Collection – one of the most obscure and compellingly gruesome museums in London.

From here on our route becomes increasingly civilized, passing through

ABOVE: Memorial to Sir Thomas More, on the corner of Serle St and Carey St, Lincoln's Inn

that a concerted effort was made to save the heath for public access. At that time the secretary of the Open Spaces Society and founding member of the Ramblers, Lawrence Chubb, met Arthur Crosfield, a merchant from Merseyside, and formed the Kenwood Preservation Council (KPC). The KPC skillfully masterminded a campaign, which brought together Crosfield's wealthy but altruistic business acquaintances with Chubb's passion for conservation. Together they managed to purchase strategic pockets of land, preventing developments that would have destroyed much of the heath, and with it the public's ability to enjoy this vital "green lung" for London. Today our great view from Parliament Hill is one of six protected views classed as London Panoramas.

ABOVE: The Senate House was George Orwell's inspiration for the Ministry of Truth

the British Museum; the Bloomsbury Group's old stomping ground; St Pancras churchyard; and then taking you on a lazy stroll up the Grand Union Canal through the bustle of Camden Lock market, to **PRIMROSE HILL**. The wider, leafier streets, tasteful cafés and celebrity residents are all evidence that this once down-at-heel district of London has completely transformed itself over the last hundred years. North of here lies the wonderful wild expanse of Hampstead Heath, perhaps London's most prized green space.

The public's "right to roam" across of the heath was a battle hard-fought over many decades. But it was not until 1919

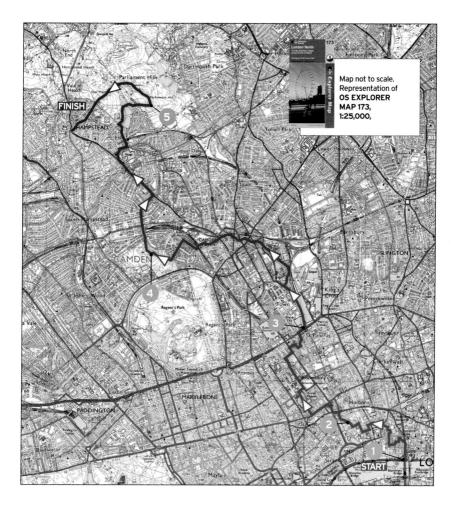

Map not to scale.
Representation of
**OS EXPLORER
MAP 173,
1:25,000,**

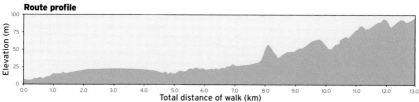

Route profile

Elevation (m) / Total distance of walk (km)

CHECKED BY
✔ **Metropolitan Walkers**

1 Starting underneath Blackfriars Bridge (the road bridge not the train bridge), ascend the steps to road level and turn away from the river (north) and cross at the lights to New Bridge St. Keep on the L side of New Bridge St. Just before Ludgate Circus turn L into the small arcade called Bride Court. Turn R at the end, and immediately L up three steps to Bride's Ave passing between The Bell pub and St Bride's Church. Continue L past the church to arrive on **Salisbury Court** (Samuel Pepys' birthplace is on the R). Turn L and then immediately R into Salisbury Square and bear R up four wide steps into a courtyard behind an office building (this is Hanging Sword Alley, once a notorious spot for eighteenth-century muggers, and home to Dickens' body-snatcher Jeremy Cruncher in *A Tale of Two Cities*). Exit the far L side of Hanging Sword Alley and turn L on Whitefriars Street and then next R into **Ashentree Court** (go down the steps in the courtyard to view Whitefriars crypt). Exit via **Magpie Alley** and turn R up **Bouverie Street** (L then R for **Temple** detour), and cross Fleet Street at the pelican crossing, going down the narrow alleyway of Bolt Court opposite the lights. Follow signs to Dr Johnson's House in Gough Sq. Exit the square with Johnson's house on your L, and turn L and then R on Fetter Lane. Cross at the lights and pass the statue of John Wilkes, turning L down Bream Buildings. Continue down Bream Buildings and cross Chancery Lane to the small

arcade, Chichester Rents, directly opposite. Turn L at the bottom arcade, then R onto Carey Street.

2 Before the Seven Stars pub, there are two boundary stones at ground level marking the division of the old parish of St Clement Danes (anchor), and St Dunstans in the West (S.D.W): these are the oldest remaining boundary stones in London. Pass the Seven Stars pub and turn R, up **Serle Street**. Turn L at **Lincoln's Inn Fields** to the Royal College of Surgeons of England then cross the square and make your way to the far L corner. Take the first R down the alley to the L of the Ship pub. Cross Holborn diagonally and go up Southampton Row to the arcaded Sicilian Ave (London's first open-air shopping arcade). At the far end of Sicilian Ave, cross at the lights and turn L down Bloomsbury Way passing St George the Martyr church on your R. Turn R down Museum St and cross at the zebra crossing to the British Museum. You can walk straight through the museum taking the far exit to Montague Place and turn R to **Russell Square** (if the museum is closed turn R then L down Montague St). Turn L at Russell Sq passing the Senate House, and continue straight on past SOAS into Woburn Square, through Gordon Sq and turn R up to Tavistock Square. Cross Woburn Place to the BMA over the zebra crossing. Turn L and then first R into Woburn Walk. At the end of Woburn Walk turn R and then first L into Cartwright Gardens. Follow the road round to the L and L again into Mabledon Place which leads to Euston Rd where you cross at the lights. **Cut**

it short: head home from King's Cross rail or tube station.

3 To continue, turn R past the British Library and L down Midland Rd. Continue up Midland Rd passing St Pancras International on your R, then a row of antique dealers on your L, and cross at the lights near the underpass. Turn L and enter St Pancras churchyard. Walk through the gardens and exit to **Camley St** (north exit). Turn L and fork R, continuing up Camley St, and descend the steps to the Grand Union Canal towpath. Turn R and follow the towpath for about 30mins until you reach Camden Lock: here you need to walk around the lock and market to continue along the towpath. Take the next exit (about 3mins) and turn R on Gloucester Road. Turn L into **Fitzroy Road**, passing No 23, before crossing Regent's Park Rd at the zebra crossing to enter **Primrose Hill**. Head up the hill to the summit.

4 Descend the far side of Primrose Hill and exit bottom R, turning L up Primrose Hill Rd past St Mary the Virgin church. Continue up this road and turn R into England's Lane. Follow England's Lane to the end and turn L up Havistock Hill. Cross over at the lights to Belsize Park tube station and turn L uphill towards the Royal Free Hospital. Turn R down Hampstead Passage (the little path snaking between the Royal Free Hospital and St Stephen's Church), and turn R on to **Pond Street**. Cross the zebra crossing at the bottom of Pond St. Continue on L on South End Rd, crossing to the Garden Gate pub. Turn L, crossing over South Hill Park Road, and onto the clear path up towards the heath. Pass the first of Hampstead's ponds and then take the R hand path after the second pond. At the far side of the second pond follow the path bearing R, marked "No Cycling": now make for the brow of **Parliament Hill**.

5 Descend the hill the same side as you came up but bear R onto a dirt track. Follow the unsurfaced track/desire-line in a south easterly direction over a cycle path and head slightly uphill to the Old Burial Ground (tumulus), which is encircled by iron railings. Continue with the tumulus on your R until you meet another surfaced path (this one is the Boundary Path): turn L and follow this path until you reach a crossroads with a drinking fountain. There is a long straight avenue of trees ahead of you (known as Lime Avenue). Follow Lime Avenue: roughly half way up it, an overground section of the River Fleet flows under the path. Exit the heath and cross East Heath Rd, and go down Well Walk. Fork R into Flask Walk and continue uphill to the Flask Pub.

Getting There
Blackfriars Underground station will be closed from March 2009 until late 2011. The next nearest tube stations are Temple or Embankment, which are both on the Circle and District lines. Buses 45, 63, 100, and 388 all stop at Blackfriars Bridge. Hampstead station is on London Underground's Northern Line. See www.tfl.gov.uk for the latest transport details.

i Visitor Information
St Bride's Church
Fleet St
020 7427 0133
www.stbrides.com
Opening hours are unreliable, so it's advisable to check in advance.

The Hunterian Collection
The Royal College of Surgeons of England, 35-43 Lincoln's Inn Fields
020 7869 6560
www.rcseng.ac.uk/museums
Admission is free, and the museum is open Tues-Sat, 10am-5pm

Eating & Drinking

Seven Stars
53 Carey St, Holborn
020 7242 8521
Dating from 1602, this pub is one of the few buildings that survived the Great Fire, and is one of London's smallest and oldest. It's said to have been established by exiles during the Dutch Civil War (1566-1609), and its name is a reference to the then seven provinces of the Netherlands. The exotically named landlady, Roxy Beaujolais, serves up the kind of food you'd expect in any fancy central London restaurant, but at a fraction of the price, prepared with more care, and in surroundings that are infinitely more pleasant.

The Flask
Flask Walk, Hampstead
020 7435 4580
Tucked away in a wee alley off the high street, The Flask gets its name from the provision to the poor of Hampstead of flasks to collect the spa waters at the well, fed by the Fleet. Today the pub serves good food, Young's ale

and ... tap water. The hand-painted glass screens separating the main bars are the work of the artist Jan Van Beers, and have graced the pub since it was re-built nearly 150 years ago.

Sleeping
YHA St Paul's
36 Carter Lane, EC4V 5AB
0845 371 9012
www.yha.org.uk
A large YHA with 190 beds, including some larger family rooms. Enjoying a great location, some 90m/100yards from St Paul's Cathedral, the hostel was the choirboys' school in an earlier incarnation.

More Info
Historic London by Stephen Inwood (Macmillan). Superbly written history that reads like an intimate biography of the capital. It's a perfect read for the adventurous backstreet urban wanderer. Includes some "mystery solving" routes.

More Walks
www.innerlondonramblers.org.uk/walksideas.html
A small but growing selection of quality urban routes available to download free. Developed by the Inner London Area of the Ramblers.

Rural Walks around Richmond by Richmond Ramblers (Ramblers). Twenty-one walks in a single London borough - further afield than our featured walk, but rich in green spaces, including Richmond Park, Bushy Park, Barnes and the Thames. Eight of the walks described have details of wheelchair-accessible sections.

Walla view!

Walla Crag

You could stick a pin anywhere on a map of the Lake District and be guaranteed to land on a great viewpoint. Shortlisting the region's "greatest views" takes a little more time and footwork, but we reckoned Derwent Water was as good a place to start the hunt as any.

As a walking destination, Derwent Water (from the ancient Brythonic for "valley thick with oaks") ticks all the boxes. An exquisite lake tapering away to a smouldering backdrop of high peaks, it's cradled by some breathtaking fells, including mighty Skiddaw and Blencathra. A constellation of pretty, wooded islets litter its surface, rippled every quarter of an hour or so by the wake of a launch chugging from the marina in Keswick to a series of wooden landing stages, from which you can set out on a network of wonderful lakeside trails – all without the encumbrance of a car.

The route we settled on features three classic views of the lake: from Peter Randall-Page's Hundred Year Stone at Calfclose Bay;

Friar's Crag on the outskirts of Keswick itself; and picture-postcard-pretty Ashness Bridge. However, the panorama that gets our "best in show"rosette is from a lesser known vantage point overlooking the lake's eastern shore, where the locals go to stretch their legs after work and remind themselves what a wonderful part of the world they live in. Sitting 300m/984ft above the waterline on the rocky top of Walla Crag, you survey a stupendous sweep of Lakeland scenery, ranging over Keswick to the cloud-swept bulk of Skiddaw, and southwards to the lumpy summits of Borrowdale.

These views are just as dramatic as those to be had from Cat Bells, on the opposite side of Derwent Water – only here you won't have to share your picnic spot with hordes of other visitors. And if you've any weary children on the expedition, rest assured the route can be cut short from roughly the midway point with a fun boat ride back to town – leaving plenty of time for tea and buns on the square.

At a glance

Where Walla Crag, near Keswick, Cumbria.
Why Terrific views over Derwent Water, minus the crowds of Cat Bells; Ashness Bridge: lakeland at its picture-postcard prettiest; Friar's Crag: the definitive lakeside panorama.
When Mid-May, for the Keswick Mountain Festival.

Downsides The last stretch towards Keswick can get busy, especially on weekends and during the school holidays; proximity of traffic on Borrowdale Road during the mid-stage of the walk along the lakeshore.
Start/Finish Moot Hall Information Centre, Keswick (NY266234).

Duration 3hrs.
Distance 10.2km/6.3miles.
Terrain Mostly on clear paths at easy gradients, with short sections through town, along tarmac the lanes and gravel beaches of the lakeshore. Suitable for children aged seven and upwards, and there's a boat near the end.
Maps OS Explorer OL4.

On your way

The town of Keswick sits astride a key intersection of the Lake District's main travel arteries, and as such has always served as an important trading hub. Granted a Royal Charter by Edward I in 1276, its Saturday market is still going strong after 700 years. The town's name derives from the Old English for "cheese" ("cese") but the chief commodities sold here were traditionally wool and leather – until, that is, the discovery in 1500 of an exceptionally large, solid lump of graphite in nearby Borrowdale.

The graphite was found to be the perfect substance to write with, and when the Italians dreamed up a way of encasing it in wood, Keswick launched a world-beating pencil-making industry that would thrive

for two hundred years or more. Forced to seek alternatives during the trade embargo of the Napoleonic wars, the French finally shattered this monopoly by discovering how to mix the more widely available powdered form of graphite with clay, which could be moulded into spaghetti-thin rods and fired in kilns. The quirky Cumberland Pencil Museum on Great Bridge tells the full story.

Rallying after the Great Pencil Slump, Keswick re-invented itself during the late-eighteenth and nineteenth centuries as a tourist destination, thanks in no small part to the descriptions of its landscapes penned by Romantic poets such as Wordsworth and Coleridge (both bards lived in the Lake District in the early 1800s).

Opium, in tincture form as laudanum, is usually cited as the main cause of the fallout between the pair. Coleridge had started using the drug at least four years earlier, allegedly as an antidote to joint pain, toothache and stress, but by the time he and his family took up residence in Keswick the addiction had started to take its toll not just on his friendships, but also the poet's marriage and artistic output. The sojourn in the Lakes was to last only four years: in 1804 Coleridge accepted the offer of a job in Malta and took the opportunity to escape his failing marriage.

Crammed with tea rooms, souvenir shops and, above all, outdoor gear stores, Keswick today is prospering on the back of the boom the Romantic poets started. It's awash with walkers year round, many of whose first target is the lakeside fell of Cat Bells to the southwest – a hill much featured on TV. Our route, however, sidesteps the tide of walkers heading up Cat Bells in favour of a less frequented, but no less rewarding viewpoint on the opposite shore of the lake.

One of the great things about the vista from **WALLA CRAG** is that you don't get to see it until you're right on top. A prominent feature of Derwent Water from this angle are the many wooded islets scattered across it. Looking from left to right, the longest, thinnest member of the group is St Herbert's Island, named after St Cuthbert, the Celtic-Christian hermit and acolyte of Lindisfarne who first preached the gospels here in the mid-seventh century. Over the years, his shrine became a popular pilgrimage destination. Rampsholm, immediately in front of it, takes its name from the Viking word for "wild garlic", while Lord's Island, the oval, wooded outcrop closer to the shore, was the site of a mid-fifteenth-century manor belonging to the Earl of Derwent, of which now only the foundations survive.

Great controversy attended the appearance in the 1770s on the next island to the right, Derwent Isle, of an Italianate-Palladian villa, which Wordsworth famously complained ruined the view. It was one of several constructions erected by an eccentric resident named John Pocklington. Others included a mock fort, which became the focus of a peculiar "battle" during Keswick's annual regatta: teams were invited to storm the stronghold's supply of beef and beer while its owner fired on them with a canon.

Centuries before Pocklington's siege became a part of the local festival calendar, Derwent Isle was owned by the monks of Furness Abbey, who after the Dissolution lost it to the Crown. Later, it fell into the hands of a foreign mining company, whose German workforce fled there after a series of racial attacks and murders forced them out of Keswick. In order to avoid ever setting foot in the town again, the miners made

ABOVE: Peter Randall-Page's Hundred Year Stone

ABOVE: Sunset on Skiddaw, from the shores of Derwent Water

their own bakery, pig house, vegetable garden and brewery on the island. It is now the property of the National Trust, who rent its villa – though part of the rental agreement ensures open access to the public on a few days each year.

On the opposite, western shore of the lake you can make out the buildings of Lingholm, the late-Victorian mansion where Beatrix Potter and her family spent nine summer holidays. Red squirrels she encountered there as a child inspired her to write *The Tale of Squirrel Nutkin*, published in 1901. Potter, of course, bought an estate in the Lakes after she made her fortune as a childrens' writer. On her death in 1943, aged 77, she bequeathed fourteen farms and 4000 acres of land to the National Trust, along with her flocks of Herdwick sheep – a gift that would form the kernel of the future Lake District National Park.

One landmark that would have been familiar to the young Beatrix Potter is **ASHNESS BRIDGE**, an old packhorse bridge below Walla Crags, the image of which, set against the backdrop of the lake and Skiddaw, has graced many a Lakeland calendar over the years.

Two equally famous viewpoints punctuate the return leg of our route along the shore of Derwent Water, the first of them the enigmatic "split boulder" emerging from the shallows of **CALFCLOSE BAY**. Created by renowned sculptor Peter Randall-Page, the **HUNDRED YEAR STONE** was commissioned by the National Trust to mark its centenary, and forms a striking counterpoint to the giant landscape sweeping into the distance beyond it.

The beautiful symmetry of Derwent Water is revealed to similarly great advantage from **FRIAR'S CRAG**, a wooded headland opposite Derwent Isle from which pilgrims used to embark on the short boat trip to St Herbert's Island. A memorial stands on it to the writer, critic, poet and painter John Ruskin (1819–1900), a passionate promoter of the region who lived on the shores of Coniston Water in a house stuffed with priceless art treasures.

Ruskin rated this view as one of the finest in Europe – comparable with Lake Geneva. And who are we to argue...

walk it | 05
Walla Crag

CHECKED BY
✔ **Penrith Ramblers**

1 With your back to the Moot Hall Information Centre, leave the Market Square on the pedestrian street leading off to the L (Main St). At the bend, where Station St runs to the L, keep walking straight ahead down St John's St, past the Parish Church of St John's on your R and the B&Bs lining Ambleside Rd. Just before the road starts to climb a hill, turn R onto Springs Rd, which winds via two bends up to Springs Farm.

2 Cross the stream, and pass to the L of the farm buildings and around a bend to a fork in the track, where you keep L to reach a gate leading into the woods. Having climbed through the trees for 5mins, the path then forks again: follow the footpath sign to R in the direction of "Rakefoot Farm, Walla Crag and Castlerigg Stone Circle", as indicated. With fine views over Derwent Water and Cat Bells opening up below you, the trail skirts the edge of a wood. Ignore the path arriving from your R; keep going straight ahead to cross a footbridge. Shortly beyond this the path bends L to meet a lane. Turn R onto the tarmac here, and follow it uphill to Rakefoot Farm.

3 From the farm, keep to the signposted track leading R up

the side of a drystone wall in the direction of **Walla Crag**, as indicated by a FPS. But after the footbridge, instead of sticking close to the wall, head straight on via a narrower trail above the beck to your L. After 5mins, this path starts to bend to the R and level off, arriving

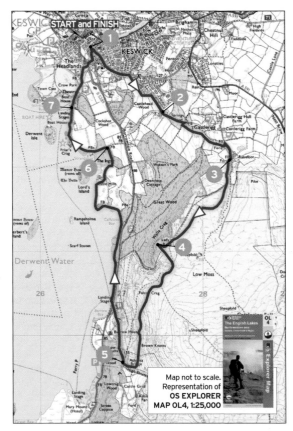

Map not to scale.
Representation of
**OS EXPLORER
MAP OL4, 1:25,000**

Route profile

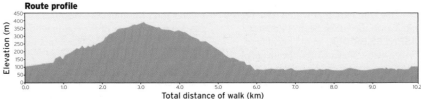

Elevation (m)

Total distance of walk (km)

eventually at another fork where you should keep L. From here, it drifts closer to the wall, before dropping into a dip known as Lady's Rake. Beyond the hollow you'll see a stile on the R leading to our featured viewpoint at Walla Crag.

4 With the viewpoint behind you, bear R to cross the stile over the wall and walk a dozen paces to a small cairn, where you should head L along the clear path arcing into the distance across the moorland in the direction of the lake. This descends steadily for just over a 2km/1.25miles, crossing a stream and arriving eventually at a drystone wall. The trail drops sharply from the wall, then swings R for the descent to **Ashness Bridge**.

5 Follow the lane downhill from the bridge past the Barrow House Youth Hostel as far as the main Keswick-Borrowdale road. Directly opposite the junction you'll see an opening in the wall, with steps leading down to the jetty. At the water's edge, turn R: you may have to improvise a route across the shingle and tree roots until a clear path emerges. And often, the path is completely submerged – in which case, use the path along the side of the road for about 10mins until a hole in the wall is reached allowing access to a narrow path leading to the shore. The going gets easier as the trail meanders around the eastern fringe of Derwent Water, skirting **Calfclose Bay**, site of Peter Randall-Page's "**Hundred-Year Stone**", and crossing a bridge and stretch of pastureland. Immediately after the NT-owned Stable Hills cottage, look for a gate leading L off the main track, which enters a nature reserve.

6 At the far end of the reserve, turn L onto the track running back to the lakeside at Strandshag Bay and follow the obvious waterside trail from here for the remaining stretch back to Keswick, passing the **Friar's Crag** viewpoint on your L and, eventually, the boat landing stages.

7 To return to the town centre from the boat jetties, head R up the lane past the theatre and follow the path running alongside the park/crazy golf course. This leads to an underpass that emerges at the bottom of Lake Rd. Follow Lake Rd up to the T-junction at the top, and turn L opposite George Fisher's gear shop to reach the Market Square.

Getting There
Keswick can be reached by rail and National Express buses. For details of the Keswick Launch Company's boat services on Derwent Water, which include a stop at the jetty just below Ashness Bridge, go to ✎ www.keswick-launch.co.uk, or telephone ✆ 017687 72263.

Visitor Information
Moot Hall Information Centre (TIC)
Moot Hall, Market Square, Keswick.
✆ 017687 72645
✎ www.visitcumbria.com

Eating & Drinking
The Dog & Gun
2 Lake Rd
✆ 017687 73463
With its exposed stone walls, oak beams, open fires and slate floors, this is much the most atmospheric and traditional boozer in Keswick. In addition to a famously tasty

goulash, they serve Lakeland's definitive pint of Old Peculier, and it's a 2-min stumble from the Moot Hall Information Centre in the centre of town.

Sleeping
Barrow House Derwentwater YHA
Borrowdale, Keswick, CA12 5UR
✆ 0845 371 9314
✎ www.yha.org.uk
A grand, 200-year-old mansion set in vast grounds that's bang on our route and close to the lakeshore, with its own waterfall and hydro-electric generator.

Keswick YHA
Station Rd, Keswick, CA12 5LH
✆ 0845 371 9746
✎ www.yha.org.uk
A better hostel option if you want to be in the thick of things, close to the shops, museums and pubs.

Acorn House Hotel,
Ambleside Rd, Keswick, CA12 4DL
✆ 017687 72553
✎ www.acornhousehotel.co.uk
One of the nicest in a long string of lookalike, upscale B&Bs lining Ambleside Rd – passed at the start of our featured route.

Bridgedale
101-103 Main Street, Keswick, CA12 5EB
✆ 017687 73914
An economical, homely, dog-friendly B&B just east of the market square, opposite the Co-Op.

More Info
✎ www.lake-district.gov.uk The National Park's homepage.
✎ www.english-lakes.com. Engaging background on Derwent Water, along with the rest of the region.

walk | 06

DORSET

The Jurassic Pyramid

Golden Cap

It is always of long-established peace, to me, that Golden Cap whispers. So high, so far, so lonely, you cannot be in the world ...
The Marches of Wessex, by F.J.H. Darton, 1922.

Opinion differs as to the origins of the name "Golden Cap", the giant table-topped hill rising sheer from the Dorset coast between Lyme Regis and Bridport. While some insist it derives from the helmet of pale yellow sandstone crowning the clifftop, others claim the canary-coloured gorse bushes that once spilled down its flanks must have been the original inspiration. Either way, the views from the little plateau at the summit – the highest ground between the Wash and Land's End – are sensational, extending from Start Point in south Devon across the spectacular sweep of Chesil beach to Portland Bill in the east, and inland across a landscape of low hills and pretty thatched villages.

Ascents of Golden Cap tend to come in two forms: short and sharp (straight up the east flank from the beachside hamlet of Seatown); or short and soft (from the Langdon Hill car park half-way up its northern side). True to the maxim that half the pleasure of

any feast lies in the expectation, our route adopts a more convoluted approach, admiring views of the hill before savouring the views from it.

The terrain along the way – ancient green lanes, hidden sea combes, bracken-covered commons, windy clifftops and patches of fragrant woodland that are carpeted with bluebells in early spring – is as varied as any on the British coastline. Moreover, a string of tempting diversions lie in wait to lure you off the path, not least the climb down to the secret smuggler's beach at St Gabriel's Mouth. Fossil hunters will also wish to rummage on the beach for the famous ammonites and other Jurassic sea creatures petrified in the Cap's lower flanks, which are perennially on the verge of collapse.

Our figure-of-eight route, starting and ending at the Anchor Inn in Seatown, can be divided neatly into two stages. If you're short of time, or feel more inclined to potter on the beach than spend a full day on the trail, limit yourself to the second loop over Golden Cap, with perhaps a sidetrip up Doghouse Hill and Thorncombe Beacon to the east, which offer equally thrilling views.

At a glance

Where Golden Cap, Seatown, 6km/4.3miles west of Bridport, Dorset.
Why Famous fossil-hunting sites; ancient meadows, flower-filled hedgerows and thatched villages; a great little seaside pub.
Downsides Proximity of the busy

A35; crowds in Seatown during the summer holidays.
When Late May to June, while the clifftop thrift is in flower.
Start/Finish The Anchor Inn, Seatown (SY420918).
Duration 4hrs 15mins.
Distance 13.5km/8.5miles.

Cut it short Complete one of two loops in our figure-of-eight route.
Terrain Clifftop paths, traffic-free country lanes and tracks, open heathland and stream valleys, involving several short, steep climbs and descent.
Maps OS Explorer 116.

On your way

Judging from the presence on its crown of four prehistoric burial mounds, people have appreciated the views from **GOLDEN CAP** for many thousands of years. The panorama from its summit, soaring 191m/626ft above the waves, has an undeniably epic quality. Stand on the razor-sharp cliff edge and you're confronted by a vast sweep of sea, framed far below by a ribbon of pale-orange shingle and cliffs arcing into the distance. It's a vista that has inspired poets, painters and lovers for many centuries, and one guaranteed to leave you feeling spiritually refreshed as well as out of breath.

It might seem sleepy enough, but the idyllic countryside spreading from the base of the cap has seen more than its fair share of conflict. In the village of **CHIDEOCK**, just northeast of the hill, the castle erected in the fourteenth century to repulse the French saw bloody fighting between Roundheads and Cavaliers during the Civil War, when it was reduced to rubble. Local villagers put the honey-coloured masonry to good use, however, beefing up the cob cottages that still distinguish the settlement – which would be one of Dorset's prettiest were it

not for the traffic rumbling through the middle of it along the A35.

You can still make out the ground plan and moat of the old castle in the field at the end of Ruins Lane (crossed by our route). Another vestige of Chideock's medieval past is hidden in the Perpendicular-style Church of St Giles, on the main road, where a fine black-marble tomb of a knight reposes under the window in the south aisle.

The lumpy land on which the castle keep once stood is today dominated by a wooden **MARTYRS' CROSS** commemorating the death of four Catholic men killed during the post-Reformation pogrom of Elizabethan

times. Under the local gentry (the Arundell family), Chideock was staunchly Catholic, and the lords of the manor regularly sheltered fugitive clergymen as persecution intensified through the sixteenth century. But in 1594 the Sheriff of Dorset arrested Lady Arundell's own priest, along with a relative of the family and a couple of their Irish servants. The four were later tortured and executed in Dorchester for high treason.

Oil portraits lining the walls of the little Romanesque chapel attached to Chideock Manor, five minutes' walk north of the village crossroads, commemorate those local men killed for refusing to renounce their faith at the turn of sixteenth century. The church also holds a famous oil painting by Bridport artist Francis Newberry. Locked away for most of the year in the sacristy, the *Blessed Martyrs of Chideock* is only displayed once or twice each year; photos of it hang in the small museum attached to the chapel.

While flax and hemp grown to supply Bridport's sail-cloth and rope industry occupied the villages inland from Chideock in the eighteenth century, the inhabitants of **SEATOWN**, the hamlet at the foot of Golden Cap, made their living mainly through smuggling. The local gang of freetraders was led by a shadowy figure known as "the Colonel", whose favourite landing place was the remote beach at **ST GABRIEL'S MOUTH**. The collapse of its Saxon chapel aside, nothing much has changed in this isolated hamlet since Seatown's smugglers used to land barrels of brandy on the flint-pebbles beside it, while lookouts stationed on the summit of Golden Cap kept watch for Customs & Excise Men. These days, St Gabriel's is owned and managed by the National Trust, which rents out its old farms

LEFT: Looking west towards Charmouth from the top of Golden Cap

as holiday cottages, and maintains the perilous looking wooden ladder-steps leading to the beach – an access point to one of the Jurassic Coast's fossil-hunting hot spots.

Golden Cap is deservedly this area's most popular target for walkers, but the views are no less impressive from the top of **THORNCOMBE BEACON**, a stiff thirty-minute climb up the cliffs east of Seatown. The hilltop, from where you gain a superb bird's-eye-view over Bridport and its hinterland, is crowned with a fire basket erected in 1988 to mark the 400th anniversary of the Spanish Armada – the basket is a replica of those dotted in a chain along the English coast as an early warning system against foreign invasion.

Due north of Thorncombe Beacon lies an area of commonland known as **EYPE DOWN** – another fine viewpoint where, if you're lucky, you might spot a peregrine falcon or two darting around the paragliders who also frequent the skies above it. In 2004, the Ramblers and Open Spaces Society successfully campaigned to prevent the enclosure of the down. It's a particularly lovely spot in early spring,

when bluebells speckle the hilltop.

Chesil Beach, stretching east from below the Down, is rife with tales of smugglers. It is said that privateers used to be able to tell which stretch of the shingle bank they were on at night by the size of its pebbles. Shipwrecks were also commonplace. None, however, caused more of a stir than the loss of the Dutch privateer, the *Hope*, when it ran aground on the night of the 16th January, 1649. The ship's crew were able to clamber to safety, but they received little succour from the "merciless battalion" of locals who started to flood in once rumours reached taverns in the area that the *Hope* had sunk with a cargo of £50,000 in gold and silver (around £4million in today's money). The plunder continued for over a week, as more and more bullion came to light amid the pebbles – "a scene of unparalleled lawlessness" according to one onlooker.

In the 1990s, divers searching for the wreck of the *Hope* found a large anchor. Subsequently dated to the mid-seventeenth century, it was purchased by the landlord of the Anchor Inn and now enjoys pride of place on the terrace in front of the pub at Seatown.

Seatown and the Pitchfork Rebellion

Trouble descended on Chideock from the sea in May 1685, when three mysterious ships appeared off the beach at Seatown. They carried a shoddily equipped, rag-tag invasion force of around a hundred men marshalled by the Protestant renegade James Scott, the 1st Duke of Monmouth, who had sailed to England from exile in Holland to seize the throne from his uncle, James II – a Catholic. Seatown was the rebels' first land-

fall, but given its Catholic leanings, couldn't have been more poorly chosen. Once his scouts learned of the area's religious affiliations, however, the Duke pressed on to Protestant Lyme Regis, where he established his headquarters.

The so-called Monmouth Re-bellion would, ultimately, last less than a month. Denied the support promised back in the Hague, the "Pitchfork Army" of 6000 farm labourers, artisans and non-

conformists who marched north to take Bristol under Monmouth's banner, were all too easily cut down by the muskets and can-onfire of the King's professional soldiers. The Duke escaped the battlefield at Sedgemoor, on the Somerset Levels, but was hunted down and beheaded at the Tower of London shortly after; 300 of his supporters were executed, and 800 others transported to the West Indies.

walk it | 06

Golden Cap

Part I:

1 Cross the car park in front of the Anchor Inn in Seatown, and keep to the cliff edges as the coast path ascends Cliff Ridge, then drops into a dry combe before scaling Doghouse Hill. After a climb of a little under half an hour, you'll reach the top of **Thorncombe Beacon** (SY435914).

2 After descending a short way from the hilltop, our route swings inland from Thorncombe Beacon around the lip of a steep field to a stile on your L, which you cross (signposted "Eype Down"). Continue across the field to another stile and climb over this. Just before reaching Downhouse Farm, look for a track cutting sharply uphill to your L through woods, signposted "Eype Down". Ignore the yellow arrow pointing to your R, and take the steep track uphill through the trees. This eventually brings you out on Eype Down. Ignore the yellow arrow to the R through the woods and. Keep walking in the same direction across **Eype Down**.

3 At the four-way signpost reached after 5mins, turn L for "Quarry Hill – Chideock", bearing R at the fork 5mins later to reach a tumulus. This marks the start of a short descent to the A35, which you cross. Follow "Quarr Lane" (sic) directly opposite for 2mins until you see a waymarked farm track peeling L off the lane through a metal gate, just before a row of bungalows.

The route reaches a second metal gate shortly after; cross this and head uphill to L along line of wind-bent hawthorn trees.

4 Once on the lumpy summit plateau of Quarry Hill, it's worth making a short detour L for a fine view over the valley. Follow the distinct path around the west rim of the hilltop and you'll reach a metal gate after 5mins leading onto access land. From the northern-most spur of the hill, you then drop sharply downhill, aiming towards the top R corner of the field below which a gate leads to a crossroads of old droveways. Turn L here onto Hell Lane.

5 After dropping through a stone cutting, the muddy track reaches a stream after 15mins, just beyond which a waymarked stile leads to the L. Bear L up the slope, making for the gap between the oak trees and coppice, and then on to the projecting corner of the field hedge beyond. The yellow arrow waymarks on the corner fence are the first in a series that guide you around field borders and over a succession of stiles to the **Martyrs' Cross**, sited amid ruins of the old castle on the northern outskirts of **Chideock** village.

6 From the castle, follow Ruins Lane through the houses to Main Street (the A35). Turn R when you reach the main road, cross and then turn L down a path cutting between houses just before Rose Cottage B&B. This pathway leads through more houses and over the village green, emerging on a tarmac lane where you bear L and follow the

slope down through the caravan park to Seatown.

Part II:

7 The second leg of our route follows Seahill Lane north through **Seatown** village from the car park in front of the Anchor Inn, turning L after 5mins up a side lane signposted for "Langdon Woods" and "Sea Hill House". After the B&B, proceed uphill along an old farm track, skirting the south edge of Landgon Woods. At the far end of the wood, go through gate straight ahead and bear along the R fork, diagonally across the field to a second gate, with **Golden Cap** now rising to your L.

8 At the second gate, a signpost indicates the "Bridleway St Gabriel's". Follow the path along the L edge of the field, as it first contours around the base of Golden Cap, then drops sharply down the hill's northwest side, past a three-way signpost on your L to the bottom corner of a field. Here, another signpost points L to the ruined chapel at St Gabriel's.

9 Keep to the path as it passes the red-brick NT holiday cottages. Continue via the five-bar gate immediately to L next to some houses, signposted "To Coast Path". At the path junction 5mins later, either follow the NT Permissive Path for the recommended diversion to **Gabriel's Mouth** (involving a steep climb down wooden ladder steps, closed due to landslips at the time of writing), or turn L onto the coast path to begin a steep, zigzagging ascent of

Golden Cap (SY407923). Continue across the summit plateau to the trig point.

10 The route off the top drops down the east side of the hill, turning R after a stile for the remaining stretch down to Seatown. Note that as you near the village there has been a re-routing of the coast path due to landslip, but it's correctly drawn on current OS maps and well waymarked, bringing you out on Seahill Lane, where you turn R for the Anchor Inn.

Getting There

Chideock is 1km/0.6miles north of Seatown and lies on FirstBus route X53 and FirstDorset

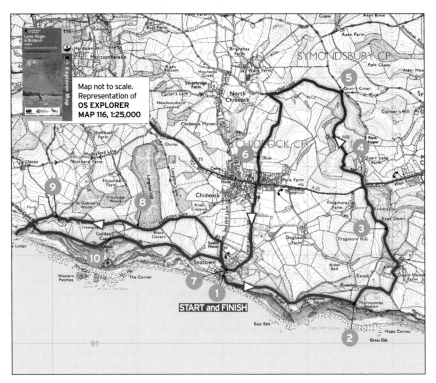

Map not to scale.
Representation of
**OS EXPLORER
MAP 116, 1:25,000**

START and FINISH

Route profile

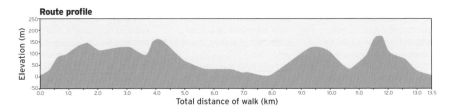

route 31 between Exeter and Poole, both of which pass through Bridport. The nearest railhead is at Axminster. For timetable information, telephone ☎0871 200 2233 or go to 🖱www.travelinesw.com.

ℹ️ Visitor Information
The National Trust's Golden Cap estate office
Charmouth
☎01297 561900

🔪 Eating & Drinking
Next to the Anchor Inn in Seatown, a small shop sells beach essentials, sweets and pasties, but there's a much better stocked store just up the hill at the entrance to the caravan park.

The Anchor Inn
Seatown
☎01297 489215
Perfect location, slap on the beach at the foot of Golden Cap. It's a brewery-owned pub that's worn around the edges, but genuinely hospitable, serving hand-pumped Palmers ales (from nearby Bridport) and fairly priced meals, which you can eat surrounded by interesting maritime photos in the bar, or outside in their breezy cliff-edge terrace overlooking the beach.

Garden Café
Downhouse Farm
Secluded little café, nestled beside a working farm with superb views over the hedges to Lyme Bay. Seated out in the flower-filled garden, you can tuck into home-baked cakes and top-quality cream teas, or order more substantial main meals.

ABOVE: The view north from Quarry Hill

🏠 Sleeping
Seahill House
Seahill Lane, Seatown, DT6 6JT
☎01297 489801 or
☎07989 940793
Single-storey, one-bedroomed self-catering cottage above Seatown on the lower slopes of Golden Cap. It's smartly furnished in contemporary style, with a cosy wood burner, and has fabulous views over our route from its sea-facing decked terrace.

National Trust Camping & Caravan Field
St Gabriel's
☎ 01297 561900
Small, basic campsite, offering a water supply but no other facilities, in a wonderful spot on the far side of Golden Cap.

📄 More Info
🖱www.nationaltrust.org.uk/ main/w-goldencap. The NT owns

not just Golden Cap, but also St Gabriel's and Thorncombe Beacon.

🖱www.chideock.co.uk. The village website holds some interesting history pages.

🖱www.seatown.ukfossils.co.uk. Tips on where to find and how to identify fossils in the rocks below Golden Cap – a complete skeleton of a hitherto unknown dinosaur came to light here in 2008, after a large chunk of the cliffs collapsed.

More Walks
The Dorset Jubilee Trail, A Rambler's Guide (Ramblers Dorset Area). A comprehensive guide with maps to this 145-km/90-mile walk across Dorset from Forde Abbey to Bokerey Dyke. The route was inaugurated in 1995 to celebrate the sixtieth anniversary of the Ramblers.

The Druids' Playground

Brimham Rocks

Just as the human eye seems primed to pick out recognizable shapes from the clouds, so it is with rock formations – and from Brimham Moor in North Yorkshire rises an outcrop guaranteed to fire even the most jaded imagination.

Scattered over a level hilltop three miles east of the former lead mining town of Pateley Bridge, Brimham Rocks is one of the North of England's best loved natural wonders – a mass of giant gritstone boulders eroded into phantasmagorical forms that have been likened to dancing bears, begging dogs, canons, mushrooms, cartoon characters and even a French president.

Our Georgian ancestors believed these weird eminences to have been man made. In 1786, one noted antiquary described them as the work "of artists skilled in the power of mathematics", identifying their creators as the same ancient "Druids" who erected the standing-stone circles at Avebury and Stonehenge.

Not until the birth of geology in the Victorian era did the processes behind the boulders' formation begin to be understood. By that time, the railway network had been extended from Harrogate towards the mines of Nidderdale to the northwest, and the

Brimham outcrop was for the first time accessible to less well off visitors.

Brimham lies today under the stewardship of the National Trust, and teems with daytrippers on sunny weekends. Its curious boulders nevertheless retain their mystique – not least because of the great swathe of wonderful countryside they overlook. From the escarpment ringing two sides of the hilltop, you can enjoy superb views northeast over the Vale of Mowbray, and northwest up the walled pastures and reservoirs of Nidderdale to Great Whernside, where the Nidd finds its source.

To put Brimham in its proper context, our route approaches the boulders along the river southeast from Pateley Bridge, via a delightful waterside path. Delving into the thickly wooded tributary valley of Fell Beck, it then winds towards the hill's base over land inhabited since Neolithic times. Having crested Brimham Moor and explored the famous boulders, you'll then descend back to Pateley Bridge along a bracken-covered hillside, followed by an enjoyable ramble over farmland criss-crossed with ancient drystone walls. To wrap things up, the final leg follows Pateley's "Panoramic Walk", offering more fine valley vistas.

At a glance

Where Brimham Rocks, Pateley Bridge, 16km/10miles northwest of Harrogate, North Yorkshire.
Why Fantastic rock formations and views; pretty woodland and riverside paths; industrial history.

When Pateley Bridge hosts the lively Nidderdale Festival in July.
Downsides Crowds, particularly during school holidays.
Start/Finish Nidd Bridge, Pateley Bridge (SE157655).

Duration 4hrs.
Distance 14km/8.7miles.
Terrain Riverside and waymarked woodland paths initially, then clear footpaths across farmland.
Maps OS Explorer 298.

On your way

"Could Brimham be transported to
Salisbury Plain, Stonehenge itself would be
reduced to a poor & pygmy miniature,"
enthused the *Gentleman's Magazine* in
1860. The comparison may be invidious,
but it conveys the astonishment that
generally attends first glimpses of these
famous rocks.

Rising from a cloak of purple heather
and rosebay willowherb, the outcrops are
scattered over a fifty-acre hilltop,
buttressed on its northern and western
flanks by steep escarpments. Some are the
size of houses, others little larger than the
children that scamper around on sunny
weekends, but no two are alike.

Names dreamed up by visitors and
guides over the years point to resemblances
both real and imagined. There's the
"Dancing Bear", with muzzle and paw
raised; the "Camel" and the "Turtle" side
by side; "Donald Duck", complete with

beak and flat feet; and the uncannily
realistic profile of "De Gaulle" himself,
with nose raised disdainfully.

Although the names of some of the
formations here (eg the "Smartie Tube")
clearly date from modern times, those of
the most famous boulders – including the
one at our featured viewpoint, the
"Druid's Writing Table" – imply ancient
roots. No evidence, however, has ever
come to light connecting Brimham with
the white-robed mistletoe worshippers of
yore. Rather, the druidic connection
probably dates from the mid-eighteenth
century, when these curious outcrops
were believed by visiting scholars to
have been fashioned for long-forgotten
ritual purposes.

In fact, the rocks at Brimham, formed
in the Carboniferous period 320 million
years ago, originated in the gritty sands
lining a massive river delta. Swept down
from the high ranges of what are now
Scotland and Norway, the sandy gloop,

flecked with quartz crystals and feldspar, became buried under later deposits, compacting over time into dark-brown gritstone. This was then thrust to the surface by plate movement for the elements to work their magic on.

The erosion responsible for the rocks' dream-like shapes occurred mostly in the wake of the last Ice Age, when the desert landscape that predominated hereabouts was devoid of plant life. Wind-blasted sand, blown at ferocious speeds along the ground, scoured the base of the outcrops, wearing away the bottoms of the boulders to narrow pedestals.

The most extreme example of this is the iconic "Druid's Idol" – a bulbous, 200-tonne monster precariously perched on a collar of only 30cm/12inches. Sometimes, the connecting stem wore away completely to leave the boulder literally rocking in the wind. Local legend holds that the "White Rocking Stone" – which used to sport a coat of whitewash and could be seen all the way from Harrogate – can only be moved "by honest people".

Plenty of other old tales and superstitions swirl around these stones. Edmund Bogg, in his 1895 travelogue *From Eden Valley to the Plain of York* noted that, "[in] bygone days [they] were supposed to be the habitation of spirits… From a conversation we had with the peasantry not far from here, it seems the ancient belief had not yet fully disappeared."

One large, cave-like hollow used to be the abode of a witch called "Great Sybill", while "Lovers' Leap" is where a star-crossed couple allegedly threw themselves to their deaths after the girl's father refused to allow the pair to marry. It is said that magical spirits intervened and rescued them before they were dashed on the rocks below.

We can safely assume such stories have probably been told about Brimham Rocks for as long as people have inhabited the Nidderdale region – a very long time indeed if the carved boulder lying in a field just off our route at High Wood Farm is anything to go by. Sculpted with so-called "cup and ring" marks, the stone's patterns are believed to be between 3500 and 6000 thousand years old.

The Neolithic waymarker rests close to the course of an ancient track, used at one time by the Cistercian monks of Fountain Abbey to travel to and from their sheep pastures further up Nidderdale. The monks also mined lead in the distant hills, transferring the ore downriver to be processed. Remnants of this industry still stand around the hamlet of Smelthouses, skirted by our walk.

Indeed, lead mining was until the late nineteenth century the mainstay of **PATELEY BRIDGE**, a small town located next to an ancient crossing point over the Nidd whose industries were long dominated by two families: the Metcalfes and the Yorkes. The Metcalfes also built the large flax mill at **GLASSHOUSES** on the riverside just southeast of Pateley. Smartly renovated, the old stone building now accommodates a mix of modern businesses, including a winery where you can taste elderberry and rhubarb "wines" in the comfort of the former wheelhouse.

Despite the arrival of the railway in 1862, Pateley Bridge's industry went into sharp decline in the early 1900s, leaving the town in the unhurried time warp it still occupies today. Home to Britain's oldest sweet shop (which claims to have been established 1827), its High Street also hosts the staunchly traditional Kendall's butchers, whose legendary pork pies have, over the years, re-fuelled many a hungry rambler freshly arrived from Brimham Rocks.

1 Immediately before you cross Nidd Bridge from the town side, turn L along a public footpath. Follow this attractive riverside track for 2km/1.2miles, past a weir and large mill reservoir until you reach a road. Turn L here towards **Glasshouses**, but after a few metres go through a doorway in a wall on your R. Bear L, then R, to pass in front of the mill. At its far side, just beyond the smoke house, turn R down a track that soon bends L back to the river.

2 The riverside path is clear, running up a bank to a stile at one point, and under a disused railway. Ignore the footbridge across the river, and instead continue ahead until you reach a wide beck. Here, the path leads away from the river to cross the beck via a footbridge. Once on the far side, turn L and cross the field to reach the main road.

3 Cross to the lane opposite. When the tarmac surface ends, keep straight ahead along the track and follow it to the next road. Turn L here over the bridge, but a short way up the hill fork R onto a footpath signposted

"Pateley Bridge". You pass a pretty mill pond on the R, after which the beck flows below you through a deep ravine.

The course of the path is obvious from here on, passing through beautiful woodland as far as a footbridge, after which you bear R up a stony track; 30m/yrds before the derelict brick building, turn sharp L along a path through a birch wood, then fork R soon after along a narrower path.

Follow this as far as another fork, where you should bear R onto a track, through a gate into the yard of a house. Walk through the yard and on to the R of the building via the main track. Follow this uphill for 1.6km/1mile, past a farm, until you reach a junction with the National Trust **Brimham Rocks** access track.

4 Turn L up the track. Walk through the car park, and continue straight ahead, around the barrier, and on for 5-10mins through some amazing rock formations until you reach the National Trust Information Centre. At the point where the tarmac track bends sharply R, just in front of the centre, head along the unsurfaced track branching L, which soon after narrows to a footpath.

Follow this as it skirts more superb rocks, past our featured viewpoint of the day, until you arrive at a big spread of open heather and a

junction. Instead of following the main path sharply to the R at this intersection, keep straight ahead for a short way, then bear L down a shallow valley as far as a surfaced track.

5 Turn L onto the tarmac and follow the track for a few minutes until you reach a field. The official right of way runs along the L edge of this field, then bends R towards the houses. Head L along the main driveway when you reach it, but where it swings sharply R, bear L along a clear footpath cutting across the field to a ladder stile. Cross this and follow the wall along the end of the field, bearing L at the bottom to a second stile. Keep to the R of the next two fields on a well worn farm track with woods to your R, at the bottom of which a ladder stile leads to a footbridge over a beck.

Cross and bear R up the track. At the junction, take the track half L, which shortly after crosses a cattle grid. You're now on the Nidderdale Way. When the wall on your R bends R, fork half R across the field to a gap in the wall ahead. Go through this and bear R to a gap stile, then keep L along the wall to reach some houses. Pass to their L,

Route profile

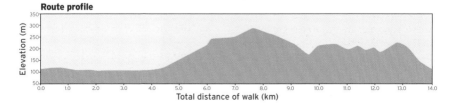

along a walled path, and turn L at the crosspath at the top. This track takes you down to White Houses.

6 At the junction, go straight over and follow the R-hand fork, which in a few metres leads to a gate. Go through this and continue for approx 500m/550yrds to a farm access track, which takes you to a road. Turn R (uphill); then L at the Nidderdale Way sign and cross the stream; soon after you're between two drystone walls.

7 At the next road junction, keep straight ahead and follow the lane for 5mins (230m/250yrds). Just beyond the entrance to Rock House, fork R by a bench onto a track, which runs past the houses of Blazefield to the B6265, which you turn L onto. Walk down the hill for 5mins, but where the road bends L, head R along a track. This soon narrows between walls. Keep L at the next fork, continuing on a tarmac lane through Knott.
You're now on the Panoramic

Walk, which takes you back to **Pateley Bridge**, with more stunning views over the valley. On reaching the hairpin bend, keep straight ahead past the entrance to the cemetery, then follow the path all the way down to the main road, turning R to regain the town centre and main street.

Getting There
Number 24 bus runs hourly from Harrogate to Pateley Bridge.

i Visitor Information
Tourist Information Centre
(summer only)
High Street, Pateley Bridge
☎ 01423 711147

Off-season: TIC Harrogate
Crescent Rd, Harrogate
☎ 0845 389 3223

Eating & Drinking
In addition to the places on, or close to, our route reviewed below, the National Trust runs a refreshments kiosk at Brimham Rocks serving snacks and light meals.

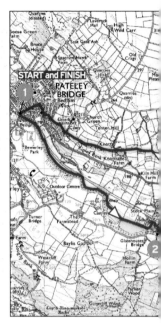

The Half Moon
Fell Beck
☎ 01423 711560
A short diversion north of our route, this roadside pub, in the village of Fell Beck, serves a decent pint of Black Sheep and proper Yorkshire ham, egg and chips.

Yorkshire Country Wines
Riverside Cellars
The Mill, Glasshouses
☎ 01423 711947
✍ www.yorkshirecountrywines.co.uk
Converted flax mill near the river that makes a great pitstop, with a tea rooms serving snacks and light meals at stone tables on a sun-dappled terrace. In winter, you can hunker down on old settles next to a log fire in the Snug for a mug of

ABOVE: Brimham's dreamlike rock formations

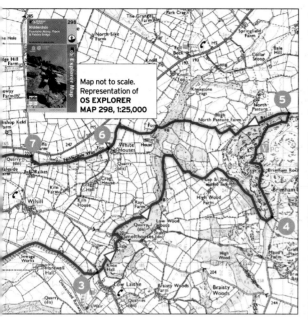

Map not to scale.
Representation of
**OS EXPLORER
MAP 298, 1:25,000**

Talbot House
27 High St, Pateley Bridge, HG3 5AL
☎01423 711597
✎www.talbothouse.co.uk
Pleasantly furnished B&B rooms in
a grade-II-listed former coaching
house. They offer deals for walkers
following the Nidderdale Way, with
transport and maps included.

🗊 **More Info**
*An Introduction to Brimham
Rocks and Moor National Trust.* Sold
at the Trust's site shop, this leaflet will
guide you around the rock formations.

🚶 **More Walks**
*Country Walks Around
Harrogate (Vol 2 West)* by West
Riding Area of the Ramblers. Two
dozen short and medium-length
routes in the Nidderdale and
Washburn Valley areas, described
by local experts. Illustrated with sketch
maps and b&w photographs, this
book provided the original inspiration
for our Brimham Rocks walk.

*Freedom to Roam Guides:
Wharfedale and Nidderdale* by
Andrew Bibby (Frances Lincoln/
Ramblers). Twelve routes in the
southern Yorkshire Dales, on land
recently opened for the public
under the CRoW Act 2000.

the winery's warming "Wassail Cup"
– not to be missed.

 Sleeping
Foxfield
Ripon Rd, Pateley Bridge, HG3 5NJ
☎01423 711685
✎www.foxfieldbnb.co.uk

Good-value, walker-friendly
B&B close to the centre of
town and the start of our walk.
It's welcoming, does great
breakfasts and boasts fine views.
Flask-filling service, boot-drying
facilities, packed lunches and taxi
transfers available on request.

The Nidderdale Way

Several stretches of our route
benefit from the waymarks and
fixtures of the Nidderdale Way, a
popular, 85-km/53-mile long-distance walk beginning and ending
at Pateley Bridge. Remaining
for most of its course within the
Nidderdale Area of Outstanding

Natural Beauty (AONB), the route
connects the open pastures of
the lower dale to the open fells
around the source of the Nidd.
The circuit, generally completed
in 5-7 days, is well served by public transport and walker-friendly
accommodation. You can also

arrange all-in "packages" through
many B&Bs in Pateley Bridge,
who will pre-book picnics and
taxis to and from the trailheads
(see "Sleeping" below). More
background on the walk appears
at ✎www.ramblers.org.uk/info/
paths/name/n/nidderdale.html.

walk | 08

BUCKINGHAMSHIRE

Chalk and Leas

Beacon Hill

The Chiltern Hills are young. A mere 10,000 years ago this entire area was flat, but at the end of last Ice Age torrents of water released by melting glaciers carved away the softer Gault and Kimmeridge clays of the Vale of Aylesbury, exposing the backbone of the Chiltern escarpment.

However, it's the tiny marine algae known as Coccolithophores we have to thank for the nature of these smooth, rounded hills. During the Cretaceous period billions upon billions of these planktonic creatures were consumed by larger marine animals and excreted onto the sea bed where they compacted to form a layer of chalk hundreds of metres thick.

Slap bang in the middle of the northern ridge, a small section folds inwards to create an amphitheatre of forested chalk foothills, peppered with smaller domed knolls and leafy hollows. From this wooded basin a sharp spur rises 260m/850ft, revealing an exhilarating view 32km/20miles northwest across the lower-lying vale to Quainton Hill, with glimpses of Oxfordshire and Northamptonshire beyond. The spur is known as Beacon Hill, and is just one of

many impressive viewpoints along the Chilterns' escarpment. Ivinghoe Beacon and Coombe Hill to the east, and Whiteleaf Hill to the south, are all contenders for the title of the Chilterns' "best view". However, we've plumped for this less well-known vantage point, partly because prior to the Countryside and Rights of Way Act of 2000 the view here was not accessible to the public - and as such the crowds of day-trippers that flock to the other sites are still unaware of it - but mostly because it provides a route that lazily avoids many of the steeper climbs in the area.

This is a short, leisurely walk on reddish-brown loam and black flint tracks that plunges you into fresh woodland then disgorges you among flower-rich meadows. You'll have plenty of time to study the glorious red kites, which were reintroduced to the area recently, and have thrived, exceeding all expectations; spread out a picnic in the pleasant leas of Grangelands Nature Reserve; or simply sit for a while on the soft knoll of Chequers' Knap watching the sun go down. And if you still have some energy left you can even take a short trot up Whiteleaf Hill.

At a glance

Where Little Kimble, 4km/ 2.5miles northeast of Princes Risborough, 5km/3miles west of Wendover, the Chiltern Hills.
Why Dense woodland with gentle hills; red kites wheeling

overhead; butterfly country.
When Late March, to witness the first of the Brimstone butterflies to emerge from their chrysalises.
Start/Finish Little Kimble train station (SP823066).

Duration 2hrs 30mins.
Distance 8km/5miles.
Terrain Mostly on clear chalk and flint paths, or woodland tracks, with gentle hills. One short, but steep climb.
Maps OS Explorer 181.

On your way

A few minutes' walk from **LITTLE KIMBLE** station takes you to **ALL SAINTS' CHURCH**. The church was built in the thirteenth century from local sarsen, flint and Portland limestone, and for decorative effect a large ammonite, found locally, was laid into the wall near the gate. Inside, there are four rare wall paintings of St George, St Christopher, St James and St Bernard. The paintings date from fourteenth century, but were only discovered during the church's restoration five hundred years later.

All Saints' also boasts medieval Chertsey tiles that outline the plot of Tristan and Isolde: a twelfth-century tale of boy-meets-girl, girl-marries-wrong-boy and an adulterous love triangle ensues. The legend is said to have inspired Thomas Malory's romance, *Le Morte d'Arthur*.

The surrounding woods are rich in archaeological remains and legend. Once home to Neolithic farmers, they were defended by a string of hillforts from Pulpit Hill to Ivinghoe Beacon. The forts were, and still are, linked by "the oldest road in Britain", the Ridgeway National Trail. **BEACON HILL** itself is thought to have been the site of a great battle between the invading Romans and the Celtic king Cymbeline. The king is said to be buried to the west of the hill, but in fact the earthwork known as **CYMBELINE'S CASTLE** or "Cymbeline's Mount" is a Norman motte and bailey construction. Shakespeare's famous romance was based on this Iron Age leader, and the surrounding villages of the "Kimbles" may have taken their names from the alternative spelling, Kymbelinus.

The short climb to the top of Beacon Hill is rewarded by the sprawling view northwards across the Vale of Aylesbury, and east to Coombe Hill, where a memorial to those who died in the Boer War crowns the summit. The most prominent feature in the foreground is **ELLESBOROUGH CHURCH**, which serves the nearby Chequers estate. Chequers was given to the nation by Lord Lee of Fareham and has been a weekend retreat for British prime ministers since 1921. You can glimpse Chequers from the far end (south) of the short ridge of Beacon Hill, but be warned, even out here you are on CCTV!

Nearby lies **ELLESBOROUGH WARREN**, which was designed in the twelfth century to introduce rabbits from France to Britain; some of the original colony's descendants still leap from the undergrowth like vernal highwaymen.

From here our route becomes ever more sylvan. Beech, ash, sycamore, whitebeam, yew and holly all grace the woodlands of Pulipit Hill. The ground flora is dominated by dog's mercury, enchanter's nightshade, and wood sorrel. The grasslands of **GRANGELANDS NATURE RESERVE** are a Site of Special Scientific Interest and support an abundant butterfly population. Brimstones are the first to emerge from their chrysalises in March, followed in mid-summer by marbled white and chalk-hill blue, while peacocks and meadow browns can be seen until September.

A short stint along the Ridgeway skirting the western slope of Pulpit Hill takes you past **THE BUTTS** – a steep coombe that was used as a firing range during World War II – and onto Chequers' Knap. The soft knoll is an idyllic spot to rest and admire the views north and west before joining the North Bucks Way to Great Kimble.

ABOVE: St Nicholas' Church, Great Kimble, the scene of John Hampden's protest in 1635

Upon arrival at Great Kimble you're greeted by two of the most important buildings in any traditional English village: the church and the pub. However, the Grade I-listed **ST NICHOLAS' CHURCH** was at one time the most important parish church in England. In 1635 John Hampden, a local landowner and MP, called a parish meeting here, where he publicly refused to pay "ship money" levied on his estate by Charles I. This ancient tax, normally voted for by parliament at a time of national crisis, obliged maritime towns and counties to supply ships, or the cash equivalent, to boost the war effort. Since this was neither a time of war, nor had the tax been approved by parliament, it became clear that Charles' intention was to convert the levy into a general peacetime tax. Hampden was arrested for his protest, but his stand against Charles I continued with his support of Pym's "Grand Remonstrance" listing 200 grievances against the King. John Hampden declared that there were two conditions under which active resistance to the Crown became the duty of a good subject: an attack upon religion, and an attack upon the fundamental laws of the land. In St Nicholas' Church the seeds of the English Civil War were sown.

CHECKED BY
✔ **Wycombe & District Ramblers**

1 From **Little Kimble** train station cross the A4010, turn R and walk for 300m to the junction with Ellesborough Road. Turn L, crossing to **All**

Saints' Church. Continue down Ellesborough Rd, crossing the road again when the pavement runs out, until you come to the sign for Ellesborough Village, just before the bus stop. Take the Aylesbury Ring path, just behind the village sign, along the edge of a private

garden and down a narrow path to a stile into a field. Continue across the field to a second stile and carry on, keeping the fence on your R, until you reach the waymarked crossing at the next stile. Here turn R uphill towards Ellesborough Church.

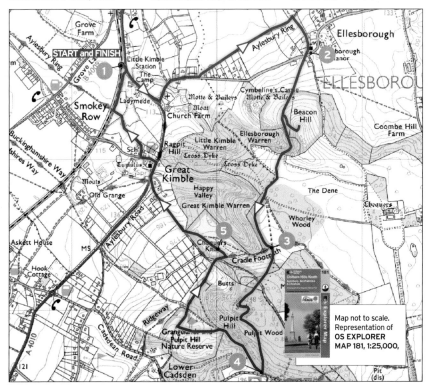

Route profile

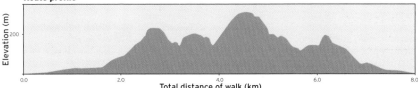

2 Pass through the churchyard and exit the main gate. Cross the road and turn immediately R and take the first path through the kissing gate on the L – then head towards **Beacon Hill**. The main path skirts the hill but you can now climb it to experience the view. The easiest route is to follow the main path to the R of the hill until just before it starts to dip, then take the narrower sheep track leading upwards to the L. Descend the same way and turn L to rejoin the main path. As you descend, **Cymbeline's Castle** is in the wooded part of the ridge ahead; surviving earthworks are visible from the fence at the far side of the grassland. The path enters **Ellesborough Warren** and climbs steps to emerge briefly to cross a field before entering woods once again. The path soon reaches a surfaced road (marked private in both directions). Cross over and pass through a gate keeping to the R along the fence through a clump of beech trees, until you reach a kissing gate leading onto signed access land. Go through the gate and up to the brow of the hill, then turn L through bushes and trees making for the far L hand side of this small enclosure.

3 Here the path crosses the Ridgeway. Climb over the stile bearing slightly R, keeping the fence on your L for approx 25m/85ft and then bearing further R away from the fence over grassland up towards the woods (ignoring a path leading off to the R). Enter the woods and pass through a kissing gate. Cross straight over a bridleway, then pass through a gap in a fence and continue for about 200m to a path junction. Turn L, crossing the Iron Age hillfort on **Pulpit Hill**, then bear R round the edge of a conifer plantation, with the bank and ditch of the fort on the R, descending to a broad track. Turn L and follow the track for about 250m until you reach a crossing path with a signpost back to the fort. Turn R downhill to meet another bridleway and the National Trust car park.

4 To continue, turn R on the bridleway and over the first stile on the L, immediately after a narrow path bears off to the R, into **Grangelands Nature Reserve**: a tree beyond the stile forms a slight obstruction. This also is access land so, keeping uphill, make your way straight on westwards through the scrub and bushes using any of the small tracks towards the Ridgeway, which runs downs a shallow valley near the western boundary of the reserve. Upon reaching the Ridgeway, turn R to continue, or L for The Plough pub (a further detour of about a kilometre up the Ridgeway beyond the pub leads to the popular Whiteleaf Hill). Pass through two gates following the Ridgeway for approx 5mins until you reach **The Butts** - a steep coombe on the western edge of Pulpit Hill. Continue on through a kissing gate and up a few steps to meet the North Bucks Way. Turn R then L through the kissing gate and then immediately L again and up onto the knoll of **Chequers' Knap**.

5 Descend the far side of Chequers' Knap to meet a path bearing L slightly downhill that rejoins the North Bucks Way. Go through the kissing gate and turn R along North Bucks Way towards **Great Kimble**. Turn R on the main road and cross to **St Nicholas' Church** and the Bernard Arms. A further 10mins' walk completes the route back to the train station. Take the road between the church and pub and turn R immediately before the school, then follow the Aylesbury Ring path over three stiles. Just before a further stile where the Aylesbury Ring crosses the railway tracks turn R and follow this path to return to Little Kimble station.

Getting There
Little Kimble Station is on a branch line from Princes Risborough to Aylesbury with hourly trains for much of the day. It's also possible to get a Chiltern Railways train direct to Little Kimble from London Marylebone.
📞 0845 7484950
🖳 www.nationalrail.co.uk

Arriva bus 300 provides a good service (hourly on Sundays) between High Wycombe and Aylesbury via Princes Risborough, stopping at Little Kimble's All Saints' Church. There are also stops at Ellesborough and Great Kimble churches should you wish to shorten the route.
📞 0870 6082608
🖳 www.traveline.org.uk

Visitor Information
Wendover TIC
The Clock Tower, High St, HP22 6DU
📞 01296 696759
🖳 www.wendover-pc.gov.uk/tourism
Open Mon-Sat 10am-4pm.

Eating & Drinking

There are no shops at Little Kimble or Great Kimble, so make sure you bring your own provisions, or check the opening times of the following:

The Plough

Cadsden

☎ 01844 343302

🖱 www.ploughatcadsden.com

Nestled between Whiteleaf Hill and Pulpit Hill, the hamlet of Cadsden gets its name from a corruption of "cat's den", a reference to the Excise Men stationed here in the eighteenth century. Few original buildings remain, and this pub has been extensively refurbished. Walkers and families are particularly welcome, and there's a log fire in winter, and a beer garden in summer. Good food and well maintained ales. Accommodation also available, including one room with wheelchair access.

The Bernard Arms

Great Kimble

☎ 01844 346172

Half a mile from Little Kimble station, this pub is convenient for our route, but it lacks the charm you'd expect from the area. Many prime ministers of the day have drowned their sorrows at this bar, but you can't help thinking the country would be in a better state if they'd headed down the road to the Red Lion (see below).

Sleeping

The Red Lion

Upper Icknield Way, Whiteleaf, HP27 0LL

☎ 01844 344476

🖱 www.theredlionwhiteleaf.co.uk

At the foot of Whiteleaf Hill,

ABOVE: The view north over Ellesborough from Beacon Hill

the Red Lion is a family-run seventeenth-century inn offering a selection of fine beers and wines, excellent food and comfortable accommodation. It's very friendly, there's usually a log fire on the go and they particularly welcome walkers.

Ramblers' Retreat

Wendover House, Church Lane, Wendover, HP22 6NL

☎ 01296 622157

🖱 www.wendoverhouse.bucks.sch.uk

The hostel is in a residential school, and is only available at weekends and school holidays. It has one dormitory with five curtained bedspaces, a private room for one, a well-equipped kitchen and plenty of washing facilities. Book at least 24 hours in advance.

More Info

🖱 www.chilternsaonb.org

One of the better AONB websites with a broad range of useful information including easy access and stile-free walks, and a recently added history section.

More Walks

🖱 www.bucks-wmiddx-ramblers.org.uk

Click on "best walks". Buckinghamshire, Milton Keynes and West Middlesex Area of the Ramblers has provided detailed route descriptions available to download free, plus a handy map-reading exercise to try out near Little Kimble.

The Secrets of Countryside Access by Dave Ramm (East Berkshire Ramblers). If you've just got the walking bug then there's nothing better to further your enthusiasm than this illustrated guide to finding, using and enjoying country paths. A mine of information and practical advice, explained in simple terms and attractively presented with over 200 illustrations, plus a foreword by Nick Crane.

Walks in South Bucks by West London Ramblers (Ramblers). A series of three books, each with around sixteen walks in the area.

High in Skye
The Old Man Of Storr

"Isle of Mists" is what the Norsemen who colonized its shores in the Dark Ages called Skye, and if you've ever been here in the *dreicht* of a Highlands summer, the air thick with drizzle and midges, you'll know only too well why. Catch this remarkable island in bright weather, however, and it's an altogether different story.

Timing is everything up here. For every cloud-free day you can expect three or four cooped up in your tent or B&B, waiting for the murk to lift. When it eventually does, the wait will seem a small price. For the landscape of Skye is, quite simply, a revelation – no more so than along the northernmost peninsula of the island, where a massive escarpment of striated shale and basalt traces the coastline.

The longest inland cliff in Britain, the Trotternish Ridge zigzags for 37km/23miles between Portree to the northern tip of Skye, where it tumbles into a belt of springy turf speckled with tiny white crofts. Most walkers who venture to the island focus on the Cuillin hills, in the far south, but the atmosphere of this area and its landforms are, in their way, just as weird and wonderful. Plus they have

something unique in their favour – something well worth travelling to the very fringes of Britain to see.

Because it stares across the Sound of Raasay to the Scottish mainland, the mighty east cliff of the Trotternish Ridge yields a breathtaking panoramic view over the mountain ranges of the Highlands, stretching from of Assynt in the far northwest to Ben Nevis in central Scotland. What's more, you don't have to climb all the way up to the scarp edge itself to get what is generally regarded as the best view of all from the Trotternish Ridge.

With the Old Man of Storr, one of Britain's most perfect views finds its perfect foreground – a towering needle of petrified lava. Withered by the elements, the monolith rises from a knot of lesser pinnacles clustered around its base like eroded Easter Island giants, tilted slightly seawards as if hypnotized by the spectacle. As well they might be. This is one walk where the payoff far exceeds the effort expended. Our featured viewpoint, from a bluff overlooking the Old Man, lies only an hour from the road – all of it uphill, granted, but along an easy path.

At a glance

Where Old Man or Storr, Isle of Skye, 9.5km/6miles north of Portree on the A855.
Why A magnificent view across the Sound of Raasay; spectacular cliffs and outlandish rock formations; Ravens and, if you're lucky, white-tailed sea eagles.

When May is officially the driest month in Skye; it's also when the Skye Music Festival takes place.
Downsides One word: midges.
Start/Finish Lay-by on the A855 at NG509529.
Duration 2hrs.

Distance 4km/2.5miles.
Terrain Mostly pitched stone footpaths through water-logged conifer woods and over an open, grazed hillside strewn with rocks and lochans.
Maps OS Explorer 408

On your way

In common with many remote Hebridean promontories, the Trotternish Peninsula feels in many respects like an island within an island. Looking across the Minch to Harris and Lewis on one side, and out over the Sound of Raasay to the mountainous northwest coast of mainland Scotland on the other, its shoreline of grey cliffs and black-sand beaches is unique in Skye, with its own distinct history, Gaelic dialect and mood.

Traces of settlement by Mesolithic hunter-gatherers, Iron-Age farmers, medieval monks and Victorian crofter-fishing communities litter the Trotternish coastline. The colonizers who made the greatest impression on this peninsula, however, were the Vikings, who held sway from the ninth until the early thirteenth centuries. Many place names have obvious Scandinavian roots: Trotternish derives from the Norse for "Trond's Headland" and Storr from "big". That said, physical remains of the Norsemens' presence were virtually non-existent until 1890, when a local crofter stumbled upon what looked like a cache of ancient silver, buried above the shore directly below the Old Man.

Comprising fragments of spiral neck rings, bracelets, brooches and ingots, as well pieces of so-called "hack" silver, which were once used as small currency, the Storr Rock Hoard is now known to date from AD935–940. Judging from its contents, drawn from as far afield as Tashkent and Turkey, the hoard must originally have been hidden here by a Norse sea trader – who perhaps used the Old Man on the mountainside above as a pointer to remind him where he'd secreted his booty.

To the eternal benefit of future generations, the merchant obviously never found his way back. Acquired by the National Museum of Scotland, the Storr Rock Hoard now resides in Edinburgh.

It's interesting to speculate what our Viking trader's supposed reference point, the **OLD MAN OF STORR**, might have looked like back when the silver was first buried. Certainly it would have been larger than today. Brittle and vulnerable to damage by frost, the basalt pillar and its neighbours – plugs of an ancient volcano – have been crumbling away since they first saw the light of day hundreds of thousands of years ago.

A large, bulbous chunk, described by local people as the "head", fell off half a century back, not long after it was first climbed by the irascible Don Whillans and his climbing partner James Barber in 1955. Measuring 48m/157ft from top to toe, the Old Man today is said to be the equivalent height of eleven double-deckers. When you approach it from below, however, the formation seems insignificant compared with the huge cliffs of the Storr looming behind, which periodically shower the moraine below with hails of rock and stone.

The great escarpment is in this perpetual state of instability because it is top heavy. The 24 layers of volcanic rock comprising the uppermost strata are, basically, too much for the crumbly rock below, which has caused gigantic pieces to collapse, exposing the spectacular geological sandwich we see today.

A wizened finger pointing heavenwards from the base of the wedge-shaped Storr mountain, the Old Man is merely the best known in a chain of similar formations created by landslip along the Trotternish Ridge. On a much bigger scale is the Quirang to the north, above the crofting village of Staffin – a wonderland of phantasmagorical pillars, needles, arches, cliffs and pinnacles, piled on a high platform overlooking the bay.

Another geological oddity worth

ABOVE: The Trotternish Ridge zigzagging above the Old Man of Storr

seeking out nearby is Kilt Rock, where the basalt strata resembles tartan, and a beautiful waterfall cascades into the sea, throwing up a cloud of spray which on sunny days is filled with rainbows.

Kilt Rock is also renowned as one of Skye's classic viewpoints, though it lacks the eerie drama of the vista from above the Old Man we've featured in our route. From this extraordinary vantage point, you get a fabulous line of sight down over the head of Loch Leathan and across the Sound to Raasay, with the peaks of Torridon, Applecross and the **CUILLIN** forming a grandiose horizon.

A long, thin, treeless arm tapering down the Sound towards Portree, Raasay dominates the midground. The island is thought to have been the traditional home of Clan MacSween, though was occupied by the MacLeods between the sixteenth and nineteenth centuries. Supporters of the Jacobite cause, the MacLeods hosted Charles Stuart here in a "mean, low hut" while he was awaiting rescue by a French frigate after the Battle of Culloden in 1745.

The "Bonnie Prince" had been escorted to Skye from his hiding place on South Uist by a 24-year-old woman named Flora MacDonald – an adventure immortalized in the famous *Skye Boat Song*. After bidding farewell to the Prince in Portree, Flora never set eyes on him again. She ended up

marrying a man from Skye and, following an ill-fated attempt at emigration to the Carolinas, settled on the tip of Trotternish to raise seven children.

Over the succeeding centuries, Raasay ("Isle of Roe Deer") saw most of its crofters cleared off the land to make way first for sheep, then for mining and, finally, a PoW camp in World War I. Now owned by the community, after being bought by the council, it boasts the largest population of any of the Hebridean islands – the majority of them staunchly Calvinist Free Presbyterians.

From the Old Man, you can easily make out the anvil-shaped summit of Raasay's highest hill, Dùn Caan (444m/1456ft), where James Boswell danced "a Highland dance" on his visit with Dr Johnson in 1773. "We returned in the evening", he recalled later "not at all fatigued, and piqued ourselves at not being outdone at the nightly ball by our less active friends, who had remained at home" – a ringing endorsement of the health benefits of hill walking if ever there was one.

A walk from the boat jetty to the summit of Dùn Caan and back can commmfortably be completed in a day, leaving plenty of time for the return ferry to Skye.

The Old Man Of Storr

CHECKED BY
✔ **Inverness Ramblers**

1 Walk to the far north end of the car park, past the interpretative panel and through the gate leading into the conifer plantation ahead. From here, a well made path ascends steadily uphill through the woods, passing a junction after 10mins, where you should keep R.

2 On emerging from the gate at the end of the trees you're greeted with an impressive view of the corrie and cliffs below the Storr's southwest face. Keep to the pitched path, which soon after reaches a junction where a path branches off to the L. Ignore this, and continue climbing up the hill until you reach a point – at NG502539 – where a fainter, non-pitched path peels R into the moraine.

3 Turn R and head along this path as it rises in the direction of the ridge above. When you reach it, look for a

Map not to scale.
Representation of
**OS EXPLORER
MAP 408 1:25,000**

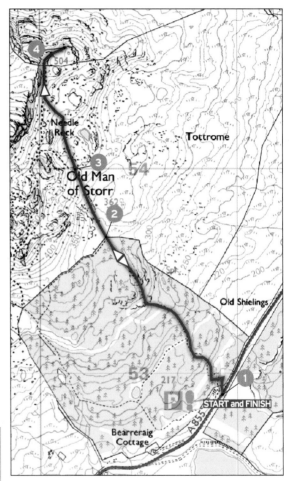

Route profile

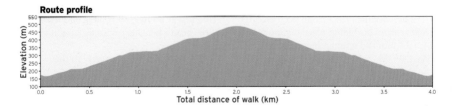

little sidetrack branching up to your R (do not continue over the broken stile and fence ahead). This will take you up to a flat-topped bluff at:

4 (NG501545) from where the view over the **Old Man of Storr** and down the Sound of Raasay to the Cuillin Hills is magnificent.
Return by the same route.

Getting There
Rapsons' Highland Country Bus 57A (Mon–Sat; 2–5 per day) stops at the layby where our walk begins en route between Portree and Uig. Portree can be reached by CityLink coaches from Inverness and Fort William, which have good connections the rest of the country. Contact Traveline Scotland ☎0871 200 2233/✎www. travelinescotland.*com* for timetable information.

Visitor Information
Portree TIC
Bayfield House
Portree
IV51 9EL
☎01478 612137

Eating & Drinking
Harbour View
7 Bosville Terrace
Portree
☎01478 612069
This famous seafood restaurant, in a former fisherman's cottage overlooking the harbour in Portree, is the place to sample the finest Loch Harport oysters, scallops from the Outer Hebrides and – if you're feeling flush – Portree langoustine. For those on tighter budgets, there's also a good chippy a little further along the harbourfront.

Sleeping
Dun Flodigarry Hostel
Flodigarry, nr Staffin, Isle of Skye, IV51 9HZ
☎01470 552212
✎www.hostelflodigarry.co.uk
Independent, family-run hostel in a wonderful location at the far northern tip of the Trotternish Peninsula. Clean, light dorms of various sizes, superb views and rock-bottom rates. Flodigarry is also on the bus route passing the Old Man.

Coolin View Guest House
2 Bosville Terrace, Portree, IV51 9DG
☎01478 611280
✎www.coolinview.co.uk
Most of the rooms in this triple-fronted 1920s town house look across Portree's picture-box harbour and down the loch to the Cuillin Hills. It makes a clean, well-run and comfortable base, only a skip from the centre.

Bayfield Backpackers
Bayfield, IV51 9EW
☎01478 612231
✎www.skyehostel.co.uk
Small hostel in the centre of Portree, with lovely views from its rear over the water. Bunks in 4- or 8-place dorms only.

More Info
✎www.skyecomuseum.co.uk. Website of the open-air Staffin Eco Museum – a route lining thirteen sites of cultural and environmental interest around the Trotternish Peninsula.

✎www.walkhighlands.co.uk/skye. This dependable walking site describes dozens of great routes on Skye, including the ascent of the Storr, behind the Old Man.

✎www.skye.co.uk. The island's official website features a region-by-region breakdown, with dozens of links to local businesses.

✎www.skye-birds.com. All about birding on the Isle of Skye.

✎ www.skyebrewery.co.uk Homepage of the island's popular real-ale brewery.

More Walks
Collins Rambler's Guide: Isle of Skye by Chris Townsend (Collins/Ramblers). Thirty walks over a range of distances and levels of difficulty. The guide explores the mountain landscapes and dramatic coastline of this spectacular corner of the Scottish Highlands and Islands.

ABOVE: The Old Man, and shattered cliffs of the Storr

Around the Devil's Rocks
Handfast Point

Some time deep in our island's mythological past, the Devil seems to have had a passionate love-hate relationship with the Dorset coast. If local folklore is to be believed, one of his favourite sleeping places was Old Harry Rocks, a surreal cluster of chalk stacks and needles tapering into the sea at the end of beautiful Studland Beach, near Poole Harbour. Yet for reasons long forgotten, he also hurled a great lump of sandstone at the heath spreading inland behind the bay; it still stands where it landed, tilted at a curious angle above a bowl of glowering heathland.

These two geological landmarks – one white, the other red – form the cornerstones of a wonderfully varied walk along the eastern rim of the Isle of Purbeck, starting in the middle of Studland Beach. Each stretch of it is dominated by contrasting colours. From the blue sea-water and golden sand lining Studland beach, you plunge into the furze of Godlingston Heath – ablaze with yellow gorse in spring and purple heather in late summer. Overlooking it, Ballard Down's springy green ridgeway – the eastern arm of a narrow chalk seam arcing across the Isle

of Purbeck to the Isle of Wight – falls away to a vertical wall of vivid white cliffs and a sea of a cobalt blue that, on sunny days at least, is decidedly untypical of England.

The terrific views over Studland Beach and Poole Harbour stay with you throughout, but grow steadily more impressive as the route progresses, culminating in a truly glorious panorama as you stride into the sea breeze along the crest of Ballard Down. The ridgetop, studded with prehistoric burial mounds, takes in a huge sweep of coast as far as the distant Needles of the Isle of Wight. Some locals claim that on a clear evening you can even see the lights of Cherbourg twinkling on the southern horizon.

Nowadays owned and run with draconian efficiency by the National Trust, Studland and its famous beach attract thousands of visitors year-round: on sunny weekends in summer, the sands can feel totally overwhelmed. The coast path itself, of course, is much quieter, but as a section of this walk crosses the beach, it's best to avoid the busiest holiday periods in the summer school holidays.

At a glance

Where Studland, Isle of Purbeck, Dorset.
Why Wide-ranging views over one of Britain's most spectacular stretches of coast; Agglestone Rock: a geological oddity; exceptionally rich flora and birdlife.

When Early spring, for the clifftop flora, and gorse and heather on the heath.
Downside Oppressive crowds on the beach in high summer; high local prices.
Start/Finish National Trust Information Centre, Knoll

Beach, Studland (SY034835).
Duration 3hrs 30mins.
Distance 10km/6.2miles.
Terrain Waymarked paths through pine forest, over heath-land, chalk downs and clifftops, with two moderate ascents.
Map OS Explorer OL15.

On your way

Although surrounded on all sides by water, the Isle of Purbeck isn't really an island. It just feels like one. Protected by the Jurassic Coast on its southern flank and by Poole Harbour to the northeast, this distinctive micro-region is hard to get to, and even harder to leave, thanks to the endless walking possibilities along its coastline.

ABOVE: Stone waypost, Ballard Down

Purbeck's heart is a hidden vale enfolded by two chalk downs, running in parallel from east to west, roughly five miles apart. Since Norman times, the only gap in the northernmost of these saddleback ridges has been guarded by Corfe Castle, whose disintegrating ruins are made from Purbeck's creamy grey limestone. The other gateway – and an even more romantic approach – is via the chain ferry that rattles across the mouth of Poole Harbour. It's only a short hop, but the transition from the chic marina of Sandbanks to the empty, windswept sand spit of Shell Bay, at the far northern tip of Studland Beach, comes as a delightful surprise.

Before the ferry placed it on the Bournemouth to Swanage bus route in the 1920s, **STUDLAND** village was deceptively remote – visible from across the harbour, but a sufficiently long haul by land to deter daytrippers. Well-heeled literati and painters from London spotted its potential as a retreat between the wars, among them Virginia Woolf, Lytton Strachey, Bertrand Russell and George Bernard Shaw, who introduced the village to the Bloomsbury group.

These days, the whole area is owned and managed by the **NATIONAL TRUST**, which goes someway to explaining why, despite the hordes of visitors in summer, Studland and its environs have remained locked in a genteel 1930s time warp. Its nature-reserve status has also made the tract of moorland behind the beach – **GODLINGSTON HEATH**

– an important wildlife haven, and a bastion of the endangered Dartford warbler (with over 130 nesting pairs present). In addition, the reserve is also among the last places in England where you stand a good chance of sighting all six native species of reptile.

Godlingston is said to have provided the inspiration for Thomas Hardy's Egdon Heath, the brooding backdrop to his great Wessex novels, and it's easy to picture Eustacia Vie, tragic heroine of *The Return of the Native*, striding through the heather towards the spectral silhouette of the **AGGLESTONE ROCK**. A giant wedge of sandstone said to have been catapulted here by Satan, the Agglestone rises from the centre of an amphitheatre of bog dotted with clumps of asphodel and cotton grass, and crisscrossed by trickling streams. Its name probably derives from the Saxon "halig", meaning "holy", suggesting cult rather than demonic status in the distant Christian past. These days, the Agglestone is more often the subject of minor indignities than acts of worship: boulder-climbers cluster on its summit, while generations of graffiti-carvers have gouged their initials around its recesses.

Evidence of pre-Christian settlement litter **BALLARD DOWN**, the great chalk ridge overshadowing Godlingston Heath, whose gently curved spine yields this area's finest view of Poole Harbour and the surrounding coast. The obelisk crowning its ridge-top, originally a London lamp standard, was erected in 1892 to mark the opening of nearby Ulwell reservoir. While walking the upland path beyond it, keep an eye out for rare Adonis Blue and Marble White butterflies, attracted by the vetches, wild marjoram and carline thistles growing in the close-cropped turf.

Before plunging into the sea to resurface 24km/15miles away on the Isle of Wight, Purbeck's cretaceous chalk seam reaches a spectacular cadence at **HANDFAST POINT** (aka "the Foreland"). Towers, pointed needles and arched stacks stand in an impressive phalanx off the headland's cliffs, like a group of frozen giants, their grassy tops mobbed by swarms of seabirds. The most distinctive member of the family is a round pillar known locally as "Old Harry", a medieval name for the Devil, who allegedly used to sleep on its summit. The stump of Old Harry's wife, who collapsed into the surf during a storm in 1896, stands alongside.

Handfast Point is a major landmark on the South West Coast Path, whose acorn waymarkers usher walkers through a small coppice and across open pasture to Studland Village. Before succumbing to the temptations of the Bankes Arms, it's worth making a short detour from the trail to the Romanesque church of St Nicholas. Appropriately enough for a stretch of shoreline that's seen more than its fair share of shipwrecks, the church, the oldest in Dorset, is dedicated to the patron saint of sailors, and stands on a site whose ritual significance long predates the building's Saxon foundations. During renovation work, pre-Christian burial cists were uncovered in the graveyard (one them containing the bones of a woman who had been decapitated). The squat tower of the church caps a pretty Norman building noted for its richly carved

arches and vaulted ceilings, which still retain patches of eleventh-century painting. Look out, too, for the sculpted corbels beneath the north and south eaves outside, some of which depict sexual acts: above the entrance porch, a couple are locked in an amorous embrace, while on the north wall a Sheela Na Gig figurine (with her head cocked at a jaunty ninety-degree angle) stretches open a grossly exaggerated vulva.

In the cemetery, a prominent tombstone opposite the main doorway commemorates Sergeant William Lawrence and his French wife, Clothilde. Lawrence ran away from Studland to join the army in 1805, and distinguished himself fighting for Wellington in the Peninsula Wars and at Waterloo. He met his wife en route to the siege of Paris, bringing her back afterwards to run a pub in his native village.

A relic of a more recent conflict huddles in a stand of sycamores a short walk north of the church, on a bluff overlooking Studland's Middle Beach. The enormous concrete bunker, known as **FORT HENRY**, was built by Canadian engineers in 1943 as part of the preparations for the D-Day landings. A massive rehearsal for the amphibious invasion, dubbed Operation Smash, was staged in the bay in front of it on April 18, 1944, watched through the long observation slit by Churchill, Montgomery, Eisenhower and King George VI. A memorial plaque recently installed beside the structure recalls the casualties incurred during the exercise.

The Python Connection

Fans of Monty Python's Flying Circus may recognize Studland Beach as the setting for the sketch series' opening sequence, when Michael Palin staggers out of the waves and collapses into the sand, uttering the immortal phrase "It's... ".

walk it 10 Handfast Point

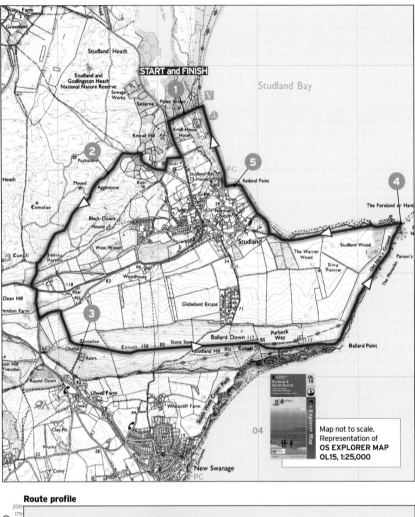

Route profile

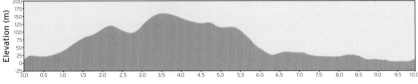

CHECKED BY
✔ **East Dorset Group**

1 From the **National Trust Information Centre** at Knoll Beach, turn your back on the sea and walk past the car park kiosks to the main road. Turn L and walk up the grass verge (passing the Knoll House Hotel) for 370m/400yrds, then cross to pick up the signposted bridleway on the R. On reaching open ground, turn L at a waypost across a grassy area to a lane at the junction of bridleways. Turn R here and follow the winding, waymarked track as far as a footbridge, which you should cross. Bear L from its far side along a narrower path through woods. You'll then come to a waypost with yellow (footpath) and blue (bridleway) arrows. Bear L here in the direction of the Agglestone, now visible ahead across the heath.

2 Follow the path through boggy furze and a series of hollows to the **Agglestone Rock**, from where you continue southwest along a clear, drier track that rises steadily. At a junction of paths continue straight ahead through two gates to the ridge and golf-course. At a red golf course warning sign take the R fork. On reaching the main road, cross over and turn L; look for the stile and footpath sign on your R. This leads across a golf fairway (keep to the yellow peg markers) to drop sharply downhill through a sycamore coppice. From the stile at the bottom of this, bear R down the hill towards the bottom corner of the field to a stile on the Studland–Swanage

road. Turn L up the broad grassy verge to a bridleway signpost near the top of the hill. From the opposite side of the road, a short track leads to a gate onto a gate on to NT land and the start of a clear track striking steeply uphill towards the granite obelisk on the ridge of **Ballard Down**.

3 At the obelisk and adjacent tumulus continue east, and follow the high ground for a little over a mile, past the trig point and downhill to clifftops leading to **Handfast Point** (aka the Foreland, or Old Harry's Rocks). There's a choice of paths as you descend, with spectacular cliff-edge tracks for those with a head for heights.

4 Having rounded the headland, veer L (west), keeping to the well-worn path (SWCP) running towards **Studland** village. Just before arriving at the lane through the village, you'll see a fingerpost indicating the alternative coast path route via South Beach. Follow this down through the trees and along the line of beach huts to Joe's Café. A short way past the café on your L, the coast path cuts up the low cliffs (between beach huts 59 & 60B) behind South Beach, past the footpath turning for the Bankes Arms, and skirts fields en-route to **Fort Henry**.

5 Follow the path beyond the bunker and thatched police post to the bottom of the lane, and turn R down to Middle Beach. From here, you should turn L, past the café and toilets, and

walk back along the beach to the visitor information centre.

 Getting There
Wilts & Dorset bus 150 runs hourly (half hourly in summer) through Studland from Bournemouth en route to Swanage via the Sandbanks chain ferry; alight at the Knoll House Hotel for the National Trust Information Centre, where our walk starts: ✆01202 673555, ✉www.wdbus.co.uk. The nearest train station is at Poole; take Wilts & Dorset bus 52 from Poole to Sandbanks (not Sundays in winter) to connect with service 50 - though note that the 50 service starts from Bournemouth train station.

Visitor Information
National Trust Information Centre, Knoll Beach
✆01929 450259
✉www.nationaltrust.org.uk

Eating & Drinking
Bankes Arms Country Inn
Manor Rd, Studland, BH19 3AU
✆01929 450225
✉www.bankesarms.com
Historic inn that enjoys a roaring trade year round; freshly cooked pub meals and real ale brewed on the premises, served inside the old building or out in the garden. If your budget can stretch to it, go for the locally caught crab or fish or the day, fresh off the boat.

National Trust Information Centre (see above)
The café run by the NT at its information centre is popular with walkers, serving a mix of hot meals, sandwiches and filled

baguettes, but you'll find better value for money at Joe's Café.

Joe's Café
South Beach
Located above South Beach, the café rustles up delicious organic ice creams, freshly ground fair-trade coffees and teas, in addition to lots of tasty hot bites, soup and home-made honey flapjack.

Sleeping
Campsite
Rempstone (SY998834; 5km/3miles east of Studland, just north of B3351). ☎01929 480570 ✐www.burnbake.com
Secluded, pleasant campsite, hidden away in the forest plantations between Godlingston Heath and the tidal inlets on the southern shores of Poole Harbour. Pitches under the trees or on prepared grass.

Bankes Arms Country Inn
(See above)
Ten smartly furnished ensuite rooms, some with sea views, above the village's busy pub. Note two-night minimum stay on weekends (or three nights on bank holidays).

More Info
Purbeck Revealed by Ilay Cooper (James Pembroke Publishing). Everything you ever wanted to know about the area, and more besides. Available direct from the author: ilay. cooper@virgin.net (plus p&p) or from shops in the Isle of Purbeck.

More Walks
The Dorset Jubilee Trail, A Rambler's Guide by Ramblers Dorset Area (Ramblers). Comprehensive guide to this 145km/90-mile route that seeks out the lesser-trodden paths winding through Dorset's quiet villages, secret valleys and rolling downs. The Dorset Jubilee Trail was established to celebrate the 60th anniversary of the founding of the Ramblers.

Walks Around the New Forest National Park by New Forest Ramblers. Seventeen walks with sketch maps created by members of the New Forest Group. Samples a range of different terrains.

ABOVE: The Pinnacles off Old Nick's Ground at dawn

In Search of the Picturesque

Wintour's Leap

From Tintern to Chepstow our admiration was scarcely left idle for a single moment. In fact, though Gilpin and most of the guide-books pass slightingly over it, we question whether any part of the Wye is grander than the last part of its course, particularly when the river is full, the sludgy shores covered, the tide just on the ebb, and the sun declining.

The Penny Magazine, 1835

The Wye Valley, whose sinuous border divides southeast Wales from England, was where the very concept of walking to viewpoints was invented. In 1782, the Reverend William Gilpin, originator of the term "picturesque", published his *Observations of the River Wye* to help those in search of the "beautiful" and "sublime" locate the most sketch-able spots in the valley. It became Britain's first mass-selling guide book – at a time when restrictions imposed by the Napoleonic wars were forcing monied, educated travellers to seek inspiration closer to home rather than amid the classical ruins and must-see cities of the continental "Grand Tour".

Armed with Gilpin's guide, the likes of Coleridge, Turner, Thackeray and Wordsworth all came to the Wye, leaving in their wake a glut of aquatints and engravings of Tintern Abbey, and poems eulogizing the forests and cliffs. These served to cement the image of the valley in the popular imagination as a wild, fabulously romantic place. But it wasn't until the completion in 1874 of the railway line between Chepstow and Monmouth that the Wye became the object of Britain's first proper tourist boom.

Visitors still pour through in droves, but with the railway line from Chepstow long uprooted they tend to do so via the A466, which looks down on the river from an angle Gilpin would have dismissed as decidedly "un-picturesque". To really understand what all the fuss was about, you have to experience the Wye Valley as the early Victorians would have done: from the footpaths winding through it. Viewed at river level, the Wye's limestone escarpments and hanging forests can seem in places less like a Welsh border landscape than one transplanted from the Amazon basin – a hidden landscape as exotic and wild as any in the country.

At a glance

Where Chepstow to Lancaut, Monmouthshire, Wales.
Why Magnificent riverine forest; Britain's oldest surviving Norman castle; a ruined twelfth-century chapel, set in a remote riverside nature reserve
When Try to time your walk to coincide with high tide, ideally around the hour before sunset when the views of Wintour's Leap cliffs are most dramatic.
Downsides A very short section follows a main road.
Start/Finish Chepstow Castle, Bridge Street (ST533941).

Distance 8km/5miles.
Duration 1hr 45mins–2hrs.
Terrain Mainly well made woodland paths, some of which are steep, narrow and crumbling in places. The route also crosses a short scree slope.
Maps OS Explorer OL14.

The Lancaut meander
from Wintour's Leap

On your Way

It may be a beauty spot today, but the **WYE VALLEY** was also one of the major crucibles of the industrial revolution, its woodlands shrouded for centuries in smoke and soot. Iron was mined in Roman times, and the forests were heavily coppiced to provide charcoal for the smelting works that blazed through the medieval era. Britain's first blast furnaces roared to life here in the 1500s, churning out the world's first brass, along with fine-quality tin plate, copper wire and paper. The trade boom went into overdrive once the old salmon weirs were pulled up in 1662, which rendered the river navigable all the way to Monmouth. Produce poured down in flat-bottomed "trows" to be shipped out of Chepstow, which until the rise of Cardiff and Swansea was Wales' busiest port.

It was the strategic importance of the Wye, flowing into the Severn at the main crossing point between England and Wales, which inspired William the Conqueror to erect a castle overlooking the river mouth in 1067 – only a year after the Battle of Hastings. Known to the Normans as "Stringuil" (from the Welsh for "bend in the river"), **CHEPSTOW** flourished for nearly a thousand years until the closure of its boat-building yards in the 1900s.

These days, despite having preserved a wonderful crop of early Georgian houses, the town feels like it's fallen on hard times, barely spared a passing glance by the traffic streaming over the nearby Severn Bridge. It deserves a couple of hours of anyone's time, though – not least to visit the splendid castle, built by William the Conqueror's master builder, William FitzOsbern, as a launchpad from which to subdue the troublesome Welsh princes. The oldest surviving stone fortress in Britain, it still strikes an imposing silhouette, and provides superb views up the Wye through its tracery windows.

Beginning at Chepstow Castle, our walk heads north up the river to explore one of the most dramatic, but least visited, corners of the valley, where the Wye performs one of its spectacular horseshoe meanders, creating a lush, narrow-necked peninsula enfolded by wooded cliffs. The name of this isolated spit of land – **LANCAUT** – derives from that of an early Welsh saint, Cewydd, to whom a

The Piercefield Walks

One of the great highlights of tours to the Wye Valley for eighteenth- and nineteenth-century visitors was Piercefield House, a now derelict country mansion just north of Chepstow, on the opposite banks of the river to Lancaut. In its prime, the stately Neo-Classical pile ranked among the grandest country seats in Britain. Visitors used to pour in to drool over the fashionable architecture and walk the network of paths cut through the estate's forest to a succession of famous viewpoints.

However, bad luck dogged the succession of mega-rich sugar barons, bankers and mine owners who occupied Piercefield, and by the 1920s the house and its pathways had been abandoned. Today,

it lies derelict just above Chepstow race course, the elegant facade and pavillions entwined with weeds and tree roots.

Most of the paths through Piercefield's adjacent woodland have also become overgrown, along with the follies that punctuated them, and trees obscure the once famous views. But you can still get a sense of what the grand tour of this area would have felt like by following the Wye Valley Walk between Chepstow and Tintern, whose earlier sections make use of one of Piercefield's former trails, passing a stone's throw from the house itself. Free leaflets outlining the three-hour linear route are available from Chepstow TIC (see Visitor Information).

ABOVE: The roofless ruins of St James Chapel

chapel was dedicated on the riverbanks during the Saxon era of the early seventh century AD. The monks who staffed it farmed the rich fields and traded salmon caught in weirs nearby. Made from wicker, the funnelled baskets they used, known as "putchers", were still a common sight on the Wye until three decades ago, since when salmon stocks have been wiped out.

Conflict between the English and Welsh has always been a feature of life on the Lancaut bend, and a shaping force on the landscape. Spread over the fields above, the iron-age fort of **SPITAL MEEND** was the focus of major earth works ordered by the Mercian King Offa (757–796AD) as part of his bid to construct a ditch along his western border. Stretching from the Dee to the Severn, **OFFA'S DYKE** is today considered one of the most remarkable structures to have survived from the Dark Ages in Britain. It made use of natural features – rivers, cliffs and mountains – as well as 130km/81miles of hand-dug trenches. Many thousands of men would have been employed in this excavation work – a testament both to the great power Offa must have wielded, and to his loathing of the Welsh.

The nineteenth-century travel writer, George Henry Borrow, noted that, "it was customary for the English to cut off the ears of every Welshman who was found to the east of the dyke, and for the Welsh to hang every Englishman whom they found to the west of it." The story is probably apocryphal, but it underlines the potency of the dyke as a symbol of enduring national differences – and mutual antipathy.

Our route actually cuts through a surviving section of Offa's Dyke to give access to the **LANCAUT NATURE RESERVE** – an impenetrable jungle of oak, ash, maple, yew, small-leaved limes, whitebeams and wild service trees, overshadowed by some of the most grandiose crags in lowland Britain. From their feet, the forest falls to a strip of tidal banks and salt marsh where you might be lucky enough to spot an otter or porpoise sloshing through the muddy water.

The great viewpoint over Lancaut is **WINTOUR'S LEAP**, the lip of a vertical limestone rock face surging 91m/300ft from the water's edge. It takes its name from a Civil War general called Sir John Wintour, who is said to have galloped over the escarpment and swum the river to escape his roundhead pursuers in 1645. Now all but forgotten and overgrown, this dramatically beautiful, deserted stretch of the Wye was until the end of the nineteenth century busy with traffic ferrying limestone blocks down to Chepstow from Lancaut's quarries. Stone from here was used to clad Avonmouth Docks, built as a rival for Liverpool in the 1870s; it was also burned for use as fertilizer in the little **LIME KILNS** passed by our route.

Staring across the horseshoe bend to the cliffs of Wintour's Leap, **ST JAMES CHAPEL** is the one of the Wye's hidden treasures, and the perfect spot from which to savour views of the river's wild lower reaches before tackling the path back to Chepstow. It was built by the Normans in 1120, possibly as an infirmary – a theory to which the presence in the surrounding fields of an unusual number medicinal herbs lends weight. Services were held here until 1865, when the chapel's Norman font was removed to Gloucester. It has since fallen into ruins.

1 Leaving the car park in front of **Chepstow Castle**, turn L past the TIC onto Bridge Street, and cross the Victorian iron bridge over the **Wye**. A lane cuts straight uphill from the end of it: follow this, ignoring the R turn half-way up for the Offa's Dyke Path (ODP), and cross the main road again at the top to enter another lane (Mopla Rd). Continue for 140m/150yards to a metal kissing gate on your L where the road bends. Go through the gate, and head uphill past the remains of a medieval windmill (marked "Lookout Tower" on OS maps). As the field narrows towards the top of the rise you arrive at another metal kissing gate on the R. Go through this and keep the stone garden wall on your L for 140m/150yards to reach another taller wall where you turn L along a short narrow passage between a wall and fence. At the end, turn R for a few yards along a driveway

to another kissing gate on the L, and pass through this into a field. Cross to the far side of the field, where you'll another kissing gate.

2 The trail divides here. One path goes straight ahead,

under a small bridge into the entrance to the Lancaut Nature Reserve. However, you need to turn R, passing in front of Pen Moel house, along the base of the ha ha and through the trees on to the main road (B4228), where

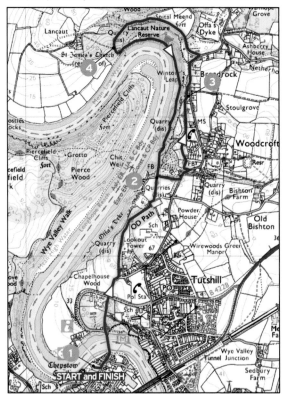

Map not to scale.
Representation of
**OS EXPLORER MAP
OL14, 1:25,000**

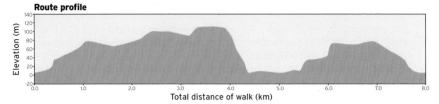

Route profile

you should turn L. After a minute, a sign points the way sharply L up Old School Lane, past the school (now a private house), just beyond which a metal gate marks the entrance to Woodcroft Quarry (long abandoned). Once past the quarry gates, the path passes dramatically along the top of the quarry walls with fine views across the Wye, eventually emerging at the B4228.

3 Follow the main road for 2mins until you reach a junction with Lancaut Lane, cutting back to the L. Three mins' walk down this brings you to the remains of **Offa's Dyke** (to the R of road in **Spital Meend** field), just after which a panel on the L marks the entrance to **Lancaut Nature Reserve**. Keep to the path as it drops steadily downhill. A short way beyond the **lime kilns** on your R, the path then forks: bear L, and keep L at the next junction to reach a metal stile leading oneards to **St James' Chapel**.

4 From the ruined chapel descend along the side of a barbed-wire fence to the riverbank, and turn L along the Wye across another metal stile. Keep to this winding path for the next 30mins or so, staying as close to the water's edge as possible (ie don't be tempted uphill by misleading climbers' and quarrymen's trails). Our path doesn't start to rise until after it crosses a scree stonefall (waymarked with yellow paint arrows). From here it climbs to Pen Moel house (**2**), reaching the little bridge and the corner of the ha ha passed earlier.
Follow the route described in paragraph 1 in reverse to return to Chepstow.

 Getting There
Chepstow is well served by public transport; the train and bus stations are both a ten-minute walk across town from the trailhead. Timetables can be viewed online at www.traveline-cymru.org.uk, or phone 0871 200 2233.

Visitor Information
TIC Chepstow
Bridge St (opposite the castle entrance)
01291 623772
You can pick up free glossy leaflets on the Lancaut Nature Reserve, which features a handy route map and lots of interesting background detail on the area.

Eating & Drinking
The Boat Inn
The Back, Chepstow, NP16 5HH
01291 628192
Occupying a prime spot on the riverbank, opposite the provocative Union Jack daubed on the Gloucestershire cliffs. Serves real ales and reasonably priced food.

Coffee 1
1-2 Beaufort Sq, Chepstow
NP16 5EP
01291 637403
The most fragrant coffee stop in town, with stripped wood floors and good views of comings and goings on the square outside.

Sleeping
Afon Gwy
28 Bridge St, Chepstow, NP16 5EZ
01291 620158
www.afongwy.co.uk
Congenial pub-B&B backing on to the river, with views of the castle from its rather worn rooms. The bar downstairs opens onto a congenial riverside terrace.

More Walks
Lower Wye Rambles by Lower Wye Ramblers (Ramblers). Our featured route is one of 16 half-day walks described in this neat little guide. It's available online, direct from the group's website www.lowerwyeramblers.org.uk, the Ramblers website www.ramblers.org.uk, or TIC Chepstow.

ABOVE: Chepstow Castle – the oldest surviving stone fortress in Britain

The Great Wall of the North
Hadrian's Wall

No towers are seen
On the wild heath, but those that fancy
builds,
And save a fosse that tracks the moor with
green,
Is nought remains to tell of what may there
have been
Sir Walter Scott, from *Harold the Dauntless* (1817).

If any hills were destined to form a border, it's the line of Whin Sill outcrops marching across the moors above Haltwhistle in Northumberland. Angled slightly towards the sky, the faces of these blue-grey crags stare defiantly towards Scotland, presiding over the rough, bleak expanse of peat bog where the Pennines merge with the Cheviots. Traditionally the realm of cattle reivers and raiding bands of Picts, this historical no-man's land is where the Romans decided to draw the northwestern boundary of their empire in the second century AD. To keep at bay the "barbarians" who routinely rampaged across it, they erected a 118-km/73.5-mile battlement from coast to coast across the backbone of northern England, fortifying it with the most ambitious structure ever built in

Roman Britain: Hadrian's Wall.

More than 1800 years on, the north's "Great Wall" conjures up more vividly than any other monument in the country the atmosphere of those distant times, and the lives of the men who built and patrolled it. Walk along the ramparts today and you tread on steps worn smooth by leather-sandalled legionnaires, gaze at the same views the imperial sentries who staffed the watchtowers would have stared across, and hear curlews and skylarks calling out on the moor just as they did.

Scott was exaggerating when he said "nought remains to tell of what may there have been". Plenty of vestiges do survive and our walk cherry-picks the finest of them, flanking Britain's most intact Roman fort at Housesteads. The Great Whin Sill here erupts into a series of ridges, and half of the route tracks their crest for the panoramas they afford of the wall. The other half loops over the lower, wilder and less frequented heathland to the north, giving a taste of what the Roman border may have looked like to those it was built to repel. Along the way you'll recognize several iconic vistas, the most famous of

At a glance

Where Housesteads Roman Fort, 11km/7miles northeast of Haltwhistle, Northumberland. **Why** The most dramatic stretch of Hadrian's Wall; Britain's best preserved Roman fort; archeo-logical museum. **When** Winter, with snow on the moors. **Start/Finish** Housesteads NT Visitor Centre (NY794684). **Duration** 2hrs 30mins.

Distance 8km/5miles. **Terrain** Undulating paths, often muddy, with sections over boggy moorland, plus a couple of short, stepped ascents and descents. **Maps** OS Explorer OL43.

them looking east from Cuddy's Crags towards Sewingshields.

This is country ideally seen under a dusting of snow, or just after dawn, with shreds of mist trailing from the hills, and the ancient stonework lit up by early morning sunlight. Rainy days, on the other hand, should most definitely be avoided – not merely because of the dampening effect on the views, but for the corrosive impact walkers' boots can have on the monument when the ground is wet.

On your way

Work on **HADRIAN'S WALL** began in the wake of Emperor Hadrian's visit to Britain in 122AD. Uprisings were breaking out across the empire, which at that time stretched from Iraq to the Western Sahara, and rather than continue attempts to push their rule further northwest into the wilds of Scotland, Hadrian decided to consolidate his forces in northern England.

Stretching from the mouth of the Tyne to the Solway Firth, the new border followed the course of the old Stanegate military road connecting Coria (Corbridge) with Lugucalium (Carlisle). Soldiers from three legions were drafted in to build the wall, which was to be made of stone in the east, and of turf in the west, reinforced by castles every Roman mile (1620 yards/1.48km), and by two watchtowers between each of these. Its purpose was more to control trade and levy taxes than repulse invasion. But only a couple of years into the project, Hadrian's original plans had a dramatic overhaul. More than a dozen large, front-line forts were added to the design and a massive ditch, or **VALLUM**, dug on the wall's southern flank, suggesting that local reaction to the Roman rampart, and the restrictions it imposed on movement, may have been less than passive.

If you track Hadrian's Wall on Google Earth, it's the traces of the mighty vallum earthwork which are most clearly discernable today, scratched in straight lines across the moors. But on the ground, the stone defences are what dominate the landscape – no more so than at **HOUSESTEADS**, where they snake along the top of a line of low cliffs. Known in its day as Vercovicium (literally "the place of effective fighters"), Housesteads ranked among the largest of the wall's fortresses, and is now the most fully intact. Abutting the wall where it runs over a high escarpment on the Whin Sill edge, its ground plan preserves the outlines of barrack blocks, a hospital, granaries, an officer's house, an army headquarters and even dedicated latrines. Between 800 and 1000 auxiliaries (the second-grade soldier of the Roman army, ranked lower than legionnaires) would have been garrisoned here – mostly Tungrians from Belgium, supplemented by Germanic cavalry.

By the standards of the time, the soldiers were well paid, and over the years a thriving township and field system grew up alongside Housesteads fort, where merchants supplied the troops with food, clothes, pottery and other essentials. Although

All the way...

If our little sampler has given you a taste for walking the wall, you might like to tackle the full 140km/84miles of the Hadrian's Wall Path. Running from Wallsend in the east to Bowness-on-Solway in the west, the route, waymarked throughout by the National Trail's acorn symbol, climbs through the arable land lining Tynedale to the Whin Sill escarpments of Housesteads, then on to the richer pastures of Cumbria, winding up on the salt flats below the Lakeland Fells.

An estimated 7000 walkers complete the walk each year end-to-end, collecting stamps in a dedicated Path Passport. It takes around a week to cover the distance comfortably. Be warned through: the path is not nearly as easy as it's often described, with a few long stages involving relentless ups and downs. And there's precious little shade when the sun beats down in summer.

marriage by Roman rites was forbidden, there was nothing to stop the men getting hitched according to local laws, and many did, which would have blurred the divide between civilian and army life.

After a little over a decade of use, Housesteads and most of the wall were abandoned in favour of a new frontier further north, the so-called Antonine Wall, erected between the Clyde and the Forth. But with the accession of Marcus Aurelius in 164AD, it was re-occupied, and remained in service until the Roman withdrawal from Britain in the fifth century.

During the years after the fall of the empire, much of the old masonry was deployed to build defensive "bastles" to defend against cross-border raiders. Only in late 1700s, when wealthy antiquarians such as local estate owner, John Clayton, bought up farms holding portions of the wall, were efforts made to preserve what remained of Hadrian's brainchild. One such parcel of land included Housesteads, which explains why its fort and adjacent stonework are in such good shape.

East of Housesteads, the wall dips into **KNAG BURN**, formerly an important crossing point in the Roman frontier, where you can see the vestiges of a fourth-century customs post. **KING'S HILL**, just beyond it, is one of several locations whose name connects this area with Arthurian legend. Another is **KING'S WICKET**, where our walk veers northwest into the moors. This prominent niche in the Whin Sill ridge was, in medieval times, also known as **BUSY GAP** because of the amount of traffic that used to pour through it. Scottish bandits and reivers (cattle thieves) frequently used to camp here, dispatching smaller bands further south in search of plunder. If any of their victims dared pursue them, the fleeing reivers would make a beeline for the gap,

knowing that their main force would be on hand to help.

Sewingshields – just east of our route's turning point, but a worthwhile extension offering a superb view – has yielded traces of what archeologists think might have been a Dark Age fort.

Local legend asserts that one of its incumbents, for reasons now long forgotten, once threw a chest of treasure into the peaty waters of nearby **BROOMLEE LOUGH**. He then cast a spell, declaring that the riches could only be recovered by "twa' twin yands (horses), twa' twin oxen, twa' twin lads, and a chain forged by a smith of kind (the seventh in an unbroken line of blacksmiths)". In the course of time, a young smith called Ridley duly heard the story and, having located what he thought was the chest, attempted to haul it out of the lough with the help of his specially recruited twin horses, oxen and lads. But just as the box broke the surface the chain shattered and the chest sank to the bottom, never to be seen again. The young man, it turned out, had mistakenly included an ancestor who hadn't been a smith.

Another echo of the same obscure period in English history resides in the name of **CUDDY'S CRAGS**, west of Housesteads. "Cuddy" refers to Saint Cuthbert, whose relics are believed to have rested here en route between Lindisfarne and Durham, when the Holy Island was under attack from Vikings in 875AD. With its perfect view of the wall winding through the pine woods of **HOUSESTEADS CRAGS**, and on over the great wedges of the Whin Sill, the hilltop can seem an ethereal place, especially at dawn, when the sun pierces the eastern horizon and illuminates the blankets of transparent mist that invariably envelop the cliffs.

walk it 12 — Hadrian's Wall

CHECKED BY
✔ Hexham Ramblers

1 Head from the car park towards the National Trust visitors' centre, turning R though the arch

after the refreshments counter. The path continues over the **vallum** and uphill to the museum: follow the grassy rise between the museum entrance and Housesteads Fort on your R until you reach the gate

Map not to scale.
Representation of
OS EXPLORER
MAP OL43,
1:25,000

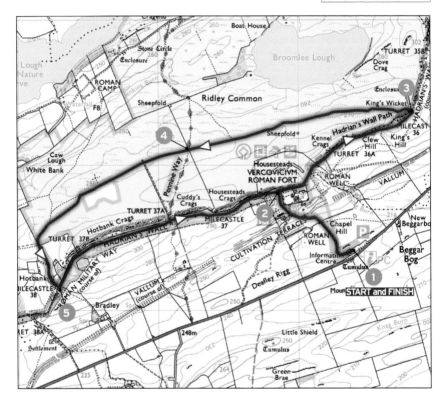

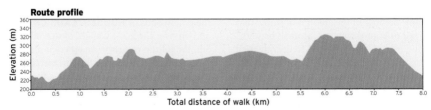

Route profile

opening on to the **Hadrian's Wall** long-distance footpath.

2 You're now on the wall itself. Turn R (E) to follow the perimeter of the fort, which the trail skirts before dropping down to **Knag Burn**, where it passes through the remnants of a fortified gateway to follow the south side of the wall up Kennel Crag. This is the first in a line of three distinct crests you'll cross, the last of which – **King's Hill** – holds the remnants of Milecastle 36. As you pass the crest of King's Hill the Wall turns N (L) and you look to **Busy Gap** (aka "King's Wicket"); a short way down the slope look for a stile on your L (at NY798693).

3 Climb over the stile, but instead of following the trail, keep close to the foot of King's Hill, bearing R up the rise, following a low bank across the bog (marked on OS maps as earthworks). When you reach a break in this bank, turn L onto the clear footpath, and follow it on to the boggy moorland of Ridley Common. Though faint initially, the path grows more pronounced as it approaches a conifer plantation (at NY793693; not drawn on OS maps), which it cuts through the middle of, emerging from the far side to continue in a straight line along the high ground, with views over **Broomlee Lough** to the north.

4 Crossing the stile near the intersection with the Pennine Way, our path then skirts and passes a lime kiln at another junction, where you should keep straight on. Gradually the trail bends L, eventually meeting another path. Bear L at this junction, and follow the clear path over a gate into the yard of Hotbank Farm.

5 Passing the farm buildings on your R, you cross a stile beyond the yard to rejoin the main Hadrian's Wall path at Milecastle 38. Turn L on it and follow the trail uphill and along the edge of a small wood, as fine views of Crag Lough and Steel Rig are revealed to the west. This next section over Hotbank and **Cuddy's Crags** strings together the most famous panoramas on the wall. A final stretch past Milecastle 39 and through the long pine wood on top of **Housesteads Crags** brings you back to the fort, where you turn R through the gate and follow the path downhill past the museum to the National Trust visitor centre, car park and bus stop.

Getting There
 Running between Newcastle-Upon-Tyne and Carlisle, the **Hadrian's Wall Bus** (the aptly named "AD122" (timetables at ✍www.hadrians-wall.org) stops at Housesteads and all the major sites along the wall half a dozen times daily between the end of March and October. The nearest railhead is at Haltwhistle, 11km/7miles southwest, from where local buses run to the site out of season.

ℹ Visitor Information
National Trust
Bardon Mill, Hexham, NE47 6NN
✆01434 344363
There's also a small visitor information point at the site shop in Housesteads.

✗ Eating & Drinking
Twice Brewed Inn
Military Rd, Bardon Mill
✆01434 344534
✍www.twicebrewedinn.co.uk
Friendly local pub on the roadside near the Once Brewed visitor centre

and Vindolana fort. Meals are served all day, and there's a pleasant little garden. Handy if you're staying at the nearby hostel.

Sleeping
Gibbs Hill Farm
Once Brewed, NE47 7AP
✆01434 344030
✍www.gibbshillfarm.co.uk
Attractive B&B rooms and bunkhouse beds on a working farm, just under 5km/3miles west down the B6318 from Housesteads (you can get there on the bus).

The Old Repeater Station
Military Rd, Grindon, NE47 7AN
✆01434 688668
✍www.hadrians-wall-bedandbreakfast.co.uk
3km/2miles east of Housesteads on the old military road (B6318), Hospitable, walker-friendly B&B that's conveniently placed for our route. They serve copious evening meals by prior arrangement.

YHA Once Brewed
Military Rd, Once Brewed, NE47 7AN
✆0845 371 9753
✍www.yha.org.uk
Most of the bunks in this purpose-built hostel next to the visitor centre are in small dorms; and they offer cooked suppers.

More Info
✍www.northumberland nationalpark.org.uk. The national park's website features an annually updated visitors' guide, helpful for planning your trip.

✍www.nationaltrust.org.uk. The NT owns approx 9.5km/6miles of the wall, running west from Housesteads, and over 1000ha/2471 acres of farmland in the area.

🖝 http://vindolanda.csad.ox.ac.uk. Everything you could want to know about the fascinating Vindolanda tablets, unearthed at a fort near Housesteads and regarded as the richest source of insights into Roman life on the wall.

🖝 www.ramblers.org.uk/info/paths/name/h.hadrianswall.htm. Comprehensive list of information about the path, including guides, maps and accommodation.

Hadrian's Wall (English Heritage). Glossy A4 guidebook, which you can purchase at the site shop in the visitors centre, featuring a site-by-site rundown and an easily digestible slice of history.

Hadrian's Wall Path by Helen and Mark Richards (Cicerone). Detailed guide to the long-distance trail.

Hadrian's Wall Path National Trail Guide by Anthony Burton (Aurum). Official guide to the national trail. Includes 1:25,000 OS map extracts, detailed route descriptions and notes on history and nature.

🚶 More Walks

Walking the Tyne: Twenty-five Walks From Mouth To Source by J B Jonas (Ramblers Northumbria Area). A route along all 133km/83 miles of this great river, divided into 25 linked, mainly circular walks of 8km/5miles to 14.5km/9miles, with suggestions for lunch stops, time estimates, public transport details, and notes on stiles, terrain and places of interest. Follows the North Tyne from Hexham to the source.

Walking the North Tyne: Seventeen Walks from Hexham to the Source by J B Jonas, (Ramblers Northumbria Area). Complementing *Walking the Tyne* (above), this volume follows the North Tyne branch of the river through remote northern countryside from Hexham to the source near Deadwater in the Kielder Forest area, including a walk alongside Kielder Water. Divided into sections, most of which are circular (3km/2miles to 12km/7.5 miles). Sketch maps, photos, route descriptions and practical information.

ABOVE: Housesteads: the best-preserved Roman fort in the country

This Scarred Land
The Norber Erratics

Since the Countryside and Rights of Way Act was passed in 2000, the area of land within the Yorkshire Dales National Park freely open for walkers has leapt from four to sixty percent – an amazing transformation. This relatively short route takes you through one of the most striking of the newly opened areas, above the pretty beck-side village of Clapham.

From the limestone crags spread over the hilltop of Thwaite Scars, you gain a cracking view of a dale that deserves to be much better known than it is. Enclosed on three sides by pale-grey escarpments, the walled fields and green lanes of Crummack Dale are ringed by an almost lunar landscape, scoured by a glacier 15,000 years ago.

The same ice flow was also responsible for one of the great geological oddities of the national park. Contrary to appearances, the Norber Erratics – a collection of sandstone boulders daintily perched on little limestone legs at the mouth of Crummack Dale – were not the work of some forgotten Neolithic tribe. Over thousands of years, they were transported a kilometre down the valley by glacial action, and dumped by the melting ice.

The Norbers provide a memorable finale to a walk through landscape dramatically shaped by the action of water and ice on stone. Lying on the lower flanks of Ingleborough, this is classic Karst country, where the moors are pock-marked with pot holes and sinks, and the hillsides encrusted with the crinkled slabs of giant limestone pavements. Even in the so-called "dry combes", formed millennia ago by meltwater, the sound of rushing streams is never far from the surface, emanating from the mouths of caverns whose inner recesses form one of the most extensive cave systems in Europe.

Generally speaking, to experience the text-book formations of Karst landscape involves long trudges across often featureless moorland, where it's all too easy to become disoriented. Here, however, you get to see some of the defining features of this terrain – including a meltwater ravine, limestone pavements, one of the dales' most famous showcaves and, of course, the extraordinary Norber Erratics – without venturing more than an hour from the nearest tearooms. Only a short section crosses pathless high ground – the section over Thwaite Scars – and this is laced with numerous sheep trails.

At a glance

Where Crummack Dale, Clapham, 8km/5miles north-west of Settle, North Yorkshire.
Why Varied limestone scenery; the Norber Erratics: weird glacial boulders; Clapham: one of Yorkshire's prettiest villages.

When May/August for the Gaping Gill bosun's chair, at Ingleborough cave.
Start/Finish The New Inn, Clapham (SD745691).
Duration 3hrs.
Distance 9.5km/6miles.

Terrain A mixture of limestone farm tracks, clear streamside paths and fainter trails over open moorland and pasture. Nav & Tech rating of 3 in poor visibility.
Maps OS Explorer OL2

On your way

A dozen or more streets clustered along the banks of a fast flowing beck, **CLAPHAM** is a typical dales estate village. The Norman tower of its church hints at the settlement's considerable age, although most of what you see today dates from the late eighteenth and nineteenth centuries, when Clapham and its surrounding farms were directly managed by the local landowners, the Farrer family of Ingleborough Hall.

It was the Farrers who originally dammed Clapdale Beck to form an ornamental lake – an early experiment in hydro-electricity. The outflow, which now gushes down a spectacular waterfall at the top of the village, used to drive a generator powering the hall and estate mills, as well as Clapham's street lights.

Exotic shrubs and trees carpet the woodland around the lake – the legacy of Reginald John Farrer (1880–1920), a renowned botanist who collected flora in China, Tibet and northern Burma. Born with a harelip that kept him out of school, he lived a solitary life as a boy, developing an interest in natural history by exploring the fells above his family's estate. After a failed literary career, he would later introduce more than one hundred plants to Britain, but is most famous for an unconventional method of propagation: to plant seeds on less accessible cliffs he is said to have fired them from a shotgun.

The moorland above Clapdale where Reginald undertook his first "plant-hunting" expeditions is dominated by the stepped profile of Ingleborough (723m/2372ft). Although it was once believed to be the highest mountain in England, the loftiest of the "Three Peaks" is neither spectacular nor a compelling hill to climb. Its interest lies rather in its unusual atmosphere, particularly

around the limestone zone of its lower flanks, whose unique geology was a prime inspiration for creating the Yorkshire Dales National Park in 1954.

Capped with a thin coat of millstone grit, the mountain comprises a 300-metre layer of "Yordale Beds", alternating strata of shale and limestone that rest on a giant, 250-metre plinth of pure limestone. Having run off the less porous beds below the summit, water disappears underground when it reaches the limestone lower down – a consequence of the acidic properties of rain, which rapidly dissolves away the chalky, alkaline limestone.

The largest of all the potholes resulting from this process is mighty Gaping Gill, on the southeast side of Ingleborough, directly above Clapham, where Fell Beck plunges through a plughole in the moor into a 110-metre vertical shaft. Twice the height of York Minster's towers, it's the tallest unbroken waterfall in Britain, though one whose base is glimpsed only by the most intrepid of cavers – except, that is, for a couple of weekends in summer. Each May and August bank holidays, the Bradford and Craven potholing clubs take it in turns to rig up an electric bosun's chair, winching paying passengers down to the gill's main chamber.

The first person to complete the full descent was the legendary French speleologist, Édouard-Alfred Martel who, in 1895, took 23 minutes to climb down a rope and wood ladder to the floor of the cave. The achievement is often credited with kickstarting caving as a sport in this country.

Having poured down Gaping Gill, the water of Fell Beck flows through a seventeen-kilometre labyrinth of subterranean passageways to re-emerge near the mouth of **INGLEBOROUGH CAVE** in Clapdale, one of three showcaves in the national park. Open to the public since 1837, it's still a popular attraction, taking visitors down half a kilometre of chambers filled with stalagmites and stalactites.

Most of the rainwater draining southeast off the hills does so underground. During the last Ice Age, however, it flowed largely through a series of ravines created by the melting ice. A fine example of one of these is **TROW GILL** – a miniature, 25-metre-tall gorge fringed by stands of fir trees at the top of Clapdale. Only a short way off our circuit, it is one of the more memorable landmarks on the path up Ingleborough, which clambers up the piled rocks at the far end of the defile.

It was here in 1947 that a couple of young cavers came across the decomposed remains of a man thought to have been a Nazi spy. A broken ampoule suggested he committed suicide by ingesting cyanide. This theory, however, has never been borne out by German intelligence records. The real identity of the Trow Gill skeleton remains a mystery.

To the east of Clapdale rises the rocky expanse of **THWAITE SCARS**, with its fractured limestone outcrops and pavements of clints (blocks) and grykes (fissures). Walking up here in early summer, with the magnificent view of Crummack Dale unfolding to the east, you'll find a wealth of plant life thriving amid the rocks, including wild thyme, early purple orchids, yellow rockrose and bird's foot trefoil.

To the south, Thwaite Scars straggles downhill to the margins of a field dotted with mysterious boulders, much darker in colour than the crags above. These otherworldly lumps are made of sandstone, dumped here by glaciers after being swept from the cliffs at the head of Crummack Dale. Known as the **NORBER ERRATICS**, they rest on pedestals fifty or sixty centimetres thick. Protected from the corrosive effects of rainwater by the boulders above them, the plinths are all that's left of a limestone layer that has completely worn away over fifteen or so thousand years.

The ancient trackway of Thwaite Lane carries you from the fields below the Norbers back to Clapham. You're walking here on an ancient footpath originally carved out by the Cistercian monks of Fountain Abbey, who used it to travel to and from their landholdings in Cumbria. Just before entering the village, the lane passes through a pair of short tunnels drilled through the limestone to carry the old right of way under the grounds of Ingleborough Hall, the Farrers' original seat. The Victorian mansion is nowadays run as an outdoor pursuits centre.

BELOW: The much-frequented path up Ingleborough, via Clapdale, approaches Trow Gill

1 From the main road bridge over the beck in the centre of **Clapham**, walk up the E (R) side of the stream, along Church Ave. Having passed the entrance to the national park car park, cross the footbridge immediately on your L, turning R on the far side up Riverside. Follow the road all way to the top, past the viewpoint over the falls. The entrance to the Clapdale trail and Ingleborough Cave lies ahead of you. Having paid the small admission fee at the meter, follow the Drive

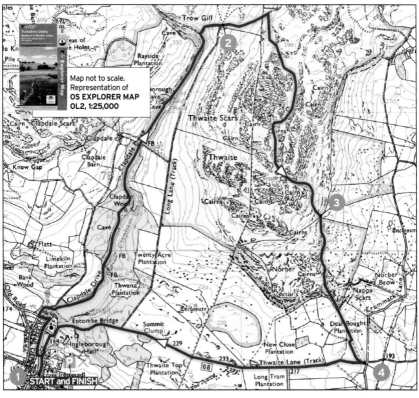

Map not to scale.
Representation of
**OS EXPLORER MAP
OL2, 1:25,000**

Route profile

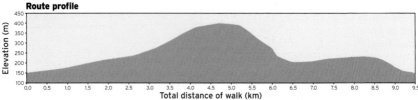

down to the lake, then northwards along the banks of the beck for 2km/1.25miles, through tree plantations and fields, past the entrance to **Ingleborough Cave**, and on to the point where the Drive bends L (NW) into **Trow Gill** (worth continuing to visit). The drystone wall on your R here makes a right-angle bend, shortly before the track passes through a gate. Turn R after the gate; keep to the wall as it makes an "S" bend, then continues up a steep slope to meet the head of Long Lane.

2 Ignore the trails fanning L (N) from here, and instead follow the track E, roughly in the same direction you've been walking, as it winds uphill in parallel with the wall on your R. Swinging L (NE) away from the wall, it then passes through a gate in another wall. Turn half R on its far side, heading for the gap in the rocks above, and continue uphill in a SE direction towards the crest of **Thwaite Scars**. A tangle of sheep trails crosses the hilltop: keep heading towards the highest ground, marked by a sharp cairn, from where the view across Crummack Dale to Moughton Scars is superb. Having explored the limestone crest, improvise a route SE down the escarpment to a ladder stile next to a wall junction at SD766703.

3 Cross the stile and bear R down the slope to reach the **Norber Erratics**, scattered across the western half of a large area of open grassland. To leave the field and continue with the route, head for the drystone enclosure in the bottom L corner of the field at SD767696.

A ladder stile here leads to a path that follows another wall downhill, then joins a farm track which eventually meets Thwaite Lane.

4 Turn R onto Thwaite Lane and follow it W for 2.5km/1.5miles, with Robin Proctor's Scar rising to your R, keeping L at the fork when the track arrives at a tree plantation. Continue down through the tunnel to reach the north side of Clapham, next to the church. Keep L of the beck, and follow Church Ave downhill to regain the car park and village centre.

Getting There
Buses between Horton-in-Ribblesdale and Ingleton stop at Clapham; you can pick up this service in Settle. For timetable information, consult traveline 0871 200 2233; www.traveline.org.uk.

Visitor Information
There's a Park Information Point in Clapham Village Stores and Post Office, on the main street through the village 015242 51212. Otherwise, contact Settle TIC, Town Hall, Cheapside, Settle 01729 825192.

Eating & Drinking
Croft Café, Clapham
In a delightful setting next to the beck, this cosy little café does a roaring trade in home-made cakes and speciality teas and coffees, which you can enjoy indoors or outside on tables next to the stream.

The New Inn
Clapham. 015242 51203.
Traditional, hearty Yorkshire fare of mostly beef, lamb and pork,

with a token veggie pasta option thrown in. You can take your meals to a rear patio in summer.

Sleeping
Brook House
Station Road, Clapham, LA2 8ER
015242 51580
www.brookhouse-clapham.co.uk.
Tasteful and reasonably-priced B&B next to Clapham Beck, with modern amenities such as wireless internet connection. They also do gourmet evening meals, made using locally farmed produce.

The New Inn Hotel
Clapham, LA2 8AH
015242 51203
The village pub, a former coaching inn, offers smart ensuite rooms, some boasting 4-posters and fancy quilts – the priciest option in the village.

More Info
www.claphamyorkshire.co.uk. Clapham's village website features a rundown of visitor-oriented local businesses.

www.yorkshiredales.org.uk The national park's homepage.

More Walks
Yorkshire Dales by David Leather (Collins/Ramblers). Detailed route descriptions for thirty walks across the dales, with Harvey maps and contextual information on the local history and wildlife.

Freedom to Roam Guides: The Three Peaks and the Howgill Fells by Sheila Bowker (Frances Lincoln/Ramblers). Twelve routes recently opened up by the CRoW Act of 2000.

walk | 14
GLOUCESTERSHIRE

On the Edge

Coaley Peak

Think of the Cotswolds and you probably don't think of "great views". Pretty ones, maybe – what with all those honey-coloured thatched cottages, immaculate village greens and endless corn fields. But not proper, jaw-dropping panoramas, of the kind that stop you in your tracks and have you rummaging in your pack for your camera.

In which case, think again. The Cotswolds start sedately enough in the south and east, rolling out of the Avon Valley and Oxfordshire plains in a wave of plump hills that wouldn't look out of place on a yoghurt pot. But the range comes to a sudden, and uncharacteristically dramatic, conclusion in the west and north, shelving away nearly 300m/1000ft in about as far as your average dog-walker can flick a frisbee.

Constantly twisting and turning as it progresses north, this mighty escarpment was formed when the layer of yellow limestone, so distinctive of the region, tilted eastwards to form what geologists call a "classic cuesta" – that's a "scarp and dip slope" to the rest of us. For local people, the cliff, cloaked for much of its length in beech woods, is simply "the Edge", and

quite apart from being a prime spot for dog-walking and paragliding, it offers one of Britain's most fantastic views. Looking west from the wooded ridgetop, the entire Severn Vale unfolds at your feet, stretching across the great silver-brown river to the Forest of Dean, the Welsh mountains and the Malverns in the far distance.

The panorama shifts subtly as you travel north. But for pure impact, few vistas along the Cotswold Edge can hold a candle to the one from Selsley Common, just southwest of Stroud. A topograph stands next to the tumulus marking the optimum spot, picking out features as far away as the Sugar Loaf and Hay Bluff – an amazing sweep of scenery given the hill's rather diminutive height.

Beginning at Coaley Peak Viewpoint on the B4066, our route approaches Selsley Common via the Cotswold Edge, and then swings south into the landscaped valley of Woodchester Park, bringing together two contrasting facets of the Cotswolds in one exceptionally satisfying walk. If you're keen to see inside Woodchester's haunted mansion, check in advance to make sure it's open.

At a glance

Where Coaley Peak in the Cotswolds, 6km/3.8miles southwest of Stroud, Gloucestershire.
Why Ancient beech forests and flower-covered pastureland; William Morris stained glass windows at Selsley church; Woodchester Mansion – an unfin-

ished Gothic masterpiece.
When May, for the glorious display of wildflowers that bedeck Selsley Common.
Start/Finish Coaley Peak Viewpoint car park (SO794013).
Duration 4hrs.
Distance 14km/8.7miles. 16km/

10miles with extension to Selsley.
Terrain Mostly easy walking over open common land, and on well-made forest trails or tracks, with a few short but steep ascents/descents.
Maps Ordnance Survey OL168.

On your way

As with many hilltop viewpoints featured in this book, **COALEY PEAK** obviously held considerable appeal for our ancient ancestors. The presence on the ridge of a various tumuli and a major burial chamber – the **NYMPSFIELD LONG BARROW** – shows this was an important mortuary site five thousand years ago. Excavation work carried out on the barrow, just to the right of the car park, revealed it contained seventeen skeletons of men, women and children. Typical of the seven-chambered tombs found along the length of the Cotswold Edge, its slab and dry-stone design features a "horned" entrance, partly reconstructed after the mound was opened by amateur archeologists in 1862.

The sea breezes funnelled up the Severn Vale may be uplifting or bracing depending on the season, but the sense of space and distance you gain from this high ground are a year-round feature of the Cotswold Way, a long-distance trail winding 160km/100 miles from Chipping Campden in the north to Bath in the south. Our route makes use of a newly established variant of this popular waymarked path to cross the beech woods lining the escarpment. Every now and then, the path dips out of the trees to reveal glimpses of the River Severn and distant Malverns as you approach **SELSLEY COMMON**, where the leaf canopy yields to an upland common of flower-rich limestone pasture. "If up on this hill for pleasure you ride/The prospect is pleasant on every side/ And if you do walk, the pleasures are still/To be seen from each corner of Selsley Hill", waxed one anonymous local poet in 1841. Come here in late spring and, in addition to the amazing view over Stroud and the Severn Vale, you'll be treated to a blaze of early purple orchids, cowslips, buttercups, daisies and other wild flowers.

Since Saxon times, local villagers have resisted attempts to enclose the common, exercising traditional grazing rights on it to this day. The hollows and lumps that riddle the hill are mostly the remains of quarry

The Woodchester Ghosts

Woodchester Park and its Gothic mansion may make the perfect destination for a day walk, but you'd have to be thick-skinned indeed to survive a night there.

Both the grounds and house are said to be haunted by ghosts, ranging from a ragged dwarf and a Roman centurion to a headless horseman, and a man who wanders the lakesides after having been mauled to death by his own dog. There have even been reports of a coffin on floating on the lake.

Interest in paranormal Wood-chester intensified in 1998, when a team of volunteers who spent the night there as a sponsored stunt claimed they witnessed a glass being thrown by a poltergeist. Staff also began to report hearing strange noises and voices while on duty. The stories attracted the attention of the reality TV programme, *Most Haunted Live*, who have since made three films at Woodches-ter, recording all manner of spooky occurrences. Stones have been thrown, furniture moved and groans heard. One night during a vigil, the crew's power supply mysteriously failed, and a glowing orb was caught on camera.

Mediums who joined the *Most Haunted Live* team insisted the hauntings relate to two French masons who died while working for William Leigh, and a woman who was allegedly strangled to death in the manor house. Investigations continue...

workings and prehistoric tumuli, although some are believed to be vestiges of a lookout camp used by rebel soldiers during the Second Barons' War of 1263–67, when Simon de Montfort and his allies mounted an uprising against King Henry III and his eldest son, Edward Longshanks.

If you've the legs for it, a worthwhile detour from Selsley Common is the drop down to the village to see the resplendent stained-glass windows of **ALL SAINTS CHURCH** – the work of William Morris and his Art and Crafts collaborators, Maddox-Brown and Rossetti. The crowning glory of the display is Morris's famous Rose Window, depicting Christ in Majesty and the Days of Creation.

At precisely the same time William Morris & Co were busily decorating Selsley church, work was underway just over the hill on a still more extravagant architectural project. **WOODCHESTER PARK** had been a baronial hunting estate for centuries, but the landscaped grounds and house that survive today are the legacy of one Victorian squire, William Leigh. The son of a wealthy Liverpool merchant, Leigh bought the mansion in the 1840s – due, it is said, to local resentment in his home county, Staffordshire, brought about by his conversion to Catholicism.

Whatever the spur for the move, William Leigh poured his inheritance into his new home, pulling down the existing Georgian mansion and erecting in its place a fashionable French-Gothic pile. The design, featuring some of the finest nineteenth-century stonework in Britain, was the brainchild of a hitherto unknown 21-year-old architect from Stroud named Benjamin Bucknall. His brief was to devise a plan for a house combining the style of a country mansion with the grandeur of a cathedral and somberness of a monastery.

ABOVE: William Morris's famous Rose Window at All Saints Church, Selsley

Initially, the project progressed well, with over one hundred tradesmen employed full time on the site. But by the 1870s, Leigh's health had begun to fail and his fortune was all but spent. When he died in 1873, work on the mansion ceased, never to resume. The building stands today largely as it did when the stone masons downed tools – seemingly complete from the outside, but a cavernous shell inside. Elaborately carved fireplaces are suspended from walls with no floors, doorways lead nowhere and upper corridors open on to voids.

Saddled with death duties, William Leigh's descendents were forced to sell the house. It is now owned by the local council, who lease the building to a trust dedicated to its preservation. The landscaped grounds, with their extensive forests and chain of five lakes, were subsequently acquired by the National Trust, who've laid out a network of waymarked paths around the woods and lakesides (see More Info, below).

Woodchester attracts plenty of visitors on those weekends when it is open, but during the week, when the mansion is closed to the public, you can expect to have the grounds almost to yourself – which only accentuates the eeriness of the place.

walk it | 14
Coaley Peak

1 From the **Coaley Peak** Viewpoint car park, first head L along the meadow to the topograph for our featured view over the Severn Vale. Then retrace your steps and a little way past the car park pass the **Nympsfield Long Barrow**. In the bottom R corner of the field, the Cotswold Way (henceforth referred to as CW) – waymarked with yellow arrows and a national trail acorn icon – leads into beech woods. Follow the waymarks as they guide you gently downhill through the trees to emerge at the bottom limits of the woods and then along the side of a field. Shortly after re-entering the woodland, the trail forks, with the CW continuing L.

2 After just under an hour, you reach a major path junction at the base of Pen Hill where the CW divides. Take the path peeling R, signed "Cotswold Way North via **Selsley Common**". After a few yards fork L downhill along the edge of woods. Cross the private access road shortly after to re-enter the woods, and after a few minutes fork R uphill to emerge on the sloping side of Selsley Common.

Once on open grassland, climb up to the main path marked by benches and continue to the prehistoric tumulus known locally as the "**Toots**" (labelled as "Long Barrow" on OS maps; SO827031), on the far side of which stands a small topograph. (For an extension to **All Saints Church** and Selsley village, follow the path contouring down the hillside to L below the Toots, aiming for the church tower. This meets the road at a kissing gate almost opposite the church. The pub lies another 10mins' walk down the road past the church and over the junction beyond on Bell Lane. To rejoin the route from

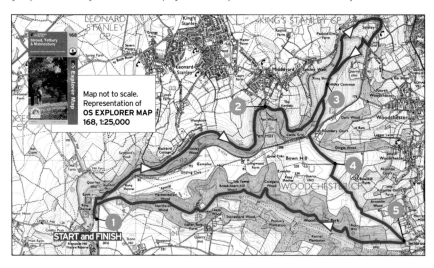

Map not to scale.
Representation of
**OS EXPLORER MAP
168, 1:25,000**

START and FINISH

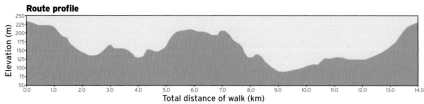

Route profile

there, follow the A4066 uphill over cattle grid, and in front of the "30 mph" sign on the roadside start climbing half right on a visible path up the common. On meeting a track, keep heading up and at each junction bear R to reach the top of the plateau to find the tumulus and topograph described above.)

3 Retrace your steps along the path skirting the western edge of the common as far as a line of electricity posts (head towards rotating blades of the wind turbine on the horizon). These run to the B4066, which you cross diagonally to the R to pick up the footpath pointing the way to "Inchbrook", down a smartly surfaced, private access road towards Bowhill Farm.

4 At the junction 5mins later (marked with a sign for "Equestrian Centre"), bear R through a small metal gate along a path running next to a drystone wall until you reach a metal gate on your L. Yellow waymark arrows point the route down the field border on your L and onwards via a series of other stiles across fields. Just after a field boundary cuts sharply to the R, look for an old stone stile to your L. Cross this and keep to the line of telegraph poles as they drop downhill.

5 Roughly 45mins after leaving the Toots, you emerge from a belt of trees at a track leading to the R through the National Trust's **Woodchester Park** estate. Follow this for about an hour around the north side of the valley, catching glimpses of some of the five lakes on your L, to reach the mansion (though

note that you should bear R at a fork in the track after 20mins). A motorable track runs W from the mansion up to the head of the valley, and onto the main B4066. Turn R when you reach the park gates, and cross the road to find a kissing gate leading on to CW; Coaley Peak Viewpoint and Nympsfield Long Barrow lie a few mins away to your L.

Getting There
Cotswold Green's bus 35 from Stroud will get you as far as Nympsfield, a 10min stroll from Coaley Peak Viewpoint.

Visitor Information
TIC Stroud
Subscription Rooms, George Street
☎01453 760960

TIC Nailsworth
George Street
☎01453 839222

Nailsworth Town Information Centre
Fountain Street
☎01453 839222

Eating & Drinking
In addition to the two pubs listed below, Woodchester Manor has a pleasant little café serving light meals, snacks, cakes, teas and coffees when the mansion is open.

The Bell
Selsley
☎01453 764910
A typical Cotswold pub by the roadside, offering real ales and home-cooked meals. At roughly the midway point of the walk, it's a good place to break for lunch, with benches outside overlooking the Nailsworth Valley.

The Rose & Crown
(See below)
Just south of the start point, this 400-year-old coaching inn, made from local stone, claims to be the highest pub in the Cotswolds. A popular local watering hole with a welcoming fire and wood-panelled interiors, it boasts a smart restaurant serving modern British food, and a garden to the rear.

Sleeping
The Rose & Crown
3 The Cross, Nympsfield, GL10 3TU
☎01453 860240
Good value B&B above a quality pub, only ten minutes' walk from Coaley Peak Viewpoint.

More Info
✎www.nationaltrust.org.uk. Maps for walks around Woodchester estate can be downloaded free from the NT's Woodchester page.
✎www.woodchestermansion.org. uk. Home page of the Woodchester Mansion Trust, listing opening days.
✎www.nationaltrail.co.uk/Cotswold. Info and inspiration for would-be walkers of the Cotswolds' famous long-distance footpath.

More Walks
Favourite South Cotswold Walks Book One (South Cotswold Ramblers). Eighteen attractive half-day walks, several of which can be combined into day walks, in the Cotswolds AONB. A fully revised and extended issue of a best-selling book first published in 1995.

More Favourite Walks in the South Cotswolds (South Cotswold Ramblers). Fifteen fully graded and illustrated walks in the Cotswolds. See ✎www.southcotswoldramblers. org.uk/books for updates.

Atop Auld Reekie
Salisbury Crags

Yonder the Shores of Fife you saw;
Here Preston-Bay and Berwick Law;
And broad between them roll'd,
The gallant Firth the eye might note,
Whose islands on its bosom float,
Like emeralds chased in gold.
Sir Walter Scott, *Marmion* (1808)

No book of walks based around great British views could possibly omit Arthur's Seat, the dramatic dollop of Scottish wilderness rising unexpectedly from the heart of Edinburgh. The plug of an extinct volcano, the hill and its outlying ramparts soar 251m/823ft above the medieval roofscape of the Royal Mile, providing a view that's as revelatory as any in the country. On a clear day, you can survey not just the entire Scottish capital, but also its majestic context. To the north: the Firth of the Forth, the Ochils and Trossachs; to the south, the Pentland Hills rolling away towards the English border. On days with exceptional visibility, you can even make out the faint line of the Atlantic in the west.

If such a site had existed in ancient Greece or India, you can be sure it would be encrusted with temples and marble-paved pathways. As it is, the route to the top – a typically Scottish mix of muddy paths and steep, rock steps – leads only to a trigpoint and metal-capped topograph. The miracle is that such wild land survives slap in the middle of one of the world's most elegant cities.

Arthur's Seat sees more than its fair share of walkers, joggers, dogs and camera-toting tourists. Even so, a climb to the top is, whatever the famously unforgiving Scottish weather throws at you, always an event. There's nothing quite as romantic as a view over a beautiful city, and few cities in the world are as exotic as this.

The route we've chosen may not be the easiest or most direct, but it certainly offers the most spectacular views. Beginning at the Scottish Parliament Building, it hugs the edge of Salisbury Crags, gaining the summit of the hill by means of the fantastic zigzagging path up "Guttit Haddie" – an ascent which will make you feel you've earned the superb panorama from the top.

At a glance

Where Arthur's Seat and Salisbury Crags, Holyrood, Edinburgh, Scotland.
Why The ultimate vantage point over the Scottish capital; historic monuments, including the new Scottish Parliament Building and Holyrood Palace; the UK's largest concentrations of geological SSSIs.
When May 1 at dawn, for the annual Dew Gathering party.
Downsides Summit rocks can be very slippery; busy on weekends.
Start/Finish Scottish Parliament Building (NT268738).
Duration 2hrs.

Distance 5km/3miles.
Terrain A mix of surfaced and unsurfaced paths, and rock steps – over gradients that are steep in places. Also some very simple scrambling on the summit rocks.
Maps OS Explorer 350; Insight Fleximap: Edinburgh.

On your way

Arthur's Seat is the highest point in a sprawling, 650-acre expanse of open crags, moorland and lochs in the centre of Edinburgh known as **HOLYROOD PARK**. A former royal hunting reserve, "Holyrood" probably derives its name from the old Scots for "Holy Cross", a reference to a supposed fragment of the True Cross brought here by the mother of King David I in the early twelfth century.

The relic later occupied pride of place in the Augustinian abbey David founded in 1128 in the shadow of the hills. Holyrood lay beyond the protection of the city ramparts and was thus prone to repeated attacks by the invading English. Apart from the walls of the nave (which still stand), the rest of the building was comprehensively demolished in 1550, but by then the Scottish monarchs had already begun to favour the site as a residence instead of the windier heights of Edinburgh Castle.

The palace subsequently erected next to the ruined abbey was where Mary Queen of Scots spent six eventful years in the 1560s, during which time she married twice, and witnessed the murder of one of her closest friends and advisors, David Rizzio, who was brutally stabbed in her private apartments by a group led by her jealous husband, Lord Darnley. Although it ceased to be the permanent royal house when James VI left for London in 1603, successive monarchs have continued to use the palace, including Bonnie Prince Charlie, who held court here for five weeks en route to Derby in 1745.

Our walk begins opposite the entrance to Holyrood Palace, in front of the new **SCOTTISH PARLIAMENT BUILDING**. The brainchild of Catalan architect Enric Miralles, the innovative complex was intended to represent the relationship

The Seventeen Coffins

A strange, and rather unnerving discovery was made on Arthur's Seat in 1836. While hunting rabbits in the rocks below the summit, a group of boys came across a collection of seventeen miniature coffins hidden in a hollow. Initially, witchcraft was suspected. The local press raved about "weird sisters ... who retain the ancient power to work their spells of death by entombing the likenesses of those they wish to destroy".

It wasn't long, however, before residents in the old city began to suspect the objects were related to the murders committed in the previous decade by Burke and Hare. The infamous pair of Irish navvies had killed seventeen people in the slums of central Edinburgh, selling their corpses to Dr Robert Knox for dissection in his medical college.

Burke had expressed some remorse after his trial, where he was sentenced to death. Perhaps the seventeen figurines had been carved by him to give his victims make-believe burials? Or maybe it was a friend or relative of the pair who knew about the murders and made the models to assuage their guilt at not exposing the crimes? In an attempt to solve the riddle once and for all, tests were recently carried out on DNA extracted from Burke's skeleton, which is displayed in the Surgeon's Hall on Edinburgh's Nicolson Street (along with his death mask and a macabre set of objects made from his skin). Samples were also taken one of the miniature coffins. The results, however, proved inconclusive.

Only eight of the figurines and their caskets have survived to the present day. Bought by the state in 1901, they're now kept at the National Museum of Scotland, where they provide a great source of fascination for visiting school children.

between the Scottish people and their natural environment. But since it was opened by the Queen in 2004 – more than three years late, and £404million over-budget – opinion has been divided between people who regard the building as sensational, and those who tend to consider the vast sum it cost as a waste of public funds.

A recent poll designated the Scottish Parliament as the World's Eighth Ugliest Building, but whether or not you like the architecture, you can't fail to be impressed by its location, set against the spectacular rock wall of **SALISBURY CRAGS**. It was while scrutinizing these glaciated basalt cliffs, which tower in a forbidding arc above Edinburgh's old city, that local naturalist James Hutton (1726–97) realized the rocks must have been formed not by rainwater deposits, as theory at the time had it, but by molten matter forcing itself into gaps between older sedimentary layers. His eureka moment paved the way for later theories of "geological time", and the birth of geology as a modern science.

At the base of the cliffs, where the crags give way to scree, a track known as the Radical Road stands as a reminder of a turbulent spell in Scottish history. In 1820, popular anger over the recession that followed the Napoleonic Wars spilled into a full-blown rebellion – the so-called Radical War, when artisans marched for economic reform. It was to diffuse these tensions (and avoid what the establishment feared might be a repeat of the French Revolution) that Sir Walter Scott convinced the government to pay unemployed weavers to dig a cart track around the bottom of the crags.

Our route steers a more radical route still, along the precipitous top edge of Salisbury Crags to reach the cliffs' culminating point – **CAT NICK**. Many would

ABOVE: A "Brocken spectre", Arthur's Seat

argue this summit, a spot favoured by suicide jumpers that falls to a near vertical, 46-metre/150-feet rock face on its western flank, affords a more impressive view than Arthur's Seat itself, being closer to the city. It's certainly a fine platform from which to pick out Edinburgh's principal landmarks.

Dropping to the col connecting Salisbury Crags with the bigger hill behind (a pass known as "the Hause"), we next follow a flight of zigzagging stone steps up a steep, heavily eroded gulley known as **GUTTIT HADDIE** (Scots for "smoked haddock fillet") – a nickname derived from a landslide in the eighteenth century which left a scar on the hillside resembling a filleted haddock. A final scramble at the hilltop brings you to the rocky crown of **ARTHUR'S SEAT** proper, revealing a stupendous view east across the Firth of the Forth to the open sea, with the distinctive conical profiles of Bass Rock and the Berwick Law dominating the mid-distance.

The name of the hill suggests an Arthurian connection. One of the earliest known references to the legendary king crops up in a sixth-century saga, *Y Gododdin*, thought to have been written in

Edinburgh about the occupants of the castle, the Gododdins (or Votadini, as they were known to the Romans). A more plausible explanation lies in the Gaelic term *ard-na-said* – "height of arrows" – a nod perhaps to the site's strategic role in Medieval times. Traces of a ruined fort can still be discerned amid the rocks of Crow, the southeasterly of Arthur's Seat's three summits.

While archeological remains underline the ancient military importance of the hilltop, Edinburgh's inhabitants have in more recent centuries tended to associate the site less with historic events than with weird, and even supernatural ones. A particularly chilling evocation of the spooky side of the city crops up in the Gothic masterpiece by Edinburgh novelist James Hogg, *The Private Memoirs and Confessions of a Justified Sinner* (1824). The sinner in question is a dour young religious fanatic called Robert Wringhim, who is incited by a mysterious doppelganger to murder his own half-brother, George.

A foggy morning on the summit of Arthur's Seat is chosen for the grim deed. But just as Robert is about to push his sibling over the cliffs, George spies a terrifying apparition projected on to the clouds below the crags. He turns in time to catch his brother, whom he chases down the hill screaming at the top of his voice.

Walk around the summit on a chilly autumn morning, with sun breaking through the mist, and you may well encounter a vision of precisely the same kind that inspired Hogg's terrifying account: a Brocken spectre. Caused by sunlight casting a shadow onto cloud below a ridge, this peculiar light effect is a common occurrence on Arthur's Seat.

Following in the footsteps of Hogg's Justified Sinner, we descend the hill via its northern side down a narrow valley called **HUNTERS BOG** (aka "The Dry Dam"). The path brings you out alongside the skeleton of **ST ANTHONY'S CHAPEL**. No-one knows for sure when this eerie structure was originally built, nor why, though it would almost certainly have been connected in some way to the nearby abbey. One theory holds that the building, dedicated to the patron saint of skin ailments, served as an annexe to the hospital at Leith, donated by James I in the fifteenth century for the treatment of a condition known as "St Anthony's Fire". The waters contained in a well nearby, still visible next to a large grey boulder, were believed to be curative.

An echo of this old belief survives in the adage, "if you wash your face in dew from Arthur's Seat on the morning of May 1 you will be beautiful". Large crowds used to gather for the annual "dew gathering". "In the course of half an hour," wrote an eyewitness in 1826, "the entire hill is a moving mass of all sorts and sizes. At the summit may be seen a company of bakers, and other craftsmen, dressed in kilts, dancing round a Maypole. On the more level part . . . is usually an itinerant vender of whiskey, or mountain (not May) dew, your approach to whom it always indicated by a number of 'bodies' carelessly lying across your path, not dead, but drunk." Having died out in the 1930s, the event has seen a resurgence, though it's more restrained than in centuries past.

Panorama

The term *panorama* – from the Greek *pan* ("all") *horama* ("view") – was originally dreamed up by the itinerant Irish artist, Robert Barker in 1792, to describe his wide-angle images of Edinburgh.

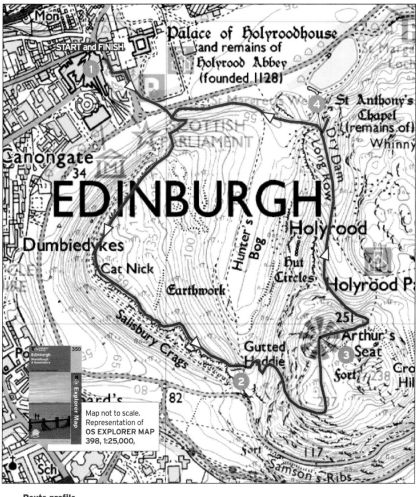

Route profile

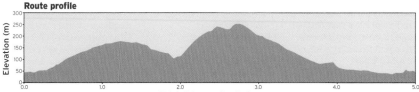

Elevation (m)

Total distance of walk (km)

CHECKED BY
✔ **Edinburgh Ramblers**

1 With your back to the new **Scottish Parliament Building**'s main entrance on Horse Wynd, cross the road and turn R, following the walls of **Holyrood Palace** around to the car park. Cross Queen's Drive via the zebra crossing. Ignoring the pitched path and steps straight ahead, turn L onto the asphalt cycleway. When you get to a fork in the path, bear R (past the "No Entry" sign, which applies to bikes not pedestrians!). Keep to the tarmac. A minute or two later you'll arrive at an unmarked path cutting up the shoulder of the hill to your R, then a second junction, where you should bear R (SW) up the edge of the cliffs .

Follow the trail up the top of **Salisbury Crags** to **Cat Nick**, and down the far side via a steeper, and more slippery path that eventually brings you out at the col below Guttit Haddie.

2 Go straight across the pass, ignoring the other paths that converge here to pick up a pitched trail leading into what look like vertical crags, with the eroded gulley of **Guttit Hadie** to your L. Almost immediately, a flight of flagstone steps takes over, zigzagging steeply uphill. After around 15mins, it levels off, turns sharply L around the south shoulder of the hill, swings over a crest, drops into a slight dip then begins a short, sharp scramble through the rocks to the summit of **Arthur's Seat**.

3 To descend, follow the worn path winding down

the eastern spur of the hilltop, which is steep and rocky to begin with but soon eases off. At a shoulder where it reaches grass (NT277730), turn L onto a trail dropping down the L (west) side of **Hunter's Bog** valley. A fork reached after 5mins offers the choice between a more exposed line along the low ridge to your L, or the route along the valley floor. Both will get you down easily enough, but the latter (lower) path takes you closer to **St Anthony's Chapel**, off to the R at the bottom of the valley.

4 From the ruined chapel, drop back to the valley floor and follow the path running parallel with Queen's Drive towards the Parliament Building, which soon rejoins the asphalt cycleway featured at the start of the route.

Getting There
Edinburgh's Waverly Station lies a 15-20-min stroll from the start of our route. The Scottish Parliament building can also be reached via Lothian Bus services 35 and 36, which run via the centre.

i Visitor Information
Edinburgh TIC
3 Princes Street
☎ 0845 225 5121
🖳 www.edinburgh.org

Historic Scotland Ranger Service
Holyrood Park Education Centre, 1 Queen's Drive, Holyrood Park
☎ 0131 652 8150
🖳 www.edinburgh.org

✗ Eating & Drinking
Henderson's
94 Hanover St
☎ 0131 225 2131

An Edinburgh institution for decades, located in the New Town. It serves up great organic veggie food in a bistro-style setting, and there's often live music in the wine bar.

The Bow Bar
80 West Bow (a continuation of Victoria St)
☎ 0131 226 7667
Fantastic little wood-panelled freehouse in a street just below the Royal Mile. Antique brewery mirrors and railway-carriage tables give the place a traditional atmosphere, and they serve a generous selection of hand-pumped cask ales and single malts from across Scotland.

🛏 Sleeping
University of Edinburgh
Pollock Halls of Residence, 18 Holyrood Park Rd, Newington, EH16 5AY
☎ 0131 651 2007
🖳 www.edinburghfirst.com
Only available outside term time, but a well placed, bargain option close to the start of our route and the city centre. Options range from rock-bottom budget to three-star rooms with views.

Smart City Hostel
50 Blackfriars St, Old Town EH1 1NE
☎ 0131 452 9072
🖳 www.smartcityhostels.com
Edinburgh's awash with backpackers hostels, but this one, as its name suggests, is smarter – and larger – than most, and they offer individual rooms as well as dorm beds. Only 1min off the Royal Mile (or 10mins walk from the start of our route), it has a lively café serving food and drink all day.

Galloway Guest House
22 Dean Park Cres, Stockbridge,
EH4 1PH
📞0131 332 3672
Like most of the city's best-value
B&Bs, this welcoming guest
house lies a short bus ride (or
a twenty-minute walk) west of
the city centre. Located down a
quiet residential street opposite
a leafy park, it's friendly, warm
and traditional, with ten spacious
rooms. Book ahead.

 More Info
The Holyrood Park
Education Centre, opposite the
southern entrance to Holyrood
Palace, has brochures on the
park's archeology, geology and
wildlife, in addition to a splendid
3D model of the whole estate.
✎www.undiscoveredscotland.
co.uk.edinburgh. Heaps of
background on the city's nooks
and crannies, including all of the
sites featured on our walk.

✎www.royal.gov.uk/output/
Page580.asp. The history of
Holyroodhouse, from the Queen's
own "Royal Residences" site.
✎www.trutv.com. Stick "Burke"
into this site's search field and
you'll hit a naccount of Burke &
Hare's grisly Old Town murders.
✎www.edinburghsdarkside.
blogspot.com The "Arthur's Seat"
link in this great little site features
photos of the famous miniature
coffins (see box).

ABOVE: Our Dynamic Earth and the Scottish Parliament, from Salisbury Crags

Castles and Kippers

Embleton Bay

The ruins of Dunstanburgh Castle cast a melancholic spell over one of the emptiest, most beautiful stretches of the Northumberland coast, where a spur of the Great Whin Sill ridge tapers into the sea just south of the Farne Islands. Rising from a headland protected on two sides by sheer cliffs and on the other by a deep ditch hewn from solid rock, the fortress was erected in the fourteenth century, ostensibly to ward off marauding Scots, but also as a symbol of the power and rank of its redoubtable creator, Thomas Earl of Lancaster.

Thomas Plantaganet, as he was also known, was the wealthiest baron in England at the time. This was his main power base and its awesome size reflects not merely the omnipresent threat from the north, but also the earl's long-standing rivalry with his cousin, King Edward II of England.

Today the crumbling gatehouse, towers and ramparts barely hint at the building's original proportions, but they stand as a perfect complement to the heart-stopping vista of windswept dunes and rocky coves that unfurls from their base.

The finest view of Dunstanburgh, as featured on innumerable magazine covers and postcard racks, is to be had from Embleton Bay, to the north of the castle – a huge sweep of golden sand and crashing surf backed by a freshwater lagoon.

Starting at the fishing harbour of Craster, where you can steel yourself for the walk ahead with a plate of locally smoked kipper, our route winds across Embleton Bay to reach Low Newton-by-the-Sea, a tiny cluster of stone fishermen's houses overlooked by a coast-guard's post. The pocket-sized pub at Low Newton's heart, the Ship Inn, has to be one of Britain's most delightful watering holes, cowering out of the wind next to the green. The perfect turning point for our route, it serves its own home-brewed beer, and fresh lobsters caught by the landlady's son-in-law.

This is a walk that should ideally be saved for a bright, windy day, when the sea colours are at their most vivid. Bring a kite, and pair of field glasses to spot the seabirds that congregate here in impressive numbers – Embleton ranks among the northeast's top birding hotspots. And if you're lucky you might even catch a glimpse of a basking seal.

At a glance

Where Craster to Low Newton-by-the-Sea, via Dunstanburgh Castle, Northumberland.
Why Magnificent Dunstanburgh Castle and adjacent beach; Craster and its famous kippers; Newton Pool Nature Reserve.

When Early Sept, for the Alnwick Food and Beer Festival.
Downsides Proximity of an unsightly golf course behind Embleton Bay.
Start/Finish Craster TIC (NU256198) at the entrance to

Craster village on the right.
Duration 3hrs 30mins.
Distance 12km/7.5miles.
Terrain Gentle coastal paths crossing low cliffs, sandy beaches and dunes. Some muddy stretches.
Maps OS Explorer 332 and 340.

On your way

Recent archeological digs have yielded evidence of settlement at Dunstanburgh stretching back thousands of years, but it was in the early fourteenth century during the lifetime of Thomas Plantagenet, Earl of Lancaster, that the site became the region's main stronghold.

The castle owes its ambitious scale primarily to the troubled relations between the Earl and his cousin, King Edward II of England. Although close in their youth, the two fell out over Edward's fondness for one of his young courtiers, Piers Gaveston – a man of inferior rank on whom the Prince and future King lavished favours, privileges, titles and land – despite furious attempts by his family to separate the pair.

Historians have long considered the two were gay lovers. However, the civil strife that erupted after Edward's accession to the throne was sparked not by disapproval of the king's suspected bisexuality, so much as by his companion Gaveston's knack of putting powerful noses out of joint.

When Edward departed to France to marry twelve-year-old Princess Isabella in 1308, he appointed his favourite as Regent. This outraged some of the older barons at court, who considered the choice a breach of protocol. Lancaster and his allies – the so-

called "Ordainer Earls" – eventually lost patience and raised an army to attack the king at Newcastle. Edward and his friend managed to slip away from the ensuing siege (leaving the young Queen Isabella behind to fend for herself), but Gaveston was eventually captured at Scarborough and, after a mock trial, beheaded in 1312.

Dunstanburgh was intended as a response to castles built by Edward's father in Wales a generation before. Several wars with the Scots made little impact on the structure, but it suffered a terrible pounding in the War of the Roses. Among the few buildings to survive the Lancastrian cannonades were the huge twin-towered gatehouse, which John of Gaunt later re-modelled into a keep, and three-storey Lilburn Tower, a medieval skyscraper propped up on basalt pillars.

The lords of the manor in this area were for centuries the Craster family, descendants of Earl Thomas based at a fifteenth-century tower house which still stands on the outskirts of nearby **CRASTER**. The same branch of the dynasty was responsible for the village's little harbour, on which a plaque records a dedication to a brother killed in Francis Younghusband's invasion of Tibet in 1906.

Part of the family's wealth derived from same durable stone that Earl Thomas chiselled out of the Great Whin Sill to create

Craster Kippers

You can't go far in Craster without being assailed by the unmistakable aroma of smoked fish. The source of the village's trademark smell is L Robson & Son's famous smoke house - the last of four such factories which, at the height of the herring boom in the nineteenth century, kept a fleet of twenty boats and hundreds of "herring girls" busy here. Overfishing and pollution have decimated North Sea herring stocks, and today the salmon and herring filets smoked by the Robsons over oak sawdust has to be imported, but the produce remains as succulent and fragrant as ever.

To sample it, and take a peep at the curing sheds in action, visit the factory shop above the harbour, or its adjacent seafood eastery, the Craster Fish Restaurant (see "Eating & Drinking").

ABOVE: Dunstanburgh castle from the coast path

Dunstanburgh. Rock from several quarries hereabouts used be transported via a network of overhead cables and bins to the jetty, where it was shipped to London for use as kerb stones. Craster's elderly inhabitants can still recall the dismantling of the aerial railway at the start of World War II. It was said at the time the measure was to prevent the installations being used as a navigation aid by enemy bombers, but in truth the quarry buckets interfered with a **SECRET RADAR POST** hidden on the ridge north of the village.

Our route takes you right past the station's surviving concrete bunkers, from where a great view extends over Dunstanburgh Castle and out to sea. Amid the wooded slopes just below them on the west flank of the hill, amateur archeologists recently uncovered terraced gardens made by Italian PoWs held here in the 1940s, along with huts decorated with murals showing nostalgic scenes of Mediterranean life.

Another vestige of the trawler industry that formerly flourished along this coast is the pretty enclave of cream-washed cottages at **LOW NEWTON-BY-THE-SEA**, 6.5km/ 4miles north of Craster at the turning point of our route. Ranged around a little green, the terrace of eighteenth-century houses faces a natural harbour shielded from the waves by an off-shore reef. Most of the boats moored here these days tend to be leisure dinghies, but a couple of local fishermen still work out of the village, supplying its pub, the heavenly Ship Inn (see "Eating & Drinking"), with fresh lobster. Before leaving Low Newton, take a stroll north up the hill above the village to the coastguard lookout station (reached via a path turning right off the main road just north of the pub). The view from its little terrace back over the beach to Dunstanburgh is magnificent.

Another short but worthwhile detour from our route is to the **LOW NEWTON NATURE RESERVE**. Centered on a freshwater lagoon surrounded by fens and scrubwood, the site attracts birdwatchers from all over the region; from a pair of hides (one of which is wheelchair accessible) you can sight rare waders and wildfowl including pochard, teal and warblers. Keen birders should explore the cliffs below **DUNSTANBURGH CASTLE**, which shelter one of Northumberland's largest seabird colonies, with large numbers of nesting kittiwakes, fulmars and razorbills in the summer months. Finally, keep your eyes peeled, too, for grey seals basking on the rocks.

1 On leaving the TIC at **Craster**, turn R and walk down the main road towards the village. After a couple of mins, you reach a turning on your L (Norwell Brow). Head to the end of the cul de sac, from where a path continues ahead, veering R shortly after through the gorse. Having passed the last gardens and houses, you then emerge through a gate onto open pasture, with a low, gorse-covered ridge to your L. Instead of keeping to the path, it's worth drifting up to the ridgetop, where (at NU255204) you'll find the remains of Craster's World War II **secret radar post** and a fine view up the coast to the castle. From there, improvise a route dropping diagonally via sheep tracks through the gorse bushes to reach the bottom RH corner of the field.

Map not to scale. Representation of **OS EXPLORER MAP 332 and 340, 1:25,000**

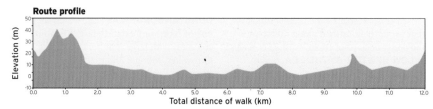

Route profile

(Elevation (m) vs Total distance of walk (km))

2 Here a five-bar gate leads to a signposted junction: bear R across the adjacent field along a fainter trail leading to the main coast path. Shortly after meeting this, you arrive at another gate. Instead of bearing R along the broad path to the entrance to **Dunstanburgh Castle**, head L via Earl Thomas' medieval ditch, with the steep bank rising to your R. Once you've reached the shoreline beyond the castle, keep to the coast path on the dune as it skirts Embleton golf course. After 5mins or so you'll reach the point where the black rocks on your R give way to the sand of Embleton Bay; a path leads down to the beach.

3 Walk along the beach for approx 10–15 mins, passing a gap in the high dunes on your L marked by an orange life ring on a post. Eventually you'll see a second, almost identical gap and life ring at NU 244230, which you should head through (if you reach the river you'll know you've gone too far). The second gap leads to a footbridge across a stream, then, shortly after, a path junction from where a surfaced track leads L to the golf course clubhouse.

4 Ignore the track to the clubhouse, and the second footbridge immediately on your R, and instead head straight along a clear path running along the bank of Embleton Burn. After a few mins, this reaches a tight R bend in the river, from where you can swing R to follow the sand. Once back on the beach, keep L, with the huts on the high dunes above you, heading north around the point to Low Newton harbour.

5 The hub of **Low Newton-by-the-Sea** consists of a three terraces of old fisherman's cottages enclosing a little green. Our path re-commences behind the Ship Inn. Follow the little lane running down the back of the north terrace (Farm Rd), turning L when you arrive at the end of the houses to follow the track down the back of the pub and out along the foot of the dunes (a continuation of Farm Rd). When you reach a fork just before a detached cottage, bear L on to a narrower path towards **Low Newton Nature Reserve**; you'll see a turning to the two hides on your R shortly after. Note that after heavy rain this section can be impassable and you may have to detour back the way you came along Low Newton beach.

After 10mins or so, the northern end of the golf course is reached. Keep L at the fork and continue uphill through the dunes past the holiday cabins, then back down to the perimeter of the golf course again. The path crosses a little stream, and soon after rejoins the sandy trail followed earlier along the bank of Embleton Burn to the junction (**4**).

For the next section of this walk, you retrace the outward route in reverse, back along the beach (or the soft sand path running along the top of the dunes if you prefer), turning R onto the coast path at the south end of Embleton Bay where the rocks take over. Keeping to the edge of the golf course, the path winds towards the castle, the entrance to which is in the main gatehouse on the south side of the complex (visit recommended).

6 From the castle, it's plain sailing all the way back to Craster via the main coast path, which keeps to grassy pasture all the way to the village. To return to the TIC and car park, follow the lane that takes over from the path (Dunstanburgh Rd) with the houses to your R, then bear R at the first junction on to West End. You'll see the TIC after 5 mins on your L.

Getting There
Regular buses, run by Arriva Northumbria and Travelsure, operate year round between Alnwick and Craster. Alnmouth, the nearest railhead, lies 13.5km/ 8.5miles south; the station is a stop on the east-coast main line between London and Scotland. For bus and train timetable information, contact Traveline
☎0871 200 2233 or
🖱www.traveline.org.uk.

Visitor Information
Craster TIC
Quarry Car Park
☎01665 576007
🖱www.visitnortheastengland.com

Eating & Drinking
The Ship Inn
Low Newton-by-the-Sea
☎01665 576262
🖱www.shipinnnewton.com
Fresh, welcoming seaside pub serving its own micro-brewery beers and wholesome meals made from locally sourced ingredients in a cosy, bare-boards bar. The lobster comes straight from Newton Bay (fished by the landlady's husband) and they do some interesting veggie options, as well as old-fashioned puddings. Pub perfection!

Craster Fish Restaurant
L Robson & Son, Craster
☎01665 576223
This is the place for the definitive Craster kipper experience. The décor is faded 1970s chintz, but the seafood platters, washed down with a bottle of salty Picboul de Pinet, are terrific. For those on tighter budgets they also serve standard battered cod, chips and mushy peas.

Jolly Fisherman
Craster
☎01665 576461
The fame of Craster's village pub rests largely on its clifftop location, legendary fresh crab soup (the recipe for which the landlord insists Rick Stein has vowed never to divulge) and chips fried in dripping, but in truth the place has become decidedly rundown and no longer deserves its popularity. Save your appetite for the Ship Inn at Low Newton.

Sleeping
Harbour Lights
Whin Hill, Craster, NE66 3TP
☎01665 576062

www.harbourlights-craster.co.uk
Quality, welcoming B&B just above Craster harbour, boasting fine views up the coast to Dunstanburgh from its two cosy guest rooms. Breakfast options include Robson's smoked salmon.

Cottage Inn
Dunstan, Craster, NE66 3NZ
☎01665 576658
www.cottageinnhotel.co.uk
This is a large, upscale – but reasonably priced – B&B option set in six acres of woodland on the edge of Craster, with ten rooms (most of them en suite) and popular licensed restaurant.

Crow's Nest
c/o The Ship Inn, Low Newton-by-the-Sea, NE66 3EW
☎01665 576262
www.shipinnnewton.co.uk
Converted barn offering pleasantly furnished, well equipped self-catering accommodation with a double bedroom, right next to the area's nicest pub. You could start and end our route from here rather than Craster.

More Info
www.english-heritage.org.uk. Although it's owned by the National Trust, English Heritage manage Dunstanburgh Castle. Click on their "Research & Conservation" page for a fascinating report on recent archeological findings.

www.nationaltrust.org.uk. As well as the castle, the NT owns Embleton Bay and Low Newton-by-the-Sea.

Queen Isabella: Treachery, Adultery, and Murder in Medieval England by Alison Weir (Ballantine Books, 2005). A compelling biography of Edward II's troubled marriage to Isabella of France, and its violent aftermath (Isabella led the rebellion that eventually deposed the king).

Piers Gaveston: Edward II's Adoptive Brother by Pierre Chaplais (OUP). This controversial, scholarly biography of the king's favourite argues their relationship was not sexual but one of "adoptive brotherhood," an old convention within the laws of chivalry.

ABOVE: Grey seal near Dunstanburgh

walk | 17

Clifton Suspension Bridge

Gorge-ous Bristol

No other city in England enjoys as spectacular a situation as Bristol, the West Country's carbuncle-ridden, but undeniably charismatic capital. Piled up the flanks of a steep-sided hill, its cluttered core rises from the banks of the River Avon in a quintessentially English jumble of cobbled quaysides, half-timbered pubs, church spires, concrete car parks and glass-sided office blocks, all overshadowed by the great tower of the University's Wills Building. Walking through the streets and gardens that break up this architectural anarchy, breathtaking views regularly open over the old Floating Harbour and Victorian suburbs below, framed by the whale-backed hulk of Dundry Hill and distant Mendips.

Our route threads together the pick of Bristol's viewpoints, starting with the most iconic of them all: the magnificent panorama over the Avon Gorge and Brunel's suspension bridge from the Clifton Observatory. From there, it loops through the Leigh Woods Nature Reserve on the opposite side of the bridge, before plunging down a hidden, forested valley

to the river bank and a compelling walk along the harbourside.

Mile for mile, the route packs in as much variety and interest as you'd expect from one of Britain's oldest and most cosmopolitan cities. In the course of the first couple of hours alone you get to clamber over huge Iron-Age ramparts, spot some of the world's rarest plants, admire the graceful lines of the *SS Great Britain* – from *below* the surface of the water – and enjoy Bristol's skyline over a pint of Somerset scrumpy. Throw in a couple of sidetrips – to see the cathedral's exquisite Norman chapterhouse, or the Elizabethan Red House on Park Row – and you've the makings of a very memorable day's walking.

Don't, however, make the mistake of thinking that because this route is urban it's a soft option. Far from it. Bristol, as any local cyclist will confirm, is built on some calf-busting gradients, and our walk tackles a couple of them head on. Allow a full day if you intend to complete the whole circuit, and take in the sights along the way.

At a glance

Where Clifton Suspension Bridge and Avon Gorge, Bristol.
Why The Floating Harbour, home of the *SS Great Britain*; Britain's best preserved Norman chapterhouse; magnificent Georgian architecture.

When Early August, during the annual Balloon Fiesta.
Start/Finish Clifton Suspension Bridge (ST565733).
Duration 4hrs 30mins.
Distance 12.5km/7.8miles.
Cut it short Cabot Tower,

Brandon Hill (ST579729), 9.5km/6miles.
Terrain Urban; docks; woodland; with some short, stepped climbs; and muddy paths.
Maps Geographer's A-Z: Bristol (132507); OS Explorer 155.

Brunel's Clifton Suspension Bridge - the architect
died five years before its completion

On your way

Many modern travellers passing through Bristol never set eyes on them, but to generations of mariners arriving by ship on the river, the mighty cliffs of the Avon Gorge must, like the Pillars of Hercules, have seemed like a gateway to another world. Thought to have been formed by the rushing meltwaters of a vast frozen lake further inland, the escarpments are made of carboniferous limestone encrusted with fossilized shells and coral, which millennia of wind and rain have smoothed into angled slabs.

The orientation of the cliffs, which face southwest towards the afternoon sun and are sheltered from the prevailing winds, account for the existence of a unique microclimate. Average temperatures are one degree higher on the eastern side of the gorge than the west, giving rise to a habitat that supports some 24 species of rare plant, among them two trees only found here (the Bristol and Wilmott's whitebeams) and several endemics, such as Bristol rock cress, Bristol onion and honewort.

Roman conscripts once manned a fort overlooking the gorge, built on top of one of three, much older, Iron-Age strongholds. Stones from the outpost were later used to erect a wind-powered snuff mill on the same spot, which ended its days after a fire in 1777. These ruins were, in turn, bought by the artist William West who in 1828 installed in the tower a camera obscura with which he and his students used to scrutinize the surrounding countryside for painting subjects. You can see the camera in action for yourself at the renovated **OBSERVATORY**, where an additional ticket gains visitors access to a tunnel plunging inside the cliffs, known here as St Vincent's Rocks, to the Giant's Cave.

CLIFTON, the ultra-smart, old-money enclave where our route begins, was where the slave traders, tobacco merchants and sugar barons of the eighteenth century fled to escape the hoi polloi of the port. Over time it became a fashionable resort; wealthy visitors from all over the country poured in to benefit from the salubrious breezes and uplifting panoramas, renting apartments for the summer season in one of the spectacular crescents erected on the lip of the Avon Gorge.

The Slave Trade

A truth Bristol has only in recent decades begun to acknowledge is that the city's world-beating prosperity in the eighteenth and nineteenth centuries was inextricably linked to the African slave trade. Local merchants spearheaded the campaign to abolish the Royal Africa Company's monopoly over slave shipment in 1689, and dispatched the first private slaver to the West African coast soon after. A confirmed 2108 slave ships left Bristol docks over the ensuing century, laden with guns from Birmingham and other metal goods that would be exchanged for slaves to work on the sugar plantations of the Caribbean (many of them estates owned by Bristol-based tycoons). An estimated half a million Africans fell victim of this so-called "triangular trade", which saw the fruits of their forced labour return to Bristol in the form of raw sugar cane. Recent studies have speculated that at least half died during the trans-shipment, and that a third of those who survived perished within a year at "Seasoning Camps", where they were tortured into submitting to their new lives, a process often compared to breaking in horses.

Pero's Bridge, a modern footbridge across the Floating Harbour connecting Narrow Quay with Millennium Square, was named after the black slave of a famous sugar baron.

The **SUSPENSION BRIDGE**, however, was a relative latecomer to the neighbourhood's architectural landscape, the rest of the Georgian village having been in existence for half a century or more by the time its foundation stone was laid. Although plans to span the gorge had first been mooted as far back as 1753, the project didn't get under way until 1829, when a competition was held to find a suitably grand design. Thomas Telford, the principal judge, rejected all those submitted (he preferred one of his own), but the second competition was won outright by 24-year-old Isambard Kingdom Brunel, with his design for a suspension bridge flanked by a pair of Egyptian-style towers. Brunel's blueprints had to be drastically scaled down, after a series of financial setbacks, but the bridge did eventually open for traffic, in 1864 – five years after the great engineer's death.

On the opposite side of the gorge lies **LEIGH WOODS**, a 200-acre zone of protected forest gifted to its present owner, the National Trust, by the Wills family of tobacco magnates in 1909. Criss-crossed by trails, the mixed forest is dominated by the massive earthwork ramparts of **STONELEIGH CAMP**, an Iron-Age fort excavated from around 300BC by the Dobunnis ("the dark-haired people"), a tribe of Iberian origins.

NIGHTINGALE VALLEY buttresses Stoneleigh to the south. A deep, sheer-sided ravine cloaked in dense forest, the combe forms an unexpected, but utterly delightful, pocket of wilderness where you might spot peregrine falcons swooping overhead. From its bottom, our route swings directly under the suspension bridge – another spectacular view – and follows the **AVON RIVER TRAIL** east towards the old port area.

By the end of the eighteenth century, the notoriously tricky approach to Bristol docks along the Avon was starting to prove a disincentive for larger ships, which often had

ABOVE: "The Harrowing of Hell", Bristol Cathedral

to wait hours for the waters to rise, lurching dangerously in the mud. It was thus decided to excavate a whole new "cut", running 1km to the south. Furnished with a series of sluices designed by Brunel, the river's original course then became a floating harbour, immune to the effects of flooding, silting and currents, and with a constant depth guaranteed. The works revived the Welsh trade in leather, grain and stone. Ultimately, however, it failed to attract the heavier cargoes of the industrial revolution, and soon the docks went into decline from which they only recently recovered, following a massive £450million redevelopment. The old wharfs that survived the blitz of World War II have been converted into flats, offices and arts centres, while a former industrial wasteland along its northern side now accommodates the At Bristol centre.

The harbour's defining sight, however, has to be the **SS GREAT BRITAIN**, the world's first iron-hulled, ocean-going steam ship. Built in Bristol's Great Western

Dockyard, she was designed by Brunel to carry 382 passengers and crew across the Atlantic. Her maiden voyage to New York on July 26, 1845, took a record-breaking fourteen days, but in spite of her formidable speed in the water the *Great Britain* never proved viable as a liner. She ended her days as a coal hulk before being wrecked and left to rot in the Falklands. A "glass sea" was recently constructed at the ship's waterline to provide a protective air-tight chamber around the hull, and visitors can now walk underneath to admire the elegantly curved flanks and propeller from below – an amazing spectacle.

Berthed alongside the *SS Great Britain* is the *Matthew*, a replica of the square-rigged caravel used by John Cabot to reach North America in 1497. The Italian-born navigator (whose name was actually "Giovanni Caboto"), set sail from Bristol in search of the Northwest Passage to the Indies, only to find his westward progress interrupted by what we now know as the coast of Newfoundland. He was lost at sea the following year trying to repeat the trick.

Survivors of the four-hundred-year maritime boom for which Cabot's transatlantic voyages paved the way still litter the harbour, but you'll be hard pushed to find any remnants of the Norman town that rose around the confluence of the Frome and Avon Rivers, let alone its Saxon predecessor. One exception endures in Bristol Cathedral, whose pinnacled towers overshadow **COLLEGE GREEN**, just north of the Floating Harbour. Don't be put off by the rather ill-proportioned, nineteenth-century facade. Inside, an airy, light nave leads to a rare example of a "Hall Church", so called because its aisles are of the same height.

The cathedral's real gem, however, is its Norman Chapterhouse – one of the finest specimens of its kind anywhere in the world. Constructed between 1150 and 1165, the serene little stone chamber, finely vaulted and richly carved, is one among only a few vestiges of the Augustinian Abbey that originally stood on the site. Just opposite the entrance to it, on the wall next to the Chapel of the Blessed Virgin Mary, look out for a worn bas relief showing a newly risen Christ brandishing a crucifix. The plaque, known as "The Harrowing of Hell", dates from before the Norman Conquest and is regarded as one of the finest examples of Saxon art surviving in Britain. It was found under the Chapterhouse floor after a fire in 1831, having been put to use as a coffin lid.

A left turn off nearby **PARK STREET**, with its über-fashionable clothes shops, brings you to the foot of **Brandon Hill**, a breezy park overlooking the city. At the top stands the **CABOT TOWER**, built in 1897 to mark the 400th anniversary of the Italian navigator's historic voyage. A pair of platforms, reached via a spiral staircase, provide unrivalled viewpoints over Bristol and its hinterland.

From Brandon Hill, our route picks a convoluted path via old stone-lined alleys through the residential district of Cliftonwood, with its brightly painted Victorian terraces, to regain Clifton village. After a tour around the elegant squares and Georgian shopping arcades, no more fitting a finale to this city walk could be conceived than a stroll along **ROYAL YORK CRESCENT**, the longest of its kind in Britain, and the one with the most extensive panorama, which sweeps across the entire southern half of the city and its enfolding hills.

As you make your way back up the hill towards the suspension bridge, look out on the left for the top entrance to the old Clifton Rocks Railway. Opened in 1893, the funicular functioned for forty years, shuttling holiday makers to and from river level. Its last incarnation, before closing in 1953, was as a secret BBC transmission base in World War II.

CHECKED BY
✔ Brunel 20s-30s Walking Group

1 From the **Clifton Observatory**, cross the **suspension bridge** and take the first R into North Rd. Continue around the bend until you reach a layby/gate into **Leigh Woods** on your R. After the gate, take the middle of the three paths, which leads to a clearing (with a terrace of white cottages on your L). Bear R at the fork in the path here to reach the

overgrown ramparts of **Stoneleigh Camp**. At the breach in the ancient ring mound, head R for a good viewpoint over the gorge (at ST561732). Retrace your steps from here back to the layby/gate onto the road, but turn L to follow the well made path down **Nightingale Valley**.

2 At the bottom of the valley, walk under railway line and turn R, then follow the asphalted **River Avon Trail** along the

riverbank for just over 1km. Passing under the flyover (the "Brunel Way"/A3029), you next turn L on to an old iron rail bridge.

On the far side, a R turn will

Map not to scale. Representation of **OS EXPLORER MAP 155, 1:25,000,**

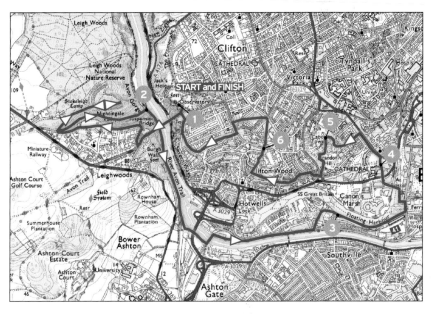

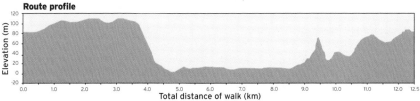

Route profile

take you along the wall of the old red-brick wharf. Follow the riverside path along the south side of Cumberland Rd as far as a green iron footbridge (Vauxhall Bridge). Cross this and keep to the pavement skirting the north side of Cumberland Rd, past Spike Island. Turn L down Hanover Pl just after Spike Island, then R, diagonally opposite the Orchard Inn, to follow the footpath past a diving school on to Gasferry Rd, which leads to the **SS Great Britain**.

3 Once on the waterfront of the Floating Harbour, turn R, and follow the quayside E to Prince St Bridge. Cross this, and turn L, passing the bronze Cabot Statue and the Arnolfini to Pero's Bridge, which you should then cross. On the far side, head straight over Millennium Square, and follow the path past the At Bristol centre to your LHS to reach Anchor Rd. Cross at the pedestrian crossing, and take the path leading diagonally opposite to the R, past Sustrans' office to **College Green**, with Bristol Cathedral on your L.

4 Cut across College Green and follow Park St uphill, taking a L turn after 150m on to Great George St to reach Brandon

Hill park and **Cabot Tower** (ST579729). Either end your walk here, or continue to Clifton Suspension Bridge via the following route:

5 Follow the path downhill from Cabot tower to the bottom-most corner of park, where steep stone steps zigzag under the trees onto Jacob's Wells Rd. At the Bag O' Nails pub on the roundabout, look for a walkway under modern blocks of flats on the opposite (W) side of the road. After the zebra crossing, pass through this and follow White Hart steps and World's End lane steeply uphill on to the far west end of Cliftonwood Cres, where a great viewpoint is hidden at the end of a gap between a row of 1970s terraced houses and the coloured Victorian-Georgian terrace beyond.
Then follow Cliftonwood Cres west, past the Lion pub, on to Argyle Pl and, after approx 500m, Ambra Vale East, from the end of which a signposted footpath cuts sharply uphill (to R) towards Clifton Village.

6 At the top of the path, cross over Goldney Ave and Clifton Hill to enter the site of former Church of Andrew's and

the graveyard. Follow St Andrew's Walk (aka "Birdcage Walk") through the tree tunnel to a junction on Queen's Rd, and from there turn L to cut diagonally across Victoria Square. Head under the archway to Boyce's Ave, past the Albion pub, and onto Clifton Down Rd/Regent's St. Turn L, then second R on to **Royal York Cres**. This ends at Sion Hill, which in turn leads back to the Clifton Suspension Bridge.

Getting There
Buses 8 & 9 run from Bristol Temple Meads station to the Clifton Suspension Bridge. You can also travel from Temple Meads by waterbus with the **Bristol Ferry Boat Company** ☎0117 927 3416 ✆www.bristolferry.com

Visitor Information
Bristol TIC, At Bristol Centre ☎0906 711 2191 (50p per minute).

Eating & Drinking
Spike Island Café
Cumberland Rd (nr *SS Great Britain*)
No-frills cafeteria canteen serving artists who work in the building above. It's airy and cool, and dishes up tasty light meals, soups, salads, cakes, fair-trade coffees and teas at artist-friendly prices.

Shipshape and Bristol Fashion

Before the construction of its Floating Harbour, Bristol's exceptionally high tide (a daily variation in water levels of 13m/43ft) would leave any ships standing to in the Avon Gorge tilted at perilous angles, with their keels stuck fast in the mud. Cargoes could shake loose and be spoiled if they weren't stowed tightly, or "shipshape" style in the holds. Vessels that regularly docked here also had to be extremely well built to withstand the pressures of being beached, whence the expression "Bristol fashion", meaning "of sound quality".

Arnolfini

16 Narrow Quay
www.arnolfini.org.uk/about/cafebar.php
Revamped art-centre café, with a good-value menu of salads, dips, hot soups, chunky sandwiches, toasties and more substantial mains. If the in-your-face modern decor gets too much, take your meal to the waterfront tables outside.

Bag O' Nails

141 St George's Rd
0117 940 6776
Staunchly traditional, single-roomed pub boasting a Victorian tiled bar, stripped wood floors and its original gas lamps and brass pumps. It's a Mecca for serious beer aficionados, with no less than nine real ales and a huge choice of bottled ciders and ports. But don't expect much in the way of food beyond rolls and pork scratchings.

The Albion

Boyce's Ave, Clifton
0117 973 3522
www.thealbionclifton.co.uk
Bristol's poshest gastro-pub occupies a handsomely renovated Georgian building just off Victoria Square. The interiors are all warm wood, exposed brickwork and fire-light, and there's a flagstoned summer patio under awnings outside. Some punters come here to drink, but the contemporary British cuisine is what makes this place really special.

Sleeping

Bristol International Youth Hostel
14 Narrow Quay, BS1 4QA
0870 770 5726
www.yha.org.uk
Well equipped YHA bang on the waterfront opposite Pero's Bridge; the situation couldn't better, and there's a sociable common room to hang out in with old cable reels as tables.

Mrs Delia Macdonald

Park House, 19 Richmond Hill, Clifton
BS8 1BA
0117 973 6331
Delightful address in one of Clifton's oldest Georgian residences (built 1797), only a short hop from the top of trendy Park St and (optional) end of our walk at Brandon Hill. It's not the cheapest B&B in town, but has oodles of period charm.

Mrs Susan Moore

21 Royal York Crescent
BS8 4JX
0117 973 4405
A comfortable en suite room on the garden side of a beautiful ground-floor flat, on Clifton's most elegant Georgian crescent. Located only a short stroll from the end point of our route, it's particularly recommended for garden lovers.

More Info

www.travelbristol.org. A one-stop information bank on getting to the city, whether by air, rail, road, cycle, boat or on foot.

www.venue.co.uk. Bristol's answer to *Time Out* – an indispensable guide to what's on and where, with lots of listings, and they often feature top walks in and around the city.
www.visitbristol.co.uk. Nicely designed site of the local visitor information centre, jam-packed with tips on how to plan your journey, find your way around and unwind after your walk.

www.cliftonrocksrailway.org. The full story on the Avon Gorge's defunct funicular railway, which used to run via a tunnel between Clifton and the Avon, and is ear-marked for renovation.

The Naked Guide to Bristol by Gill Gillespie (Naked Guides Ltd) Wittily written insider's guide to the city, with a particularly readable history section and fully updated listings.

More Walks

Bristol Backs: Discovering Bristol on Foot by Bristol Ramblers (Ramblers).
This gem of a book, produced by Bristol Ramblers and supported by Bristol City Council, leads you on 27 city walks of between 3km/2miles and 17.5km/11miles. Included are a selection of street-based heritage walks, green trails, waterside strolls and a sculpture trail, with plentiful background descriptions.

Walk West by Geoff Mullett (Avon Ramblers).
Thirty country walks within easy reach of Bristol and Bath, of between 6.5km/4miles and 22.5km/14miles. The series is supported by a dedicated website to allow readers to check the status of the routes. *Walk West Again* is available in traditional printed form; the other two, *Walk West* and *Walk West 3*, are ebooks (go to: www.walk-west.co.uk).

The Devil's Steps
Bedruthan

After decades the doldrums, the north coast of Cornwall is very much in vogue again. Newquay has had a sexy makeover, with Rick Stein and Jamie Oliver putting its seafood on Britain's gastronomic map. And the bucket-and-spade brigade have returned in appreciative droves. All the more reason to avoid the place like the plague you might be thinking. On the contrary: in spite of the recent tourist boom, long stretches of this exceptionally beautiful coast remain wild and unspoilt – even at the height of summer – and present a mouthwatering prospect for walkers.

It has the weather to thank for that. Jutting its jaw defiantly into the Atlantic, north Cornwall faces the full might of the ocean, and for much of the year the gales howl in with umbrella-defying ferocity, blowing mountainous waves against the slate cliffs, and twisting any exposed blackthorn trees into improbable angles. What little vegetation there is tends to be stunted by the salt winds. Wiry herbs and Jurassic-looking mosses spring in clumps from the cracks in herringboned stone hedges, while thrift and Alexanders spill from the shelter of gorse bushes.

This is an austere, storm-scoured landscape, synonymous with shipwrecks and smugglers, which can seem unremittingly bleak one minute, and dazzlingly vibrant the next. Catch the right day on any stretch of the coast between Newquay and Padstow and you'll be startled by the translucent blue-green colour of the sea and brilliance of the sand – not to mention the breathtaking views. Our route includes a Cornish classic: the clifftop vista over Bedruthan Steps, where a rank of colossal, pointed stacks march out of the breakers against a dramatic backdrop of slate escarpments.

Meandering past a succession of picture-postcard coves, windswept headlands and old-fashioned holiday resorts, this stretch of the coast path running north of Bedruthan ranks among the prettiest in the southwest. Moreover, it's backed up by an unusually good bus service. Should the weather close in, or if you decide to cut the route short and kick back on one of the beaches, rest assured that the local bus company, Western Greyhound, will soon be on hand to whisk you back to where you started.

At a glance

Where Mawgan Porth, northeast of Newquay, to Harlyn Bay, west of Padstow, Cornwall.
Why Seven perfect sandy beaches, and dramatic cliffs; distinctive marine flora; some of Britain's best surfing.
When Spring, for abundant coastal flora.
Downsides Heavy congestion in summer on the beaches and coast road.
Start/Finish Mawgan Porth (SW850672)/ Harlyn Bridge (SW878753).
Duration 5-6hrs.

Distance 17km/10.5miles.
Cut it Short Porthcothan, 8km/5miles, or Constantine Bay, 11.6km/7.2miles.
Terrain Mostly level clifftops and sandy beaches, via well worn, waymarked footpaths.
Maps OS Explorer 106

On your way

People have defied the elements to scrape a living from this coast for more than 3000 years. During the Bronze Age (1300–700BC) a sizeable farming community of between thirty and fifty homesteads survived in wood and stone huts just inland, trading Bodmin tin and lead ore as far afield as Brittany and the west of Ireland. You can see their burial mounds on the clifftops at Park Head and Harlyn Bay, and the remains of a late Iron Age fort at Redcliffe Castle (overlooking Bedruthan Steps). For most of its history, however, this area and its Celtic inhabitants existed on the margins of the known world, beyond the reach of Britain's conquerors. Only with the rise of tin-mining and the big pilchard boom of the sixteenth and seventeenth centuries did it experience anything resembling prosperity – and little of this trickled down to the peasantry.

The sheltered, sandy coves were perfect for smuggling though, and the locals were not averse to a spot of "wrecking" to supplement their meager fishing incomes. Dozens of ships met grisly ends on the rocks between Mawgan Porth and Trevose Head. When the *Samaritan* ran aground here in 1846, the good folk of **MAWGAN PORTH** reportedly acquired a sudden penchant for fine silk clothes and cognac.

BEDRUTHAN STEPS, or **CARNEWAS BAY** as it's also known, takes its name from the stairs hacked down to the three tidal beaches lining the cliffs by freetraders in the eighteenth century – not, as local guides would enjoy telling Victorian visitors, because the Devil once used the three pointed stacks in the bay as giant stepping stones. At low tide you can clamber down to the beach, but don't be tempted to venture into the surf: the rip currents have claimed several lives over the years – hence the

closure of the site in the winter.

Visible inland from the National Trust's low-roofed café at Carnewas are the transmitter masts of RAF St Eval, where an ancient village was requisitioned in 1938 and all but demolished to make way for a World War II radio and air base. Marooned amid the disused runways, a lone-standing thirteenth-century Norman church is virtually all that survives of the former settlement of Trevisker, where archeological excavations have yielded traces of settlement dating back more than 3300 years.

You pass several prominent burial mounds on the coast path winding north from Carnewas, along a fabulously convoluted, rocky line of cliffs that delves suddenly inland at **PORTHCOTHAN**. DH Lawrence and his wife Frieda stayed in one of the holiday cottages overlooking the narrow bay for a while in the late 1930s – before being forced out by wartime paranoia (Frieda was German, and the couple were unfairly suspected of signaling to U-boats from the clifftops). Though small by Cornish standards, the white-sand beach is a real gem.

TREYARNON BAY, the next beach north, is a slightly larger version of Porthcothan, with a youth hostel and well-developed surf scene – the latter thanks to its proximity to neighbouring **CONSTANTINE BAY**, the most spectacular sweep of white sand and breakers on this part of the north Cornish coast. Margaret Thatcher and family used to take one of the many holiday homes nestled in the lanes behind it. Dennis would doubtless have enjoyed a round or two at golf links, whose manicured fairways you skirt en route towards the boney shoulder of **TREVOSE HEAD**, a bare dollop of fractured shale crowned by a solitary white lighthouse to the north. Built in the mid-nineteenth century after the wreck of

ABOVE: Trevose Head lighthouse was built in the mid-nineteenth century after the wreck of the *Samaritan*

the *Samaritan*, the light, powered by a 35-watt bulb that's visible some twenty miles out to sea, was automated only in 1995. The neatly painted lighthouse keepers' cottages below it have now been converted by owners, Trinity House, into holiday cottages.

Don't be tempted to cut across the neck of Trevose Head or you'll miss the extraordinary geological feature (marked as "Round Hole" on OS maps) on its western fringe, where the sea has worn away the slate beneath the clifftop and caused a large patch of ground to collapse thirty or more metres inland. The chasm has no fence around it, allowing you to peer over the edge to listen to the sound of waves emanating incongruously from its depths.

Descending Trevose Head, fabulous views open up to the north and south, embracing a huge expanse of coast stretching all the way from Hartland to St Ives. From this lofty vantage point, it's easy to appreciate why the shoreline of north Cornwall has always struck fear into the heart of sailors heading up the Bristol Channel. The infamous westerlies still claim lives each year, and Padstow's lifeboat station ranks among the busiest in the country. Its new £5.5million boathouse, on the southeast flank of Trevose Head overlooking Mother Ivey's Bay, holds memorials to volunteers who have perished in these treacherous seas over the years. RNLI Padstow's darkest day was April

1900, when eight crew members drowned after their lifeboat overturned while trying to rescue the trawler *Peace and Plenty*, which had got into difficulties in a big storm off Trevose Head. Three of the fishing boat's crew also died in the disaster.

A stone's throw below the new lifeboat station, on a bluff overlooking **MOTHER IVEY'S BAY** (aka Polverton Bay), the coast path passes the elegant white beach house of TV chef and local restaurateur, Rick Stein. The celebrity's Art Deco bolthole, originally built by his father and uncle in the 1930s, enjoys a sea view to die for, only slightly marred by the clifftop caravan park.

HARLYN BAY, a ten-minute walk around Cataclews Point from Mother Ivey's, holds still more dazzling turquoise water. It's tempting to speculate that the same gorgeous colours enjoyed by people here today were the reason ancient inhabitants of this coast buried their dead overlooking the bay. Some 130 Iron Age graves were exhumed in the fields behind the beach by archeologists in 1900, many of them containing metal implements and pottery. Harlyn's most valuable treasure, however, came to light half a century earlier, when a local labourer digging on the clifftop above **ONJOHN COVE** (an especially beautiful spot at the northwest corner of the bay) found a pair of exquisite, wafer-thin gold neck ornaments. Known to archeologists as "lunulae", the necklaces were fashioned in the form of crescent moons and are thought, because of their delicacy and fine ornamentation, to have been objects of great ritual significance. Identical lunulae were discovered in Ireland, where they're believed to have originated around 2300–2000 BC. The Harlyn necklaces are now the prize exhibits of the Royal Cornwall Museum in Truro.

A cursed field

A field behind Harlyn Bay has for centuries had been associated with a sinister curse which, according to local belief, has claimed several lives. The story dates back to the sixteenth century, when the landowners, the Hellyars, ran a lucrative fish-export business shipping salted Cornish pilchards to Italy. A Latin inscription carved above the door of their processing house (which still looms over the north end of the bay) recalls the fortune the trade earned for the family. Lucri Dulsis Odor, "Sweet is the Scent of Riches", proclaimed the line etched across the lintel. But for the impoverished fisher families in the village, the declaration was replete with irony.

Resentment came to a head when a cargo of pilchards was once returned to Harlyn. Hungry families from miles around flocked to the harbour in the hope of a handout. But instead, the squire gave orders for the rotting fish to be ploughed into one of his fields as fertilizer. Incensed by this act of stone-heartedness, a local white witch, Mother Ivey, cast a curse on the pasture, saying that if ever its soil was broken, death would follow.

The Hellyars ignored her, but would come to regret their skepticism when, within weeks, the family's eldest son died after being thrown from his horse. In World War II, a member of the local Home Guard dropped dead soon after digging defensive trenches into the cursed field, and in the 1970s, a metal detector enthusiast met an untimely end there.

Recent experience suggests the malevolent spell has lost none of its potency. Despite Southwest Water's hiring of a vicar to exorcise the field before laying a pipe through it a few years back, the project's foreman died of a heart attack before the job was finished. The grass has not been disturbed since.

walk it | 18

Bedruthan

1 Walk north along **Mawgan Porth** beach until you see the South West Coast Path sign at the limit of the dunes, pointing R up a path that winds towards the clifftops. A breezy 20-minute walk above Trerathick Point and Cove and brings you to our featured viewpoint of the day, overlooking **Bedruthan Steps** and **Carnewas Bay**. The National Trust visitor centre and café stand one field back from the cliff edge. A paved path runs from there down to the start of the steps leading to the beach, which is covered at high tide.

2 A classic view of the famous rocks extends from the north end of the bay, as the path winds beyond ancient herringbone walls to a headland dotted with Bronze Age tumuli. The next stretch skirts a series of craggy, wild coves before descending on the inlet of Porth Mear. From there the path climbs again to the clifftops, past a spectacular blowhole, before rounding the headland to approach **Porthcothan**. The bus stop is opposite the village shop, on the main road, a minute's walk inland from the beach.

3 To pick up the coast path again, you can either ford the stream at the top of Porthcothan

Map not to scale.
Representation of
**OS EXPLORER MAP
106, 1:25,000**

Route profile

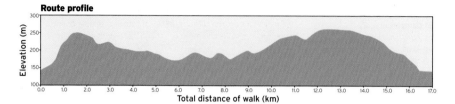

beach, or else head through the dunes to the road and cross the stream via the bridge. The path turns R (north) off the track running from the bridge back to the sands.

Only the odd drystone wall and a single campsite interrupt the SWCP's winding progress north from Porthcothan, as it bends around a succession of rocky promontories, finally descending to sea level again at **Treyarnon Bay**, one of Cornwall's loveliest little beach resorts.

4 Cross to the far side of the beach and follow the lane past Treyarnon YHA, beyond which the path hugs the shoreline faithfully as it crosses north to the bottom end of **Constantine Bay**.

5 If you're catching the bus here at Constantine rather than carrying to Harlyn, turn R just before reaching the sand and follow the lane east past a small car park, then on through the village to the shop at the crossroads. The bus stop stands on the opposite side of the road from the stores. Otherwise, walk towards the rocks at the far north end of the beach, where the coast path skirts a golf course and continues on around windswept **Trevose Head**, passing the lighthouse en route.
Views extend far up the north

Cornish coastline as you drop down to Mother Ivey's Cove along the edge of a long, straight field border, with the Padstow Lifeboat Station off to your left. Skirting Rick Stein's glamorous Art Deco house, the path then descends to **Mother Ivey's Bay**, past a couple of pretty holiday cottages and a rather less attractive static caravan park. One last headland – Cataclews Point – has to be rounded before the day's work is done. As you bend south, you walk right past the Cellars house, the Hellyar family's former herring factory. It stands on ground separating two exquisite coves: Big Guns and **Onjohns Cove**.

6 Keep to the edge of **Harlyn Bay** to reach the Harlyn village. The bus stop for the return journey to Morgan Porth and Newquay, or east to Padstow, is next to the bridge at the far southeast side of the beach.

Getting There
The nearest train station is Newquay 8km/5miles away; www.nationalrail.co.uk or call Traveline 0871 200 2233 for details.

Western Greyhound bus 556 runs more or less hourly between Newquay and Padstow, via the coast road just inland from our route, stopping at Mawgan Porth,

Bedruthan Steps, Porthcothan, Constantine Bay and Harlyn Bay bridge. For current timetable information call 01637 871871 or www.westerngreyhound.com

Visitor Information
Newquay TIC
01637 854020
www.newquay.co.uk
National Trust
Bedruthan Steps
01637 860563

www.nationaltrust.org.uk/main/w-carnewasandbedruthansteps.
A rundown of facilities and what to do at Carnewas Bay, which is fully owned by the NT.

Eating & Drinking
In Mawgan Porth, the "Cornwall Fresh" store, housed in a converted petrol station, does a fantastic range of pasties, croissants and freshly made sandwiches.

Fire
Mawgan Porth
01637 860372
Funky little bistro behind the beach at Mawgan Porth, with gorgeous views from its big windows. Their coffee and egg-and-bacon breakfasts are famous, but they also open all day for light lunches (try Thai-style chicken burgers or lamb kofta kebabs), and more elaborate evening seafood suppers.

The Falcon
St Mawgan
☎01637 860225
Indisputably the nicest pub in the area, though you'll have to plod up the valley from Mawgan Porth for half an hour to reach it. Swathed in wisteria, it's a welcoming, traditional Cornish hostelry, set in the midst of a pretty slate village, where you can enjoy hand-pumped local ales and quality food.

National Trust Café
Bedruthan Steps
Typical NT tea room serving proper Cornish cream teas and a range of light meals, only 100m from the cliff tops and the famous view of Bedruthan steps.

YHA Café
Treyarnon (see below)
With its trendy burnt-orange and surf-board décor, this beachside café is packed in the summer, but it also serves as a cosy shelter from the wind in winter, with a real fire. Good value meals, cream teas and fresh coffee dished up year round.

Sleeping
The Falcon
St Mawgan, TR8 4EP
☎01637 860225
✉www.thefalconinn-newquay.co.uk
A couple of comfortable en-suite rooms at the best country pub in the area (see above for a review).

Bedruthan House Hotel
Bedruthan Steps PL27 7UW
☎01637 860346
✉www.bedruthanhousehotel.co.uk
Opposite the entrance to the NT visitors' centre, on the main coast road, this unpretentious B&B in a

family-run hotel on the roadside is a 5min walk from the clifftops. All rooms are en suite, and they do evening meals on request.

Treyarnon Youth Hostel
Tregonnan, Treyarnon Bay PL28 8JR
☎0870 770 6076
✉www.yha.org.uk
Few YHAs in Britain occupy as splendid a site as this one, a stone's throw from the golden sands of Treyarnon Beach. It's one of the YHA's flagship properties, with rooms as well as dorms, and a great little café – though you'll have to book well in advance. Open all year.

More Info
✉www.swcp.org.uk. Home of the South West Coast Path Association.
✉www.cornwall-online.co.uk. Hosts lots of interesting background on the area.
✉www.meynmamvro.co.uk/article2.htm. Photos and history of the Harlyn Bay lunulae and other treasures unearthed locally.

More Walks
✉www.trailsfromthetrack.com (Devon & Cornwall Rail Partnership). A growing number of routes available online, all starting from rural train stations in Cornwall and Devon. Includes the Maritime Line walks developed in partnership with Carrick Ramblers. Printed leaflets are also available free from local stations and TICs.

Ten Walks Around Falmouth by Philip and Barbara Roberts (Carrick Ramblers). Neat little A5 book of walks along the coast, creeks and rivers around Falmouth. All walks are specially selected by the Carrick Ramblers, and are between 6.5km/4miles and 11km/7miles. Sketch maps and route descriptions are on facing pages for easy reference.

Ten Rambles in the Roseland by Carrick Ramblers (Ramblers). Walks of 6.5km/4miles to 11km/7miles around the Cornish peninsula of Roseland, just east of Falmouth.

Ten Walks Around Truro by Carrick Ramblers (Ramblers). Walks of 6.5km/4miles to 11km/7miles around Cornwall's only city.

ABOVE: Heading out of Porthcothan on the coast path

The Ups and the Downs
The Seven Sisters

The South Downs are not all downs, there are a lot of ups as well.
Eddie Izzard, on his favourite national icon

It's as if the sea formed the Seven Sisters expressly to test the skill of sailors. From the base of these sheer chalk cliffs on the Sussex Downs, a shelf of submerged rock slices into the English Channel, posing a lethal hazard for passing ships. As many as 87 have been lost along this isolated stretch of coast since the seventeenth century, earning it the nickname "the mariners' graveyard".

Recently incorporated into the South Downs National Park (Britain's youngest national park), the iconic coastal hills may strike fear into the hearts of unwary mariners, but they provide some of the most remarkable coast walking in Britain.

It's hard not to feel exhilarated as you climb aboard the Seven Sisters' "rollercoaster". To one side, the lush green turf of the clifftops, speckled with hoary stock and clumps of pink thrift. On the other, the massive ramparts of chalk swooping in graceful curves to Beachy Head and the distant Belle Tout lighthouse.

The crash of invisible surf rising from the shingle far below may well entice you to take a peek over the edge for a glimpse of the yellow horned-poppy and sea kale growing along the base of the cliffs. But such temptation should be resisted, especially after heavy rain or rough seas, when the Seven Sisters become notoriously crumbly and unstable.

Our walk takes you on an undulating ride from Went Hill Brow on to Baily's Brow, Flagstaff Point, Brass Point, Rough Brow, Short Brow and Haven Brow, where the Cuckmere River breaches the range creating a broad alluvial valley. A short meander around the beautiful estuary of Cuckmere Haven and a final climb past the old coastguards' cottages up to Seaford Head completes the trip.

The optimum time for any walk here has to be around the summer solstice (which occurs on June 21st). With the sun setting at its most northerly point, dramatic shadows are cast on the cliffs, picking out the runnels and huge, vertical towers. Catch an especially clear evening, and the Seven Sisters can seem like giant spectres guarding the Sussex coast.

At a glance

Where East Dean, 5km/3miles west of Eastbourne, to Seaford, East Sussex.
Why Precipitous white cliffs and sweeping sea views; spongy downs turf underfoot; beautifully preserved smugglers' beach.

When June, when the sun sets at it's most northerly point casting dramatic shadows on the Seven Sisters.
Start/Finish East Dean, Tiger Inn (TV557978) / Seaford, Martello Tower (TV485985).
Duration 3hrs 30mins.

Distance 12.75km/8miles.
Cut it Short Exceat Bridge, 7.3km/4.5miles
Terrain Springy downs turf on top of the cliffs. But keep well clear of the cliff edges.
Map OS Explorer 123.

On your way

Until the lighthouse at Belle Tout (pronounced "toot") was completed in 1832, the only reliable warning light for ships was provided by Jonathan Darby, the vicar of St Jude's church in **EAST DEAN**. He became so concerned about the danger to sailors that he excavated a makeshift lighthouse and rescue-centre twenty feet up the face of the cliffs at **BIRLING GAP**. Darby spent night after night in his cave and saved many lives until 1726, when, rather unfairly, he died from exposure. Parson Darby's cave still sits beneath Belle Tout lighthouse.

Locals often profited from the sailors' misfortune, and "wreckers" hung false lights from the Seven Sisters to lure cargo ships to their doom. One unfortunate vessel to strike the cliffs was the *Coonatto*. This three-masted clipper weighing 633 tons was en route from Adelaide laden with wool and copper ingots when she ran around in the early hours of 21 February 1876. Inquisitive "wreck hunters" can find the ship off **FLAGSTAFF POINT** (TV537966) during spring low tides, when the large teak and iron frame of its hull protrudes from the foreshore.

However, contrary to popular belief there is no general right of access to beaches, cliffs or foreshore in England and Wales. The Ramblers has been campaigning to change this with the proposal of a continuous path around Britain's coastl with "spreading room" on either side. At the time of writing, these proposals were included in the Marine and Coastal Access Bill, and looked likely to become a reality.

High above the beach the "rollercoaster ride" of ups and downs reaches a crescendo at the top of **HAVEN BROW**. The reward for surmounting the highest "sister" is the magnificent view across the tranquil Cuckmere valley from 78m/255ft. The only inhabitants of **CUCKMERE HAVEN** moved into the coastguards' cottages on the far side of the beach in 1818. The Navy built these cottages to provide a permanent base for Customs & Excise Men to tackle the prolific trafficking of gin, brandy and tobacco up the Cuckmere River to Alfriston. One notorious smuggler lived at the Manor House in East Dean. James Dipperay amassed a large fortune from the supply of contraband and, when he was finally arrested, betrayed his fellow local smugglers in return for his own freedom. His colleagues were deported to Australia, and Dipperay retired a wealthy man.

The wild meanders of the **CUCKMERE RIVER** were first tamed in 1846 by cutting a straight channel from the shoreline to **EXCEAT BRIDGE**. The channel was built to improve drainage, prevent flooding and create land for pasture. Today the valley is

In the Guard's Van

The creation of the Vanguard Way was a combined effort by the Vanguards Rambling Club, the Ramblers and the YHA. The 100km/62.5-mile route opened in 1981 and links East Croydon to the Sussex Heritage Coast, by way of the Selsdon Nature Reserve, the North Downs, High Weald and the South Downs – "from the suburbs to the sea" is its motto. The way takes its name from the walking club, whose members, after a long day's stomping on the South Downs, were in the habit of retiring to the Berwick Inn. Invariably they would catch the last train back to London, and on one occasion - for an unspecified reason – ended up in the guard's van.

ABOVE: The straight channel cut in 1846 to tame the Cuckmere River's wild meanders

further protected by earthbanks along the river's course and the extensive maintenance of shingle banks to the west of its mouth. But climate change and rising sea levels have placed an impossible burden on resources, and there are plans to allow the valley to return to its natural state. It is hoped that if the process is managed carefully and gradually it will result in a self-sustaining tidal estuary of saltmarsh and mudflats.

The fate of Cuckmere Haven could have been very different if the Luftwaffe had fallen for the plan to create a night-time decoy. The Army and Navy were in favour of the scheme, but the RAF reckoned the Germans would not be fooled. An exact replica of Newhaven harbour's lighting system was laid out in the valley south of Exceat Bridge, with a control panel housed in a Nissan hut close to where the **GOLDEN GALLEON** pub is today. It seems the RAF were right, and Cuckmere Haven was left relatively unscathed. The same can not be said of Seaford. Despite its lack of strategic importance this small town suffered 36 air attacks, resulting in the death 23 citizens, with hundreds more injured. Over 140 high explosive bombs and countless incendiary bombs fell on the town during the war – more than any other town in Sussex, with the exception of Brighton and Eastbourne.

EXCEAT suffered a different blight. The village was a flourishing settlement until the fifteenth century, and is said to have served as a naval base for Alfred the Great. But a series of poor harvests, frequent raids by French pirates, and the Black Death, led to rapid depopulation and its eventual desertion. Today it's occupied by the Seven Sisters Country Park centre and, on the far side of the bridge, the Golden Galleon pub. It also marks the departure of the South Downs Way from the Vanguard Way. Our route follows the latter, which skirts the western edge of Cuckmere Haven and climbs past the coastguards' cottages to **SEAFORD HEAD**.

Seaford town was first recorded in 788AD as "Saeford" but there were earlier Roman and Celtic settlements here at the mouth of the River Ouse. The town became an important port and was granted membership of the Cinque Ports Federation. But the gradual silting of the Ouse coupled with a great storm in 1579 caused the river to burst its banks, diverting its course further west. A port was built at the new river mouth and Seaford's influence was gradually eclipsed by the "New Haven". Today the town is unremarkable but for the moated **MARTELLO TOWER** on the seafront which houses Seaford Museum.

There are 74 Martello towers lining England's coast, from Folkstone to Seaford. Seaford's tower was the last link in this defensive chain built to repel the French during the Napoleonic Wars. The towers were inspired by a round fortress at Mortella Point in Corsica, which so impressed the Commander-in-Chief of the Mediterranean, Admiral Sir John Jervis, that he resolved to erect one "on every part of the [English] coast likely for an enemy to make a descent on". "Martello" is believed to be a corruption of "Mortella".

walk it 19

The Seven Sisters

1 From outside the Tiger Inn at **East Dean**, cross the village green to the Frith & Little Deli and turn L then fork R down the road marked "No Through Rd". Follow this surfaced road past a few houses until you reach a gate. Go through the gate and head fairly steeply uphill, ignoring a cross path, and through two smaller gates onto the access land at National Trust's Crowlink. Follow the path through the woods up to the crest of Went Hill where you'll see a barn with a red roof in the distance. Make for the barn in the direction of the sea, keeping to the R of the barn and following the

bridleway down to a gate at the bottom of the field. Go through this gate and through another gate before turning R onto the South Downs Way (SDW). (**Birling Gap** is 2mins to the L downhill.)

2 Here is where the 4km/2.5mile rollercoaster of the Seven Sisters starts: it'll take approx 45mins to traverse all Seven Sisters. Cross Went Hill Brow (Sister No 1); descend into Michel Dene; ascend Baily's Hill (Sister No 2); and down into Flathill Bottom; briefly up Flat Hill (an uncounted Sister!) and down to Flagstaff Bottom; up to **Flagstaff Point** (Sister No 3); down to Gap Bottom; up to Brass Point (Sister No 4); down to Rough Bottom; up

to Rough Brow (Sister No 5); down to Limekiln Bottom; up to Short Brow (Sister No 6); down to Short Bottom; and finally up to **Haven Brow** (Sister No 7).

3 Here take the L fork leading steeply down and away from the SDW. Continue along the cliff and over a stile. The path skirts the edge of Cliff End to the R, descending to **Cuckmere Haven** where you need to double back along a path at the base of the cliff to reach the beach. Cross the beach to the mouth of the **Cuckmere River** and follow the path tight against its canalized bank, which makes a beeline to **Exceat** (about 20mins), where you cross **Exceat Bridge** to get to the Golden Galleon.

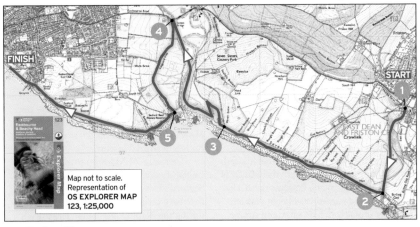

Map not to scale.
Representation of
**OS EXPLORER MAP
123, 1:25,000**

Route profile

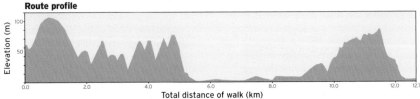

4 At the far end of the **Golden Galleon**'s car park go through the gate and follow the Vanguard Way south for 20–30mins, ignoring paths to L then R, before emerging on the west side of Cuckmere Haven with the coastguards' cottages in front of you, and our great view of the Seven Sisters from **Seaford Head**.

5 Passing the coastguards' cottages on your L continue uphill to Hop Gap and then R following the cliff edge through Seaford Head Nature Reserve, and walk for a further 30mins past Hope Bottom and along the esplanade to get to the **Martello Tower**. (**Seaford** station is 10mins further down the esplanade, and R up Dane Rd.)

Getting There
Both Eastbourne and Seaford are easy to reach by train, see ✎www.infotransport.co.uk or call traveline on ☎0870 608 2608 for details. Regular bus service 12 runs every 20mins Mon–Sat (hourly Sun) between Eastbourne (Arndale Centre), via East Dean, Exceat (Golden Galleon) and Seaford station. See ✎www.buses.co.uk or contact Brighton & Hove Buses on ☎01273 886200 for route details and timetable.

Visitor Information
Eastbourne TIC
Cornfield Road, Eastbourne
☎0871 6630031
✎www.visiteastbourne.com

Seven Sisters Country Park Visitor Centre,
Exceat
☎01323 870280
✎www.sevensisters.org.uk

Eating & Drinking
The Tiger Inn
The Green, East Dean
☎01323 423209
Idyllic country pub on the village green. Serves Harvey's Best and Horsham ales, and good pub lunches from 12.30pm to 2.30pm (if you're too early, or late, try the Hiker's Rest next door). Evening meals served from 6pm onwards. Open all day at weekends, and 12noon–3pm and 6pm–11pm weekdays.

Golden Galleon
Exceat Bridge, Exceat
☎01323 892247
Situated where the Vanguard Way and South Downs Way part company. A popular haunt for weary walkers deciding, over a pint of Haveys, Spitfire or Timothy Taylor, which path to choose. An extensive and above average menu, which can be devoured in the large garden overlooking Cuckmere Haven. Open every day until 11pm.

Sleeping
The Boathouse
Birling Gap, BN20 0AB,
☎01323 423073
Just up the track away from the hubbub of the multi-purpose Birling Gap Hotel, the Boathouse is a quieter alternative. Accommodation is unfussy, friendly and affordable. Situated just yards from the cliff edge; the view across the Channel comes at no extra charge.

Foxhole Campsite & Camping Barn
Seven Sisters Country Park (TV524984). ☎01323 870280
✎www.sevensisters.org.uk
Space for twenty tents, plus a traditional Sussex barn sleeping up to 35. Discount of £1 for anyone

arriving by "sustainable means". Book ahead using the form on their website or call them.

More Info

A Companion on the South Downs Way by Peter Anderson and Terry Owen (Perrambulations). One of the more interesting and informative of the many guides to the South Downs Way National Trail.

✎www.sevensisters.org.uk. The country park's website is good source of local information, and includes details of an easy access trail.

✎www.ramblers.org.uk/info/paths/name/s/southdowns.htm. For more accommodation, a list of guidebooks and contacts for the South Downs Way National Trail.

More Walks
Walks in the Weald by Heathfield Ramblers (Ramblers). Thirty-six walks from 5km/3miles to 16km/10miles across varied terrain.

Walks to Interesting Places in Sussex & Kent by Heathfield Ramblers (Ramblers). Details 21 walks from 4km/2.5miles across easy terrain, including some linear routes returning on preserved railways.

25 Favourite Walks in West Surrey & Sussex and *Another 25 Favourite Walks in Surrey, Sussex and Hampshire* by Godalming and Haslemere Ramblers (Ramblers). Two books with a varied selection of enticing walks north of Guildford to the Sussex coast. Distances vary from 5km/3miles to 24km/15miles.

Gower Power

Rhossili

"The wildest, bleakest and barrenest I know – four or five miles of yellow coldness going away into the distance of the sea," was Dylan Thomas' uncharacteristically downbeat description of Rhossili beach, at the far western tip of the Gower peninsula in South Wales. True enough, under a leaden sky, with a gale howling off the Bristol Channel, this sweeping bay can feel like the the end of the world. But time your visit for fine weather, when the water sparkles brilliant blue-green and the sand takes on its radiant straw colour, and you'll understand why in a recent poll Rhossili was ranked eleventh in a list of the world's fifty most beautiful coastal locations.

The classic view of the beach, featured on countless tourist office brochures, is from the low cliffs at its far southern end, near Rhossili village. From here, the sands stretch north in an exhilarating arc, bounded on one side by ranks of breakers and on the other by an elegantly sloping moorland ridge. It's a perfect postcard vista – down to the lonely cottage plonked midway along the bay, which only serves to underline how pristine the landscape is.

But if you thought this perspective was a winner, try walking along the crest of Rhossili Down just inland. Studded with prehistoric cairns and burial chambers, the highest ridge in the Gower provides an even more breathtaking view. But don't just take our word for it. The route we outline strings together both Rhossili's golden viewpoints, so you can make your own mind up which is the best.

Starting in Rhossili village, it strikes steeply uphill to follow the undulating ridge of the Down north, then drops back to sea-level down a steep, grassy slope. After a short link section across the dunes via a path cutting through a campsite, you'll reach the sea to begin a glorious mile-long section of uninterrupted sand and surf. This brings you to the foot of the cliffs, from where a short final climb leads back to the start.

If you're doing this walk in summer, be sure to bring your swimming togs and shades: the beach is one of Europe's surfing hot spots. Adrenalin junkies might also be tempted to sign up for an accompanied parascending flight from the Down, which is something of a Mecca for British flyers.

At a glance

Where Rhossili Down, Gower peninsula, Swansea, Wales.
Why World-class coastal scenery; ancient monuments spanning 9000 years; seabird colonies on tidal islets.
When Mid-winter. Migratory purple sandpipers and other rarities, such as great northern and red-throated divers, flock to the beach.
Downsides Crowded car parks and cafés in summer.
Start/Finish Rhossili village (SS415881).

Duration 2hrs.
Distance 7.3km/4.5miles.
Terrain Mostly gentle seaside paths, with a short, sharp ascent and descent over stretches of bracken-covered moorland.
Maps OS Explorer 164.

On your way

Before the last Ice Age, this stretch of coast formed part of a line of hills running 112km/70miles inland, overlooking a plain where the Bristol Channel now flows. Judging from the wealth of Mesolithic remnants uncovered in the area, the forest carpeting it provided a rich source of food for early Welsh hunter-gatherers, at a time when the climate was cooling and the ice line would have been only a couple of hour's walk north of here.

Sea caves concealed in the limestone cliffs of the southwest Gower have yielded a wealth of famous archeological finds – most notably the "Red Lady of Paviland", a skeleton stained with red ochre and adorned with shell necklaces and ivory rods, which the local curate who found it in 1823 mistakenly believed to be the bones of a Roman-era prostitute. In fact, modern carbon-dating techniques have shown the "Red Lady" was a 25–30-year-old male, and that he lived not 2000, but 29,000 years ago, making these the oldest remains of a modern human ever discovered in Europe.

Most of the prehistoric vestiges to have come to light at **RHOSSILI** itself date from a more recent period in the late Bronze Age, by which time sea levels would have been what they are today. In a tiny cave on the far side of Burry Holm (the headland bounding the north end of the beach) a narrow opening in the rock leads into Culver Hole where, during excavations in the 1920s, an ossuary containing the bones of thirty or more individuals was discovered, along with eleven urns of human ashes.

Rhossili appears to have been continuously inhabited through the Roman era and Dark Ages, as Celtic missionary-saints began to spread Christianity along the Welsh coast. The name of the beach itself derives from the old Welsh for "moor" – "*rhos*" – and the now forgotten "Saint Suilen" or "Saint Sili", who probably founded the first church here in the sixth century AD. It would have served as a waystage on the coastal pilgrimage circuit, with travellers passing through en route to the shrine of Saint Cenydd just inland.

Later enlarged by the Normans, the settlement became engulfed in sand over the course of the fifteenth century, forcing a move to higher ground on the headland above the bay. The precise whereabouts of the old village, meanwhile, became forgotten, and remained a mystery until a powerful spring tide in the 1970s uncovered ruins at the foot of Rhossili Down; they're now protected as an ancient monument.

One remnant, however, had clearly been deemed too valuable to leave for the sand to swallow. Spanning the entrance to Rhossili's church of st mary's is an incongruous early-twelfth-century archway, complete with trademark Norman dog-tooth mouldings, which must have been salvaged from the deserted medieval village. St Mary's other claim to fame is a small memorial plaque to local boy Edgar "Taff" Evans, a member of Scott's ill-fated 1910–1913 *Terra Nova* expedition to the Antarctic. The Welshman was the first to perish on the long walk back from the south pole, collapsing from exhaustion, frostbite and the effects of repeated head injuries, at the base of the Beardmore Glacier on February 16, 1912. His body was the only one never recovered.

The church stands at the start of the path up the steep, south side of **RHOSSILI DOWN**, at 193m/633ft the loftiest of the Old Red Sandstone ridges slicing through the Gower peninsula. A glorious view over the beach and surrounding coastline extends from its spine, along which the area's Iron Age settlers buried their dead chiefs in a row

of fourteen chambers and cairns. The name of one group, Swayne's Howes, is of Norse derivation ("servants' village"), but the mounds predate the arrival of the Vikings by at least two thousand years.

The house at the base of the hill, surveying the sands from the safety of a raised plateau, is Rhossili's much photographed **OLD RECTORY**, built in the 1850s. This exposed spot was chosen because the resident priests used to minister to both Rhossili and the neighbouring parish of Llangennith. A ghost is said to haunt the cottage, taking the form of a mysterious voice which fills the corridors with cold air

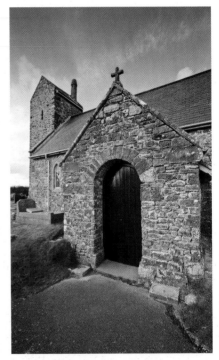

ABOVE: Rhossili's Church of St Mary's, which features a Norman archway

The Dragon's Head

One of the great landmarks of the Gower peninsula is the long, narrow, weirdly shaped promontory running into the sea at the southern perimeter of Rhossili bay. It's easy to see why the Vikings who pillaged this coast in the centuries before the Norman conquest called it the "Wurm", or "Dragon". From dry land, Worm's Head looks every inch like a coiled serpent, petrified at the precise moment it was about to spring into the waves – an illusion enhanced by the presence at its nose of a blow hole through which plumes of sea spray are periodically blasted.
The peninsula is actually composed of two rocks, connected to the shore by a tidal causeway, and to each other by a neck of land known as the Devil's Bridge. The entrance to a large sea cave can be seen on its tip. Henry VIII's antiquarian, John Leland, remarked that according to the locals, "a Dore within the spatius Hole hathe be sene with great Nayles on it," and that this concealed a tunnel leading to Carreg Cennen Castleβ! in Camarthenshire. No such door exists, but the cave was found to contain numerous stone-age tools and the bones of animals long-disappeared from this coast, including mammoth, rhinoceros, bear, wolves and reindeer.

For Dylan Thomas, who used to love walking on it while a boy, Worm's Head was all, "rubbery, gull-limed grass . . .sheep-pilled stones . . . pieces of bones and feather." It's still a wonderfully wild and windy place to blow away the cobwebs, but if you attempt to follow in the Swansea bard's footsteps, keep an eye on the tide: the causeway connecting it to dry land is only crossable for a few hours each day. Precise timings for the "safe window" can be checked at the National Trust Visitor Centre in Rhossili (opposite the hotel), and at the coastguard station at the start of the path down to the causeway.

and whispers into your ear, "why don't you turn around and look at me?" (a fact not advertised by the National Trust, which rents it out as a holiday cottage). Local superstition holds that the spirit is that of a sailor shipwrecked on one of the many vessels that have been blown ashore here over the centuries, spilling their cargo for the locals to plunder. Whether the villagers ever actively lured any ships onto the rocks using lanterns, as is sometimes suggested, remains a matter of controversy, but there's no doubt that several fortunes were made in the area from washed-up booty.

In 1800, a Rhossili fisherman and his wife working in a cove just west of Culver Hole hit the jackpot when they stumbled upon a hoard of Portuguese gold moidores and doubloons glittering in the rocks. Seven years later, a further 12lbs/5.5kg of Spanish dollars were dug up on the main beach, sparking a mini gold rush. Rumours circulated at the time that the coins must have come from a galleon carrying the dowry of Catherine of Braganza, said to have been wrecked here during the reign of Charles II in the late-seventeenth century. No record exists of any such disaster, but that doesn't mean to say it didn't happen – a curtain of silence often closed around such events so that those who benefited from them could hold on to their loot.

A graphic reminder of how treacherous the Bristol Channel winds can be for shipping are the blackened timbers protruding from the sand at the southern end of **RHOSSILI BEACH**. Picked clean by the waves like the carcass of some giant sea monster, the wooden shell is all that survives of a Norwegian barque called the *Helvetia*, which ran aground during a fierce storm in 1887. Visible at low tide, the timbers have had a major battering in recent years; only fragments now remain.

walk it | 20 Rhossili

CHECKED BY
✔ **West Glamorgan Ramblers**

1 From the car park opposite the Worm's Head Hotel, walk back up the lane through **Rhossili** village, passing the church on your L, until you reach the sharp bend in the road. A lane peels away L and heads straight on before the curve; follow it to the end, where a gate leads on to National Trust access land. Bearing R, the path up the south flank of Rhossili Down is steep, but easy to follow, flattening off only as it approaches the trig point (193m/633ft).

2 Keeping more or less to the highest strip of ground, the ridgetop path winds north through a mix of bracken and heather. Superb views extend in all directions, from Exmoor to the Brecon Beacons, and west to the Preseli Hills.
Having passed the second of the ridge's three prominent peaks, the path falls slightly to a fork (at

SS419897). Here you can either follow the track downhill to the L, to the ruined World War II signaling post, or keep right and press on through the heather along the rocky ridgetop. Either way, you'll arrive after 10-15 mins

at the third and final highpoint of **Rhossili Down** (SS419897)

3 The trigpoint marks the start of a steep, 150-m/492-ft descent to Hillend Campsite. Take care here if the grass is wet.

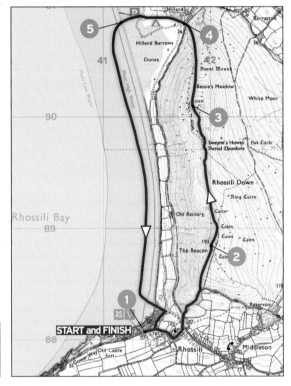

Map not to scale.
Representation of
**OS EXPLORER
MAP 164, 1:25,000**

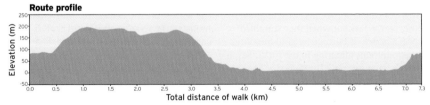

Route profile

162

4 Ignoring the path that veers L/due south from the foot of the hill along the bottom of Rhossili Down via the **Old Rectory**, head through the main gates of the campsite, and bear immediately R, past the front of the pub-café to the main reception and car park gate. From here, a track leads W, skirting the bottom side of the campsite to a paying car-park. Next, follow the fenced track through the dunes to reach **Rhossili beach** itself.

5 A steady, 45-min plod along the tidal sand below Rhossili Down takes you south from here to the start of a short, steep ascent up the cliff. The steps emerge next to the Bay Bistro and Coffee House – the perfect spot to celebrate the end of the walk. If the tide is in your favour (check at the National Trust shop before setting off), it's well worth setting aside another couple of hours for the walk out to Worm's Head (see box).

✕ Eating & Drinking
The King's Head

Llangennith

📞01792 386212

✎www.kingsheadgower.co.uk
This is the nearest decent local to our route, serving reasonably priced meals (Thai food is a speciality), Felinfoel bitter from Llanelli, and (or so they claim), "the largest selection of single malts outside Scotland."

King Arthur Hotel

Higher Green, Reynoldston

✎www.kingarthurhotel.co.uk
Real-ale aficionados might wish to try this pub, 5miles northwest at Reynoldston, which pulls the best pint in the Gower.

Bay Bistro and Coffee House

Rhossili

📞01792 390519
Serves tasty meals, cakes and hot drinks, in a sunny dining room or on a terrace with stupendous views of the beach.

🛏 Sleeping
YHA Rhossili

Middleton, SA3 1PJ

📞01792 401548
Basic bunkhouse in a converted Victorian school.

Western House

Llangennith, SA3 1HU

📞01792 386620

✎www.westernhousebandb.co.uk
Inexpensive, family-run B&B in a 100-year-old farmhouse, with brightly decorated rooms and friendly surfer hosts. Great breakfasts, and it's dog-friendly.

Hillend Campsite

Rhossili, SA3 1JD

📞01792 386204
At a prime site sandwiched between the north end of Rhossili Down and the dunes, this is much the nicest site in the area, with smart toilet blocks and a considerate clientele (read "no all-night surfers' parties").

📖 More Info

Portrait of Gower by Wynford Vaughan Thomas (Robert Hale – London). This definitive guide to the Gower region was written in the 1970s by a much loved Welsh broadcaster.

✎www.nationaltrust.org.uk. The NT owns Rhossili and the Down, and runs the site visitor centre and shop – good, not least, for checking tide times.

✎explore-gower.co.uk. Informed background on the region's beaches, caves, castles and prehistoric monuments.

✎www.enjoygower.com. General info, with an emphasis on the area's beaches – worth a browse for its photos.

🚶 More Walks

Valeways Millennium Heritage Trail by B Palmer and G Woodnam (Vale of Glamorgan Ramblers). Fascinating 99km/62-mile circular walk with various spurs linking up many places of historical, geographic and geological interest, developed by a partnership of the Ramblers, Vale of Glamorgan Council and other organizations. Published with an attractive descriptive booklet and sixteen route cards presenting map and route details in easy sections.

Walking Around Gower by Albert White (West Glamorgan Ramblers). Ten circular walks of between 8km/5miles and 21km/13miles around the Gower peninsula, going out along the coast and returning inland, including extensive notes on scenery, wildlife and history. Available from the NT shop at Rhossili Down.

Walking Around Northern Gower and the Swansea Valley by Peter Beck and Peter J Thomas, based on an original work by Albert White (West Glamorgan Ramblers). Ten circular walks that can be split into shorter circuits, giving options of between 8km/5miles and 21km/13miles, in the former mining area north of Swansea and the Gower peninsula.

On the Trail of the Green Knight

The Roaches

"Great crooked crags, cruelly jagged, the bristling barbs of rock seemed to brush the sky," was how the nameless author of *Sir Gawain and the Green Knight* described Staffordshire's Roaches in the fourteenth century. Seven hundred years on, the mighty gritstone cliffs, whose knotted, lumpen faces loom above the main Leek to Buxton road, strike a no less imposing profile.

Guarding the southwest approaches to the Peak District, the rocks preside over one of the most dramatic landscape changes in mainland Britain. To the west, green pastureland and low wooded hills, with the Cheshire plains stretching into the distance. In the other direction, an expanse of dark, moody moors entangled by miles of salmon-red gritstone walls.

The Roaches' top edge, which can be accessed via several breaks in the escarpment, is the perfect platform from which to admire this dramatic transition – and provides as compelling a walk as any in the Peak District, boasting superb views along its whole length. The ridge holds four distinct summits, the most prominent of them Hen Cloud, the Midlands' answer to

the Rock of Gibraltar.

Saving Hen Cloud for a grand finale, our route gets under way by following in the footsteps of Sir Gawain: along the ridge's high tier and down the far side through a tract of twisted oaks and beech trees straight from the pages of a medieval romance. Hidden in the depths of this fairytale forest is Lud's Church, a kind of miniature gorge draped with mosses and ferns, which scholars have identified as the inspiration for Sir Gawain's Green Chapel. From there, we loop back up to the ridge and retrace our steps to the foot of Hen Cloud – the final climb of the day.

Although strong walkers could easily complete this circuit in an afternoon, it's a route definitely best expanded over a full day, which will give you ample time to enjoy the vistas from the Roaches' edge, watch peregrine falcons swooping over the crags and savour the contrasting atmospheres of high moorland.

Route-finding is easy – except for the final stretch around the flank of Hen Cloud, where the path gets intermittently submerged under ferns during the summer months.

At a glance

Where The Roaches, north of Leek, Staffordshire Peak District. **Why** Weird rock formations; sightings of peregrine falcons and red grouse; Lud's Church: a hidden cleft with its own micro-climate and flora.

When June, when the peregrine falcons are nesting. **Start/Finish** Roaches Gate car park (SK004622), 1.6km/1mile west of Upper Hulme. **Duration** 4hrs 30mins–5hrs. **Distance** 13.5km/8.5miles

Terrain Clear or well waymarked paths over fairly easy gradients, though with a long stretch on exposed scarp where sudden changes of weather are frequent. **Maps** OS Explorer OL24.

On your way

Your typical Peak District gritstone edge, characteristic of the Dark Peak region to the north and west of the park, tends to fall away to near vertical cliffs. The Roaches, however (the name derives from the French for "rocks", "roches") are tilted gently skywards, which lends an eerie presence to the summits and phantasmagorical shapes worn out of their sides. In places, the outcrops stand like petrified heads staring mutely across the Staffs-Cheshire border, their features blurred by millennia of wind and rain.

Until the 1970s, the entire Roaches ridge lay within the boundaries of the Brocklehurst estate, owned by the Swythamley family, an aristocratic dynasty on the decline who used the area as a grouse reserve. It was they who erected the curious Gothic cottage at the foot of the rocks known as **ROCKHALL**, to house their gamekeepers. Complete with crenellated roofs and arched windows, the folly also served as the unlikely venue in 1872 for a royal visit, when Princess Mary of Cambridge (a cousin of Queen Victoria) and her German husband, the Prince of Teck, descended for a spot of scrambling and shooting. A local reporter enthusiastically recorded that, "[the] Princess deployed capital mountaineering powers, and during a portion of the ascent the Prince of Teck gallantly adjusted a rope for her support."

Little could onlookers have imagined that a century later the same crags would be crawling with rock climbers. Since those working-class legends of the sport, Joe Brown and Don Whillans, met here in the 1950s, the Roaches has served as one of the Peak District's foremost sites, with routes ranging from easy scrambles to E7s. Salford-born Whillans, equipped with little more than a pair of plimsoles and his mother's washing line, is credited with the first lead on the most famous of all: "the sloth", so-named because its ascent involves prolonged spells of dangling upside down in mid-air.

By Whillans' day, the Brocklehurst estate was on its last legs and the cottage a hovel inhabited by a couple of eccentric hermits, Dougie (aka Lord of the Roaches) and his consort Annie. Judging by the invective they hurled on visiting climbers (and vice versa, by all accounts) the pair little appreciated the rising chorus of karabiners and belay plates clanking above their rooftops. Rockhall now serves as the **WHILLANS MEMORIAL HUT** in honour of the climbing hero who cut his teeth on the rocks above it.

Overshadowed by some of the more

ABOVE: Rockhall, aka the Whillans Memorial Hut

ghoulish formations in the Roaches, the cave around which Rockhall was originally built played host over the centuries to a succession of smugglers, thieves and deserters. In the Napoleonic wars its inhabitants were an old crone named Bessy Bowyer and her daughter – descendents of a notorious Scottish renegade-bandit, or "moss trooper". The daughter reportedly possessed an uncommon voice and used to wander at night among the rocks singing, "songs that sounded foreign to English ears." Local legend has it that she was abducted, and that her ghost still haunts a small, circular tarn on the ridgetop known as Doxey Pool. The pond has, since the Domesday Book, been associated with female occult phenomena (in the medieval dialect of the northwest Midlands, "doxey" meant a fortune teller, healer or "wise woman"). It's also said that the peaty depths of the pool are inhabited by a mermaid who lures unwary walkers to a watery grave.

The pink grit trail winding northeast from **DOXEY POOL** arrives soon after at a pronounced dip in the ridge known as **ROACH END**. Here our path continues along the ridge, then swings northwest, through the ancient forest at the head of the Dane Valley to one of the Peak District's great curiosities. Although it looks like a stream gorge, **LUD'S CHURCH** was originally formed by landslip. During the summer, its sides – no more than 15m/49ft apart and 100m/328ft long – hold cascades of ferns, mosses and grass that glow a luminous green when viewed from below.

It's easy to see why literary historians connect this chasm with Sir Gawain's Green Chapel. In the poem, the "hideous oratory" where he travelled for his appointment with the dreaded Green Knight had, "a hole in each end and on either side/And was overgrown with grass in great patches/All

hollow it was within, only an old cavern/Or the crevice of an ancient crag."

The site's present name derives from the mid-fourteenth century, when it hosted congregations of a religious sect known as the Lollards (later corrupted to "Luds"). As the first group ever to openly oppose the teachings of the Catholic church, the Lollards were considered heretics and burned at the stake, which is why they chose to assemble in this remote spot.

Our path passes directly through the little chasm, and continues out the other side through the forest lining the upper reaches of the Dane river. "Wonderfully wild was their way through the woods", recounts the narrator of *Sir Gawain and the Green Knight*. Little can have altered here in many centuries – save perhaps for the appearance in the 1930s of some incongruously exotic animals. Released from a nearby zoo, five Bennett's wallabies and three Tibetan yaks survived on this windy moorland top for a couple of decades.

The yaks are long gone now, but you may still be lucky enough to catch the bizarre sight of the sole surviving wallaby hopping through the heather. Another rarity to look out for are the peregrine falcons who, after a hundred-year absence, returned to nest on a ledge above Rockhall Cottage in the summer of 2008.

Shortly after passing above the peregrines' nest, the path descends into the **WINDYGATES GAP**, the saddle separating the Roach from **HEN CLOUD**. Until 1765, when a toll road was constructed further south, this pass lay along the route of the main cart track over the southern Pennines. Traversing some of Britain's harshest, bleakest terrain, the new toll road profited as an artery along which raw materials mined in the hills were brought down to the potteries of north Staffordshire.

The Roaches

1 From the main car park at Roaches Gate (SJ004621), follow the old cart track uphill towards the gap in the rocks, keeping your eye out for a side path peeling L towards the old larch plantation and **Rockhall** Cottage (**Whillans Memorial Hut**). Cross the enclosure diagonally, passing in front of the building, and follow the path out the other side through the trees. After a couple of mins in the woods, the route cuts sharply R, ascending steeply via a flight of stone steps to the ridgetop via a narrow cleft to a small cairn. Once on level ground, turn L (north).

2 From here on, the path along the flat edge of the escarpment is impossible to lose as it wriggles around a succession of outcrops, past **Doxey Pool**, and on to the highpoint of the Roaches (505m/1657ft) ridge, marked by a trig point. During the descent, you pass a number of striking rock formations (including the famous Bearstone Head), before arriving at a saddle known as **Roach End** (SJ996645).

3 Keep heading straight along the line of the watershed, following the route signed "Concession Path to Danebridge".

4 At (SJ977653), a major path intersection, flagged by a fingerpost, is reached; our route bends R here in the direction of Gradbach, following the line of a drystone wall. Fine views over

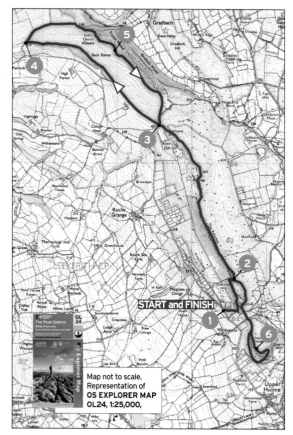

Map not to scale.
Representation of
**OS EXPLORER MAP
OL24, 1:25,000,**

Route profile

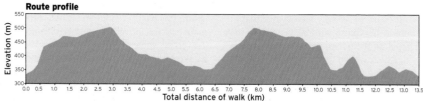

the Dane Valley to the prominent peak of Shutlingsloe open up to the north as you enter the forest, shortly after which a signposted path veers R towards **Lud's Church** (SJ987657). Look out for the engraved sign on a stone on the right marking the entrance to the chasm.

5 Follow the muddy track through the chasm and out the other side, via some steps leading onto a path which contours L downhill through the trees. At the signpost go R in the direction of Roach End and start the ascent out of the woods, then cross open moorland back to Roach End (**3**). Once back on the ridgetop, retrace the outward leg past the Roaches trig point and on as far as the head of the steps above Rockhall, marked by a cairn. At this point, take the trail bearing L around the sides of the rock outcrops ahead, rather than the one that drops R through the middle them, as it's much easier going.At **Windygates Gap** (SJ007621), pause to admire the views from the memorial bench. The gate in the drystone wall nearby leads straight across a field to a second gate, beyond which you'll have no trouble following the path climbing steadily to R up Hen Cloud.

6 From the summit of **Hen Cloud** (SJ008616), the path winds sharply down the southeast flank of the hill into beech woods, then swings R to join the driveway of Roaches' Hall (former seat of the Swythamleys). Turn R onto this and follow it for 1min. Directly opposite the final beech tree on the L, a path

cuts uphill to the R through the bracken; after a short distance take the right fork in the path. This section, between The Roaches Hall driveway around the lower flank of Hen Cloud, is very indistinct – especially when the bracken is high. Don't be tempted up climbers' trails that intersect the path, but keep contouring northwards under Hen Cloud until the path bends around the base of the hill to rejoin the trail you followed earlier to the summit at (SJ008618). Cross the field again, only this time turn L downhill to regain the car park.

🚌 Getting There
First Potteries bus 118, running between Leek and Buxton, will drop you at the village of Upper Hulme, a 20-30-minute walk from Roaches Gate car park. The nearest train station is 12miles away at Stoke-on-Trent. Call traveline ✆ 0871 200 2233 or visit

✎ www.staffordshire.gov.uk/transport/publictransport for timetables.

ℹ️ Visitor Information
Leek TIC, 1 Market PI, Leek
✆ 01538 483741
✎ www.staffsmoorlands.gov.uk

🏠 Sleeping
The Roaches Tea Rooms
Paddock Far, Roach Rd, Upper Hulme ST13 8TY
✆ 01538 300345
✎ www.roachestearooms.co.uk
Self-catering cottages in a former farmhouse right under the rocks. They also offer basic camping in a field opposite; with views across the valley.

YHA Gradbach
Quarnford
Buxton, SK17 0SU
✆ 0845 371 9118
✎ www.yha.co.uk
Well set-up hostel in a secluded vale on the Lud's Church side of the escarpment.

🍴 Eating & Drinking
At the time of writing, there was no decent pub within easy walking distance of the Roaches, but breakfast, lunch and "lite bites" are available at The Roaches Tea Room (below). Real-ale fans should make for Leek, seven miles away, where the Wilkes Head on St Edward Street serves hand-pulled Whim bitters, as well as guest beers and proper farm cider, in a tiny, three-roomed pub dating from the eighteenth century.

📖 More Info
✎ www.roaches.org.uk. A lively introduction to the area and its places of interest.

✎ www.thebmc.co.uk/Feature. aspx?id=2243. History of the Don Whillans Memorial Hut (aka Rockhall).

🚶 More Walks
Stone Circles by Stone Ramblers (*Ramblers*). Eleven walks from the villages around Stone, Staffs, between 4km/2.5miles and 13km/8miles, including short options for the longer routes. Full colour OS maps and photos.

Ramblers' Choice by City of Birmingham Ramblers (Meridian Books). A collection of the Group's favourite walks in the Midlands from 5-16km/3-10miles.

The Corpse Road

Crackpot Hall

There's a hint of mischief about Alfred Wainwright's famous assertion, made in his *Companion to the Pennine Way*, that Swaledale was, "the most beautiful of the Yorkshire Dales". Mischief, because he must have realized he'd be putting a lot of proud noses out of joint by making it. But if you had to single out any one dale as the loveliest, or the most quintessentially "Yorkshire", few would deny Swaledale a place on the shortlist.

The most remote of the large dales, it extends across the far north of the park, narrowing as it winds into the wild moors of the watershed. Our featured viewpoint of Crackpot Hall lies deep in the valley's far western extremity, Upper Swaledale, overlooking a secluded enclave of green pasture and drystone walls, dotted with stone barns, or "laithes", set against a backdrop of bracken-covered fells. Out of the wind on the valley floor, the tiny village of Keld, one of the prettiest in the British uplands, completes the picture-postcard scene.

This idyllic corner of the dales, however, was not always as tranquil as it seems today. Look a little closer and you'll notice slips of spoil and the grey skeletons of abandoned mine workings scarring the hillsides. For Upper Swaledale was, in the late eighteenth century, the epicentre of a furious lead rush. At its peak, a pall of acrid black smoke and toxic dust would have hung over the dale, disgorged by dozens of crushing yards and smelthouses. And these were merely the most visible signs of an operation whose tentacles burrowed deep inside the hills themselves, honeycombing the limestone.

Largely reclaimed by nature, the vestiges of Swaledale's industrial past today stand less as blots on an otherwise bucolic landscape than intriguing monuments to a lost way of life. The route we've describe passes a succession of them, in addition to one of the national park's finest waterfalls, Kisdon Force on the River Swale.

Beginning in the tiny village of Muker, the route follows the bank of the Swale north to Keld, then returns down the opposite flank of the dale over Kisdon Hill, following the course of a historic path used in former times to transport dead bodies to the nearest consecrated ground – hence its chilling name, "the Corpse Road".

At a glance

Where Crackpot Hall, in Upper Swaledale – 17km/10miles southeast of Kirkby Stephen, or 37km/23miles west of Richmond.
Why Text-book Yorkshire dales landscape; spectacular waterfalls; vestiges of old lead mines.

When In late May/early June Swaledale hosts a lively arts festival, with venues in both Muker and Keld.
Start/Finish The Farmers Arms, Muker (SD909979).
Duration 4hrs.

Distance 11km/7.5miles.
Terrain Clear paths and old mine tracks, well signposted and fixtured, with proper ladder stiles, and footbridges spanning the becks.
Maps OS Explorer OL30.

On your way

The view down Swaledale from the path above Crackpot Hall, with the old farm buildings in the foreground and the Swale twisting east across a patchwork of lush fields, is one of the classic dales vistas. What photographs of this picturesque spot fail to convey, however, is the presence, on the hillside immediately behind, of a sprawling slag heap – a legacy of the lead-mining boom that raged here at the end of the nineteenth century.

Lead had been extracted from the fellsides of Swaledale since at least Roman times. Later, Cistercian monks used the metal as a source of revenue for their abbeys further east. But in the late 1700s, when war with France cut off supplies of cheaper foreign lead, the price rocketed, causing small concessions to proliferate across the dale, and especially above Keld.

Production techniques were crude and labour-intensive. Initially, lead was obtained by damming streams, then releasing the

water to wash away the topsoil containing the ore – a process known as "hushing". When the surface was eroded completely away, veins of the metal were pursued underground. Reached by cutting vertical shafts and horizontal drainage adits in the hills, the ore would be brought to the surface and crushed on so-called "dressing floors" by boys wielding hammers known as "buckers". It would then be sifted and smelted, before being cast into "pigs" (ingots).

Vestiges of old lead workings can still be seen at **SWINNER GILL**, a narrow side valley cutting north into the moors from Swaledale, which our route crosses by means of an old miners' footbridge. Continue up the gill beyond the bridge a short way and you'll come to **SWINNER GILL KIRK**, a cave where Dissenters used to worship in secret in the seventeenth century.

Swinner Gill formed part of the large Parkes mine, which in the late eighteenth century became embroiled in a violent conflict with its neighbour, the Beldi Hill mine, centered on the land above Crackpot

Hall. The property, and most the land in this area, belonged to Lord Smith of Muker Manor, who leased it to a mine company. However, it had originally formed part of the estate of Phillip Duke Wharton, a notorious Jacobite (supporter of James Stuart) who'd had his land impounded after allegedly drinking the health of the Old Pretender in the local pub.

When a rich seam of lead was discovered at the Beldi Hill mine, one of Wharton's descendents (by marriage) – George Denny, Lord of Pomfret – claimed he was entitled to royalties, and took his case to the High Court.

As the legal process rumbled on, the miners themselves became caught up in the dispute. Encouraged by Pomfret, men from the Parke excavations cut their rivals' water supply, slashed smelting bellows, and diverted streams into Beldi Hill's shafts. Matters came to a head on 6 June 1769, when a mob of three hundred, "did unlawfully, riotously, beet, wound and ill-treat" one of Lord Smith's miners, "and

with great force and violence throw him into . . . a hush gutter."

Despite such tactics, Pomfret lost his case, and eventually all his land, after taking it to the High Court. Beldi Hill survived for a few more decades, but like its neighbours closed when the price of lead began to fall.

Having lain derelict since subsidence forced its abandonment in the 1950s, **CRACKPOT HALL** is currently under renovation by the Gunnerside Estate. Dating from the 1700s, the building standing today originally served as a keeper's lodge, though records exist of a farm on the same site with an old "ling" (heather) roof.

Traditional stone flags clad the rooftops of the nearby village of Keld, crossing-point of the Pennine Way and Coast to Coast Path. **KELD** is also the springboard for the short ramble to **KISDON FORCE**, where the Swale crashes over a series of dramatic limestone steps in the river.

In common with Crackpot Hall, and many place names in this part of the world, the word "force" has Norse origins.

Swaledale Sheep

Originally introduced by the Norse herders who colonized this region a thousand years ago, the Swaledale sheep is as characteristic of the Dales as the region's stone barns and walls. The breed is particularly well suited to the harsh conditions of life on the high fells, thanks to its thick wool, which has served inhabitants of the Yorkshire uplands faithfully over the years. When the bottom dropped out of the lead market in the nineteenth century, many former miners fell back on shepherding, as well as a cottage industry that would become a mainstay of the Swaledale economy: knitting. Whole families, including the men and children, were engaged in producing socks and other garments for sale to the "stockinger", who toured the villages of Upper Swaledale every couple of months collecting the finished goods in his covered cart for sale in the market at Kendall. Because it was paid per piece, the work had to be done at a fast - or "terrible" - pace. Children were taught at a young age how to speed-knit using long, curved needles, or "wires", one of which would be secured in a wooden sheath.

Over time, a whole culture evolved around dales knitting, with its own special songs and rhymes, which the families would sing to keep time as they worked in the light of their peat fires, swaying back and forth to the rhythm of the clicking needles.

ABOVE: Kisdon Force, near Keld, on the River Swale – one of a string of waterfalls passed by our circular route from Muker

"Crackpot" is a corruption of the Viking for "chasm haunted by crows"; "Keld" was the Viking for "spring"; and "Muker" derives from the term for "narrow acre". Unlike lower reaches of the dale, which were colonized by Anglo-Saxon farmers, Upper Swaldale was settled in the tenth century by Scandinavian herders who grazed their sheep and cattle on the high fells in summer, and down in the valley in winter.

Aside from their Norse roots and pretty stone roofs, Keld and **MUKER** have in common the medieval trackway connecting them via the top of Kisdon Hill. It's known as the **CORPSE ROAD**, a transmission from the time before the construction in 1580 of the parish church in Muker, when the dead of Upper Swaldale had to be carried to the nearest consecrated ground down the valley in Grinton – a distance of 22km/14miles.

The walk used to take two days, with an overnight halt at the Punchbowl Inn in Low Row en route. Coffins were encased in wicker baskets and carried by pairs of pallbearers working in relays. During rest breaks they used to place their load on flat stone plinths called "coffin stones", spaced at regular intervals along the road; several of these can still be seen.

You might well be tempted to pause yourself before the steep descent from Kisdon Hill to Muker. The view over the village rooftops and down the valley to Gunnerside is as glorious as any in the dales – and all the more lovely for having a decent pub, the Farmers Arms, at the bottom of it.

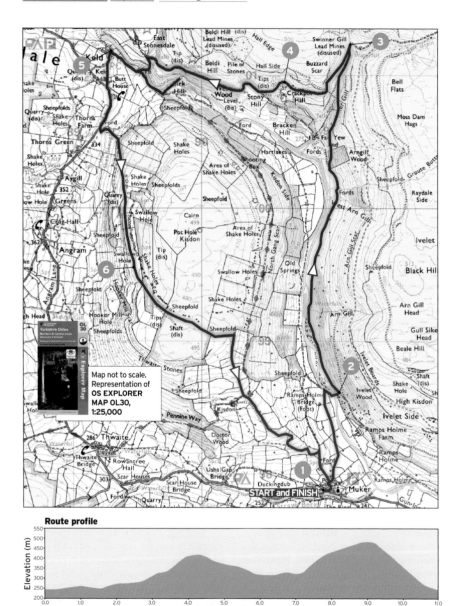

Route profile

1 With your back to the Farmers Arms in **Muker**, turn L along the main road (B6270), then L again into the village. At the top of a short rise, you arrive at a tiny "square". Take the R fork in the lane here, past the old post office (signposted "Gunnerside & Keld"). This leads to a squeeze-stile and the start of a flagstone path that runs north across seven fields to the river. Turn R when you reach it and cross Ramps Holme Bridge (footbridge) to the far bank. Climb up the steps ahead then bear L along a path (signposted "Keld") to join a broad, stony track.

2 Continue N along this old mine track, rising steadily with the river to your L and patches of woodland on your R. After just under 2km/1.2miles, a narrow path peels R towards **Swinner Gill**, a tributary of the Swale, just after a side stream crosses under the track, next to a fence corner. Follow this fainter path through the bracken up the R side of the Gill, which you cross near a mine entrance from which water gushes. Having forded the stream, the trail cuts up the L (W) side of the ravine to a stone bridge, near the mouth of the Swinner Gill mine, where you get a fine view back down the valley.

3 It's worth making the short detour upstream from the bridge to visit **Swinner Gill Kirk**. Then return to the bridge, and bear R along the broad, upper track, which contours SW past the ruins of an old forge, and on through a gate in a drystone wall to **Crackpot Hall**.

4 Follow the track down past Crackpot Hall, and on at an easy gradient above a wooded gorge, with Kisdon Force falls visible below. A footbridge crosses a tributary stream near the beautiful East Gill Falls. Turn L just after it on to the Pennine Way, which drops down to a larger footbridge spanning the River Swale. Having climbed the steep rise on the far bank, turn L along the Pennine Way, then L again at a fingerpost down a narrower side path to reach the famous **Kisdon Force** waterfalls. Having seen the falls, retrace your steps to the turning down to the footbridge, but instead of dropping R back to the river, continue straight ahead to Keld, a short way further along the path.

5 Turn L to follow the lane through the village, taking your first L at the public toilets past Butt House. Bear L at the War Memorial onto the Reeth-Kirkby Stephen road (B6270), and follow the tarmac for 300m/330yrds, until you see a footpath sign on your L (marked "Bridleway Muker 2 miles"), pointing the way down an old walled cart track to a ford and footbridge at Skeb Skeugh. This track – the famous **Corpse Road** – continues from the river up the flank of Kisdon Hill, passing an isolated farmhouse on the L.

6 A short way beyond the farmhouse, the track swings gently L to pass through a gate, with limestone crags below on the R. From here on it becomes grassier, bending L as it cuts via a series of gates across the open moorland on top of Kisdon Hill. Not long after you begin to descend in earnest, the path runs along a wall for a short way, then veers sharply R, following a series of walled farm tracks and fields back down to Muker.

Getting There

Harrogate District's bus 30 runs 2–3 times daily to Muker from Richmond (Mon–Sat). Timetables may be consulted at ✑www. yorkshiretravel.net, or on ☎0871 200 2233. On Sundays in summer, additional services are laid on from Darlington, Hawes, and Leeds.

Visitor Information
Reeth TIC
Hudson House, The Green, Reeth
☎01748 884059

Eating & Drinking
Muker Village Stores & Teashop
Muker
Two Victorian-era sitting rooms with open fires and outdoor patios where you can steel yourself for your walk with a wide selection of quality teas, coffees and Cocketts of Hawes' famous toasted teacake.

The Farmers Arms
Muker
☎01748 886297
Typical dales pub with an open fire, stone flags and lots of local character. In the heart of the village, it serves Theakston keg ales (including a fine pint of "Old Peculier") and tasty bar meals.

The Tan Hill Inn
Tan Hill
☎01833 628246
This legendary watering hole, marooned on a windswept moor, is officially the highest pub in Britain. You can walk there in a

couple of hours from Keld on the Pennine Way – an adventure in itself – and if the Theakston and Black Sheep ales prove too much of a temptation, they offer inexpensive B&B and camping on the premises.

Sleeping
The Village Stores B&B
Muker, DL11 6QQ
☎01748 886409
🖳www.mukervillage.com
Pleasantly furnished, good-value rooms (all en-suite) overlooking Straw Beck; run by the same owners as the shop. Transfers to trailheads available on request.

Swale Farm
Muker, DL11 6QG
☎01748 886479
Simple, but light and clean rooms, in a family-run B&B on the outskirts of the village.

Chapel House
Muker, DL11 6QG
☎01748 886 822
Spacious B&B accommodation in a converted 1930s chapel, just past the gallery near the pub.

More Info
The Old Hand-Knitters of the Dales (1951) by Marie Hartley and Joan Ingleby.
This social-history classic is the definitive account of the dales' knitting industry, and its cultural legacy in North Yorkshire.

🖳www.brigantesenglishwalks. com. Baggage service for walkers in the Upper Swaledale area. It's primarily aimed at people following the Pennine Way, but can also assist if you're only walking a single stage of the long-distance route, say, to the Tan Hill Inn.
🖳www.swaledale-festival.org.uk.

Homepage of the annual music and performing arts festival held in early summer, including one or two venues in Upper Swaledale.

More Walks

Freedom to Roam Guide. Wensleydale & Swaledale: the Northern Yorkshire Dales by Andrew Bibby (Frances Lincoln/ Ramblers). Fully illustrated guide featuring twelve tempting hill walks in the region, backed up by 1:25,000 OS maps and lots of engaging background on local history, geology and wildlife.

Yorkshire Dales by David Leather (Collins/Ramblers). Detailed route descriptions for thirty walks across the dales.

BELOW: The curlew's call is one of the dales' defining sounds

walk 23

The Mermaid's Rest

Sandwood Bay

For the Viking mariners who used to round Cape Wrath, the far northwestern tip of the British mainland, Sandwood Bay was a place of deliverance – one of the few spots on this rugged coastline where they could safely land a longboat and take on fresh water after crossing the North Sea.

Sandwood remains a sanctuary of sorts, only today it's somewhere people go not to escape the elements, but to experience them more fully. Staring out to sea from here, the next landmass is, quite literally, Greenland, which ensures the beach catches the full ferocity of the Atlantic. Come on a calm, sunny day and the turquoise water, rose-white sand and resplendent cliffs flanking the bay can look almost tropical. But when the weather's stormy, a mere stroll along its foreshore – with huge waves pounding in and sand blowing at hurricane force into your face – might feel like an expedition.

All of which, of course, adds to the allure of the place. A ninety-minute walk from the nearest road, it takes a significant effort to reach. The trail is rough at times, and a bit monotonous by the standards of the region. And there's precious little shelter should one of those freak hail storms suddenly sweep off the ocean, firing ice pellets the size of quails eggs into the machair.

The prize at the end of the walk, though, is a glimpse of a beach as pristine as you'll see anywhere. No litter, no signs, no telegraph posts or interpretative panels, no facilities of any kind. Just the sound of the wind in the dunes, the relentless, jade-green surf crashing in and the watchful presence of a lonely rock stack – "Am Buachaille", "The Herdsman"– standing off the cliffs to the southwest.

No-one lives at Sandwood any more. Once the home of a small crofter-fishing community, the land overlooking the loch behind the bay became deserted after the Clearances of the mid-nineteenth century. Little wonder that such a place should be associated with numerous legends, ghost stories and supernatural occurrences, from phantom longboats to mythic water horses.

More than trepidation, however, Sandwood Bay tends to inspire those who make the effort to reach it with something more akin to reverence – and gratitude that such a wild place can still exist on an island as crowded as ours.

At a glance

Where Sandwood Bay, 12km/7.5miles northwest of Kinlochbervie, Sutherland, in the northwest Highlands.
Why Britain's wildest and most beautiful white-sand beach; spectacular dunes and cliffs; "Am Buachaille" rock stack;

sightings of great skuas and red deer.
When July–Aug for the most frequent public transport; and pick a windy day to see the beach at its most dramatic.
Downsides No pub or shop near the trailhead.

Start/Finish Blairmore, 5.2km/3miles northwest of Kinlochbervie (NC194600).
Duration 3hrs.
Distance 13.6km/8.5miles.
Terrain Uneven, rocky tracks and paths, waterlogged where they pass alongside lochans.

A viking longboat is said to be buried
under the sifting dunes of Sandwood Bay

On your way

"Extreem wilderness" was how the first cartographers labeled this far northwestern rim of the Scottish coast in the seventeenth century – an indication of the fear its awesome cliffs and hinterland of bleak moorland and sandstone mountains evoked in travellers.

Watching the breakers crash against the foot of the **AM BUACHAILLE** sea stack to the south of Sandwood Bay, and the swell thumping the base of the still larger cliffs of Cape Wrath to the north, it's amazing to think that mariners have braved these volatile seas for a thousand years or more.

Longboats carrying Viking invaders and traders used to stop at Sandwood to take on fresh water from the loch behind it. Clues to their presence linger in many local place names: "Wrath" derives from the ancient Norse word "hvarf", meaning "turning point"; and Sandwood comes from "sandvat", "sand lake" (via the Gaelic "seannabhat", and the Elizabethan "sandwait") – a reference to the freshwater loch behind the beach.

Later, in 1588, the Spanish Armada passed this way on its ill-fated odyssey around the British Isles. One can only imagine the horror with which, after the ordeals they endured off the Irish coast, its sailors must have regarded Sutherland's unforgiving shoreline, whose northwesterlies and rock ramparts have wrecked countless ships over the centuries.

Local legend holds that during high winds, the masts and rafters of lost ships sometimes protrude from the huge dunes behind Sandwood's beach. Because of the strength of the winds here, these dunes are some of the most dynamic in Europe, forever shifting and changing form, like the headlands behind them.

They're part of a precious ecosystem rare in coastal Britain for the total absence of human settlement. Inland from the dunes, machair – shell-sand grassland hosting around two hundred different kinds of flowering plant – yields to peaty moorland interspersed with reed beds and little lochans. It's a paradise for local wildlife, which includes familiar species such as badger and rabbit alongside rarities like corncrake and great skuas.

Remnants of ancient shielings (seasonal stone swellings) and "lazybeds" (strip mounds fertilized with kelp) show Sandwood was inhabited centuries ago. In the 1820s, it even became over-populated, as dozens of families of refugees from

The John Muir Trust

Sandwood Bay, and most of the land between it and Kinlochber-vie, falls within a 4650-hectare estate owned by the John Muir Trust. Established in 1983 in memory of the Scottish-born writer and environmental luminary John Muir, the trust sets out to protect wild places throughout Scotland, both by purchasing and managing property, and education and campaign work.

The Sandwood Estate is the most northerly of its eight principal sites; others encompass parts of the Cuillin Hills in Skye, the Quinag massif, Knoydart and mighty Ben Nevis itself. As well as holding land, the JMT also gives grants to individuals and schemes working to raise public awareness of wilderness issues. One project it has supported to great effect is the Carrifran Wild Wood in Dumfrieshire, described on p314.

ABOVE: Sandwood's spectacular dunes are some of the most dynamic in Europe

"cleared" land further north settled here. However, they too were evicted in 1847, packed off on a specially chartered steamer to Australia so that the land they had farmed could be given over to more lucrative sheep.

Built by the estate as a fishing retreat, a lone cottage, **SANDWOOD LODGE** is the only vestige here from this tragic episode in Scottish history. Its roofless ruin stands just off the path to the beach from Blairmore – a melancholic monument to the cruelty of the Highland Clearances. The house is said to be haunted by the ghost of the same shipwrecked sailor who, on windy nights, marches up and down **SANDWOOD BAY** in his seamen's boots, brass-buttoned tunic and mariner's cap searching for his lost crew.

A few years back, a couple of walkers bivouacking near the ruins reported a still weirder phenomenon, when a thundering of horses' hooves in the middle of the night caused the walls of the cottage to tremble. As any superstitious Highlander will tell you, Sandwood Bay – with its churning surf and icy loch – is prime territory for "Each Uisge" – the dreaded "Water Horse" of Gaelic legend. For which reason, the hikers may have had a lucky escape.

The most feared of all Scottish folklore's supernatural ogres, Each Uisge is said to take two forms – both equally lethal depending on your gender. As a horse, he seduces men who jump onto his back, then drags them into the nearest loch or sea to devour them whole (all except for the liver, apparently, which he lets float to the surface). Women, on the other hand, fall foul of his charms when the Water Horse adopts the shape of a handsome man. Which is why Highlanders are traditionally suspicious of figures standing alone at the water's edge.

The most famous of all the many spooky goings on reported at Sandwood Bay, however, was one that occurred on the 5th of January, 1900. A local crofter named Alexander Gunn had followed his collie to the foot of the cliffs south of the beach, where he found his dog trembling with fear. Above them, reclined on a rock ledge, was a seven-foot-long figure, yellowish in colour, with green eyes and long, reddish-blond hair.

Until his death 44 years later, Gunn insisted he hadn't made the whole story up, and that what he'd seen was, in fact, the last recorded sighting in Britain of a mermaid.

CHECKED BY
✔ **Inverness Ramblers**

1 The path to Sandwood Bay starts near a small car park at Blairmore, maintained by the John Muir Trust. Cross the road running past the car park and look for a turning on the opposite side, where an unsurfaced track runs past a ruined croft. Pass through the gate ahead and follow the track northwest.

2 After 10mins this drops downhill slightly to skirt the southern tip of Loch Na Gainimh. Continue on the same track above the lochan's southeast shore as far as a T-junction, where you should turn L to reach the northeast corner of the loch. From here, the track bends R, passing a fork where you keep R again. At the next fork, reached a minute or two later, bear L. The correct way at each of these turnings is obvious, as it's more worn.

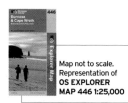

Map not to scale.
Representation of
**OS EXPLORER
MAP 446 1:25,000**

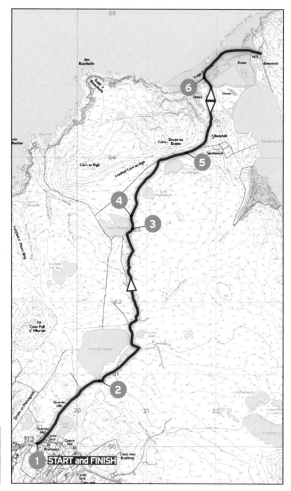

START and FINISH

Route profile

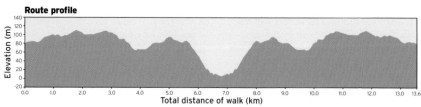

3 A gentle descent ensues to Loch a' Mhuilinn, which the path skirts via its boggy eastern shore. It can get quite muddy here, and you may need to pick a drier route through the lumpy ground to your R.

4 Once clear of Loch a' Mhuilinn, the trail becomes a proper footpath that rises gently uphill at first, giving fine views east across the moorland lining Strath Shinary. Passing two more small lochs on your R, you then arrive at a fork, where you should keep L (again, the way ahead is obvious); a R turn here would take you to the remnants of **Sandwood Lodge** visible just down the hill.

5 Shortly after the fork, pass through the gate in the drystone wall, where you'll be treated to your first glimpse of **Sandwood Bay** and the mighty cliffs beyond it. Keep to the main path as it drops towards the lagoon behind the beach; this eventually emerges in the middle of the bay.

6 To reach our featured viewpoint, turn R when you reach the sand and head towards the far, northeastern end of the beach. Having forded the stream, you can then clamber up the rocks ahead to the top of a bluff surveying the whole bay to the **Am Buachaille** rock stack in the distance.

Return by the same route.

Getting There
Between May and Sept, Tim Dearman buses run a service to Kinlochbervie from Inverness via Ullapool (Mon–Sat; plus Sun in July & Aug). For current timetable information, phone ✆01349 883585, or visit ✎www.timdearmancoaches.co.uk.

From Kinlochbervie, you can reach Blairmore by Subsidized Taxi (Allan Bruce ✆01971 521477). Sponsored by the Highland Regional Council, this wonderful service is aimed primarily at local senior citizens, but visiting walkers are welcome to use it; and the fare for the 5-km/3-mile trip is only 70p per person. There's a phone box at Blairmore car park – handy for summoning the taxi for the return leg (mobile phone reception up here is patchy).

Visitor Information
Durness TIC
Sutherland, IV27 4PN
✆01971 511259
✎www.visithighlands.com

John Muir Trust
41 Commercial St, Edinburgh, EH6 6JD
✆0131 554 0114
✎www.jmt.org

Eating & Drinking
In addition to the Old School Restaurant, reviewed below, the Fishermen's Mission in Kinlochbervie serves up hearty plates of fish and chips, and other inexpensive café meals – though note that at the time of writing it was in the process of being bought by the local community, and may not be open for 2009.

Old School Restaurant & Rooms
Inshegra, Kinlochbervie, IV27 4RF
✆01971 521383
Smart little B&B-cum-restaurant in a converted school overlooking Loch Inchard. This is the closest accommodation to the start of our route, and it's one of the nicest places to stay in the area, with a licensed restaurant occupying an old classroom. The menu's dominated by prime Scottish steak and local seafood, though they also serve veggie haggis.

Sleeping
Kinlochbervie Hotel
Kinlochbervie, IV27 4RP
✆01971 521275
✎www.kinlochberviehotel.com
This is the upscale option. Light and airy ensuite rooms, some of them with sea views, in an efficiently run three star on the edge of the village. Their restaurant serves seafood straight off the boat, and locally sourced hill lamb and venison.

Find Out More
✎www.jmt.org/sandwood-estate.asp. The JMT's Sandwood page features a colour fact sheet on the bay, its geology, wildlife and management.

✎www.durness.org. Lively little village website with a page devoted to the local Countryside Ranger Service, which organizes guided walks in the area.

ABOVE: John Muir Trust sign

To the Devil's Chair

The Stiperstones

The Stiperstones in south Shropshire extend across classic border terrain – an area of overlap and ambiguity, where accents merge, landscapes shift, and stories of supernatural and heroic deeds abound. This distinctive ridge is often eclipsed by its near neighbour, the bigger, better known Long Mynd. But it has an unforgettable atmosphere – one more akin to that of the Welsh mountains than the rolling pastures eulogized by AE Housman in *A Shropshire Lad*.

Erupting at regular intervals from its mantle of purple heather and lime-green whinberry bushes are outcrops of wild, jagged tors, interlaced by ancient tracks. The rocks sparkle in the sunlight as you pass, and giant ravens the size of small dogs caw from their wind-sculpted tops, surveying a heath alive with lark, grouse and curlews.

Although they only rise to 536m/1758ft, these lonely outcrops afford some of the finest views in central England. In clear weather you can see from the Malverns to the Peak District, northwest to Cader Idris and, if you're lucky, all the way to Snowdon, 93km/58miles northwest.

When mist enfolds the ridge, on the other hand, the stones take on a more sinister mood, inducing a sense of claustrophobia. Local legend asserts that witches congregate around them, and that the Devil himself keeps a seat here.

His eponymous "Chair" is one of four prominent quartzite outcrops skirted by our route in the course of its north–south traverse of the ridge. It approaches the Stiperstones from the gentler east flank of the hill, via a meandering trail across verdant sheep country. The starting point is the hamlet of Bridges, on the floor of the East Onna valley, famed for its excellent pub and youth hostel. From there it crests a series grassy ridges, grazed by Shropshire sheep, as it approaches the Stiperstones ridge. Fine panoramas extend back to the Long Mynd and Church Stretton area as you climb.

Once on open moorland, you've a rocky, but level walk ahead, punctuated by the outcrops themselves, where you'll want to hunker down in the stones to enjoy the views and quiet. The return leg back to Bridges crosses more pasture and riverine fields, winding up at the Horseshoe Inn for one of the best pints of ale in the county.

At a glance

Where The Stiperstones ridge, 12km/7.5miles northwest of Church Stretton.
Why The finest views in the county; weird rock formations; a great pub: the Horseshoe Inn; sightings of raven, peregrines and red grouse.

When First week of June, for the annual Church Stretton Walking Festival.
Downsides No public transport during the week, or in winter.
Start/Finish The Horseshoe Inn, Bridges (SO393965).
Duration 3hrs 30mins.

Distance 12km/7.5miles.
Terrain Field paths giving way to uneven, rocky tracks on open moorland. Some small boggy sections towards the end of the route.
Maps OS Explorer 216, OS Explorer 217.

On weekends and bank holidays between May and September, it's possible to travel to Bridges from Church Stretton on the county council's walker-friendly Shropshire Hills Shuttle – a model service that allows you to improvise innumerable routes around the villages at which it calls.

Using the Shuttle, possible extensions to our walk take you down the deep, steep-sided combes, or "dingles", cleaving the western flank of the Stiperstones hill. Huddled at the bottom of these are a string of pretty Shropshire villages around which is scattered the detritus of former lead mines: rusting wheelhouses, crushing yards and grassed-over spoil heaps. Lead was excavated and smelted here since the time of the Romans, but the industry, which also produced barytes used in paint and paper manufacturing, peaked in the 1850s when it accounted for around ten percent of national production.

Mining continued in places until World War I. Since then, however, this part of Shropshire has reverted to a rural area, with sheep far outnumbering humans.

On your way

The Stiperstones ridge owes its distinctive appearance to a seam of Ordovician quartzite, forced upwards 480 million years ago by the same geological upheavals that formed Snowdonia. This was subsequently shattered and sculpted over successive Ice Ages into a string of sharp-edged outcrops, the most prominent of them the **MANSTONE** (536m/1758ft), **CRANBERRY ROCKS** and sharp-edged **DEVIL'S CHAIR**.

Local legend attributes the creation of these giant rock piles to the Devil himself, who is said to have rested here during journeys between Ireland and England. Once, he decided to fill one of the valleys nearby, Hell's Gutter, with rock carried in his apron from the Emerald Isle, but was foiled when its strings broke. Some locals insist that in the heat of summer you can still smell the brimstone sizzling on the stones.

The Devil's Chair, a razor-backed heap of pale-grey quartzite rising from the midpoint of the summit ridge, is where Satan is believed to reside when fog engulfs the hilltop. On the night of the winter solstice, he is also supposed to take up residence here, summoning all the witches, ghosts and evil spirits to elect their king for the year.

One of the many ghosts in attendance on the longest night is that of Wild Edric, a Saxon earl who rebelled against the Normans and is thought to ride across the moors hereabouts in the dead of night.

Mystery and legend surrounds the historical figure of Edric himself – a thorn in the side of William the Conqueror and his Marcher Lords, and leading light in the border rebellion that rumbled on for years

ABOVE: The Horseshoe Inn, Bridges – the start and end point of our route

ABOVE: Derelict tank at Near Gatten Farm – a surreal landmark amid the sheep fields of Shropshire

after the Conquest. Some say he was slain in the Battle of Stafford, others that he became an ally of the Normans in their expedition against Scotland in 1072. Either way, his ghost is still said to haunt the Stiperstones, returning from the dead when the country is threatened with invasion (his last appearance was in the run up to the Falklands War).

These days, the Stiperstones crest enjoys added protection as a National Nature Reserve. Rarities here include ring ouzel, raven, peregrine falcon, red grouse and emperor moth. Local biodiversity has been given a boost by the "Back to Purple" project, in which conifer plantations have been steadily replaced with the heather plants whose flowers cloak the ridgetop in a blaze of colour during late summer.

Almost as prolific at ground level are whinberry (aka "bilberry") bushes. For centuries, local people would flock here in season to harvest the eye-wateringly bittersweet, dark-purple berries, formerly used in the dye industry (as well as to bake delicious crumbles). Elderly villagers still recall the days when the "whinberry higgler" used to tour the villages buying up the crop for the dye factories in neighbouring Staffordshire.

From the time of Emperor Hadrian, however, the real economic mainstay of this border area was lead. Hadrian's mark has been identified on several "pigs" (or ingots) unearthed in the area, and remnants of mines and smelting chimneys still litter the western slopes of the hill, particularly around the village of Snailbeach.

Ruins of miners' allotments and hovels rest in the "dingles" on the western slopes of the Stiperstones hills. Many of them were originally squatters camps on common land: a local bye-law stated that any man who could build a chimney and light a fire in it between sunset and sunrise might lay claim to the plot afterwards.

Around many of the mining settlements look out for patches of unusual vegetation, colonized by plants such as sheep's fescue (*Festuca ovina*) which thrive on the high lead levels of heavy metals and salt in the soil.

An engaging account of the area's mining heritage is on view at the Bog Centre, on the roadside at the southwest tip of the hill; it also holds a small café (see "Eating & Drinking") and serves as a handy stop on the Shropshire Hills Shuttle.

Further around the Shuttle's circuit, Snailbeach, the largest former mining village in this area, also hosts a volunteer-run vistor centre (Easter–Oct only), where you get a taste of what life was like in the old underground levels by joining guided tours. Full details, along with a great virtual surface tour, are posted on the centre's website: www.shropshiremines.org.uk.

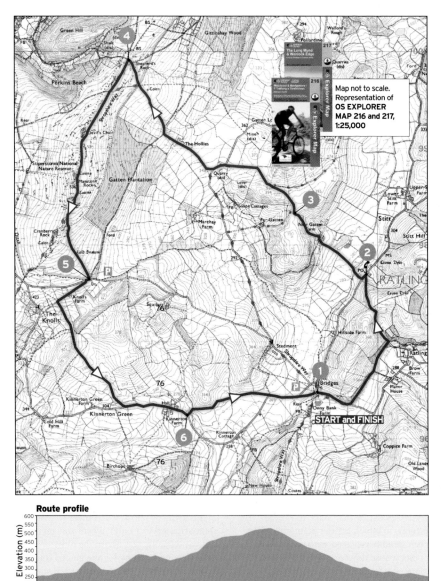

Map not to scale.
Representation of
**OS EXPLORER
MAP 216 and 217,
1:25,000**

Route profile

CHECKED BY
✔ Shrewsbury & Mid-Shropshire
Ramblers

1 Turn R out of the Horseshoe Inn, and R again up the lane past the YHA for 5mins until you reach stile and waypost on your L, pointing the route of the Shropshire Way. Bear R from the stile along the side of Darnford Brook, through a conifer plantation. After the next stile, turn L out of the woods up a stony farm track which swings steadily R towards a saddle between two low hillocks. Beyond the metal gate just after the pass, the track descends gently to the R through sheep pasture.

2 Once at the road at the bottom of the hill, turn L and immediately R up the lane towards Near Gatten Farm. Follow the track through the farm (past the old tank!), and up a smaller track which starts where the main one bends R towards red-brick houses (a waypost marks the turning). Keep heading uphill, through the metal gate and on to a low pass that's almost identical to the previous one.

3 At the pass, a stile on your R leads to a path arcing around the side of the ridge to another stile, where you bear R as indicated (although the views are better from the low hills to your L). The official

right of way drops to a metal gate and onwards across level marshland. On emerging at the metalled road, turn L and very soon after R towards Hollies Farm, via the Shropshire Way. Just beyond the farm buildings, the path passes through a metal gate, shortly before reaching a waymarked trail junction, marked with a fingerpost. Keep to the track bearing R, then turn L uphill towards the heath, as shown by a second waypost. Having passed a third metal gate you're on open NT-owned access land, where the paths diverge. Our route ascends gently to the R, reaching the ridgetop at Shepherd's Rock.

ABOVE: A raven soaring on the thermals above the Stiperstones

4 Turn L (SW) opposite the cairn and follow the broad, rocky track along the ridgeline to the **Devil's Chair** and then **Manstone Rocks** (536m/1758ft), where a trig point marks the highest point on the crest. The final outcrop is **Cranberry Rocks**, from where the path drops L through the heather to an interpretative panel and car park at SO369977. (For the Bog Field Centre, follow the road to your R out of the car park for 10mins.)

5 The return leg to Bridges starts diagonally opposite the car park exit, where a stile leads to a path between gorse bushes. This passes Knoll's Farm soon after: go through the yard gate, keeping the farm buildings to your L, until you reach a field and, soon after, a second gate where waymarkers indicate a bifurcation in footpaths at SO365974.
Turn L here, through a coppice and over a little plank bridge, ignoring the gap in the hedge to your R. Keep the trees to your R as you drop down the slope over the stile in the bottom corner of a marshy field. Continue across boggier ground fringed with gorse. From here, the path ahead across pasture is clearly visible. Proceed with the field border to your L – there's still a bit of wet ground to negotiate. After a couple more stiles you reach open fields at a low ridge, from where the route downhill is dry and well used. Follow the shallow combe down, keeping to the R of a grassy stream bed until you reach the hedge, where another stile opens onto the road at SO373963.
Turn L onto tarmac here. Follow the lane for 5mins, past Kinnerton

Farm, until you see a waypost pointing L through a metal gate.

6 From the turning, a broad, unsurfaced track fords a stream and rises to your R to cross a low grassy spur. Ignore the first gate on your R, instead taking the next R across a field to a stile at SO384964. In the final meadow (with a solitary oak in its centre) aim for the bottom R corner, where a path rises through a metal gate (wayposted) rejoins the road. Turn L towards Bridges and then R onto a signposted footpath, at a point where the road bends to your L – this brings you out directly opposite the pub.

🚌 Getting There
The trailhead for this walk is the pretty village of Bridges , 9km/5.5miles east of Church Stretton, or 30km/19miles southwest of Shrewsbury on the A49.
You can get there on the Shropshire Hills Shuttle minibus ✎www.shropshirehillsshuttles.co.uk, which runs from Shrewsbury to Bridges direct on weekends and bank holiday Mondays from May–Sept.

ℹ️ Visitor Information
The Bog Field Centre
Stiperstones Nature Reserve (SO356978)
📞01743 792484
✎www.bogcentre.co.uk

Church Stretton VIC
Church St, next to library
✎01694 722535

🍴 Eating & Drinking
The Horseshoe Inn
Bridges, SY5 0ST
📞01588 650260
✎www.horseshoeinnbridges.co.uk

Delicious, home-prepared bar snacks and main meals served in an oak-lined interior, with a crackling fire and top-notch Three Tuns ale from nearby Bishops Castle. Country pubs don't come much more alluring than this, and they host regular live-music sessions.

🛏️ Sleeping

The Horseshoe Inn
(As above)
Rooms with exposed wood beams and modern facilities in a detached stone cottage behind the pub. Comfortable, reasonably priced and perfectly placed for our route.

Bridges YHA
Bridge, Ratlinghope, SY5 0SP
📞01588 650656
✎www.yha.org.uk
Large, pleasant "Y" set in lovely gardens at the foot of the Long Mynd, just around the corner from the pub – and it's slap on the trail.

📱 More Info
✎www.shropshirewalking.co.uk. Dedicated site for walkers featuring short routes based around villages and inns, town trails, and GEOcaching hot spots.

✎www.churchstretton.co.uk. Local info for the town of Church Stretton.

✎www.shropshirehillsaonb.co.uk. The Stiperstones falls within the Shropshire Hills Area of Outstanding Natural Beauty, introduced here.

🚶 More Walks
Rambler's Guide to the Shropshire Way by Shropshire Ramblers (Pengwern Books). Guidebook for the whole of this 225-km/140-mile circular trail from Wem, with useful background and maps.

Tor Stories
Bowerman's Nose

Dartmoor has always been synonymous with ghoulish goings on. William Crossing's 1912 guide to the region – a 576-page magnum opus of legendary status locally, reminiscent of Wainwright, Tolkien and the Old Testament rolled into one – is packed with scary stories associated with the moor and its landmarks: an abbot who killed his horse and crawled into it to survive a blizzard; golden frogs; haunted crossroads; tin miners disappearing into the fog for days, only to be found by clairvoyant dowsers. Come here when the mist is down, and those eerie tors crowning the moorland hilltops will raise the hairs on the back of your neck. But under a big, sunny sky, Dartmoor's huge horizons and magnificent views can also inspire an exceptional sense of freedom.

Encompassing 368 square miles (953 square kilometres) of rolling moorland, peat bog, rocky rivers and gorges draped in deciduous forest, this is the largest and wildest expanse of open country in southern Britain. The gently curved hilltops at its heart, which rise to above 600m/1968ft in places, are crossed by few roads. You can walk for hours and only hear the sound of the wind in the grasses and the chirruping of larks high overhead. Yet Dartmoor was in former times a major population centre. The region holds more Bronze Age sites than any other in the UK, along with ruined Saxon villages, disused mines and Victorian quarries.

For the walker, the old tracks winding across the moor between these vestiges offer inexhaustible possibilities. Taking "great views" as its cue, our route squeezes the maximum impact from this unique landscape, starting at the quintessential Dartmoor village of Widecome-in-the-Moor, before climbing to the high hills encircling it via a series of spectacular viewpoints extending across the whole of Devon. Along the way, you're assured close encounters with wild ponies, a giant oak chair the height of a two-storey house, and prehistoric hut circles where local people would have enjoyed just the same uplifting views 3000 or more years ago. If you've the legs for it, a worthwhile detour is to the wonderful Warren House Inn, Dartmoor's highest pub.

At a glance

Where Widecome-in-the-Moor, northeast of Newton Abbot, Dartmoor, Devon.
Why Prehistoric hut circles, menhirs and stone rows; possible sightings of dippers, ring ouzels and wild Dartmoor ponies; the Giant's Chair.

When September, to coincide with Widecombe Fair.
Start/Finish Widecombe-in-the-Moor village green (SX719768).
Duration 5-6hrs.
Distance 16.5km/10.2miles.
Cut it Short The Giant's Chair,

13.2km/8.2miles.
Terrain Mostly open, gently undulating moorland, with some stretches across pasture and along quiet country lanes; includes a few short, steep ascents.
Maps OS Explorer OL28.

On your way

The landscape of contemporary Dartmoor bears little resemblance to what it would have looked like 5000 years ago. At that time, the 160 or more tors so prominent on hilltops today would have been engulfed by a vast broadleaf forest. When the climate warmed allowing Neolithic farmers to penetrate the uplands, however, most of the trees were burned off to make way for fields. But because the soil is so acidic, the forest never recovered. Only a few carefully protected fragments of it now remain, sheltered by inaccessible folds in the moor.

Following the disappearance of the tree cover, farming and herding continued through the late-Bronze Age, when tin and copper (the main constituents of bronze) were extensively mined in the area, and Dartmoor's inhabitants lived in large stone enclosures. You gain a vivid sense of what life must have been like for them at **GRIMSPOUND**, where a circle of heaped boulders ring the ruins of 24 huts dating from 1500–1300BC. Huddled in a hollow flanked by Hameldown and Hookney Tors, it's a superbly atmospheric site with fine views across the valley to ridges serrated by lonely stone rows and menhirs. Paved entranceways, L-shaped porches, hearths for peat fires and sleeping platforms are still discernable in some of the hut circles. Grimspound's chef d'oeuvre, however, is the monumental entrance on the south side of the enclosure, made from a pair of huge granite door jambs.

Pollen samples extracted from Grimspound suggest the site was probably deserted around 1300BC, when the climate grew suddenly colder and wetter. Seven or more centuries elapsed before the weather improved sufficiently to permit farming again. Just to the southeast of **HOUND TOR**, one of Dartmoor's most spectacular rock formations, you can see the remains of longhouses constructed around 500AD by Saxon settlers, alongside remains of later medieval cottages. A giant pile of weirdly shaped boulders, towers and clefts, Hound Tor has long fascinated visitors to Dartmoor. Conan Doyle was inspired to write *The Hound of the Baskervilles* after a visit, and the tor remains the subject of numerous local legends. In 2007, a walker claimed to have spotted a large, black, bear-like "beast" ambling around it. More bizarrely, an episode of *Eastenders* was also once filmed here.

From the approach to Hound Tor, a dramatic view opens up to the east across the head of the Becka Valley to Hay Tor – a colossal rhino horn of granite. The track cutting across the slope below it is all that's left of the stone tramway carved between 1776 and 1820 to transport rock, quarried nearby, to the harbour at Teignmouth (some of which ended up being used to build the old London Bridge). The route was recently converted into a long-distance footpath, the Templer's Way, named after the engineer responsible for the work.

Another famous Dartmoor rock formation rises to the north of Hound Tor, at the tip of Hayne Down. **BOWERMAN'S NOSE**, a 6.6-metre/21.5-feet tall pillar, stands alone above a so-called "clitter" of granite blocks that have fallen over the years from the outcrop of which it once formed the core. Resembling an old man in a flat cap, the statue stares mutely across a glorious sweep of walled pasture and moorland. Local legend has it that Bowerman was a hunter turned to stone by a coven of witches whose cauldron he mistakenly spilled.

On a quiet verge to the west of Bowerman's Nose rests a monument to a victim of an act of more earthly cruelty.

With a blank headstone standing at its head, the humble grave of **KITTY JAY** is the last resting place of a pauper's daughter who left the workhouse to enter the service of a local landowner in 1790 and fell pregnant by the son of the household. Cast out by the family and with no prospect of future employment, Kitty hanged herself. But suicide being deemed a mortal sin at the time, she could not be buried in a churchyard. Instead, her body was placed in a rough hole dug on the borders of the parish, at a lonely intersection of moorland tracks from where Kitty Jay's spirit could not return to haunt the god-fearing locals. For decades, fresh flowers have mysteriously appeared on it, said to have been placed there during the night by a hooded figure, while passersby leave lucky pennies and crosses made from twigs.

A construction of a rather more imperious nature stands in a field just west of Kitty Jay's grave. Placed at the head of a beautiful combe, the **GIANT OAK CHAIR** strikes an unlikely silhouette when seen from the village of Widecombe-in-the-Moor far below. It was commissioned by the

ABOVE: The Giant's Chair: an oak chair the size of a two-storey house is placed at the head of a beautiful combe

landowner and is made of English oak.

Visible in the valley below, **WIDECOMBE-IN-THE-MOOR** could be a contender for the crown of "most picturesque village in Britain". Enfolded by bracken-covered hills and a chain of craggy tors, the focal point of its pretty thatched cottages is the incongruously large Church of St Pancras. Often dubbed the Cathedral of the Moor, the Perpendicular-style church was built of local granite in the mid-fourteenth century, when Dartmoor stood at the epicentre of a boom in the wool trade and could afford such flights of ostentation. It was struck by lightening in the Great Thunderstorm of 1638 while an afternoon service was taking place inside. Eyewitness accounts at the time described a unnerving darkness, followed by an immense thunder clap and a "great ball of fire" that smashed through one of the widows and tore apart the roof, killing four members of the congregation and injuring many others.

Widecombe-in-the-Moor, of course, owes its fame – and enduring popularity as the moor's principal honeypot – to its annual fair, held on the second Tuesday of September; or more accurately, to the old folk song about the event featuring Uncle Tom Cobbley and All The ditty's long list of characters has furnished local shops with a lucrative sideline selling souvenirs to the stream of tourists who pass through in the summer to photograph the ponies on the green, and soak up the mood of the high moors.

The ideal antidote to the brouhaha of the green is the wonderful Rugglestone Inn, on the edge of the village, where you can contemplate your day's boot work over a perfect pint of Dartmoor Best.

For those who may find their navigation skills a little impaired afterwards, rest assured that help is at hand in the form of a team of local llamas, who accompany walkers on routes of various lengths to great viewpoints in the area. Picnic lunches and stops for cream teas may be included in the itineraries; see ✎www.dartmoorllamawalks.co.uk

Letterboxing

Dartmoor offers a terrific way to keep any children you may be walking with busy for hours while you recline and enjoy the views. Hidden in nooks and crannies on all of the tors in the national park are little "letterboxes", made from old ammunition cases or empty pill boxes. These contain a small stamp, an ink pad, notebook and instructions to help others find the spot (in the form of a simple grid reference or more cryptic clue), which you're supposed to pass on. The idea is that once located, collectors take an impression from the stamp, leave another with their own personal print in the letterbox's visitors' book, then replace the box where they found it. At the end of our walk, with enough determination and short side trips to tors adjacent to the route, you could end up bagging a dozen or more stamps.

"Letterboxing" is thought to have been invented by a local guide, James Perott, in 1854, after he left a glass jar at Cranmere Pool in the far north of Dartmoor for people to leave their calling cards in. Since then, countless other boxes have appeared across the moor. No official organization regulates the activity, although the Letterbox 100 Club publishes a full catalogue of clues. To become a fully-fledged member, you have to have collected one hundred stamps. Special badges are issued for people notching up 1000, 2000, 3000, 4000 and, unbelievably, 5000 letterboxes.

walk it 25   Bowerman's Nose

CHECKED BY
✔ **South Devon Ramblers**

1 Leave **Widecombe-in-the-Moor** village green with the Old Inn on your RHS, and follow the lane to the L past the church (turning signposted "Rugglestone Inn 1/4 mile"). Follow it downhill for 5mins to Venton Bridge, just before which a footpath crosses a stile to the L and runs over a field alongside a stream. Once you've reached the road, turn L and immediately R up the lane with a wood to your L. After a level start, the road begins to steepen as it nears the hamlet of Bonehill, levelling off at a break in the wall with granite posts each side and Bonehill Rocks rising to the R. You can take a short diversion south from here to Bonehill Rocks to hunt for the letterbox. Otherwise turn L opposite the car park, away from Bonehill, and follow the path uphill to Bell Tor.

2 From the foot of Bell Tor, a path drops down to the east, skirting the boggy, flat ground below to reach the road at SX739779, where you should turn L. After cattle grid, ignore the five-bar gate on your R and continue instead to the gate/stile and finger post, which leads on to Holwell Lawn and pony club access land. Follow a R fork across the field (E) past jumps until you arrive at a breach in an old drystone wall. Here you turn L and follow the wall in a northerly direction as far as a second wall running at right-angles to the first. A signposted stile then leads you to the start of a clear path, which forks L through bracken-covered moorland up to **Hound Tor**. It's well worth having a look around the rocks.

3 Skirt the west side of the tor, dropping down the far side to the car park. Turn L onto the junction at Swallerton Gate, walk past the house (on your L) and follow the middle of three lanes N (signposted "Manaton"). Some 5mins later you arrive at a metal five-bar gate: cross and follow the path to the R over Hayne Down and Bowerman's Nose rock formation (SX742804).

4 From Bowerman's Nose, retrace your steps back to the metal five-bar gate, on the far side of which a path strikes westwards (to the R), uphill across pasture and over hilltop via a series of five stiles and gates. The track eventually drops down to a road, on the far side of which stands **Kitty Jay**'s Grave.

5 Our route then continues along the wooded lane behind the grave, passing the **giant oak chair** to the L, shortly before arriving at another road just north of Natsworthy Manor.

6 You can cut the walk short here by turning L for Widecombe. Otherwise, look for the gate and signposted path diagonally opposite (to the L). This leads initially along the south flank of a conifer plantation but after 5mins starts to drift L. At a fork in the path 5mins later, bear R, heading for the saddle pass in the ridge above. Keep to the well worn path as it drops down the other side to **Grimspound**.

7 From the southern gateway of Grimspound, a clear path strikes SE, steeply uphill, to Hameldown Tor, where it begins

a 3-km traverse of Hamel Down. A useful navigation aid in poor visibility is the corner of the drystone wall at SX706792. The path hugs this wall, but peels L at Hameldown Beacon, arcing along the shoulder of the descending slope to the corner of another drystone wall at SX707776, where it turns L.

8 Follow this wall to a gate and the start of Green Farm Lane, where a chain and "No Access" sign block progress. Waymarks to the L lead instead around the boundary of Kingshead Farm via a series of stiles. They then bifurcate, with a R turn leading through a field down the side of an old stone wall; the farmhouse should be to your bottom R (if you reach a sign for "Widecombe" pointing the way you've come you'll know you've missed the turning and should backtrack to the path junction). At the farm driveway, turn L and drop steeply downhill via the lane for 5 mins, where you turn R for the village centre.

i **Visitor Information**
Dartmoor Information Point, Church House, Widecombe-in-the-Moor
☎ 01364 621321

The High Moorland Visitor Centre
Princetown
☎ 01822 890414
✐ www.dartmoor-npa.gov.uk

Letterbox 100 Club
✐ www.letterboxingondart-moor.co.uk. The letterboxing homepage, with complete clue catalogue. (See box opposite for more information.)

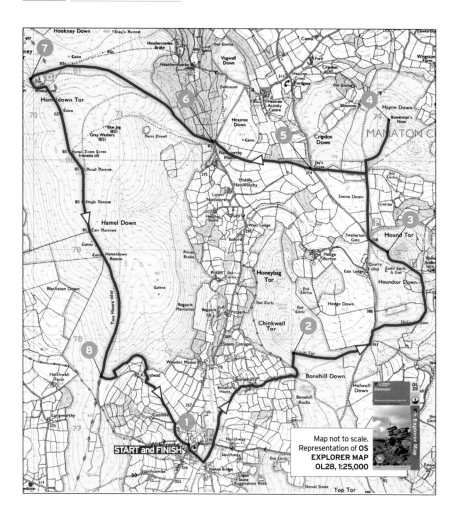

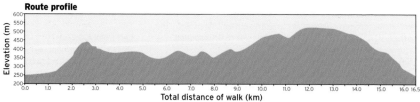

Route profile

Eating & Drinking
Rugglestone Inn
Widecombe-in-the-Moor
☎01364 621327
✐ www.rugglestoneinn.co.uk
Cosy, traditional Dartmoor pub,
located next to a pretty stream on
the outskirts of the village. Real
ales and quality home-cooked
food are served in an interior
warmed by an open log fire and
wood burner, or on picnic tables
out in the garden, where ducks will
relieve the unwary of their crisps.

Hound of the Basket Meals
Hound Tor car park
This mobile snack van is a modern
Dartmoor legend, serving around
twenty sorts of tea, tasty Brixham
crab sandwiches and garlic ham-
burgers. They even have their very
own letterbox stamp.

Warren House Inn
Postbridge
☎01822 880208
✐ www.warrenhouseinn.co.uk
The most famous pub on Dartmoor
– the third highest in England - at a
lonely spot slap in the middle of the
moors. With low oak beams and a
fire that has burned continuously
since 1845, it holds oodles of traditional atmosphere, and serves great
food (including a justly popular
rabbit pie) as well as hand-pumped
local ales. The catch is, the pub lies
a 90-min round trip from our route
(at SX674809): start at Grimspound
and follow the well-worn path west
via Headland Warren Farm – well
worth the detour, though allow
plenty of time for it.

Sleeping
Sheena Tower
Sheena Tower, Widecombe-in-the-
Moor, TQ13 7TE

**ABOVE: Ancient wayside cross, Hamel Down – probably converted
in the Dark Ages from a Neolithic standing stone**

☎01364 621308
Good value, secluded little B&B, high
on the hillside above Widecombe
(just off the Bovey Tracey road),
boasting fine moorland views. Some
en suite rooms available.

The Old Rectory
Widecombe-in-the-Moor
TQ13 7TB
☎01364 621231
In the centre of the village opposite
the post office, this charming
former vicarage is set in its own
organic cottage garden, with traditional interiors enlivened by South
American textiles. A notch pricier
than the competition, but worth
the extra.

More Info
Crossing's Guide to Dartmoor
(Peninsula Press). The definitive
guide to the region, first published
in 1912.

Dartmoor Guide
Free newspaper published annually
by the national park.

✐ www.widecombe-in-the-moor.
com. The village's information-
packed website.

✐ www.legendarydartmoor.co.uk.
A huge compendium of myths,
fables and history.

✐ www.virtuallydartmoor.com.
Combines oral history and archive
photographs with 360-degree
panoramas to explore various locations on the moor.

More Walks
*John Musgrave
Heritage Trail* (South Devon
Ramblers). The 56-km/35-mile
trail was created from a generous
legacy left by former South Devon
Ramblers chairman John Musgrave.
The trail is split into four managable
sections of between 9km/5.5miles
and 18km/11miles each. The guide
provides detailed commentary on
local heritage, maps and transport
links along the way. See also
✐ www.southdevonramblers.com/
johnmusgrave/the_trail.php.

walk | 26
SURREY

Hills, Mills and Gunpowder Cake

Leith Hill

He that in Winter should behold some of our highest Hills in Surrey clad with whole Woods ... might without the least violence to his Imagination, easily phansie himself transported into some new or enchanted Country.

John Evelyn, *Sylva*

The Surrey Hills were one of the first landscapes to be designated an area of outstanding natural beauty following the National Parks and Access to the Countryside Act of 1949. This tranquil corner of the county, where, as William Cobbett reports in his 1822 journal *Rural Rides*, "the nightingales are to be heard earlier and later in the year than in any other part of England" and "the first bursting of the buds is seen in spring, and no rigour of seasons can ever be felt," deserves special protection.

The area rises as the Hog's Back, a narrow chalk ridge just west of Guildford, and sweeps east to Kent along a row of smaller undulating hills creating a natural barrier between London's urban sprawl and the North Downs. Winding among these densely forested hills is the Greensand Way, a Ramblers-inspired long-distance path which traces a seam of greensand rock from Hindhead to Ashford in Kent. Leith Hill rises abruptly from this greensand ridge to a height of 294m/965ft above sea level, making it the highest point in southeast England. Its rapid elevation from the south opens up a superb panorama over the North Downs, the forested clay slopes of the Weald and the chalky South Downs beyond – and on a clear day some thirty miles to the English Channel. Our route, however, approaches Leith Hill from the north, along a gentle section of the Greensand Way winding through the beech and fir-combed hills; and the vista it leads to belies the minimal effort. "Should the atmosphere be clear, the view is such that can scarcely be matched elsewhere, at least a dozen counties being visible, as well as a glimpse of the sea," was how the celebrated nineteenth-century guidebook writer, Walker Miles, described it.

However, this calm backwater was not always so pleasantly wooded. It was dominated for over four centuries by the industrious Evelyn family who played a remarkable role in shaping the landscape of the Surrey Hills. One generation desecrated the area, another redeemed it.

At a glance

Where Holmbury St Mary, 11km/7miles southeast of Guildford, Surrey Hills AONB.
When April, for the Leith Hill Musical Festival.
Why Sleepy Surrey mill hamlets and "hammer" ponds; 360-degree view from Leith Hill Tower.
Downsides Infrequent public transport service.
Start/Finish Holmbury St Mary bus stop (TQ113441), one stop after the Royal Oak.

Duration 4hrs.
Distance 12km/7.5miles.
Terrain Wide well-maintained bridleways to Friday Street, then narrower forest tracks.
Maps OS Explorer 146.

The text on the plaque reads:

...E PROVIDED BY MEMBERS AND FRIENDS OF THE FEDERATION OF RAMBLING C...

...MUND SEYFANG TAYLOR ("WALKER MIL...

...RAMBLE... HELPED TO MAKE KNOWN THE BYWAYS OF THE...

1853   ...IED 19TH APRIL 1908.   BURIED IN GODSTO...

"STARE SUPER VIAS ANTIQUAS"

The view direction markers read:

LEITH 17
GIBBET HILL 69
DEVILS DYKE 26
HASSOCK 9
OXLEY'S 2
SHOREHAM GAP 24
ENGLISH CHANNEL 31
CISSBURY RING 22
CHANCTONBURY RING 24
AMBERIE 24

On your way

You reach **LEITH HILL** within an hour of setting out. The view from the summit is indeed impressive, but you'll need to fork out a modest sum to the National Trust, and ascend a further 20m/65ft to the top of **LEITH HILL TOWER** for the clear 360-degree view of over a dozen counties, which may include a glimpse St Paul's Cathedral, and as far north as the Chilterns.

Originally named "Prospect House", this Gothic folly was constructed by Richard Hull in 1766, possibly in an attempt to reclassify the hill as a mountain (ie over 1000ft). Hull was an eccentric gentleman who lived at the foot of the hill at Leith Hill Place, and insisted on his death that he be buried upside down beneath the tower, believing that the world would be "overturned" on judgement day. It seems his wish was fulfilled, as during restoration in 1984 his remains were discovered thus arranged, six to ten feet beneath the tower's base. He was left undisturbed and is there to this day.

However, it was the Evelyn family of Wotton and their domination of the Surrey milling industry from sixteenth century onwards that had a more lasting impact on the surrounding countryside. Over 400 years ago, George Evelyn learned the secret formula of producing cheap saltpetre during his military service on the Continent. The Evelyns were rewarded by none other than Queen Elizabeth I when she granted them the monopoly for the manufacture of gunpowder.

George wasted little time, and soon a number of large gunpowder mills, but also iron and paper works, sprang up along the banks of the river Tillingbourne. Many "hammer ponds" – artificial basins – were gouged along its course to power the waterwheels. The powder industry literally boomed. Indeed explosions were a frequent occurrence: one unfortunate worker was blown clean over the mill at

Walker Miles

If you look east from the top of Leith Hill Tower you'll see St Nicholas' Church at Godstone, where a distinctive sarsen stone marks the final resting place of "Walker Miles".

Born in Camberwell in 1853, Edmund Seyfang Taylor become proprietor of the family's printing and publishing firm, Robert Edmund Taylor and Son. It was through this publishing firm that he began to produce his meticulously written walks guides - most notably the Field-Path Rambles series - under the nom de "pun" Walker Miles. Even though Walker only lived to the age of 54, he published more than forty guides - thirty

volumes of FieldPath Rambles alone. He edited several outdoors journals and founded one of the first Ramblers groups, Forest Ramblers, in 1884. His prolific life and works saved many public paths from neglect.

The plaque at the top of the tower was provided by members and friends of the Federation of Rambling Clubs (now the Ramblers) in, "grateful memory of Edmund Seyfang Taylor (Walker Miles) whose Fieldpath Rambles helped to make known the byways of the countryside".

ABOVE: Friday Street's "hammer pond" powered George Evelyn's mill in the sixteenth century

Chilworth. Production became so intense that by the seventeenth century many of the surrounding hills had been stripped bare to supply the voracious mills with fresh timber and charcoal. William Cobbett in *Rural Rides* described local production as, "carrying into execution two of the most damnable inventions that ever sprang from the minds of men under the influence of the devil! Namely, the making of gunpowder and of bank-notes."

The last of the mills was decommissioned after the First World War, but their legacy is found in the sleepy Surrey mill hamlets of **BROADMOOR, FRIDAY STREET**, Abinger Bottom and Abinger Hammer – each depended on a watermill for its existence. Most of the hammer ponds are now used for growing watercress or farming trout, but our route passes the beautiful undisturbed pond at Friday Street which served a mill constructed by George Evelyn shortly after he purchased Wotton Manor in 1579. Also the short detour to the source of the Tillingbourne skirts the site of Brookmill and **BROOKWICK COPSE,** which

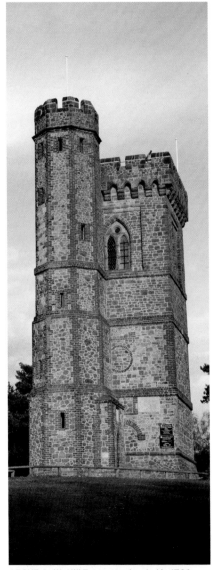

ABOVE: Leith Hill Tower, constructed in 1766 by Richard Hull, who is still buried beneath it

was enclosed by George Evelyn, despite bitter opposition at the time, to supply the mill at Abinger Hammer.

However, it is George Evelyn's grandson, the celebrated diarist John Evelyn, we have to thank for the abundance of coniferous branches shading the route today. He described the damage done by his family as "epidemical", and was determined to make amends. This, coupled with his passion for ecology, led to the publication of *Sylva or A Discourse of Forest-trees and the Propagation of Timber*; the first work devoted to the importance of tree conservation, which he delivered to the Royal Society on 15 October 1662. John Evelyn was perhaps also the first true environmentalist. A year earlier he published *Fumifugium or The Inconveniencie of the Aer and Smoak of London Dissipated*, which was a direct plea to Charles II following the Interregnum to nurture London's green spaces: "In a word, as the Lucid and noble Aer, clarifies the Blood, subtilizes it and excites it, cheering the Spirits and promoting digestion; so the dark, and grosse (on the Contrary) perturbs the Body ... And therefore the Empoysoning of Aer, was ever esteem'd no lesse fatall then the poysoning of Water or Meate it self."

Sylva and *Fumifugium* were the first such works to make clear the connection between the quality of the environment and the wellbeing of the individual. It was this revelation that sparked a profound shift in attitudes, which ultimately led to a programme of reafforestation in the Surrey Hills. You can take comfort from this if you lose yourself among the spider web of paths of **ABINGER COMMON** and **PASTURE WOOD** on the return leg to Holmbury St Mary.

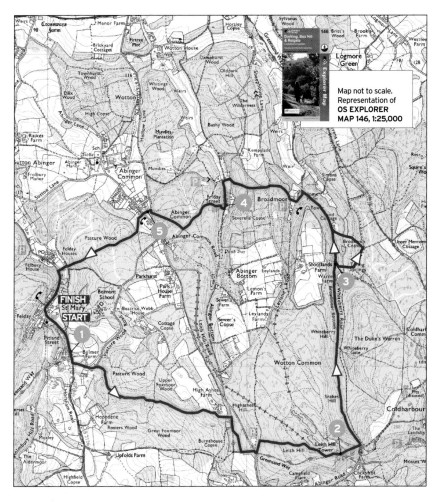

Map not to scale.
Representation of
OS EXPLORER MAP 146, 1:25,000

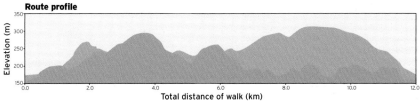

Route profile

26 Leith Hill

1 With Holmbury St Mary bus stop (one stop after the Royal Oak) on your L, turn L into Pasture Wood Road and walk past Bulmer Farm. Take the next R onto the Greensand Way (GW). Follow the GW through Pasture Wood for approx 20mins until you reach High Ashes Farm. Go past the farm and turn R at the fingerpost and continue on the GW, but take the first L to cut a corner and rejoin the GW 5mins later, where you turn L up the hill to a road. Cross the road and immediately turn L onto a footpath, ignoring the wide main track. After approximately 2mins turn R and a further 3mins fork L and continue, always on the upward path, until you meet a wide track. Turn R towards the open space ahead. Bear L towards **Leith Hill Tower** (TQ139431).

2 From Leith Hill, with the tower on your L, walk downhill on the Green Trail to a crossroads where you turn L along the GW again. There is now a pleasant descent through the woods lasting approx 20mins, passing a crossroads at Whiteberry Gate, past Warren Farm to the track junction.

3 An optional 30-min detour to the source of the Tillingbourne and **Brookwick Copse**: turn R towards Tilling Springs (signposted), and then L passing across the bridge over the Tillingbourne and uphill to a staggered gate. Turn L downhill just before the gate and follow the poorly defined track passing through holly and bracken of Brookwick Copse which eventually becomes marshland. Using the boardwalk provided follow the path uphill again to rejoin the GW at Pond Cottage. If you're not taking the detour, continue along the GW past Pond Cottage down to a road and riding stables at **Broadmoor**. Turn L up the road to Broadmoor and turn R on the path next to the Parish Council notice board. Bear R at the first fork and L at a second fork and press on uphill to a T-junction. Turn L and across two small roads and past the sign for the Wotton Estate. Continue through the woods past NT Severalls Copse down to the mill pond at Friday Street. Circle the pond round to the L and up to the Stephen Langton pub in **Friday Street**.

4 Carry on with the pub on your L up the lane and take the first R (unmarked footpath) at the gate into the woods of **Abinger Common**. Push through any overgrowth and climb the short steep woodland track which soon levels out. Continue (westerly), ignoring another path leading backwards, to reach a fork where you turn L (ignoring a small path to your R) to reach a five-way junction. Take the second R down through the woods, crossing another path. Continue for another 5mins ignoring small paths to R and L until you emerge on the road. Abinger Common bus stop is to your R (buses to Guildford and Dorking). To your L is a small green with a well, built by William John Evelyn (1893), and Goddards house, designed and built by Edwin Lutyens in 1898.

5 To continue back to Holmbury St Mary, cross the green and follow a well defined footpath through **Pasture Wood**, which starts nearly opposite the red phone box. Ignore all turnings L and R and stay on the main track until it starts to descend. Here leave the main track and head steeply downhill on a narrow forest path to a kissing gate (about 15mins). Continue straight ahead across the path junction turning L on the main road to reach Holmbury St Mary and the Royal Oak pub.

Getting There
Arriva bus 21 runs roughly every two hours (no service on Sundays or bank holidays) between Guildford and Redhill, calling at Gomshall, Holmbury St Mary, Abinger Common, Dorking and Reigate. The walk starts next to the bus stop at Holmbury St Mary (one stop after the Royal Oak). Go to www.arrivabus.co.uk or call Traveline on 0871 200 22 33 for a timetable.

The nearest train station is Gomshall (4km/2.5miles north of Holmbury St Mary) on the First Great Western line between Guildford, Dorking and Reigate.
www.nationalrail.co.uk
08457 484950 for details.

Visitor Information
Leith Hill Tower
National Trust Information Centre

☎01306 711777
✎www.nationaltrust.org.
Be sure to check opening times
and admission prices before
you leave.

🍴 Eating & Drinking
Royal Oak

Felday Road, Holmbury St Mary,
RH5 6PF
☎01306 730120
Seventeenth-century inn
overlooking the village green. It
is reported to have been visited
by Pitt the Elder and George II
on their way to Portsmouth to
review the fleet.

Stephen Langton Inn

Friday St, RH5 6JR
☎01306 730775
Named after the Archbishop
of Canterbury (1207-28) who
persuaded King John to sign
the Magna Carta in 1215. The
delicious menu features local
delicacies such as Tillingbourne
trout pâté and Abinger
watercress soup. All carefully
prepared and reasonably
priced, despite the pub's
popularity (particularly on
Saturday lunchtimes).

Abinger Hatch

Abinger Common, RH5 6HZ
☎01306 730737
Idyllic country pub on the
village green next to St James'
Church, the second-oldest
parish church in Surrey, dating
back to Norman times. The
village stocks, now preserved
next to the church, were in use
as recently as 1830.

🏠 Sleeping
Bulmer Farm

Holmbury St Mary, RH5 6LG

☎01306 730210
Seventeenth-century farmhouse
with oak beams and an inglenook
fireplace. B&B and self-catering
available. Ideally situated on
Pasture Wood Road at the start
of our route.

Holmbury Farm

Holmbury St Mary
RH5 6NB
☎01306 621443
A mile or two down the road from
Hombury St Mary towards Ockley,
this traditional farmhouse with
ancillary buildings and a tennis
court is a friendly, welcoming and
reasonably priced B&B.

YHA Holmbury St Mary

Radnor Lane
RH5 6NW
☎0845 371 9323
✎www.yha.org.uk
Ten minutes' walk from Holmbury
St Mary, the YHA provides a good
base to explore the Surrey Hills
on a budget.

📖 More Info

The Tillingbourne Story
by Gomshall & Peaslake
Local History Society (Shere).
Meticulously researched history
of the river's local and national
significance. Available from local
TICs.

✎www.lhmf.co.uk or ☎01403
240093 for **Leith Hill Musical
Festival.** The festival began in
1905 and specializes in choral
music. The composer Ralph
Vaughan Williams lived at Leith
Hill Place and was the festival
conductor for the first fifty years.

✎www.viewfinderpanoramas.
org. Topographs of over 100

viewpoints in Britain, including
views north and south from
Leith Hill.

✎www.ramblers.org.uk/info/
paths. More information on
the North Downs Way and
Greensand Way.

✎www.surreyhills.org. Website
for the Surrey Hills AONB.

🚶 More Walks

*Let's Walk...Farnham &
Beyond* by Farnham & District
Ramblers (Ramblers). Fifty routes
specially developed the group.
Walks range from 3km/2miles to
22.5km/14miles. Includes a walk
around the infamous Chilworth
Gunpowder Mills, and nearby St
Martha's Hill.

*25 Favourite Walks in West Surrey
& Sussex* by Godalming and
Haslemere Ramblers (Ramblers).
A varied selection of circular
walks with short and long options
between 5.5km/3.5miles and
25.5km/16miles.

*Another 25 Favourite Walks in
Surrey, Sussex and Hampshire*
by Godalming and Haslemere
Ramblers (Ramblers). The sequel
to the guide above, featuring
another selection of enticing
walks north of Guildford to the
Sussex coast. Distances vary
from 5km/3miles to 24km/
15miles.

Four Stations Way by Godalming
and Haslemere Ramblers
(Ramblers). Eleven-mile route
connecting Godalming, Milford,
Witley and Haslemere railway
stations. Includes Ordnance
Survey mapping.

Along The Bare Hill
British Camp

Some hilltop views inspire rapture, others a sense of doom. Some just evoke a mood of quiet, affirmatory contemplation – a feeling that all is as it should be in the world. The Malverns, on the Herefordshire–Worcestershire border, definitely fall into the latter category.

Dominating the Severn plain like the outline of a sleeping dinosaur, the range – roughly 10miles/16km from north to south – affords a sensational view across five counties. Admittedly, it's only just out of earshot of the M5, and on a clear day the messy fringes of Birmingham litter the northeastern horizon. But these blots are more than eclipsed by the vision of the patchwork floodplain of the Severn, and the idyllic farmland of deepest Herefordshire rolling west to the Welsh hills.

It's a quintessentially English view that has, over the centuries, cast a spell over many artists – most famously Elgar, whose Enigma Variations were written here. Auden penned a long love poem to the Malverns, where he taught for a spell in the 1930s,

and *Piers Plowman*, William Langland's fourteenth-century masterpiece, starts with a dream-vision of, "a fair fielde ful of folke," conceived while gazing from the ridgetop.

The classic walking route, popular since the spa boom of Victorian times, is the traverse between the two highest summits: Worcestershire Beacon (425m) in the north, and Herefordshire Beacon, aka "British Camp" (383m), in the south. Lined for most of its length with an Iron-Age earthwork, the ridge path crosses five named peaks, where outcrops of Pre-Cambrian gneiss – a kind of volcanic rock otherwise found only in the far northwest of Scotland – fall away to steep, grassy slopes carpeted in bracken, gorse and red banks of sorrel.

Once you're clear of the tree level, spellbinding views accompany the entire walk. Moreoever, thanks to the walker-friendly Hopper Bus service that loops around the hills on summer weekends, you can make it a linear trip, staying high all day and avoiding the long trudge back around the Malvern's wooded flanks.

At a glance

Where Great Malvern, Worcestershire.

Why Massive Iron Age fort; St Anne's well, with its spring-water spout and little Edwardian café; Great Malvern's eleventh-century Priory.

When Late spring sees rare High Brown Fritillary butterflies flitting around the violets.

Downsides The Malverns rank among central England's most walked open spaces, and get very crowded on weekends and summer evenings.

Start/Finish Great Malvern Priory (SO776458).

Distance 12km/7.5miles.

Duration 3hrs 30mins.

Terrain An initially steep ascent through woods and across open heathland gives way to more gentle gradients, all via clear paths, some sections of which are broad enough for wheelchairs.

Maps OS Explorer 190.

On your way

The "Bare Hill", or "Moel Fryn" as it was known to the ancient Welsh, has served as a place of spiritual and physical renewal since at least the eleventh century, when monks were attracted to the many springs and wells trickling from its lower flanks. A couple of monasteries were established on natural balconies close to the plain, drawing pilgrims from across Christendom during the Norman era. But the range was also a much troubled border. Along its spine, a long, undulating earthwork, still visible to this day, was for many centuries thought to be a survivor of the boundary dispute between Gilbert de Clare, the "Red Earl" of Gloucester, and the Bishop of Hereford in 1287. Dubbed "the Red Dyke" or "Shire Ditch" (because it separated two counties), the trench is now known to be of much greater antiquity than previously believed. Carbon-dating of its lowest layers revealed it was probably excavated more than five thousand years ago by the Iron Age settlers who resided in seasonal camps and grazed

ABOVE: The topograph, Worcester Beacon

their flocks here during the summer.

The town of **GREAT MALVERN**, at the northwest foot of the range, developed around the Norman **PRIORY** in the eleventh century, which started life as a Benedictine monastery but was bought by the locals after the Reformation for use as a parish church. Its pride and joy is the unrivalled collection of medieval wall tiles, sited behind the main altar, and some fine stained glass, including a window gifted by Richard III.

Malvern expanded rapidly during the water cure craze of the 1750s, and again with the arrival of the railway line a century later, when grand Victorian hotels and tree-lined avenues sprang up alongside the old Regency core. Wealthy benefactors paid for paths to be built around the hills, to which patients would be dispatched for bracing walks after a cold water dip, followed by a restorative round of the tea rooms, parks

ABOVE: Lady Foley's Tea Room

and promenades.

The best spot at which to savour Malvern's old spa ambience is **ST ANNE'S WELL**, nestled in a wooded combe at the foot of **WORCESTERSHIRE BEACON**. In a shelter next to the little café, ice-cold water gurgles from the mountainside into a marble font, below a panel recalling the popular rhyme that, "The Malvern Water, says Dr John Wall/Is famed for containing just nothing at all." Wall was the entrepreneur credited with mid-eighteenth-century rise of the resort, which blossomed despite the fact that local spring water was known to be devoid of health-giving minerals. Whether Dr Wall's doctorate was in medicine or spin, history doesn't record.

The tangle of pathways extending into the hills from St Anne's Well are today almost as well-used as they were in the town's Victorian heyday – albeit by iPod-wearing joggers, parascenders and dog walkers rather than ladies in crinoline skirts. Then, as now, they were maintained through the offices of the Malvern Conservators, a body set up by act of parliament in 1884 to protect the hills from quarrying.

One of the Conservators' notable recent successes has been the installation of a wheelchair-friendly route to the top of windy Worcestershire Beacon. The viewpoint is crowned with a brass "toposcope" on which is inscribed the position of every town, village and landscape feature visible from the spot. Dating from 1899, the plate was engraved from a drawing by Arthur Troyle Griffith, a close friend of Elgar (he later inspired Enigma Variation No.7). In February 2000, thieves made off with the antique, but it was retrieved by police and restored to its original position soon after.

The pass to the south of Worcestershire Beacon, where the B4218 crosses the ridgetop at **UPPER WYCHE**, marks the start

ABOVE: Malvern's eleventh-century priory started life as a Benedictine monastery

of the wheelchair route to the range's high point. In times past, this same gap through the Malverns was a landmark on an important salt route stretching from the River Severn (only 11km/7miles east of here) into the Welsh border region.

To its south rise the stepped ramparts of **HEREFORDSHIRE BEACON**, or "British Camp", as the fort carved from the hill's summit is known. Originally dug by Iron Age settlers in the third century BC, they were later re-modelled by the Normans into a motte-and-bailey castle. The view from the camp ranks alongside that from Worcestershire Beacon, only with the added interest of the Malvern Hills themselves, which taper northwards to the Midlands, rising and falling in a majestic arc.

walk it | 27

Britium Camp

1 Turn L out of the main entrance to the priory onto Church St, which will bring you out on Wells Rd (with the TIC to your R). Bear L up the rise onto Belle Vue Terrace, cross the road and look for the wrought-iron gate entrance to Rose Bank Garden next to the Mount Pleasant Hotel, where a sign to "St Anne's Well" marks the start of our footpath. Ninety-nine steps lead you onto Foley Terrace. At the top, follow a footpath sign leading to **St Anne's Well**.

2 Walk along the broad, stony track behind the café for about 2min to the first path junction, keep straight on and drop down for 2 mins to a second junction. Turn L here uphill through a wooded combe and alongside the stream. After 5mins take a L fork, which brings you out on a wide gravel track (Lady Howard De Walden Drive). Follow this track for a minute and take the middle rising track around hillside for about 3mins to a rocky outcrop. Bear L and follow the slope steeply to summit of North Hill (397m).

3 From North Hill, drop due W down a clear path to a saddle below, then up the other side to Table Hill (373m). Turn L (SSW)

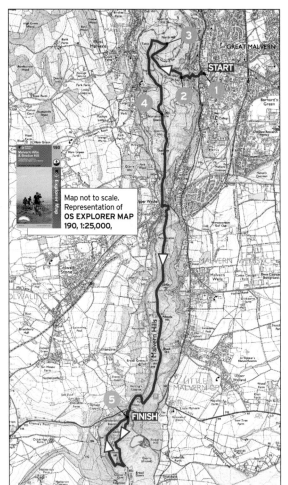

Map not to scale.
Representation of
**OS EXPLORER MAP
190, 1:25,000,**

Route profile

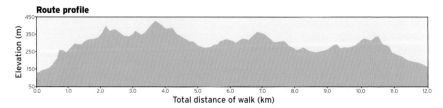

at the summit and keep to the descending path, which starts to scale Sugarloaf Hill (368m) via an obvious ridge route. The onward way from there, along the main Malvern ridge to a second pass and five-way junction (marked with a circular, stone topo-beacon) is clear. Continue uphill to **Worcestershire Beacon** (425m).

4 It's simple walking from the summit of Worcestershire Beacon all the way south, over Summer Hill and down to the road and car parks at **Upper Wyche**. The onward path begins to the L (E) of the pass, and presses steeply uphill to crest a series of four peaks: Perseverance Hill, Jubilee Hill, Pinnacle Hill and, finally, Black Hill. As you approach Wynds Point, the path drops R and follows the B432 briefly to arrive at the snack stall and hotel opposite the British Camp car park.

5 Take the lower (L) of the two paths leading from the car park, which contours around the east flank of the hill fort, above Tinker's Hill reservoir. At the saddle pass below Millennium Hill, follow the well-made footpath up towards the summit. The best views are from the very top of **Herefordshire Beacon** itself, from where a gentle descent takes you back to the car park. Buses for Great Malvern stop next to the snack bar.

Getting There
Great Malvern is served by regular rail and bus connections to most towns and cities in the Midlands and beyond. The town boasts two train stations:

"Malvern Link", to the north, is closest to the hills, but possesses less charm than "Great Malvern", further south.

Visitor Information
Great Malvern's award-winning TIC is on Wells Rd, at the top of Church St.
☏ 01684 892289

Eating & Drinking
Lady Foley's Tea Room
Eastbound platform of Malvern train station.
A town institution and a real period piece, little changed since Victorian times. Does teas and light lunches.

St Anne's Well Café
St Ann's Road, Malvern
☏ 01684 560285
www.hillsarts.co.uk/stannswell
Serves tasty vegetarian and vegan food, and famously delicious home-baked cakes. Open daily Easter–Oct; Sat & Sun in winter.

The Nags Head
Bank St, Malvern
☏ 01684 574373
Eccentric old pub serving the town's best real ales and popular

bar meals, which you can tuck into in a flagstone-floored interior.

Sleeping
Old Country Farm
Mathon, WR13 5PS
☏ 01886 880867
www.oldcountryhouse.co.uk
Quality B&B in a beautiful 600-year-old house, set in a large garden – though you'll need to catch a bus to West Malvern to reach it.

Harmony House
184 West Malvern Rd, WR14 4AZ
☏ 01684 891650
www.harmonyhouse
malvern.com
Another delightful little B&B, on the west side of the Malvern Hills, with great sunset views.

More Info
www.malvernhills.org.uk.
Home page of the Malvern Hills Conservators.

www.malvernhillsaonb.org.uk.
Geology, landscape and wildlife, from the Area of Outstanding Natural Beauty board.

www.malvern-hills.co.uk.
Privately run site featuring reams of in-depth background on the hills.

The Hills Hopper

The Hills Hopper is a special summer-only weekend (and bank holiday) service designed for walkers, which makes a circuit of the hills seven times daily. You pay a flat fare, which entitles you to jump on and off as many times as you like at stops that include Wyche Cutting and British Camp – perfect for anyone thinking of extending our featured route. Timetables are available from the tourist office, and can be downloaded from www.malvernhillsaonb. org.uk. Local bus service 675 also runs between Great Malvern and British Camp, starting at the bus shelter below Rose Bank Garden.

Three, Three, the Rivals
Yr Eifl

Ever wondered what that odd line about "the Rivals" in "Green Grow the Rushes-Oh" means – the one before the "two, two, lilly white boys, dressèd all in green-a-ho"? No-one really knows for sure, but the most convincing answer is that it refers to a trio of shapely hills on the Lleyn peninsula in North Wales. Known collectively as Yr Eifl (literally "The Fork" in Welsh), the peaks were much loved landmarks on the old Pilgrims Road to Bardsey Island, heralding the end of a long journey for weary travellers from England, who Anglicized their Welsh name to "the Rivals".

A cameo appearance in a surreal folk song of arcane origins would be not un-typical for this charismatic landform, mentions of which crop up in many old stories, legends and chronicles, suggesting it must have enjoyed greater fame among our ancestors than it does today. Largely ignored by the streams of holiday makers who pass them en route to the beaches further west, the Eifl hills nevertheless offer three irresistible reasons to travel to the Lleyn.

The first is the way they rise so abruptly from the peninsula's rocky north coast, against an epic backdrop of churning Atlantic surf and wild mountains. The second is the presence on the easternmost peak, Tre'r Ceiri, of a magnificent hill-fort, known locally as the "Town of Giants". A chaos of granite spilling down slopes of heather and whinberry scrub, the eagle's nest citadel preserves ramparts over which sentries would have stepped seventeen or more centuries ago.

A walk around it serves as a fine appetizer for the third of the Eifl's unique attributes: the stupendous views from the top of the highest hill, Garn Ganol. Thanks to its seaside location, this miniature Mount Fuji yields a grandstand view inland to the giants of the Snowdonia range, and south across Cardigan Bay to the Rhinnogs, Preselis and distant carns of St David's Head. To the west, you can also see the tops of the Wicklow Hills floating above the Irish coast, and even the mountains of County Mourne in Northern Ireland. But the real wonder, visible only on the clearest of clear days, is the silhouette on a strip of horizon beyond Anglesey and the Menai Straits of Helvellyn – an amazing 193km/120miles away.

At a glance

Where Yr Eifl, Lleyn peninsula, North Wales.
Why Views stretching from the Lake District to County Wicklow, and inland to Snowdonia; one of Britain's best preserved pre-Roman hillforts.

When Late summer, for the purple heather.
Downsides Bus services infrequent; no decent pubs or cafés close to finish point.
Start/Finish Llithfaen village (SH 356432), on the B4417,

16km/10miles north of Pwllheli.
Duration 3hrs.
Distance 6km/3.7miles.
Terrain Clear trails on open moorland, with short, but steep ascents and descents.
Maps OS Explorer 254.

On your way

Yr Eifl is one among a dozen or so low hills, here known as garns, that carbuncle the face of the Lleyn. Jutting more than sixty kilometres/thirty-seven miles into the Irish Sea from the Cambrian Coast, the promontory feels more like an island than a peninsula: remote, exposed to the elements, and with a distinctive maritime light that is at its most magical on clear evenings, when the setting sun casts a red glow across the mountains of Snowdonia just inland.

Centuries before Edward I subdued the Welsh princes and erected his "Iron Ring" of castles along the Cambrian coast, its name was synonymous with monks, pilgrims and pirates. Celtic Christians poured in their thousands across it to worship at Ynis Enlli (Bardsey Island), in defiance of perilous currents and the threat of Viking raiders.

Today, the Lleyn is a staunch bastion of Welshess: seventy to eighty percent of the local population are native Welsh speakers – the highest proportion in the Principality. It was near here that the Welsh nationalist party, Plaid Cymru, was born, and where the militant Meibion Glyndwr – Sons of Glyndwr – began their campaign of fire-bombing English-owned holiday cottages in the 1970s and 1980s.

One way to endear yourself to the Lleyn's Welsh speaking locals is to pronounce Yr Eifl correctly: ur (rolling the "r") ey-vul (with the stress on the "ey").

The Lleyn's role as a last stronghold for beleaguered Celts has deep roots, if the sixth-century chronicles of Saint Gildas are to believed. After the fall of the Roman empire, the Brythonic warlord Vortigern, leader of the ancient Britons, is said to have taken refuge here from the Saxons' westward advance. Known in Welsh as "Gwrtheryn", Vortigern it was whom Gildas blames for originally inviting the Anglo-Saxons to these shores to help him fend off the marauding Picts in the northeast. But the Germanic mercenaries stayed behind after the war and eventually usurped their former master, spreading devastation across Britain.

Vortigern ordered a chain of fortresses to be built in this distant corner of Wales, where he planned to make his last stand against the Saxons. Among them, or so it is believed, was the one encircling the crown of

The Lleyn Coastal Path

It's hard to think of a better way to spend a week than following the wonderful Lleyn Coastal Path from Caernarfon to Porthmadog. Covering a total of 146km/84miles, it winds around the whole peninsula, taking you to some of Britain's wildest and most compelling seaside landscapes, as well as making regular detours inland to hilltop viewpoints such as Yr Eifl.

Other highlights include Criccieth Castle, the whitewashed fishing village of Aberdaron, where pilgrims used to set sail for Ynys Enlli (Bardesy Island) in the Dark Ages, Porth Neigwl (Hell's Mouth), one of the UK's top surfing beaches, and a string of isolated, gold-sand coves where you can spot seals and dolphins in the summer months. Gwynedd Council pub-lishes a booklet with maps to accompany the walk, broken into eight stages, which you can download for free from ✐www.gwynedd.gov.uk, or purchase at local tourist offices. They're also available by post from Gwynedd Council's Tourism & Marketing Service, Council Offices, Caernarfon LL55 1SH; enclose a cheque or postal order for £1.

TRE'R CEIRI. Whether or not the great chief Gwrtheryn actually had a hand in the construction of the hilltop citadel is a matter of conjecture. More certain is that Tre'r Ceri was inhabited over two distinct phases: one during the late Bronze Age, between 800 and 400BC, and the other towards the end of Roman occupation, in 200–400AD.

It was from this latter period that the 150 or so drystone hut circles enclosed within the fort date. Locals refer to them as the "Town of Giants" or Cytiau Gwyddelod ("Irishman's Huts"), recalling the influx of Celtic immigrants from across the sea who settled here in the late Roman era. Between three- and four-hundred people would have subsisted on this windy hilltop, keeping cows and sheep, and cultivating crops on the terraces whose remains protrude in places through the heather. A grassed-over gateway still stands intact, as do sections of the ancient ramparts.

ABOVE: The drystone hut circles enclosed within the fort are over 1500 years old.

In *The Matter of Wales*, Jan Morris thought the whole scene, "rather homely . . . one can quite comfortably fancy the comings and goings up the track, the shouts of the watchmen at the gate, the cattle grazing in their stony enclosures, the kitchen fires smoking into the sky, the squabbling children and barking aboriginal dogs."

For a magnificent view over the Irish Sea, you have to descend from the fort and scale the larger summit to the west, **YR EIFL** (564m/1850ft). Although only half the height of Snowdon, the peak reveals a panorama of wondrous proportions, with lines of sight connecting the mountains of southern Ireland with those of the Lake District – not to mention the entire Snowdonia range spread inland.

If you half close your eyes and blot out the ribbon of little towns and roads running along the north Welsh coast from the Menai Straits, it's a vista than can have changed little since Vortigern's day.

At the western foot of Yr Eifl, a narrow, wooded sea combe named Bedd Gwrtheryn – "Vortigern's Valley" – is where local tradition holds the great warlord lies entombed, "clad in green armour."

Granite gouged from the surrounding hillsides in the nineteenth century provided pavements for London and – for reasons known only to aficionados of winter sports – top-grade curling stones. The quarrymen and their families were housed in two rows of stone cottages, cowering at the base of the hills facing the open sea.

With the quarries long closed, these houses now accommodate the Nant Gwtheryn Language and Heritage Centre, where adults from across the world attend residential courses in Welsh.

Yr Eifl

1 From the crossroads in the centre of Llithfaen, walk E

along the B4417 for a couple of minutes in the direction of Caernarfon as far as a turning on your L opposite a small chapel. Follow the lane uphill until you pass

the last of the houses to reach open moorland.

2 Head L from the fork in the track at SH359437 along the

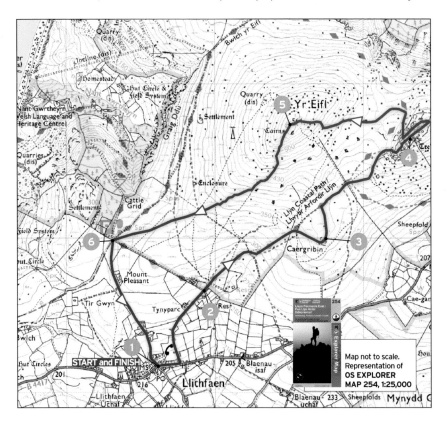

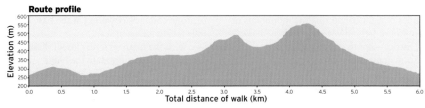

Route profile

Lleyn Coastal Path keeping the day's first objective, Caergribin, firmly in your sights. Stay on the main trail, which runs L of the hilltop, but after the black kissing gate turn R onto a narrower path for the final climb to the rocky summit.

3 Follow the little path running N off the top of Caergribin, dropping through the heather to rejoin the LCP. Turn R when you reach the latter, which continues NE to cross a drystone wall via a big ladder stile. It then drifts R before switching L up the hillside towards the southwestern entrance to the **Tre'r Ceiri** hillfort. An obvious path leads towards the summit of the hill, at the top R corner of the enclosure.

4 Having admired the view, continue ahead in the same direction, as far as the perimeter wall, then turn L, following the inside of the wall past a tunneled entrance. Keep going, and you'll soon arrive at the main gateway on the W side of the enclosure, marked with an interpretative panel – it's not far from the one through which you entered the fort. Head through this to reach a second paved entrance, where you exit the enclosure and bear R along a narrow path that soon after swings L (W) towards the pass below. Continue in the same direction from the saddle dividing Tre'r Ceiri from Yr Eifl (also known as "Garn Ganol"), and keep R when you reach a fork in the trail. The correct route is obvious, winding more steeply uphill via grassy patches through the rocks to **Yr Eifl**'s summit trigpoint and ancient cairn, from where the view is magnificent.

5 For the descent from the top of Yr Eifl/Garn Ganol, follow the trail leading SW from the summit – orientate yourself by steering towards the tip of the Lleyn if you can see it, passing between two lesser rocky summits. After a steep start, the path eases off as you lose ground. Once past a tumbledown stone wall, it bends westwards across open, bracken-covered moorland towards the junction of a forestry road and quarry track at SH353440, to the north of which lies a large council car park and toilet block. Keeping the car park to your R, head L (S) down the lane, past a row of houses and on for another 600m/650yards to regain Llithfaen village.

Getting There
Nefyn bus number 27 bus runs daily to Llithfaen from Pwllheli, the nearest railhead to our walk. Timetables are viewable online at ✎www.traveline-cymru. org.uk, or can be checked by phone ✆0781 200 2233.

Visitor Information
Pwllheli TIC, Min y Don Sgwar yr Orsaf. ✆01758 613000

Eating & Drinking
Ty Coch Inn
Porth Dinllaen, Nefyn
✆01758 720498
✎www.tycoch.co.uk
Surely one of the best situated pubs in Britain, nestled at the head of a sweeping sandy bay just up the coast from Yr Eifl. It's only accessible on foot, via a 10-minute walk along the beach. In the summer you can take your drinks outside, and sit on the old stone wall with the sand literally at your

feet, enjoying superb sea views. The food isn't up to much, but the location can't be bettered.

Sleeping
Tir Bach Campsite
Pistyll, 3.6km/2.2miles southwest of Llithfaen towards Nefyn
LL53 6LW
✆01758 720074
Well kept site, comprising just a couple of small, sloping fields on the cliffs next to the road. Facilities are basic, but the sea views are in a class of their own.

Nanhoron Hotel
St Davids Road, Nefyn, LL53 6EA
✆01758 720203
✎www.nanhoronhotel.com
Don't be put off by the rather grand façade of this roadside hotel, in the historic village of Nefyn, 6km/3.7miles southwest of Llithfaen. Its offers particularly good value for the area, and is well placed for the nearby beaches, though rates rise in the summer holidays.

More Info
✎www.viewfinderpanoramas. org. Scroll though their Wales list to find a marvellous colour-coded summit panorama from Yr Eifl, identifying all the landforms theoretically visible from the summit.

✎www.llyn.info. Online guide to the Lleyn.

More Walks
Collins Rambler's Guide: North Wales by Richard Sale (Collins/Ramblers). Thirty walks over a range of distances and levels of difficulty exploring the main mountain groups of Snowdonia National Park.

On the Bonnie, Bonnie Banks...

Conic Hill

I mind where we parted
In yon shady glen
On the steep, steep side
O' Ben Lomon'
Where deep in purple hue
The highland hills we view
And the morn shines out
Frae the gloamin'
From *Loch Lomond*, traditional

It's hardly surprising that Scots the world over are wont to burst into song at the very mention of Loch Lomond. Cradled by astounding scenery, the banks of Britain's largest lake are indeed as bonnie as the lament suggests – though it's a kind of beauty which, like that of all great actors, owes its drama less to absolute symmetry than a unique flaw. Look to the south of the loch and you'll notice clustered at its bulbous bottom end a handful of wooded islets ranged in a distinct line. This is the Highland Boundary Fault – the precise point at which the gentle, rolling Lowlands of Scotland collide with the more rugged terrain of the Highlands.

The fault slices diagonally for 250km/

155miles, from the Isle of Arran northeast to the Aberdeenshire coast. But nowhere is it so splendidly manifest as from the top of Conic Hill, overlooking Loch Lomond. A continuation of the line sketched by the islands in the lake, Conic's six-peaked ridge actually straddles the Boundary Fault, affording a front-row seat for one of the great geologic marvels of Britain.

This powerful viewpoint is far from a secret, however. Loch Lomond is a favourite playground for Glaswegians, and Balmaha, the tiny village where our route starts, among its established honeypots. But the view is no less resplendent for all that. Tapering northwards from the fringes of the distant city, across the island-speckled waters of the loch into the depths of the Highlands, it packs the full gamut of Scottish landscapes into a single glorious panorama.

Making use of the West Highland Way, our route takes you from the shores of Loch Lomond to the ridgetop in a steady, 350-metre ascent. It then drops steeply to rejoin the long-distance route for a gentle march across moorland and forest to road level.

At a glance

Where Conic Hill, Balmaha, on the southeast shore of Loch Lomond, Scottish Highlands.
Why views of the Highland Boundary Fault and Britain's largest body of fresh water; boat trips to nearby islands; terrific pub.
When Autumn, when the colours are legendary.

Downside The last half hour of the route is along a road (though this can be avoided by catching a bus).
Start/Finish Balmaha (NS420909), 10.5km/6.4miles northwest of Drymen, or 34km/21miles northwest of Glasgow.
Duration 3hrs.

Distance 10.5km/6.5miles.
Cut it short Conic ridge, 6.3km/3.9miles.
Terrain Clearly defined paths crossing conifer forest and open uplands, with some rocky, stony stretches. Expect plenty of water on the paths after rain.
Maps OS Explorer 347.

On your way

Loch Lomond owes its fjord-like splendour to the grinding action of glaciers during the last Ice Age. By that time, the Highland Boundary Fault had already existed for hundreds of millions of years. During the so-called Caledonian Orogeny era, the tectonic plate holding the lowlands drifted northwards, crumpling the land beyond it into hundreds of high mountains and valleys.

Looking down on Loch Lomond from the top of **CONIC HILL**, you can trace the precise point the plates collided. The line marks a stark shift in geology. On one side, the sedimentary sandstone of the south and east; on the other, the metamorphic shale and granite of the northwest. The hill itself is composed of what's known locally as "pudding stone" – conglomerate rock made of differently sized pebbles packed together in finer sandstone. It is thought to have originated in what was, 500 million years ago, a Himalayan-scale mountain that has since eroded away.

The boundary fault also forms an ancient cultural frontier. For many centuries, Highlanders and Lowlanders clashed along the shores of Loch Lomond. It's no coincidence that the last great clan battle to be fought in Scotland, the Battle of Glen Fruin (1603), took place in a valley running off the lake, pitting the MacGregors and their allies against the Colquhouns.

Thereafter, Highland clansmen restricted their plundering largely to smash-and-grab cattle raids – which were invariably followed up by offers of expensive "protection" to their victims. Rob Roy, born in a village on the northeastern shore of Loch Lomond, numbered among the clan leaders who perfected this form of extortion, which in time came to be known as "black mail" because the poor cattle farmers whom the reivers generally attacked could only afford to pay in grain or meat, as opposed to silver ("white mail").

Cattle were traditionally driven from their Highland grazing lands via the shores of Loch Lomond to the big market, or "tryst", at Crieff. As Glasgow grew in size, so did the scale of these mass "droves", which by the end of the eighteenth century were being squeezed from their traditional lakeside route into the hills by the imposition of heavy tolls. Herds even used to be swum en masse across the loch to circumvent the payments. Eventually, though, it was the advent of the Glasgow to Balloch railway line rather than the road charges that sounded the death knell for this ancient tradition.

Along with the railways in the 1840s came the first wave of pleasure seekers to Loch Lomond. Paddle-steamers built in the shipyards of the Clyde to transport timber and stone were converted for use as cruisers, shuttling paying passengers between the lochside villages, which over time grew into little resorts. Having made her final commercial trip in 1981, the last of the steamers, *Maid of the Loch*, came to rest at Balloch Pier, where she's currently undergoing a Heritage Lottery-funded refit.

Measuring 36km/22.5miles from north to south, and 8km/5miles at its widest point, Loch Lomond is the largest body of fresh water in Britain – by surface area, if not by volume (that prize goes to Loch Ness). The forty or so islands dotted across it (the number fluctuates according to water levels) are mostly natural, though some – such as Clairinish, at the foot of Conic Hill – are thought to be crannogs, created by the loch's prehistoric population.

Scotland holds an estimated six hundred such constructions, made by driving axe-sharpened piles around an existing islet into the lake bed. These would then be interwoven with branches and wattle, and the resulting enclosure filled with peat and clay, on top of which hearth stones would be laid. Access would have been by dugout canoe, or a wooden causeway whose surface rested just below that of the water to conceal it from would-be attackers.

It's not clear when Clairinish ceased to be occupied, but its larger neighbour – long, thin, densely forested Inchailloch – shows evidence of settlement spanning from Neolithic until Victorian times. The island's name, derived from the Irish for "old woman", harks back to the early eighth century when a female Christian missionary from Ireland named St Kentigerna founded a hermitage here. A nunnery was added in the twelfth century, with a church dedicated to the saint's memory to which worshipers from the mainland rowed every Sunday for five hundred years. Members of the legendary Clan MacGregor considered its graveyard hallowed ground; clan oaths were traditionally sworn on the memory "of those who sleep beneath the grey stones of Inchailloch".

Given over to forestry in the nineteenth century, the island is today managed as a nature reserve and technically deserted, although it receives around 20,000 visitors annually. A little boat ferries passengers across from **BALMAHA** to the jetty at Port Bawn on its south side, near the start of a trail winding through the oaks and firs to Inchailloch's summit – a famous viewpoint looking north across the loch's archipelago to the peaks north of the lake.

A former forestry settlement where the oak from Inchailloch used to be distilled to make wood vinegar (a source of acetic acid), Balmaha itself holds little of interest beyond the snug, timber-lined bar of the Oak Tree Inn, just above the village's tiny marina. But

ABOVE: The jetty at Balmaha, on the southeast shore of Loch Lomond

as the site of a large national park car park, springboard for the Macfarlane & Son boat cruises, and an overnight stop on the West Highland Way, it sees plenty of through traffic.

Walkers heading further up the eastern shore of the lake towards the start of the path up Ben Lomond also pause to re-provision at the village store, home of famous Balmaha Bears. Decked in their dapper embroidered jumpers, tammies and bespoke tartan scarves, the miniature Caledonian bears even boast their own series of childrens' books, which you can browse while ordering your mug of steaming broth.

Plodding back into the village after the circuit of Conic Hill, most walkers' thoughts tend to turn to the well-earned pint awaiting in the Oak Tree. But it's well worth setting aside half an hour for the short detour to Craigie Fort, the headland enfolding the north side of Balmaha marina. The site of a prehistoric bastion, it too affords a formidable view over the loch, at its most mesmeric around sunset time on winter evenings, when the snow peaks to the north may be illuminated in red alpenglow.

1 Apart from the short detour over the ridgetop of **Conic Hill**, our route sticks faithfully to the course of the West Highland Way, which is well waymarked and easy to follow throughout. To pick it up, walk past the national park visitor centre to the top of the car park in **Balmaha**, where you'll find the start of a broad forest trail through the conifer plantation. Bear R, and follow the track until you see a sign pointing L. From here, the path starts to narrow and rise, growing gradually steeper as it emerges from the trees and then swings L up a rocky stream bed to crest a saddle in the Conic ridge known as "Bealach Ard" ("High Pass"). Having swung around the far side of the hill, it continues northeast at a slightly easier gradient.

2 Keep an eye out for the fork in the path (at NS429922), from where a clear side-trail veers off R towards the summit of Conic. When you reach the ridge, it's worth cutting back up to the R to admire the view

Map not to scale.
Representation of OS
EXPLORER MAP 347
1:25,000

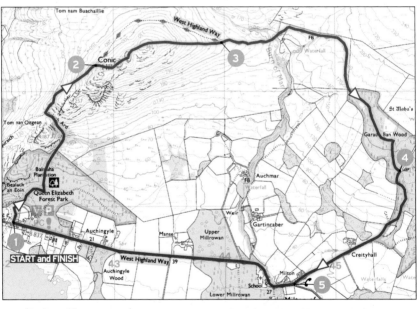

Route profile

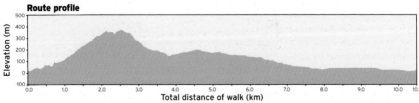

from the first bluff – arguably the best panorama of the day. This is a great place from which to appreciate the Highland Boundary Fault, tracked by Inchailloch, Inchmurrin and other islands below.

The main path, meanwhile, climbs steeply to the L (northeast) to the first in a line of four distinct summits, separated by a series of rollercoaster dips. After the final, and highest of these tops (361m/1184ft) you begin a sustained drop of 200m to rejoin the West Highland Way, where you turn R. **Cut it short:** After dropping down from the Conic ridge, turn L on to the West Highland Way instead of R, and follow it back down to Balmaha – saving 4.2km/2.6miles and the trudge back along the road.

3 It's plain sailing from here on, as the path settles into a more gradual descent to the Burn of Mar, crossed via a footbridge. It then climbs over open moorland, and across the smaller Kilandan Burn, shortly after which you start an easy descent through the remnants of a spruce forest, Garadh Ban wood.

4 On reaching the crosspaths (at NS456913), turn R and follow the broad track downhill as far as Milton of Buchanan, via the low-level route of the West Highland Way (which walkers following the long-distance trail use to avoid Conic Hill in bad weather).

5 Once on the B837, you can either wait for a bus to take you back to **Balmaha** (there's a stop in Milton, immediately to the

right of the junction where you reach the road), or else walk the mile-and-a-half on the tarmac pavement.

Getting There

Bus 309 from Balloch runs daily to Balmaha via Drymen. Balloch can be reached by bus or rail from Glasgow.

Visitor Information

Loch Lomond and Trossachs National Park Visitor Centre, Balmaha
☎01360 870470
✎www.lochlomond-trossachs.org

Eating & Drinking

If you don't feel like splashing out on a meal at the Oak Tree Inn, try a cup of homemade soup from village shop in Balmaha, where you can also pick up the usual range of intestinally challenging Scots pies.

The Oak Tree Inn
Balmaha
☎01360 870357
✎www.oak-tree-inn.co.uk
Top-notch bar meals, snacks and cakes served by an open fireplace in an elm-lined bar, or out in a light annexe backing on to the marina. The house speciality is Atlantic char, a rare freshwater fish that's a cross between salmon and trout.

Sleeping

The Oak Tree Inn
(As above)
The pub offers accommodation in either pleasant en suite rooms or walker-friendly four-bunk dorms.

More Info

✎www.west-highland-way. co.uk. Official site for Scot-

land's oldest and most popular long-distance footpath, running from the country's biggest city (Glasgow) to its highest mountain (Ben Nevis).

✎www.balmahaboatyard.co.uk. Home page of Macfarlane & Son, who run launch cruises and rowing-boat hire out of Balmaha marina, as well as the Inchailloch ferry and local inter-island mail run.

✎www.lochomond-islands.com. Detailed histories of the loch's 23 named islands.

✎www.undiscoveredscotland.co.uk. This ever dependable online guide to Scotland's backwaters features a page on Balmaha.

✎www.mwis.org.uk. Walkers' weather forecast for the Highlands.

More Walks

Walk Strathkelvin by John Logan (Strathkelvin Ramblers). Handsome book with an introduction by Cameron McNeish, historical essays by Don Martin and nature notes by Ian McCallum. Includes over seventy mainly short and easy walks (30mins-2hrs), plus some longer routes in the Campsies, canalside and disused railway-line trails around East Dunbartonshire.

Twenty Five Walks in North Ayrshire by Cunninghame Ramblers. Hand-picked walks to celebrate the 25th anniversary of Cunninghame Ramblers, from Irvine to Arran, including a great Three Towns Walk linking the coastal towns of Saltcoats, Stevenston and Ardrossan.

The Big End
Pendle Hill

With its carpet of mill towns and motorways, the Burnley Valley may not spring to mind as a source of great views. Look a little to the north, however, and the prospect improves dramatically. Standing proud of the Pennines and the Forest of Bowland, Pendle Hill is Lancashire's answer to Ayres Rock. Not as red, granted. Nor nearly as large. But a wonderfully imposing lump nonetheless, whose summit – "the Big End" – provides an unrivalled viewpoint over Yorkshire's Three Peaks to the distant fells of the Lake District, and across the coastal plain to Blackpool and the Irish Sea.

It was this awe-inspiring panorama that moved George Fox to found the Religious Society of Friends, or Quaker movement, in 1652, and which in the early 1900s proved life changing for Tom Stephenson, creator of the Pennine Way. Ask anyone locally what Pendle is famous for, however, and you're more likely to be told "witches".

On Halloween each year, the path to its summit is transformed into a twinkling necklace of lanterns as hundreds make their way to the top to commemorate the infamous Pendle Witch Trials of 1612, when eleven men and women living in the shadow of the hill were hanged for practicing black magic on their neighbours. The flying witch symbols branded on to posts along the route of the "Pendle Way" footpath are one legacy of this dark chapter; the Witches' Brew ale served in local pubs is another.

Neither, however, divert many of the walkers streaming along the nearby M6 en route to the Lake District. But if you're looking for a pre-amble to the high fells, or merely a bracing half-day walk with a magnificent viewpoint over northwest England at the end of it, Pendle Hill is unlikely to disappoint.

Our route starts in the pretty East Lancs village of Barley, looping around the hill in an anti-clockwise direction that allows you to savour its moody eastern flank before getting stuck into the ascent proper. The crux of the climb is a long flight of steps leading to an inclined summit plateau, crowned by a lonely trig point. From there, you drop down the hill's steeper western side – a slippery descent in wet weather – to skirt a couple of reservoirs for the easy walk back to Barley, where a pint of witches' brew awaits at the Pendle Inn.

At a glance

Where Pendle Hill, between Burnley and Clitheroe in north-east Lancashire.
Why Fantastic views over the Ribble Valley, Yorkshire Dales and Forest of Bowland, extending to the Lake District and Snowdonia in clear weather; red grouse, curlew and golden plover.
When Halloween, for the mass torch-lit walk to the hilltop.
Downsides A local saying insists that "if you can see Pendle Hill, it's going to rain. If you can't see it, it's already raining".
Start/Finish Barley (SD822402), 6.4km/4miles west of Nelson.
Duration 3hrs-3hrs 30mins.
Distance 10km/6miles.
Terrain Good tracks, eroded moorland and field paths – some stepped in places – with one strenuous ascent and descent.
Maps: OS Explorer Map 41.

On your way

With its steep flanks and gently shelving summit plateau, **PENDLE HILL** resembles a giant whale swimming serenely above the industrial sprawl of the Ribble and Burnley Valleys. For centuries, its moorland top served as a sanctuary for textile workers from the smoggy mill towns below, who used to climb it in wooden clogs on Sunday afternoons for a blast of fresh air. Among them was a thirteen-year-old Tom Stephenson, future journalist, rights of way activist and Ramblers' president, who made his first ascent on a February morning in 1906, and would later describe the view of snowy Pennine fells that greeted him at the top as a revelation.

Centuries before Stephenson's seminal climb, Pendle was the scene of another historic eureka moment. In 1652, while the country was reeling in the wake of the Civil War, the Christian dissenter George Fox, travelling through the region on a preaching tour, felt, "moved of the Lord to go up to the top of the very great hill" he and his companions had seen from a distance. Once at the summit, he said, "the Lord let me see in what places he had a great people to be gathered."

The vision transformed Fox from an itinerant preacher into the founder of what would become a worldwide religious movement, the Society of Friends, or "Quakers". Published posthumously, the account of his journey around the north of England would inspire the likes of William Pen and Oliver Cromwell, and provide guiding precepts for whole colonies in America: there still exists today a study centre in Pennsylvania called "Pendle Hill".

George Fox visited the district at a time when Lancashire ranked among the most anarchic and ungovernable counties in England, "fabled" in the words of one local historian, "for its theft, violence and sexual laxity, where the church was honoured without much understanding of its doctrines by the common people." And Pendle was the most notorious district of all in this Wild North-West – thanks to the famous Witch Trials of 1612, in which thirteen men and women from the area were found guilty of practicing satanic rites.

The catalyst for the famous trials was an alleged attack on a peddler named John Law, who claimed he had been paralyzed by one Alizon Devices after he had refused to sell her pins. Without being subjected to torture, Devices made a full confession – extraordinary in its frankness, and for the fact it incriminated three other members of her own family.

There followed an equally amazing set of revelations as the Devices not only admitted having committed murders by means of black magic, but also identified other practising witches in the Pendle area,

Townley's Hypothesis

A lesser known claim to fame of Pendle Hill is that it was the scene of a ground-breaking scientific experiment in 1661, when local scientist Richard Townley tested a machine on its sides that established a connection between atmospheric pressure and altitude. "Townley's Hypothesis", as his theory became known, later served as the basis of the more famous Boyle's Law, and paved the way for the invention of the barometer. Robert Boyle (1627-1691) saw an early draft of Townley's book *Experimental Philosophy* in 1661, and, or so it is claimed, originally named his own theory "Townley's Hypothesis".

ABOVE: Two long-distance walking paths, a bus route and several kinds of beer immortalize the memory of the Pendle witches

most of them from the rival Chattox family. The Chattoxes, in turn, spilled more beans on the Devices and their associates, whether out of revenge or as a vain attempt to secure clemency no-one is sure.

Of the thirteen individuals found guilty at the subsequent trials, eleven were hanged within a couple of days of the verdicts. The elderly matriarch of the Devices, a much feared witch known as Owd Demdike, died in prison before her case could be heard.

The Pendle Witch Trials were not only the single largest number of convictions made during the witch hunts of James I's reign. They were also the best documented court-room dramas of their day – due to the efforts of a clerk named Thomas Potts, who took detailed notes on the interrogations and proceedings, and then published them as the *Wonderfull Discoverie of Witches in the Countie of Lancaster*. With its florid descriptions of demonic rituals and spells, the account lifted the lid on the murky world of seventeenth-century witchcraft, revealing how witches made pacts with spirit animals, or "familiars", in exchange for secret powers which they would use to kill or inflict illness and injuries on adversaries.

The *Wonderfull Discoverie* inspired a rip-roaring novel by the Victorian author William Harrison Ainsworth, and a horror movie in the 1970s. Today, two long-distance walking paths and a bus route immortalize the memory of the Pendle witches, while a cottage industry in witchy nick nacks has sprung up to service a local tourist trade.

Pendle Witch fervour, however, reaches fever pitch at the end of October each year, with the nocturnal procession to the top of the hill held on the night of Halloween. Interest in the event soared after the ghost-hunting television show *Most Haunted* filmed a Halloween Special there; presenters and mediums later claimed the events they experienced were among the most terrifying of their careers.

While some of the old farms nestled at the foot of the hill definitely retain a spooky air, the top of Pendle itself is definitely an uplifting place. Reclined on one of the outcrops overlooking the Ribble Valley, with the Irish Sea glinting in the distance, you're more likely to hear the melancholic call of a curlew as it skims over the heather and peat bogs than the cackle of a wicked witch on her broomstick.

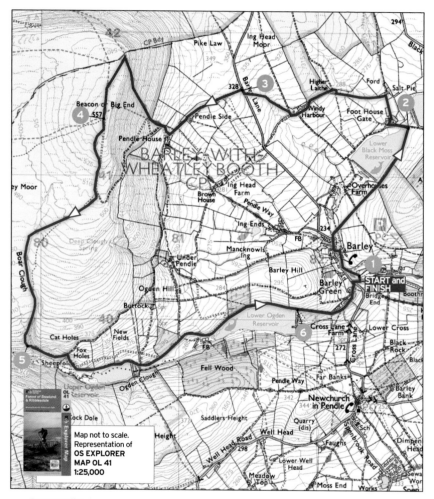

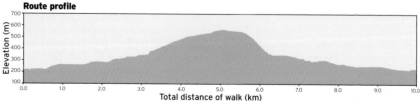

Route profile

1 Leave the car park in Barley by the path running between the toilet block and café, and follow it through the little streamside park on to the footbridge opposite the pub. Turn R at the bridge and follow the path to the road, and turn R on to the main road through the village, past the Barley Mow and Tea Rooms, and on to a bend, from where a lane heads straight on (signposted "Blacko Footpath Only")

Veering R soon after, this takes you along the eastern side of Black Moss Reservoir, with impressive views of **Pendle Hill** rising over the water.

2 When you get to the T-junction at the end of the lane, turn L along the far side of the reservoir, then R soon after through Foot House Gate. The path runs between the former farm buildings, and onwards up a lane between stone walls to Salt Pie cottage. From a stone stile opposite the cottage, this clear footpath cuts diagonally across a field L to Higher Laithe. When you reach the latter, cross the stile on to the driveway/lawn of the end house and look for a swing gate immediately to your R. Next, turn L and follow the boundary behind the houses until you arrive at a stile leading on to a black tarmac lane. Then turn R and follow the lane for a few minutes.

At Windy Harbour Farm, a short way down the lane on your R, a stile set back from the tarmac just beyond the end building gives access to a sloping, boggy field, which you cross diagonally to the L (aim for the prominent tree beyond the wall at the top). Squeeze through the opening in the drystone wall when you reach Barley Lane, and turn R. Follow the tarmac for a minute or so, as far as the turning on the L, signposted for "Pendle Side & Pendle House".

3 Head L down this track, past Pendle Side farm. Shortly before reaching the second farm, a gate to the R, marked by three footpath arrows, stands at the start of the stepped path up the eastern flank of Pendle Hill. It's a strenuous, but steady and enjoyable climb, for which you're rewarded with rapidly improving views over the Ribble Valley. When a drystone wall and stile are reached close to the edge of the summit plateau, the path switches back sharply L, levelling off as it approaches the trig point.

4 From the summit, keep heading south along the heavily eroded path lined intermittently by cairns – though be aware of the proximity of a steep slope to your L. The route drops steadily across the black peat hags of Barley Moor to a fork at SD804409, where you bear R, as indicated by the cairns, towards the head of a muddy, rocky stream gully known as "Boar Clough". Growing increasingly steep, the path then switches to the R bank of the stream, and crosses a tributary brook, before arriving at a second prominent junction at SD799398, where you'll meet a collapsed post-and-rail fence.

5 Turn L here and cross the torrent via stepping stones to follow a well worn path (part of the "Pendle Way") down Ogden Clough. Once through a wooden gate soon after, continue down the path above the northern bank of Upper Ogden Reservoir. At the dam, you drop sharply down a broken tarmac track to a stone stile beside a locked metal gate. Keep heading along the paved bridleway ahead, ignoring the concrete track cutting L just before a conifer wood, and continue instead along track between the tree plantation and Lower Ogden Reservoir.

6 At the second dam, head straight on down the lane winding around the foot of Barley Hill, passing a large United Utilities building ("Nelson Waterworks 1930") and two stone gate posts. Keep to the main track past Barley Green Farmhouse and Cottage. Soon after, you arrive at a crossroads in the village: continue straight over for the car park and café, or turn L for the pub and tea rooms.

Getting There
The Pendle Witch Hopper runs daily between Nelson and Clitheroe via Barley. Timetable details via Traveline ☏ 0871 200 2233, ✎ www.traveline.org.uk.

Visitor Information
Pendle Tourism
Pendle Heritage Centre, Park Hill, Barrowford
☏ 01282 661701
✎ www.pendletourism.com.

Eating & Drinking
The Cabin Café
Barley picnic site
Walker-friendly café, perfectly placed in the car park at the start/finish of our route, in a cosy wood cabin. They rustle up light snacks, paninis, or traditional cooked meals, as well as cakes, teas, coffees and cold drinks – and you can even order take-out picnics.

The Pendle Inn
Barley Lane, Barley
☎ 01282 661701
🖱 www.pendleinn.co.uk
Barley's village pub occupies a rather grand, early-twentieth-century building with wood-panelled walls and roaring fireplaces. The local Moorhouse brewery's witch ales dominate a decent beer menu, while filling pub food – including a popular Pendle Pie, with steak and Lancashire cheese topping – is served in the Barley Mow restaurant to the rear.

Sleeping
The Pendle Inn
(See above)
Half a dozen uninspiring, modern, en suite B&B rooms in a rear annexe that opens on to the pub car park.

Blakey Hall Farm
Red Lane, Cole, BB8 9TD
☎ 0282 863121
🖱 www.blakeyhallfarm.co.uk
Overlooking the towpath of the Leeds–Liverpool canal, this is the nicest B&B option in the area, though you'll need your own transport to get there from Barley – a fifteen-minute drive away. Classy, recently refurbished rooms, all with exposed stone walls and big

bathrooms, in a huge converted dairy.

More Info
🖱 www.pendlewitches.co.uk. Confessions of the Pendle Witches and plenty of background on the trials, with a good book list for anyone who wants to research the story in depth.

🖱 en.wikipedia.org/wiki/Pendle_witch_trials. A thorough account of whole Pendle Witch debacle.

🖱 gerald-massey.org.uk/Billington/b_pendle_hill.htm. Full text of the famous poem on Pendle Hill by the "Blackburn Bard", William Billington.

More Walks
Freedom to Roam Guide: Forest of Bowland by Andrew Bibby (Frances Lincoln/Ramblers). Compact guide with OS 1:25,000 scale maps. Features fourteen routes celebrating the magnificent scenery opened up under the right to roam in the Forest of Bowland and the West Pennine Moors.

Walks from the Limestone Link by Lancaster Ramblers (Ramblers). Great little guide to this spectacular 21-km/13-mile route, crossing the weathered limestone ridge between Lancaster and Kendal. The guide includes sixteen specially devised short circular walks along and just off the main trail.

Walks in North West Lancashire by Lancaster Ramblers (Ramblers). Fifteen short walks from the Silverdale AONB down to the river valleys and upland farms of the Forest of Bowland AONB.

More Walks in North West Lancashire by Lancaster Ramblers (Ramblers). Twenty short walks, this time widening the net to include the Lancaster Canal, the coast, and access areas including Clougha Pike.

Walks in the Lune Valley by Lancaster Ramblers (Ramblers). Sixteen walks in Lancashire's Lune Valley, one of Britain's best and most secret walking destinations. Includes the Lune Valley Ramble along the north bank.

Walks Round Lancaster City by Lancaster Ramblers (Ramblers). Five short walks that start in the centre of Lancaster and out into the countryside passing the city's most famous historical sites, including the cathedral.

ABOVE: Looking east from the Big End over the Black Moss Reservoir

walk 31

DERBYSHIRE

The Shivering Peak

Mam Tor

The Peak District is a classic British misnomer – up there with "Chelsea FC" (a Russian-owned soccer team based in Fulham) and "British Summer Time" (a contradiction in itself). Europe's most frequented national park, which annually receives more than twenty million visitors, holds more than its fair share of cliffs, gorges and high moorland. But peaks – proper pointy ones with 360-degree panoramas – are in short supply.

One corner of the park, however, stands as the exception to the rule. Enfolded by an arc of prominent summits, the head of the Hope Valley around Castleton can claim a near monopoly on the Peak's peaks. Moreover, the tops are strung together by a single classic ridge (another rarity in this region of gritstone escarpments and rolling heathland). Stretching for 3.5km/2miles from east to west, the "Great Ridge" straddles the geological fault-line where the rolling pastures of the "White Peak" collide with the millstone grit and peaty wastes of the dour "Dark Peak" to the north. In doing so it not only quickens the pulse of local geography teachers, but also provides one of Britain's

benchmark hill walks, framed by a succession of magnificent views.

Nowadays paved with flagstones to prevent erosion, the Great Ridge falls sheer on its northern flank to the beautiful Edale sanctuary, with the folds of Kinder Scout rising beyond. To the south, a finger-pattern of narrow dales delves from the top of the Hope Valley into a patchwork of green uplands and drystone walls. No trees or rocks impede the panoramas, which just seem to grow more spectacular the further west you walk, culminating in the stupendous vista of hills and dales that unfolds from the top of Mam Tor, the famous "Shivering Mountain".

To put the Great Ridge in context, our route combines the walk along it between Lose Hill and Mam Tor with a gentle foray into the limestone country on the southern side of the valley. Crossing a checker board of sheep folds and disused lead mines, it then drops back to Castleton via picturesque Cave Dale, whose narrow sides steepen and converge as they approach the fairy-tale vision of Peveril Castle – one of the Peak's great man-made spectacles.

At a glance

Where The Great Ridge and Cave Dale from Castleton, Derbyshire Peak District.

Why The perfect Peak primer, sampling the best of the park's varied interior; bird's-eye-view over Edale and the start of the Pennine Way; Peveril Castle – a splendid Norman fortress; rare

mountain hares.

When May 29th – "Garland Day" – when the "Garland King & Queen" parade around Castleton decked in flowers – an ancient fertility rite.

Downsides A couple of busy roads have to be crossed midway, and don't expect to have the ridge

to yourself at any time of the year.

Start/Finish Castleton VIC (SK149830).

Duration 4-5hrs.

Distance 13km/8miles.

Terrain Mostly well made mountain paths, with a steep initial climb across fields.

Maps OS Explorer OL1.

Mam Tor, with Lose Hill in the mid-distance, and the Hope Valley stretching east towards Grindleford

On your way

Walking the Great Ridge provides a crash course in Peak geology. As you progress westwards, you'll notice the rock change from red-brown gritstone to pale-grey shale and white limestone – laid down 300–350 million years ago when this area was submerged under a vast river delta. The various deposits were sifted by the tides into layers, then compressed before being forced to the surface by volcanic activity. Erosion did the rest, shaping the outcrops and steep hill flanks that shelve from the ridge today.

Ward's Piece, a classic lump of north Derbyshire gritstone, derives its popular name – **LOSE HILL** – from a battle that took place in the Hope Valley during the Dark Ages between Cuicholm of Wessex and Edward of Northumbria. Despite possessing greater numbers, the Wessex army lost the day after their adversaries staged a false retreat to their camp on the hilltop opposite ("Win Hill"), piling boulders on the attackers as they charged upwards.

A plaque just below the north side of the summit recalls the donation in 1945 of Lose Hill to the National Trust by GBH Ward (1876–1957), founder member and long-time president of the Sheffield Clarion Walking Club. The club, which celebrated its centenary in 2000, had purchased the land on his behalf, in recognition of their inspirational leader's contribution to rambling.

A chain of four distinct summits crenellates the narrow ridge, which dips to its lowest point at **HOLLINS CROSS**, where in times past an old mule track crossed into Edale. The path junction marks the start of a long, curving ascent to **MAM TOR** (517m/1696ft) – the "Mother" or "Shivering Mountain" – whose iconic east face looms benevolently above the head of the Hope Valley.

A hundred-metre triangle of striated, flaking shale and grit, the cliff reveals a cross-section of the layered rocks hidden beneath the surface of these rolling hills. It's in a perpetual state of collapse, periodically shedding falls of debris as water saturates the strata. Geologists speculate that the landslip will only stabilize once the cliff has reached an angle of thirty degrees – in around 1500 years' time! Until then, climbers steer clear of the incline, except in times of penetrating frost, when it makes a novel winter challenge.

Visible below are remnants of the old Sheffield Turnpike road, built in 1819 across the shifting lower skirt tails of Mam

Blue John

Castleton's lead miners were responsible for unearthing the caves that are today the village's prime attractions: Peak Cavern (aka "the Devil's Arse"), Speedwell, Treak Cliff, Bagshaw and Blue John Mine. The latter takes its name from an extremely rare and beautiful form of fluorite, unique to the hills below Mam Tor, which possesses a luminous quality when viewed in low light (the source of the term "fluorescent"). First discovered by the Romans 2000 years ago, the mineral – distinguished by its crystalline bands of purple, yellow and grey – is still mined by hand during the winter when the caves are closed to the public. Samples can be seen in gift shops around Castleton, where local craftsmen turn it into jewelery and ornaments, though be warned that much of what's on sale these days is actually made from cheaper crystal imported from China.

Tor. Subsidence continually plagued the route, however, and in 1979 the County Council, weary of continual resurfacing work, finally closed the road to motor traffic.

Vestiges of much earlier indignities inflicted on the mountain slip into focus as you approach its top. In the Bronze Age (1300–1000 BC), the tor's crest was the site of a major hill fort, whose inhabitants gouged defensive ditches and terraces around the steep upper hillside to accommodate huts and wooden palisades. Some of these were later shored up with stone.

The summit itself is crowned with an early Bronze-Age tumulus, which now lies under paving stones installed to protect it from the many boots that tramp over it each year. Little is known about the ancient Britons who claimed this lofty spot. But their settlement, which was probably a seasonal summer camp, ranks as the second highest hillfort in the country, and one of the oldest.

From Mam Tor, another NT pavement ushers walkers down to a pass where a tortuous single-track road crosses the Great Ridge into Edale. Further southeast, a still more dramatic motor route winds down **WINNAT'S PASS** (or "Windy Gates") – a spectacular limestone gorge believed to have once been an undersea ravine dividing two coral reefs. Before the construction of the now derelict Turnpike road, it offered the only way into the Hope Valley from the west, with a 1:5 gradient that was a stern test for the skills of local coachmen, requiring an additional pair of horses from Castleton for the final pull.

Huddled at the foot of the gorge, **CASTLETON** itself sprang up shortly after 1066 as the seat of William the Conqueror's illegitimate son, William Peveril, on whom the king conferred the role of Bailiff of the Royal Manor of the Peak, his northern hunting reserve. In later centuries, the village prospered as a lead mining centre, remains of which still litter the surrounding hills.

With its show caves and state-of-the-art national park information centre, Castleton now serves as the Peak District's prime visitor destination. It's well worth setting aside time to explore the ruined castle, rising from a limestone crag above, and the village church, whose nave is spanned by a finely sculpted Norman arch. But the big attraction here is definitely **PEAK CAVERN**, reached via a narrow lane leading off the square (past the chip shop). The entrance to the grotto, flanked by 85-metre/280-ft cliffs, is the largest of any cave in Britain, and until the mid-nineteenth century was inhabited by a colony of troglodyte ropemakers, the soot from whose fires is still visible on the rock walls. Accounts from early visitors record that their ragamuffin children used to act as guides, leading daytrippers through the cave by lantern light.

PEAK CAVERN also featured in Tudor literature as the venue of the King of the Gypsies' legendary meeting with the infamous brigand Cock Lorel ("the most notorious knave that ever lived"). In the course of their encounter, the pair were said to have devised a secret language, "thieves cant", "to the end that their cozenings, knaveries and villainies might not so easily be perceived and known".

Based on Romani slang, cant (also known as "pelting speech") spiced up penny pamphlets and plays of the time, and may well have been used by some of the real-life crooks and fugitives who lived alongside the ropemakers, though the story of Cock Lorel is probably a myth. It's equally uncertain quite when the cavern's ribald nickname, "the Devil's Arse" was coined. Both it, and the flatulent noises emitted from some nether corners of the cave to which it refers, remain a considerable source of amusement for visiting teenagers.

walk it 31

Mam Tor

CHECKED BY
✔ **New Mills Ramblers**

While the route described below requires neither exceptional fitness nor technical clothing to complete in fair weather, the higher sections of it, between Lose Hill and Mam Tor, are a different proposition in high winds or storms. Some experience of winter hill-walking will also be necessary if tackling the route when the paths are covered by snow – an ice axe and crampons may be essential in particularly cold conditions.

1 From the bottom R corner of the **Castleton** Visitor Information Centre's car park, a narrow lane leads on to Hollowford Rd, where you should turn L. Follow the lane for 5-10mins as far as the "Hollowford Centre", in front of which another lane branches R, signposted "Rotary". Turn onto this and follow it for 5mins until lane bends L, where you bear R, as shown, across fields and a brook, following the waymarks.

2 Immediately after passing Losehill Hall on your R (SK153838), a prominent fingerpost indicates the route L to **Lose Hill**. This leads up the side of field to a kissing gate, from where a well-made, well waymarked path runs uphill across farmland. After crossing a second brook, it then contours to a stile just below Crimea Farm (SK158847). From the farmhouse, wayposts flag the turn L up a rise to a metal gate and fingerpost visible ahead pointing the way to "Lose Hill". The path follows the line of

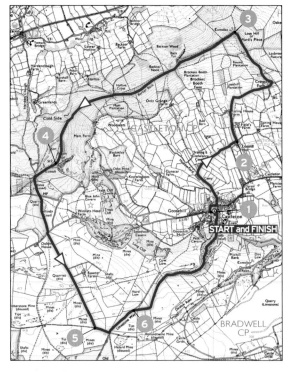

Map not to scale.
Representation of
OS EXPLORER
MAP 01, 1:25,000

Route profile

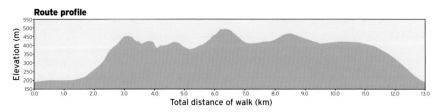

a fence and a broken drystone wall to a stile on your R, next to a cairn. Immediately beyond the latter, a second stile (onto NT land) gives access to a paved path leading directly to the summit.

3 Marked by a brass topograph, the top of Lose Hill reveals views into Edale for the first time. From here as far as the top of Mam Tor, the ridge route via Back Tor, Barker Bank and **Hollins' Cross** is well worn and paved for much of its length. Superb panoramas extend along its full length over Edale and Hope Valley.

4 Once on the summit of **Mam Tor** (SK127836), follow the NT's paving stones downhill until you reach the road, where a L turn after the gate takes you down a flight of steps to a second gate. From there, keep going straight to a third gate opening onto a metalled road. Head along the track starting directly opposite and continue over the rise to the **Winnat's Pass** road, which you should cross diagonally to the R (ignore the stile over a drystone wall).

A metal gate on the far side of the road leads on to Rowter Farm's asphalted drive, which you should follow past the turning to the farm and onwards along an unsurfaced bridleway, skirting mine workings (in the field to the R) before arriving at a T-junction (SK134814).

5 Turn L here, and then L again after 2mins over a pair of stiles separated by parallel stone walls. After the second stile, the trail bears R along the Limestone Way signposted for ''Castleton''.

6 From this point, our route drops steeply down the head of Cave Dale, with the sides of the combe gaining height as you descend. Keep your eyes peeled for mountain hares and wheatears as you approach the waypost marking a fork in the trail at SK138816; bear R through the gate, as indicated, keeping to the Limestone Way as it winds towards Castleton.

This will bring you after 20mins to a fine view of Peveril Castle and the deepest stretch of the dale, riddled with cave openings. The village lies a short walk beyond the narrow gap in the rocks marking the entrance to the valley, which used to be capped with a natural arch. For the Castle and **Peak Cavern**, turn L.

Getting There Services on the main trans-Pennine Sheffield–Manchester rail line stop at the neighbouring village of Hope, 2miles east of Castleton. Bus services into the valley are frequent on weekends .

Visitor Information Castleton VIC, Buxton Rd ☎01629 816572 ✎www.peakdistrict.org

Eating & Drinking The Cheshire Cheese Edale Rd, Hope ☎01433 620381 Snug oak-beamed pub on the outskirts of Hope. It's as old as the hills, and gets packed out in season, but serves copious meals and at least six local cask ales.

Sleeping Underleigh House Off Edale Road, Hope, S33 6RF

☎01433 621372 ✎www.underleighhouse.co.uk Award-winning B&B, in a converted Victorian barn, hidden down a country lane, with lovely hill views. Their breakfasts, served on an oak refectory table, are sumptuous. It's well placed for our route (just down the lane from Crimea Farm) and within walking distance of Hope train station.

More Info ✎www.peakdistrict.org. The national park's information-packed website.

✎www.nationaltrust.org.uk. Most of the land crossed by our route is part of the Trust's massive High Peak Estate.

✎www.cressbrook.co.uk. Top Peak District information site.

✎www.mwis.org.uk. Dedicated walkers' weather forecast for the Peak District

More Walks *Collins Ramblers Guide: The Peak District* by Roly Smith (Collins/Ramblers). Thirty walks of various lengths and levels of difficulty, exploring the main northern moors of Britain's oldest national park.

Freedom to Roam Guides: Peak District Eastern Moors and the South and *Peak District Northern and Western Moors* by Roly Smith (Frances Lincoln/Ramblers). Compact guides with OS 1:25,000 scale maps featuring fourteen routes. Each celebrates the magnificent scenery opened up to walkers in the Peak District under the right to roam.

The Welsh Knight
Cnicht

If you were Dôn, the Celtic Goddess of the Sky, and had to create the perfect viewpoint over Snowdonia, you'd be hard pushed to improve on Cnicht. Standing proud of the main range just inland from Tremadog Bay, the peak known as the "Welsh Matterhorn" affords an incomparable panorama over the tops of the Glaslyn Valley to Snowdon.

The really impressive vista from here, however, covers ground closer to home. Separating Cnicht from its neighbour, Moelwyn Mawr, is beautiful Cwm Croesor, a shapely glacial valley whose distinguishing feature is an arrow-straight line scraped along its floor towards the sea. The scar – the remains of a nineteenth-century tramway used to transport slate from mines high up on the mountains to Porthmadog – only seems to accentuate the graceful curves of the valley itself, one of the most spectacular in the Welsh mountains.

Contrary to appearances, Cnicht isn't a Welsh word, but a name derived from Middle English. The theory goes that medieval sailors out in the bay compared its distinctively pointed shape to a knight's helmet. These days, however, it's the "Matterhorn" tag

that tends to stick – a comparison the real Matterhorn might well resent. For at a diminutive 689m/2260ft, Cnicht barely deserves the status of a mountain. Moreover, the summit is accessible to anyone willing to endure an hour of aching calf muscles.

You may have to take your hands out of your pockets towards the top, but any proper scrambling is easily avoided. So if you're contemplating a first taste of Snowdonia, this is the ideal peak, with just enough gradient to make it a challenge. And the views from the top will blow away even hardened mountaineers.

An additional surprise awaits those who complete the ascent: Cnicht's summit turns out not to be a sharp point, as its profile suggest from below, but the start of a long ridge, running northeast into a tract of moorland. Experienced walkers may well be tempted to press on from here around the wonderful "Croesor Horseshoe" (see box), which loops over the mountains of Moelwyn Bach and Moelwyn Mawr. Our route, however, is a more straightforward out-and-back affair, leaving you plenty of time for a slice of cake at Caffi Croesor afterwards.

At a glance

Where Cnicht, 12km/7miles, Snowdonia, North Wales.
Why The ultimate panoramic view over the highest mountain range in England and Wales; picturesque Welsh slate mining village; the Caffi Croesor.
When This landscape looks at its

most striking after a dusting of snow, but if you do venture up Cnicht in midwinter, be equipped for ice.
Downsides Lying to the seaward side of Snowdonia, Cnicht gets more than its fair share of rain.
Start/Finish Croesor National

Park car park (SH631447).
Duration 2hrs 30mins-3hrs.
Distance 6km/3.75miles.
Terrain From open moorland above the village to exposed, rocky mountainside: steep sections towards the top.
Maps OS Explorers OL17 & OL18.

On your way

In clear conditions, the awesome 360-degree panorama from the top of **CNICHT** more than repays the slog up its southwest ridge from **CROESOR**, a former miners' village at the end of a quiet country lane. Some 200 years ago, before entrepreneur William Alexander Maddocks (1773–1828) built a cob wall across the mouth of the Glaslyn Estuary, this sharp-topped pyramid rose straight from the sea. Now it peaks eight miles from the shoreline, above the flat, green pastures and yellow sandbanks of the Traeth Mawr floodplain, unfurling into the sea.

Conceived a full two decades before Thomas Telford's toll road and suspension bridge across the Menai Strait diverted traffic through Holyhead, Maddocks' scheme was the lynchpin of an ambitious plan to transform Porthmadog into northwest Wales' main sea port. It nearly ruined him: in 1816, shortly after its completion, the embankment burst, causing a catastrophic flood. A mass mobilization of local labour managed to plug the breach, but it was the rise of the north Wales slate industry that ultimately rescued the financial fortunes of both Maddocks and his new port.

As the industrial revolution gathered pace in the mid-nineteenth century, millions of roofs were needed for new terraced houses. Blaenau Ffestiniog, at the foot of the Moelwynion, became the epicentre of a massive slate boom, and Porthmadog was its main port. A web of rail lines and tramways was built to transport the quarried stone to the harbour, which at its peak in the 1860s and 1870s shipped 52 million pieces across the globe each year. The boom made Maddocks and the quarry barons super-rich. But it also ravaged the surrounding mountainsides – damage that was just left to the elements after the industry's demise.

Today, after a century-and-a-half of battering by the Welsh weather, the heaps of spoil and ruined installations have largely merged with the mountains and stand as intriguing monuments more than mere blots on the upland landscape. Those at Rhosydd, part of a huge complex spread across the head of the Cwm Croesor, yield a particularly vivid impression of the scale of the Welsh slate enterprise, and the conditions endured

The Croesor Horseshoe

Most walkers turn around at the top of Cnicht and retrace their steps back to Croesor village. But the summit ridge marks the start of a magnificent horseshoe route that can be followed around the head of Cwm Croesor, via several small lakes and abandoned slate mines, to the tops of Moelwyn Bach and Moelwyn Mawr – altogether more imposing hills, the latter with a razor-back summit ridge edged by a dramatic, near-vertical north wall. Aside from taking in a fascinating slice of Welsh industrial history, this longer option has the advantage of rounding off the day with one final, stupendous view – over the glorious Vale of Ffestiniog and Harlech to the southwest. But it's

a circuit that should be approached with caution. The stretch beyond Cnicht crosses rough, boggy ground where it's easy to lose your way amid the old quarry workings if cloud and rain suddenly sweep in – an all too common occurrence in this, one of the wettest, and least frequented uplands of Wales. And the west ridge route off Moelwyn Mawr, with it dizzying drops to the north, can be perilous in a strong southwesterly. So save the Croesor Horseshoe for a sunny, calm day, and only attempt it if you're sure that you have the necessary navigation skills.

The full circuit from Croesor takes a full day to complete: allow 6-7hrs.

ABOVE: Cnicht's summit ridge in winter

by those men who worked in it.

Rhosydd was neither the largest, nor the most profitable of the region's quarries, but it was the highest, bleakest and most reviled. It started out life in the 1830s as an open-cast mine, going underground as new veins were discovered running deep into the mountain. In all, 170 chambers were excavated on seventeen separate levels. A couple of hundred men laboured in the wet, numbingly cold tunnels, trudging to the quarry each Monday morning and returning to their families down in the valley on Saturday afternoon. Conditions were grim, even by the standards of this notoriously inhuman industry. Exposed for six days each week to slate dust, miners died in droves of tuberculosis and typhoid. Between 1876 and 1889, average life expectancy was a mere 44 years.

Remnants of the quarry – derelict wheel houses, rusty pipes and truck chassis, piles of spoil and dripping adits – are strewn across the high saddle dividing Cwm Croesor from Cwmorthin and Blaenau. Alongside them stands the blind-eyed carcass of the barracks where the miners lived, and, further down the mountain near Llyn Cwmorthin, the remnants of a small Non-Conformist chapel in which they gathered after work to pray, talk politics and, in true Welsh style, sing hymns – Rhosydd boasted one of the finest male-voice choirs in Wales.

Of all the relics, though, the old tramway has to be the most impressive. Centerpiece of the eight-mile track, which horse-drawn trains used to follow down the valley to Porthmadog, is a spectacular incline, plunging 2600/800ft in less than two miles. The weight of the incoming supplies would balance that of the outgoing slate wagons as they negotiated a 240-metre/670-foot cliff at gradients of 1:1. Judging by the number of bogies lying bottom-up on the mountainside, accidents weren't uncommon.

Rhosydd ended production in the 1930s, though its pumps weren't finally switched off until 1948: with the threat of Nazi invasion hanging over the country, some of the deeper chambers here served as hiding places for the crown jewels, and other national treasures from the V&A and British Museum.

The site is now owned by the McAlpine consortium, who are rumoured to be considering re-opening the quarry. Modern earth-moving machinery could scrape the ceilings off some of the shallower chambers to expose valuable slate pillars beneath – an endeavour for which a road would have to built up the mountain to Rhosydd.

The best vantage point from which to survey the ravages inflicted on this area by the slate boom is the summit of Moelwyn Mawr, the "Big White Mountain" on the opposite side of Cwm Croesor from Cnicht – as featured in our "Croesor Horseshoe" box opposite. From its trig point, reached by an exhilarating climb above the Llyn Stwlan reservoir, you can look down on the rooftops of Blaenau-Ffestiniog, enfolded by vast slopes of blue-grey slag and scree, to the steam train chuffing along the narrow gauge railway to the coast. Trawsfynydd Lake and its nearby nuclear power station dominate the mid-ground, with the Rhinnogs rippling behind towards Pembrokeshire. In the other direction, a wonderful vista opens to the north and west across the Lleyn and main Snowdonia range.

1 Cross the little footbridge at the top of the National Park car park in **Croesor** and follow the path to the road. Turn R when you reach the tarmac, then head up the lane through the village for a couple of mins, past the old chapel and memorial to the local bard, shepherd and book collector, Bob

Owen Croesor. Growing steeper as it climbs, the lane becomes a slate track then, as it emerges from the trees at the brow of the hill, forks in two: bear R at the junction. The well worn track winds across open moorland, with views of Cnicht looming ahead. A little over 5mins after leaving the trees, look for a sign on your R pointing to a stile over a drystone wall. This leads you to the start of the path up the

ridge ahead, which from this angle can look more formidable than it really is.

2 The route from here onwards is obvious, wriggling up **Cnicht**'s southwest ridge. It becomes progressively steeper as you gain height, with a short, simple scramble close to the top to take you up on to the first of the hill's three summits.

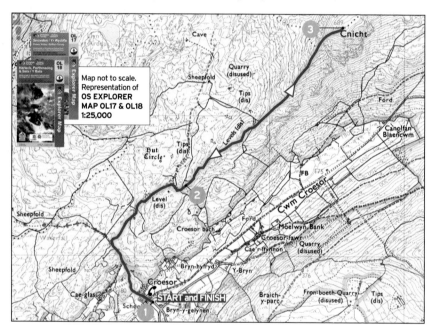

Map not to scale.
Representation of
**OS EXPLORER
MAP OL17 & OL18**
1:25,000

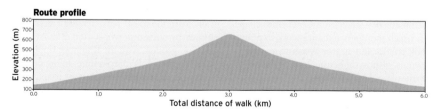

Route profile

ABOVE: Snowdon from Cnicht

From the crest, the views north take in the whole of the Snowdon massif, and Moelwyn Bach and Moelwyn Mawr to the south. Looking down the valley you'll be able to make out Tremadog and the Irish Sea in the distance. Return by the same route.

Getting There
Croesor is 12km/7.5miles northeast of Porthmadog, in Gwynedd, just off the A4085. Express Motors' bus no.98 runs there from Porthmadog on week days, though as it's tied to school hours the timings aren't all that walker-friendly. Timetable information is available online at www.expressmotors.co.uk, or by phone on 01286 881108. The nearest train station is at Penrhyndeudraeth, 7.5km/ 4.6miles southwest, from where you can take a taxi to Croesor.

Visitor Information
Beddgelert TIC
Canolfan Hebog
01766 890615

www.beddgelert-snowdonia.co.uk.

Sleeping
Places to sleep are thin on the ground in Croesor itself, but you've spoilt for choice in nearby Beddgelert (see p.000). Alternatively, try the following B&B, over the mountain near Blaenau Ffestiniog:

Bryn Elltyd
Tanygrisiau
Blaenau Ffestiniog
01766 831356
www.accommodation-snowdonia.com.
Eco-friendly guest house at a scenic lakeside location below Moelwyn Mawr – you can walk out of the garden up the mountain, and it's a short stroll from the train station. Three-course dinners available (with 24hrs notice).

Eating & Drinking
Caffi Croesor
Croesor
01766 770456
A few years back, the local

community got together to renovate a disused farmhouse a stone's throw away from the National Park car park. Perfectly placed for the ascent of Cnicht, the building now accommodates one of North Wales' coziest cafés, with boot-friendly slate floors and a roaring wood burner. Try their scrumptious home-baked bara brith, or hot soup in the winter. Open Thurs-Mon noon–5pm (closed Tues & Weds, except for groups by prior appointment).

More Info
www.penmorfa.com/Rhosydd. Highly readable website dedicated to the history of Rhosydd Quarry, with lots of evocative photographs.

More Walks
Collins Rambler's Guide: North Wales by Richard Sale (Collins/Ramblers). Thirty walks over a range of distances and levels of difficulty exploring the main mountain groups of Snowdonia National Park, including the nearby Moelwynion.

High Above the Madding Crowd

Cheddar Gorge

The Mendip Hills may not be the loftiest in the land, but they punch well above their weight when it comes to views. From the summit of Back Down (325m), the highest ground on this straggling limestone outcrop in northwest Somerset, you can, on a clear day, see right across the Bristol Channel to the Welsh coast and Brecon Beacons. In the opposite direction, the southern escarpment of the Mendips falls away to the Levels, a low-lying patchwork of boggy fields and drainage ditches studded by tortoise-shaped tors – the legendary "Vale of Avalon".

At sunset time, with the rivulets and canals glinting beneath the mysterious profile of Glastonbury Tor, this distinctive panorama can possess its own enigmatic grandeur, particularly when viewed from atop the crags of mighty Cheddar Gorge.

Somerset's own Grand Canyon is the single most impressive natural feature in southern England. Around half a million people pour through it each year to see the famous show caves and admire the cliffs from their car or coach windows. Barely a trickle of the daytrippers, however, sample the open vistas lying beyond the gorge. Higher up the valley, another world takes over: of swallow holes and invisible underground cave systems, of endless drystone walls and drovers' tracks overgrown with drifts of purple willowherb and cow parsley, where bleak little farms preside over fields pimpled by long-barrows, tumuli and other weird prehistoric earthworks.

Combining classic waymarked footpaths with less well known trails over access land, our route leads you around the dizzying rim of Cheddar Gorge via a succession of dramatic viewpoints. For those wishing to sample the atmosphere of upland Mendip, we've also devised a second loop north across Black Down, which you can do separately, starting at Back Rock, or as part of a longer figure-of-eight route.

At a glance

Where Cheddar Gorge and Black Down, Cheddar, Somerset.
Why Spectacular bird's-eye views of England's deepest gorge; herds of rare Soay sheep grazing on inaccessible cliff ledges; long-distance panoramas from the top of the Mendips; Roman lead mines; Gorsey Bigbury Henge and other prehistoric sites.

When Spring: Longwood is rightly famous for its beautiful bluebells.
Downsides Poorly served by public transport; some sections around the Gorge are busy in holiday periods.
Start/Finish Lippiatt Lane (ST462537), Cheddar village.
Duration 2hrs – 2hrs 30min for the Gorge circuit; 4hrs for the full Black Down loop.

Distance Standard Gorge circuit 6km/3.75 miles; plus 10.5km/6.5 miles for loop over Black Down.
Terrain Woodland, open moors, pasture and grassy combes; some steep sections to and from the top of the gorge where loose rocks, mud and slippery grass ledges require great caution in wet weather. Walking poles recommended.
Maps: OS Explorer 141.

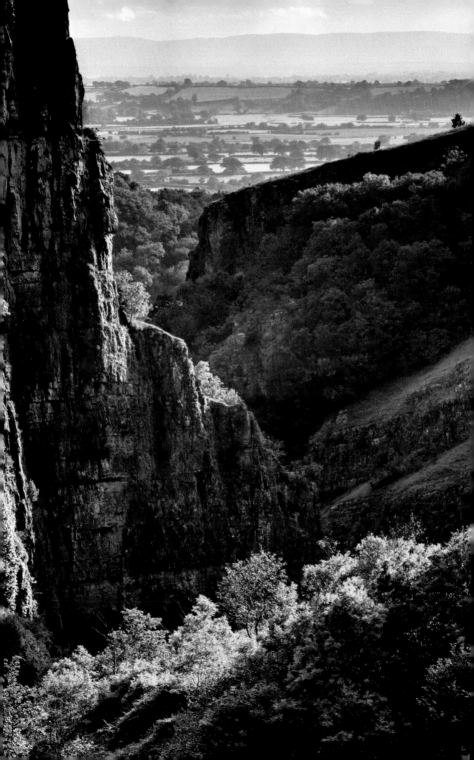

On your way

Cheddar Gorge was formed during the last Ice Age, when fissures deep under the Mendips' limestone cap were blocked by frozen water, forcing runoff from melting glaciers to scour the porous limestone surface into the deep trench we see today. Lined with forest, the canyon and its rock shelters hosted semi-permanent camps of hunter-gatherers over several millennia. A rich horde of prehistoric remains has been uncovered in Cheddar's caves, not least the complete, 9000-year-old skeleton known as "Cheddar Man".

Vestiges of Iron and Bronze Age occupations are also scattered across the whole of the region, the most impressive concentration of them around Priddy, southeast of Cheddar. The nearby escarpment, with its sweeping views over the Somerset Levels, is riddled with literally hundreds of burial mounds, rings and chambers, suggesting that in prehistoric times this area was one of major ritual importance, second only to Stonehenge in neighbouring Wiltshire. Staring across the Levels, which at that time would have formed a shallow lake broken by numerous islands, it's not hard to imagine why.

After the Roman invasion of Britain in 43AD, **VELVET BOTTOM**, one of three dry valleys that converge on the head of Cheddar Gorge, rapidly became one of the empire's principal sources of lead (some historians have argued that it may have even been one of the primary motives for Emperor Claudius' invasion). Traces of extensive mines – both deep shafts and open-cast ditches – scar the fields around Charterhouse, where a distinct earthwork (at ST502561) is believed to be the remains of an amphitheatre. Lead ingots bearing the Mendips' hallmark have been found all over Europe, and in the medieval era Charterhouse lead was used to roof many of the continent's finest churches. Mining continued on a reduced scale until the mid-eighteenth century.

During Saxon times, the whole of the region served as a royal hunting forest, with its headquarters at Cheddar, where a collection of cathedral-sized wooden palaces were erected. The ruins of these now lie buried under the local Kings of Wessex comprehensive school, on the southern edge of Cheddar. Concrete posts in front of the modern buildings delineate the ground plan of Alfred the Great's former "King's Hall".

Subsequent centuries saw control of the uplands remain in the hands of large landowners, as wool overtook lead as the principal source of local wealth. The peasantry, meanwhile, became poorer – and unhealthy thanks to the poisoning of the water supply by lead smelting upstream.

The Black Down Decoy

The Black Down plateau, a wind-swept heather moorland grazed by herds of wild Exmoor ponies, is pock-marked with rows of low mounds. Contrary to appearances, these are not of pre-historic origin, but were made during World War II when the hilltop served as a huge decoy designed to confuse Luftwaffe pilots flying towards Bristol. Electric lights were mounted on the lumps, set out to replicate the shape of Bristol docks. It is, however, doubtful the ruse ever worked. Bristol was blitzed nine times in 1940, while Black Down came through unscathed.

ABOVE: Britain's largest gorge, with the Somerset Levels visible in the distance

When the social reformer and slavery abolitionist, William Wilberforce, visited Cheddar in 1789, he described the local population as, "ignorant and brutal to a degree which is hard to conceive," urging his friend, the Bristolian philanthropist Hannah Moore, to inspect the area. Appalled at the poverty she encountered, Moore opened many free schools in and around Cheddar. The extent of her success can be measured in local parish marriage registers, which before her arrival in 1806 were filled with the crosses of illiterate brides and grooms, but thereafter boast lines of proper signatures.

The River Yeo, one of England's largest underground rivers, first sees the light of day at the mouth of the gorge, where it emerges from eighteen separate springs. These flow into a series of ponds and weirs that formerly fed paper, cloth and flour mills. The old mill buildings still stand, but they were long ago put to use as trinket shops, hotels and cafés servicing the tourism industry that nowadays dominates this lower end of the canyon.

Cheddar's gimcrackery peaks around the entrance to the show caves, outposts of Lord Bath's money-spinning Longleat Estate, which owns the whole south side of the gorge. The Natural Trust looks after the northern side, where 130-metre/430-foot High Rock stands as the tallest cliff in Britain – a Mecca for climbers since it was first scaled by a Chris Bonnington-led team in 1965.

Lesser mortals can either ascend the gorge by our more sedate route, or opt for the knee-crunching Jacob's Ladder – a flight of 274 steps that was recently scaled in a record 56 seconds. Whichever path you follow, the spectacle of the crags plummeting to the tiny ribbon of road winding along the

floor of the gorge will more that repay the effort. The finest viewpoints are on the NT's north side of canyon, accessed via sidetracks off the main path.

As you walk, look out for herds of Soay sheep grazing inaccessible ledges below you. This small, dark-brown breed was introduced from the remote Hebridean island of St Kilda, where it has survived virtually unchanged since Neolithic times, to help keep the vegetation under control. A small herd of wild Exmoor ponies also patrols the pathways, and you might encounter feral goats released by the Longleat Estate to keep the undergrowth down on their side of the valley.

Three separate nature reserves are encountered in the course of this walk, each with its own distinct character. Leaflets stacked in the interpretive panels at the entrances sketch the routes of various nature trails through them, and highlight interesting flora and fauna you might encounter, along with the location of several cave mouths, long since shored up.

In **LONGWOOD NATURE RESERVE**, you can see the exact sport where a stream mysteriously disappears into a cave system underground.

"Cheddar Man"

In 1903, the owners of Gough's Cave were blasting open a new drain to cure the problem of winter flooding when they discovered a pile of human bones protruding from the rubble. Modern dating techniques have since attributed an age of 9000 years to what

anthropologists claim is the oldest complete prehistoric skeleton ever discovered in Britain. Dubbed "Cheddar Man", it made international headlines in 1997 when genetic material extracted from its jaw was matched with a sample given by a living resident in Cheddar

village, history teacher Adrian Targett - a genealogical world record.
You can see a facsimile of Cheddar Man on display at the show caves. The original resides in the British Museum in London. Adrian Targett still lives in Cheddar.

walk it | 33 Cheddar Gorge

CHECKED BY
✔ **Clevedon Ramblers**

1 Our route begins on Lippiatt Lane, at the start of the road leading up the Gorge. Look for the "Shahnaz" Indian restaurant on your R; Lippiatt Lane leads to R of this. After 2mins, steps cut sharply to the L between "Retreat" and "Lilliput Cottage", running behind

the houses along a narrow path to meet Lynch Lane.

Turn L onto the lane (un-named at this point – passing Copeley Peak bungalow) to reach a fork in path shortly after. Bear L here following the blue arrow (ie not along the Mendip Way), via a steep path through the woods to the Pavey's Lookout Tower at the head of Jacob's Ladder.

Map not to scale.
Representation of
**OS EXPLORER
MAP 141, 1:25,000**

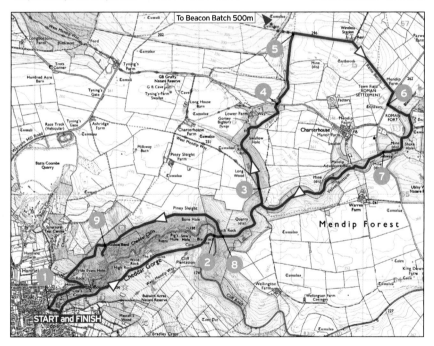

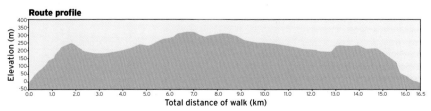

Route profile

Turn R here through a metal kissing gate; from here a well worn path climbs steadily along the cliff edges to the grassland plateau at the top of the gorge – a stiff 225m ascent – and then drops steeply down the other side through woods to Black Rock Gate. Cliff edges should be approached with caution: they are not fenced.

2 Once at Black Rock Gate, cross the B3135 and follow the path opposite into Black Rock nature reserve, up the floor of a steep-sided, wooded combe, past old quarry workings and a restored lime kiln to a four-way path junction. Bear L onto the West Mendip Way here, then R at a fork after 200m where a kissing gate marks the start of a permissive path through the **Longwood Nature Reserve**.

3 From the gateway into the reserve, a muddy path continues up the combe to a fork in the valley near the entrance to Rhino Rift cave, where it swings to the R (NE). Shortly after you reach a stream (which disappears underground) crossed by a little wooden bridge. Once on the other bank, the path bends to the R and rises through the woods to a stile. Turn L here and after a few paces cut diagonally R across the brow of the field, heading for the white bungalow beyond its bottom RH corner.
At the top R corner of the field, you'll meet a bridleway arriving from the R, which drops steeply down through a coppice of deciduous trees to a brook crossed by a railway sleeper. Cross and keep following the path around the side of the bungalow to the road.

4 Head straight across the road, and pick up the path continuing opposite the bungalow, which runs up a field alongside a narrow coppice to another stile. Ignore the waymarks leading L into the woods, and continue straight on, following a fence past some gorse bushes and onwards over the brow of the hill, from where you'll be able to see a stile and gate ahead to your R.

5 This junction, where the path runs into an old droveway, marks the start of an enjoyable detour to Beacon Batch, summit of Black Down and a fine viewpoint. Turn L onto the droveway, and continue to a swing gate, where you're confronted with a choice of four paths; take the middle one, leading straight to the top of the hill. The summit is marked by a trig point.
Return to point 5 by the same path, continuing E along the droveway to a wireless station, and thence down Rains Batch to the road. Shortly after turning R towards Charterhouse, look for a signposted path to the L.

6 This leads to a track into access land and the Blackmoor Nature Reserve. Once beyond the ponds and slag beach, keep straight ahead on the main path as it climbs the "gruffy ground", with a large mound on your R, to join a grey gravel track ending at a small car park, where you head straight on, over post stumps and along the floor of the combe to the road.
Climb the culvert, and turn R on to the road, then L shortly after into the top of the **Velvet Bottom Nature Reserve**.

7 From the entrance to the reserve, a clear path through Velvet Bottom winds gently along the floor of a deepening combe, past an outdoor activities hut and disused mine workings, and a series of old dams. At ST488549, you rejoin the main path through Black Rock Nature Reserve, turning left into the main valley.

8 Just before reaching the Black Rock Gate layby, a signboard next to a five-bar gate marked "To Cheddar" flags the onward route R, which climbs through beech woods and over a low hill into another combe. From the valley floor, a long flight of wooden steps cuts steeply uphill to regain the top of the main Gorge – the last stiff ascent of the day. From here on, the path winds at a gentle gradient through NT land along the northern rim of Gorge, above woodland. Look out for obvious side paths on the L leading to vantage points from where you get great views of the cliffs on the opposite side: one of the best is reached through a stile in a wall, flagged by a sign warning: "Danger Steep Cliffs". The path eventually begins to descend along the side of a drystone wall.

9 At the fork reached soon after, follow the wall to the corner where a stone stile leads along the edge of a precipice for the last spectacular view of the day. Then retrace your steps back to the fork, and bear L downhill towards another stone wall and five-bar gate marking the start of a steep descent through woodland. The path emerges at lane behind Hillside Cottage tea rooms. Turn L onto the lane to reach the main B3135 at the model toy exhibition, diagonally opposite the Tourist Information Office. A R turn on to the main road will take you back via the old mill ponds to the start of the route and Cheddar village.

Getting There

The nearest train station is at Weston-Super-Mare (14.5km/9miles), which is well connected by bus 126 to Cheddar (☎0871 200 2233, ✐www. firstgroup.com). Service 668 from Street to Lower Langford also stops at Cheddar. From Bristol, infrequent Eurotaxis buses (672; ☎0871 250 3333; ✐www. euro-taxis.co.uk) run to the village and caves, mostly around late afternoon or early evening; they also stop at the head of the Gorge, near the car park at Black Rock – an alternative start point for the walk.

Visitor Information

Cheddar Tourist Information Office (April–Sept daily 10am–5pm, Oct–March Sun only) Close to the entrance to the showcaves, on the south side of the Gorge.
☎01934 744071
✐www.visitsomerset.co.uk

Eating & Drinking

Cox's Mill
Opposite Cox's Cave, Cheddar Gorge
Welcoming estate-owned pub on the ground floor of a small hotel with a crackling fire in winter, flagstone floors and three or four real ales (including local Butcombe) and ciders. Serves good pub food at fair prices.

The Queen Victoria

Priddy
Six miles outside Cheddar on the village green. A Somerset institution that's changed little in a century or more. Three big wood fires (one of them open on two sides) warm a stone-lined, wood walled interior decorated with old photos of the village. Butcombe Gold and proper Somerset cider are served from barrels, along with basic pub meals.

Sleeping

Bay Rose House
The Bays, Cheddar Gorge
☎01934 741377
✐www.bayrose.co.uk
Homely B&B in a nineteenth-century cottage, with a flower-filled garden. Organic evening meals on request.

Cox's Mill Hotel

Opposite Cox's Cave, Cheddar Gorge, BS27 3QE
☎01934 742346
✐www.coxsmill.co.uk
Recently renovated hotel, occupying a former mill on the roadside, next to the old pond. Owned by the Longleat estate, it offers inexpensive singles, doubles and family rooms – some of them decked in flouncy pink satin.

Cheddar Bridge Caravan Touring Park

Draycott Road , Cheddar
BS27 3RJ
☎01934 743 048
✐www.cheddarbridge.co.uk
Within easy walking distance of the village, on the banks of the River Yeo. Well equipped and clean (its toilet block once won a "loo of the year award"), but pitch prices are steep in high summer. Over 18s only.

More Info

✐www.cheddarsomerset. co.uk. The village website hosts detailed local info pages and lots of links to visitor-oriented businesses in the area.

✐www.mendiphillsaonb.org. uk. Home page of the Mendips Hills area of outstanding natural beauty (AONB).

ABOVE: One of Lord Bath's feral goats, keeping down vegetation on the south side of the gorge

Coigach's "Little Mountain"

Stac Pollaidh

No photographs can fully prepare you for the stark beauty of Scotland's far northwest. Rising from a maze of lochans and knobbly rock outcrops, the region's mountains possess a surreal quality that owes as much to the other-wordly emptiness of their surroundings as the suddenness with which they rise from them. Quinag, Suilven, Canisp, Cul Mor and Cul Beag … each of these colossal lumps of ice-smoothed sandstone have an instantly recognizable shape. One, however, gets considerably more attention than all the rest.

It's not so much its spiky-topped ridge, nor even its diminutive height, that explain the popularity of Stac Pollaidh –"Peak of the Peat Moss". What really makes this hill special are the views to be had from it, and the relatively straightforward nature of the terrain you have to negotiate to enjoy them. Looking south and west over Loch Lugainn to the Summer Isles, and north over the staggeringly beautiful Inverpolly Nature Reserve to the peaks of Assynt, the panorama extends across Europe's largest wilderness. It's the kind of view you'd normally expect to have to mount an expedition to experience. Only here – thanks to a pitched path laid around the sides of the hill – it's safely attainable by anyone prepared to invest a few hours of effort.

The unique landscape around Stac Pollaidh owes its distinctiveness to two main factors. Firstly, the belt of Torridonian sandstone running between Skye and Cape Wrath, from where the mountains derive their peculiar shape. The second were the the "Clearances" of the nineteenth century, which initiated a process of depopulation that would never be reversed.

Buildings and roads may be few and far between as a consequence, but – in summer at least – you'll encounter plenty of other people scampering around Stac Pollaidh. An estimated 30,000 walkers make the ascent annually. This can be reassuring, of course, if such inhospitable terrain isn't generally your thing. Don't however, be lulled into a false sense of security. Only 612m/2008ft it may be, but at these latitudes the weather can deteriorate fast, making the path more difficult to follow. Check the forecast in advance, and ensure you've adequate clothing should the clouds close in.

At a glance

Where Stac Pollaidh; 23km/ 14miles northwest of Ullapool.
Why Panoramic view over Britain's greatest wilderness; possible sightings of golden eagles and red deer.
When Mid-October, for the Ullapool Guitar Festival.
Downsides Crowds in summer; erratic public transport.
Start/Finish Stac Pollaidh car park (NC108095), on the Achiltibuie road.
Duration 2hrs 30mins-4hrs.

Distance 4.5km/2.8miles.
Terrain Well made pitched paths, uneven in places, with sustained ascents/descents and a very steep climb to reach the summit ridge.
Maps OS Explorer 439.

On your way

Stac Pollaidh's serrated cap separates **LOCH LUGAINN** and Loch Sionascaig, on the broad peninsula of Coigach, to the north of Ullapool. The mountain and its larger siblings have long fascinated geologists. Comprised of chocolate-red sandstone, they rest on a bedrock of Lewissian Gneiss, formed 1500 million years ago, and one of the oldest known rocks in the world. Completing the geological picture is the layer of limestone lining some of the area's larger glens, where fossils of reindeer and wolves have been discovered, and vestiges of polar bear found in hidden caves.

Nearby Knockan Crag (✍www. knockan-crag.co.uk), 5km/3miles past the turning for Stac Poillaidh/Achiltibuie on the A835, was the focus of much scholarly debate in the late nineteenth century. Schists encrusting the clifftop here seemed much older than the limestones lower down, but it wasn't until 1907 that the puzzle of their origin was finally solved.

Knockan was found to lie on the so-called "Moine thrust fault" along which tectonic plate movement had displaced whole layers of rock, forcing them upwards and sideways. An interpretative centre perched just above the main road, complete with a turf-roof rock room and sculpture trail, tells the story of this conceptual breakthrough, showing how ice and erosion also played their part in shaping the region's distinctive landforms.

The climate of the northwest has seen some dramatic fluctuations since the last ice age. Pollen identified in the sediment at the bottom of a loch next to **STAC POLLAIDH** suggests that around 4200 years ago a sudden rise in temperature, accompanied by the onset of much windier and wetter weather, resulted in the disappearance of the pine forest that once carpeted the whole region. Today, it's hard to imagine the vast expanse of peat bog and bare rock covered in trees, and still harder to picture it dotted with little villages.

But this rough terrain was once home to a thriving community of Gaelic-speaking herders and subsistence farmers, who lived in tiny sod-and-stone huts, rearing goats and black cattle. Huddled together in clachans (townships), they supplemented their diet with herring, a hardy strain of oats and, later, crops of potatoes.

The humble spud fuelled a surge in the population of the Highlands. But it also contributed to the downfall of the region's distinctive culture. Increased pressure on land resulting from the potato boom made it easy for the local landowners to entice people to new settlements on the coast, where they could be put to work as cheap labour gathering two lucrative cash crops: herring and kelp (a kind of seaweed used in the manufacture of soap and glass).

In the 1820s, however, the bottom suddenly fell out of both markets, and the lairds decided they'd switch to sheep-rearing instead, which required the mass eviction of tenants remaining in the interior. This the estate owners achieved with a single-mindedness, and in some instances brutality, that has become legendary in the annals of the Highlands. Clachans were burned and their occupants dumped in an impoverished belt along the coastal strip, where old and young alike succumbed to malnourishment and infectious diseases.

Coigach was particularly badly hit by the Clearances. It lay within the domain of the most venal of all the estate owners, the Marquess of Stafford, First Duke of Sutherland, described in his obituary as "a leviathan of wealth (and) the richest individual who ever died." Having already moved them from the inland areas, the Duke later ordered a second re-location of Coigach's inhabitants from the coastal strip of the peninsula. Many, however, refused to budge, burning the eviction writs served on them.

Local newspapers described numerous so-called "deforcing" incidents, where crofters would disobey orders to shift. In one, the boat of the Deputy Sheriff and Procurator Fiscal, who'd come to serve notice on a community, was dragged by angry villagers onto dry land, leaving its passengers stranded at the mercy of the very mob they'd come to evict. The womenfolk, noted the reporter wryly, formed the vanguard of the protest.

The tone of press coverage became markedly more sombre after 1846, when the potato harvest failed and the crofters of the northwest faced starvation. The disaster must have weakened the resolve of people to cling to their land, for records show tens of thousands emigrated over the coming years rather than endure the "sheer hunger and

The New Stac Pollaidh Path

Stac Pollaidh is the most visited peak in the northwest Highlands, with upwards of 30,000 visitors annually. The erosion resulting from so many footsteps led Scottish Natural Heritage in 1999 to start construction of a path around the mountain. Paid for with £175,000 of lottery money, it is made of sandstone flags and, higher up, sand and cement laid in naturally decaying sacks.

Aside from forestalling erosion, the new path also aids navigation. In theory, if you stick to it you shouldn't get lost as the route forms a closed circle.

depression of opportunity" at home.

One particularly poignant letter to the *Inverness Advertiser* records the departure of a large contingent from Coigach. The crofters had assembled in a school in Ullapool to await the steamer to Glasgow, from where they would leave for Liverpool and then Tasmania.

"From the interest felt by friends and neighbours in those leaving," the letter of November 1853 remarked, "the school-room was densely crowded, even at that early hour, and there were many obliged to stand outside. After reading the (eleventh) chapter of Isaiah, their attention was called to subjects peculiarly suited to the circumstances in which they were placed. During the address, the concluding prayer, and singing, many were in tears."

Conned by middlemen at every stage of their long voyage to the southern hemisphere, the hapless crofters of Coigach arrived with little more than the shirts and dresses on their backs – many of them in debt to the land agents who'd paid for their passage to clear them off the land.

The majority ended up working on sheep farms in Van Diemen's Land, from where the male population had recently left for the Victoria gold rush. It's an irony indeed that these displaced Highlanders from Coigach actually contributed, in a roundabout kind of way, to the failure of the project that had originally uprooted them. Because it was cheaper, the woollen mills of Yorkshire bought Tasmanian wool rather than pricier fleeces from Sutherland. In time, the Duke's grand scheme floundered and his flocks dwindled, leaving the estate in the wild condition it remains today – and descendents of its original inhabitants scattered across the globe.

ABOVE: Cul Mor (849m), one of the giants of the Inverpolly Forest, dominates the view north from Stac Pollaidh

1 Cross the road from the car park and head up the path to the first gate. From there, the route rises steadily to your R through a recently planted wood and out on to the open moor. As you climb, fine views are revealed of **Loch Lugainn** to the south and Cul Beag to the southeast.

2 Some 5-10mins mins into the walk you reach a fork in the pitched path at NC108097. Bear R here and continue uphill (the L fork is your return route) and keep to the main path as it scales the eastern shoulder of the mountain, from the crest of which you gain your first glimpse of Suilven and the spectacular wilderness to the north.

3 At a second fork, on the far, northeastern side of the hill, a well made path peels L off the lower circuit towards the ridgetop above. Bear L here to start the steep, strenuous ascent to the ridge. A short, simple scramble runs L (E) from the lowest point in the ridge to **Stac Pollaidh**'s eastern peak - a magnificent viewpoint. But the true summit further west is a much trickier proposition involving exposed, difficult scrambling around a series of rock towers. It's best

avoided unless you're an experienced climber with a solid head for heights.

4 Return from the east peak to the low point in the ridge, and from there pick up the pitched path dropping NW to rejoin the main circuit. Turn L when you reach it, and follow the path around the dramatic western tower of Stac Pollaidh and back down the mountain to the junction passed earlier at NC108097. An easy downhill walk from there leads back to the car park and bus stop.

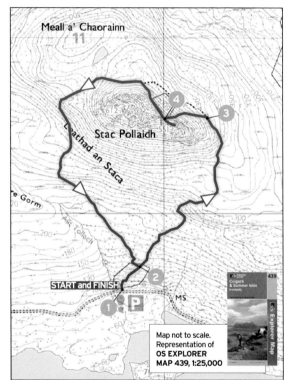

Map not to scale.
Representation of
**OS EXPLORER
MAP 439, 1:25,000**

Route profile

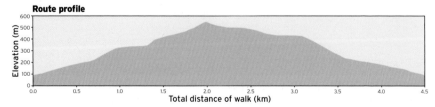

ABOVE: the jagged summit ridge of Stac Pollaidh, as seen from the Achiltibuie road

Getting There
D&E bus 811 runs daily from Ullapool to Reiff and back (Mon-Sat), passing Stac Pollaidh car park en route. Unfortunately, the gap between the outward and return services doesn't always leave enough time to climb the mountain. Timetables should be checked in advance at ✐www.decoaches.co.uk, or phone ✆01463 222444.

Visitor Information
Ullapool TIC
6 Argyll St
✆01854 612135

Eating & Drinking
Mountain Supplies Café
West Argyle Street, IV26 2TY
✆01854 613383
Good quality, reasonably priced food and drink served in a cosy first-floor café above an outdoor equipment shop.

Am Fuaran
Althandu, Nr Achiltibuie,
✆01854 622 339
Hidden gem of a pub, tucked away on the tip of the Coigach peninsula. Enjoy the sunset over a quiet pint and a plate of local poached salmon or prawns. Open

all day in summer.

The Seaforth
Quay St, Ullapool
✆01854 622122
✐www.theseaforth.com
An institution in Ullapool, the Seaforth stands opposite the pier and ferry terminal. Its ground floor is a busy all-day bar, serving sandwiches and pubby meals, while the bistro upstairs specializes in Scottish tapas: oyster goujons, salmon bruschetta, mussels and creamy Cullen Skink soup. There's also a terrific chippy at street level, voted "Best Takeaway" in the Radio 4 Food & Farming awards.

Sleeping
Woodlands
1A Pulteney St, Ullapool
IV26 2UP
✆01854 612701
Small, family-run budget B&B in the centre of Ullapool; handy for the shops and ferry terminal.

Suilven
Rhue, nr Ullapool, IV26 2TJ
✆01854 612955
✐www.bvegb.co.uk
Delightful vegetarian B&B in a stylish modern eco-house,

5km/3miles north of Ullapool on the A835. The views extend south over Loch Broom and west to the Summer Isles.

SYHA Ullapool
Shore St, Ullapool, IV26 2UJ
✆01854 612 254
✐www.syha.org.uk
Slap on the seafront and only a stone's throw from the ferry terminal, this small hostel is well situated and nicely set up, with internet access and a laundry. Dorm beds only.

More Info
✐www.northwest-highlands-geopark.org.uk. Website of the recently inaugurated Northwest Highlands Geopark, featuring a rundown of geological hotspots in the Coigach area.

✐www.ullapool.co.uk. The town's Community, business and tourism site, hosting dozens of useful links.

✐www.iainroy.com. Spectacular photogrpahs from the far northwest by local photographer, Iain Brownlie Roy, including a splendid panoramic version of our main image.

walk | 35

A Border Trinity

The Eildon Hills

Three crests against the saffron sky,
Beyond the purple plain,
The kind remembered melody
Of Tweed once more again
Andrew Lang, from *Twilight on Tweed* (1872)

Whether they're Himalayan giants or
Lowland knolls, peaks that stand proud of
their surrounding landscape cast a peculiar
spell – especially when, like the Eildon Hills
in the Scottish Borders, they sport three
distinct summits. Although rising to only
404m/1325ft, the Eildons' three-pronged
profile dominates the region around Melrose
and Galashiels, where Ettrick Water meets
the River Tweed. From the moment you set
eyes on them, you'll find yourself wanting
to scale the steep slopes of heather and
grass connecting the trio of shapely hilltops.

Ranging as far as the Cheviots and
Lammermuirs, the views are as wide-
ranging as you'd expect. Sir Walter Scott
claimed he could identify, "forty-three places
famous in war and verse" from the top of
the Eildons, on which Bronze Age tribes,
Roman sentries, and Saxon monks and

pilgrims have all left their marks.

The path up the hills from Melrose
makes for a relatively short, but lung-
stretching half-day walk – the perfect
appetizer if you're heading for wilder,
higher parts further north in Scotland.
Starting at Sir Walter Scott's beloved
Melrose Abbey, the route we've chosen
follows the course of the St Cuthbert's
Way, a waymarked long-distance route, to
the central ridge. From there it loops over
all three peaks before plunging back to the
valley floor for a leisurely amble at river-
level back to town.

The panoramas from the tops of the
Eildons can be magnificent in clear weather.
But it's the view *of* the hills from the east
that most often pops up on calendars. One
in particular attracts a steady stream of
admirers. A favourite of Sir Walter Scott,
it extends across a tight bend in the Tweed
from a natural balcony above the river near
the village of Bemersyde, just off the B6356.
It's known as "Scott's View", and is said to
be where the horse carrying the poet's hearse
paused en route to Dryburgh Abbey.

At a glance

Where The Eildon Hills, near
Melrose, Scottish Borders.
Why Ascent of three-peaked
extinct volcano; Melrose Abbey;
remains of Bronze Age hillfort
and Roman signal station.
When September, during the
Borders Walking Festival.

Start/Finish Melrose Abbey car
park (NT548340).
Duration 3-4hrs.
Distance 9km/6miles.
Cut it short Eildon Hill North,
6.5km/4.5miles.
Terrain Mostly un-surfaced
paths over open moorland that

are at times rocky and steep,
with sharp, slippery descents for
which walking poles are recommended. One short section
involves scaling a long flight of
wooden steps. The return leg of
the route is level and easy.
Maps OS Explorer 338.

On your way

Eildon is a text-book example of what geologists call a "laccolith". Some 300 million years ago, molten rock erupted into a magma chamber hundreds of metres below the valley floor, forcing the layers of sandstone above it upwards – like a giant pimple. The soft sandstone cap then gradually wore way, exposing the harder volcanic core to the elements.

Erosion has sculpted steep slopes below all three of Eildon's peaks, the most northerly of which holds a summit plateau fortified by the Selgovae tribe around 1000 BC. In its heyday before the Roman invasion, the Bronze Age bastion accommodated between three- and six-thousand people: you can still see traces of three hundred or more platforms where their turf huts would have rested.

Despite its redoubtable natural defences, the hillfort proved no match for the well-honed assault tactics of Agricola and his legions when they swept north into Scotland in 80AD. Having ousted the Selgovae, the Roman governor ordered a huge signal tower to be erected amid the hilltop ruins, but chose a site at the foot of the Eildons, near the modern village of **NEWSTEAD**, for his own stronghold.

"Trimontium" ("Three Hills") ranked among the most heavily protected military bases in Roman Britain. Ptolemy mentioned it in his *Geographia*, and all distances in Scotland were measured from its gateway. Excavations carried out in the 1900s revealed a massive ground plan, ramparts, remnants of an amphitheatre (the most northerly in the empire) and a hoard of splendid armour, including an exquisitely decorated cavalry helmet (now one of the National Museum of Scotland's greatest treasures).

Trimontium lay deserted after the Roman withdrawal, as did the old Selgovae hillfort above it. When, at the behest of King Oswald, St Aidan from Lindisfarne established a monastery in the area in 635 AD, he elected to build it on a spit of land further east, at a bend in the River Tweed called "mail-rhos", or "bare peninsula". St Cuthbert was one of the abbots before he became Bishop of Lindisfarne, and after his death his relics also resided here for a few months during their seven-year odyssey around northern England in 875AD.

The town and abbey that would later inherit the name of Mailrhos started life in the 1130s on a plot two miles upriver from the old monastery, which its Cistercian founders deemed better suited for farming. Paid for by King David I, **MELROSE ABBEY** would emerge as one of the grandest religious buildings of its day, noted above all for its splendid decorative carving. Alexander II and other Scottish kings were buried here. The heart of Robert the Bruce was also rumoured to lie under its chancery. However, it wasn't until 1996, when an archeology student unearthed a small lead casket containing a human heart, that the legend was proven to be true. A memorial stone commemorates the object's subsequent re-burial two years later.

Burned to cinders in 1385 by Richard II of England, attacked by the army of Henry VIII during the Reformation, and bombarded again by Cromwell in the Civil War, Melrose Abbey today is a battle-scarred ruin – but one whose famous decorative sculpture remains astonishingly fresh. Most of what survives – including the first known stone-carved depiction in Britain of the Virgin and Child, and a grotesque menagerie of bagpipe-playing gargoyles and dragons – dates from the late fourteenth century.

That so much of the abbey's decoration has endured can be attributed in part to the efforts of Sir Walter Scott, who lobbied successfully for renovation work to be carried out in the Victorian era. Although a native of Edinburgh, Scott developed a strong affection for the borders while convalescing from polio here as a boy. In 1812 he spent some of the earnings from his early novels on a farm overlooking the Tweed downriver from the abbey, near the site of the old monastery. The farm, Abbotsford, evolved into an extravagant Gothic fantasy, "a kind of conundrum castle . . . [which] pleases a fantastic person in style and manner."

Although the expense nearly ruined Scott and his French wife, the constant threat of insolvency had its advantages, spurring him to rattle off the best-selling Waverley series of novels. Scott's fiction, however, was never meant to be anything more than a lucrative sideline. Poetry was always his first love, and Melrose, with its abbey and epic landscape, provided him with plenty of inspiration.

The other poet associated with the Eildons hails from a much more distant past. "Thomas the Rhymer" – aka "True Tammas" – was a local soothsayer who prophesized many of the most important events in Scottish history, including the accession of James VI to the English throne. He is said to have gained his powers from a Fairy Queen he met after falling asleep under a tree at the foot of the Eildon Hills – a story told in *Thomas and the Elf Queen*. A memorial known as the **RHYMER'S STONE** now stands on the spot (the tree is long gone), reminding passersby of his prediction that, "(at) Eildon Tree, if you shall be/A brig o'er Tweed, yon there may see" – interpreted as foretelling the construction of a bridge at precisely the place one (in fact, two) now spans the river.

Some debate surrounds the true identity of Scotland's own Nostradamus, but the

ABOVE: Melrose Abbey, where Robert the Bruce's heart is buried

most likely candidate was a local laird named Thomas Learmont, who lived in the village of Erceldoune (Earlston) in the late thirteenth century. One thing's for certain: the poet's literary creations seem over the years to have become confused with the character of the writer himself.

A similar mist of obscurity shrouds the medieval alchemist and astrologer Michael Scott, regarded locally as a Scottish equivalent of Merlin. Borders folklore asserts the scholar, who served as a resident philosopher at the court of the Holy Roman Emperor, travelled to Scotland in 1236 to end his life at Melrose Abbey.

His reputation as a magician, however, derives less from the known facts of his life than from future embellishments dreamed up by the likes of Dante and James Hogg, which Sir Walter Scott further exaggerated in his epic poem *Lay of the Last Minstrel*.

It was also Sir Walter who first credited Michael Scott with the creation of the Borders' most iconic landform, claiming he "cleft the Eildon hills in three and bridled the river Tweed with a curb of stone."

1 From the car park opposite **Melrose Abbey**, head south down Abbey St, along the side of the high stone wall bounding Priorwood Garden to the Market Square. Cross it to follow the road running straight on (Dingleton Rd). This cuts under the bypass and onwards up the hill.

After 2mins, look for a gap in the pebble-dashed terrace to your L, signposted "St Cuthbert's Way & the Eildon Hills Walk". Dropping behind the houses, you cross a stream via a footbridge, then climb a long flight of 131 wooden steps, which brings you to the start of a broad, fenced path. A steady ascent over pasture ensues, via a couple of swing gates. At the 230m contour, the path emerges onto open moorland, bending R through a patch of gorse and onwards from there at a much easier gradient to a crosspaths at NT551325.

2 At the junction, turn R off St Cuthbert's Way to a rockier path winding steeply up the north side of Eildon Mid Hill. Ignore any side paths. After a while this swings L into the line of the hill for a steeper climb to the summit, marked with a trig point and antique topograph dedicated to Sir Walter Scott.

3 Pick up the path that drops SW off the hilltop. This bends L to begin a very steep descent to a path junction at NT545321. Here, you should turn L on to another path rising to a low saddle. Before passing the waypost visible ahead, bear R up the track leading to Little Hill; where the path swings L, turn

R on to a rockier side path leading, via three false summits, to the top of Eildon West Hill.

4 You follow a different path down the hill, dropping to the R (northwards) to a junction at NT549320. Do not turn R towards the woods, but keep

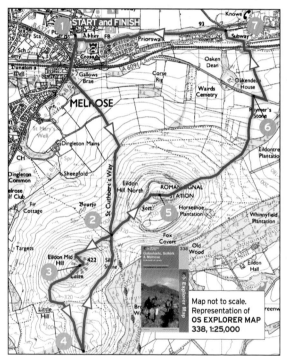

Map not to scale. Representation of **OS EXPLORER MAP 338, 1:25,000**

Route profile

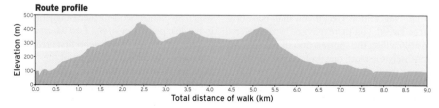

instead to the narrow path rising straight ahead of you up the hillside, which climbs to the saddle between the two main peaks, where you briefly rejoin St Cuthbert's Way. Turn L to follow its waymarks briefly then, at the point St Cuthbert's Way veers L, keep heading straight on up the clear path to the top of Eildon Hill North. **Cut it Short:** Retrace your steps to the pass after climbing Eildon Hill North, and return to Melrose by the same (outward) route (saving 2.5km/1.5miles).

5 Continue E from the summit of Eildon Hill North to begin the longest and steepest descent of the day. Bear L at the second waypost you reach (as indicated, at NT557329). The gradient eases off as the path approaches a conifer wood; pass through a gate and follow the wooded track down to the old (surfaced) road, where you turn R.

6 A short diversion up the lane leads to the **Rhymer's Stone**; otherwise follow the "Eildon Hills Walk" waymarks L down a farm track to a metal gate, then through the subway under the bypass and on down a muddy droveway to **Newstead** village.

7 Turn immediately L when you arrive in Newsteads (on to Dean Rd), and follow the lane for a few paces until you see a waypost on your R flagging a turning past pony stables. Keeping to the course of an old Roman road, this leads along a fence below a terrace of houses. At Priorswalk End, you bear R down a tarmac road (Dean Place) to the end of a cul de sac, then

on through a childrens' playground. From there, a pleasant little footpath runs at river level along a wrought-iron fence bordering the abbey grounds, emerging opposite the car park where you started.

Getting There
Direct buses run hourly to Melrose from Edinburgh. From Newcastle-upon-Tyne, you have to travel via Jedburgh and Newton-St Boswells. Timetable information for all services is available through Traveline Scotland (☎0871 200 2233, ✉www.travelinescotland.com).

Visitor Information
Melrose Tourist Office
Abbey House, Abbey Street
☎0870 6080404
✉www.visitscotland.com

Eating & Drinking
Burt's Hotel
Market Square, Melrose
☎0189 822285
✉www.burtshotel.co.uk
A terrific traditional Borders Inn on the main square, which serves fancy, French-influenced gastro renditions of Lowland cuisine, made with the very finest local produce. Their restaurant's quite pricy, but you can order less expensive meals in the congenial, hunting-and-fishing-themed "Bistro Bar", along with real ales and a large selection of single malts.

Sleeping
Braidwood
Buccleuch Street, Melrose, TD6 9LD
☎01896 822488
Smartly furnished, professionally run B&B in a Georgian town house only a stone's throw from the abbey.

Dunfermline House
Buccleuch Street, Melrose, TD6 9LD
☎01896 822411
The best fallback if Braidwood, opposite, is full, with similar views but more contemporary décor.

YHA Melrose
Priorwood, Melrose, TD6 9EF
☎01896 822521
Housed in a large, red-brick Georgian villa overlooking the abbey, this hostel has mostly 3- to 6-bed dorms, plus a couple of doubles.

More Info
✉www.melrose.border-net.co.uk. The town's exhaustively detailed website, particularly strong on rugby and history.

✉www.undiscoveredscotland.co.uk/melrose. A concise historical roundup, with links to other pages on places of interest in the area.

✉www.stcuthbertsway.fsnet.co.uk. Support for people attempting the four- to five-day walk from Melrose to Lindisfarne, a section of which is followed by our route.

✉www.scottsabbotsford.co.uk. Visitors to Sir Walter's fantasy home just east of Melrose can view the poet's immense collection historic relics, and wander the grounds.

✉www.roman-britain.org/places/trimontium.htm. The full lowdown on the Roman fort outside Melrose.

✉www.bordersbookfestival.org. Home page of the prestigious literature festival held in Melrose in the 3rd week of June.

walk | 36
GWYNEDD

Red Dragon, White Dragon

Nantgwynant

In their rush to reach the top of Snowdon, many visitors to North Wales overlook the delights of the valleys that buttress the massif. Yet the landscape to the south, in particular, ranks as some of the most superb in Wales. Clustered around the confluence of two fast-flowing rivers, with mountains looming on all sides, the village of Beddgelert is the area's prettiest village, and the launch pad for some unforgettable walks around the valley which George Borrow, writing in 1862, described as "wondrous … rivalling for grandeur and beauty any vale in the Alps or Pyrenees."

Even by Snowdonian standards, Nantgwynant holds some spectacular views. Having the highest peak in Britain south of the Scottish border as a backdrop certainly helps, as do the shimmering glacial lakes of Llyn Dinas and Llyn Gwynant on the valley floor. But what really gives the scenery here a captivating quality are the remnants of Dinas Emrys – the fortress to which the Celtic warlord Vortigern (Gwrtheryn)

retreated during the Saxon wars of the fifth century – which is thought by some to be the resting place of the old Throne of Britain.

Despite being hidden beneath a blanket of gnarled trees, the remains of the bastion cast a subtle spell over the valley. Viewed from the hills opposite, with the cloud-swept ridges of Snowdon just visible behind, it's not hard to imagine Dinas Emrys as the seat of a long-forgotten Celtic capital – or a gateway to some mythical Welsh underworld, guarded by invisible wizards.

In short, this is just the walk for anyone with a penchant for landscapes rich in romance, myth and legend. It starts by following the recently paved Fisherman's Path downriver from Beddgelert, passing a succession of tumultuous rapids to the Aberglaslyn Pass – a narrow defile through which the River Glaslyn crashes into the coastal plain. From there, our route swings northeast up Cwm Bychan, a roadless valley lined with eerie vestiges of the Victorian copper boom, to the crest of Mynydd Sygun

At a glance

Where Beddgelert, Snowdonia, North Wales.
Why Aberglaslyn Pass, Llyn Dinas lake and views of Snowdon; ruins of a Dark Age fortress; the Welsh Highland Railway.
When The rhododendrons may be a perennial pest hereabouts, but they look spectacular in early summer (May–June).
Downsides Brace yourself for

rain: this valley is officially one of the wettest places in Britain.
Start/Finish Beddgelert TIC (SH590481).
Duration 5-6hrs.
Distance 16km/10miles.
Cut it short You can catch a bus back to Beddgelert from the midway point (8km/5miles), where the path crosses the A498 at Bethania. Or turn L instead

of R when you reach Llyn Dinas to return directly to Beddgelert via the Sygun Copper mine and riverside.
Terrain Clearly defined paths along stony riversides, through woodland and over some exposed hillsides; boggy and muddy in places, and with sections over rock that may be slippery if wet.
Maps OS Explorer OL17.

mountain and our featured view.

An amble along the shores of exquisite Llyn Dinas then takes you to the halfway mark, where you can refuel at the delightful Caffi Dinas at Bethania before tackling the return leg across the rumpled skirt of the Snowdon massif itself.

Although lacking the strenuous gradients for which this region is renowned, the route is a fairly long one, and you may wish to chop it in two – easy enough to do thanks to the frequent Sherpa buses running along the A498, which will whisk you back to Beddgelert. Alternatively, skip the stretch along the lake, turning left towards the Sygun Copper Mine instead of right for Bethania to make a compact circuit that can be covered in less than three hours.

Whichever route you chose, you'll understand why this valley has featured in so many movies over the years (including one of the recent Tomb Raider series). Much of the filming took place around the campsite at the far northeast end of the lake – as spectacular a location as any in the country, and the perfect base if you're under canvas.

On your way

With its wild mountain backdrop, **DINAS EMRYS** looks every inch the seat of a legendary Dark-Age warlord. Archeological digs in the 1950s confirmed that the rounded crags rising from the floor of the Nantgwynant valley, a mile or so up the A498 from Beddgelert, were indeed inhabited during the fifth and sixth centuries by chiefs of some substance: shards of Phoenician pottery and amphorae from the eastern Mediterranean suggest its occupants were wealthy. But whether or not this was actually the last bastion of Vortigern (Gwrtheryn) himself will probably never be known for sure.

Local legend, however, asserts that it was here the "proud tyrant" mentioned by St Gildas made his base after his retreat from the Saxons. He ordered a tower to be built on top of the hill, but on waking each morning is said to have found the previous day's stonework strewn over the hilltop – a

mystery the warlord's wizard, Myrddin (Merlin), attributed to a pair of mischievous dragons buried beneath Dinas Emrys – one red and the other white. He also foretold that if ever the pair were released from their subterranean prison they would resume a never-ending fight that would consume the whole country.

The dragon story has long been interpreted as symbolizing the struggle between the Welsh (represented by the red dragon) and the English (the white one). And it's highly likely Dinas Emrys played a role in the long war between the ancient Britons and invading Anglo-Saxons during the Dark Ages. After Vortigern's demise, the citadel fell to King Abmrosius Aurelianus (b 403AD), the second son of Emperor Constantine and a leader whom Saint Gildas, writing a century later, identifies as the Welsh figure Emrys Wledig ("the Imperator"), who rallied the Britons to successfully counterattack the Saxons.

Aurelianus is regarded by many modern

Nantgwynant in the Movies

Thanks to its magnificent setting, the Nantgwynant valley, northeast of Beddgelert, has played a bit part in several major movies – most recently in 2002, when it doubled as rural China in *Tomb Raider II*, starring Angelina Jolie. Fans of the film (and there weren't many) may recall scenes set in a village overlooked by some dodgy CGI-generated mountains, where Lara had gone in search of the "Cradle of Life". The motorbike chase sequence made use of the old stone clapper bridge just

north of Llyn Gwynant, next to the campsite, watched by fifty Chinese-Welsh extras bussed in from Caernarfon. Nantgwynant's first starring role in a Hollywood blockbuster, however, was back in 1958, when the lake appeared in *The Inn of the Sixth Happiness*. Ingrid Bergman played the part of the missionary Gladys Aylward, who crosses the waters on a raft piled with children to escape the advancing Japanese army. The Chinese kids who acted in the film all came from Liverpool and had strong Scouse accents

that can clearly be heard in some scenes.

And then, of course, there's the Rupert the Bear connection. Those tartan trousers may suggest Scottish origins, but it was Nantgwynant that inspired many of the backdrops for the *Daily Express* Rupert stories. Illustrator Alfred Bestall, who took over from bear's creator, Mary Tourtel, in the 1930s, lived and worked in the valley for much of his long career. From his cottage in Beddgelert, he continued to write Rupert annuals until well into his 90s.

ABOVE: Boathouses, Llyn Gywnant

historians as the true source of the King Arthur legend, and the ghost of the mythical king is never far from the surface in this part of the world: the waters of Llyn Llydaw, at the foot of Mount Snowdon, are supposed to be where Bedivere threw Excalibur, and a pass further down the mountain, Bwlch-y-Saethau (the "Pass of Arrows") was allegedly the place Arthur received his mortal wound. In Nantgwynant itself, Llyn Dinas, the southerly of the valley's two lakes, is held by some to contain the old Throne of Britain, hidden under a stone slab by Vortigern.

The prevalence of such myths underlines Nantgwynant's historic role as a sanctuary for royalty in troubled times. After his defeat at the hands of Edward I in 1277, Llewelyn ap Iorwerth, the last Welsh Prince of Wales, came here to hide in his hunting lodge. It is said he once left his baby son sleeping in his cot while his much loved hound, Gelert, stood guard, but that on returning found the infant gone and the dog dripping with blood. Jumping to the obvious conclusion, Llewelyn killed Gelert, only to discover the boy safely asleep beneath his bed and the body of a wolf behind the house.

As he was being lowered into his grave, ever-faithful Gelert licked the hand of his master. Beddgelert was subsequently named in his honour (*bedd* = "grave" in Welsh), and you can still visit the railed-off enclosure a few hundred yards south of the village where Llewelyn is said to have buried the animal.

Both the grave and the story associated with it were, however, a complete fiction – a clever marketing ploy cooked up by the landlord of the Goat Hotel in the late-1700s to boost trade. "Gelert" was in fact a sixth-century Celtic saint, probably connected to the Dinas Emrys castle nearby.

The yarn did much to put Beddgelert on the region's tourist map. But it would be another century-and-a-half before visitors supplanted copper as the area's prime source of income. Just how important copper mining was to the area in the mid-nineteenth century can be seen in Beddgelert's main street, which is lined with little stone miners' cottages.

Most of the local male population worked in the nearby **SYGUN MINE**, whose excavations still honeycomb the rocky-topped mountain to the east of the village, **MYNYDD SYGUN**. Closed in the early

1900s, it recently reopened as a visitor attraction, where you climb underground to the top of the hill through tunnels oozing with stalactites and stalagmites.

Shafts were dug horizontally into the uppermost levels of the mine and the ore transported down to the River Glaslyn by means of an aerial tramway, the rusting pylons of which still march along the floor of **CWM BYCHAN**. Once at the **ABERGLASLYN PASS**, at the foot of Cwm Bychan, the copper ore was transferred to barges – before the estuary behind Porthmadog was drained in the early 1800s, Aberglaslyn marked the meeting point of the river and sea. Today, it lies 8km/5miles from the river mouth, but still forms a striking natural spectacle, with vertical cliffs soaring from whitewater rapids and pine forest.

The trademark viewpoint of the Pass is from the little road bridge just west of Nantmor village, where the A4085 crosses the river. A more vivid glimpse of the cataracts, however, is to be had by following the **FISHERMAN'S PATH** down from Beddgelert. Despite its ancient appearance, this route was laid only recently as an alternative to the narrow-gauge railway line just above it, which walkers traditionally followed, but whose trackbed and tunnels have recently been revamped as part of the **WELSH HIGHLAND RAILWAY**. In addition

to fixed railings to secure progress over the more slippery stretches, a new footbridge has also been constructed at **BRYN-Y-FELIN** to provide access for walkers to the gorge from the Gelert's Grave side of the river. The first steam locomotive chuffed over the adjacent railway bridge in October, 2007. By the time you read this, regular services should once again be running the whole route between Porthmadog and Caernarfon.

ABOVE: Llyn Gwynant – thought by some to be the resting place of the ancient Throne of Britain

Visiting Dinas Emrys

Hidden among groves of twisted oak trees and lichen-covered boulders, the tumbledown remnants of Gwtheryn's fortress at Dinas Emrys are an undisputed highlight of the Nantgwynant, and provide a great viewpoint over the valley. The site falls within the bounda-

ries of the former Craflwyn Estate, now owned by the National Trust. Visitors are welcome to explore the fort, but as much of it is in a fragile state you're asked to keep to a special waymarked trail. Our own route crosses this (see opposite) but you can also approach

the hillock from the NT car park just off the A498 (at SH599489), next to Craflwyn Hall. Leaflets outlining the paths are available free from the dispenser at the car park, and from the NT Warden in the converted stable block behind the main building.

walk it | 36
Nantgwynant Valley

CHECKED BY
✔ **Caernarfon/Dwyfor Ramblers**

1 Turn L out of Beddgelert TIC and follow the A498 through the village, past the bus stop on your L and village shop on your R. When you reach the road bridge, do not cross it: instead, head straight on, down the little lane running opposite, along the riverbank, past the woodcraft shop and public toilets. Cross the footbridge ahead of you and on the far side turn R through a carved wooden gate onto the riverside path, which brings you after 5-10mins to the new **Bryn-y-Felin** bridges. Cross the **Welsh Highland Railway** line via a metal swing gate to pick up the start of the **Fisherman's Path**. This winds down the L bank of the stream past an old stone sheep pen and a series of rapids to the **Aberglaslyn Pass**. Handrails have been fitted as walking aids in places where the rock may be slippery.

2 As the path approaches the roadbridge (Pont Aberglaslyn) you'll see the onward route rising L through the woods, continuing at a level gradient above a cottage. After 5mins, drop downhill to your R towards the National Park car park; go through the gate at the

bottom of the path and follow the trail L past the toilet block and under the railway arch. Soon after you'll emerge from the trees into the narrow valley of **Cwm Bychan**. Keep to the main path running in a straight line along the valley floor, ignoring

side paths cutting L towards the crest of **Mynydd Sygun**. The route steepens as it approaches the ridge, on the crest of which you cross a fence. On the far side, follow the path L as it contours around the hillside to an intersection marked with a

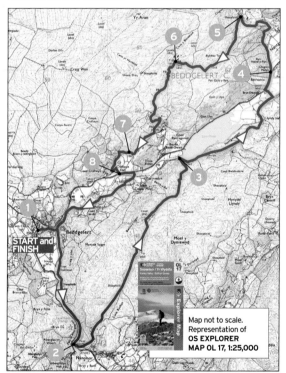

Map not to scale.
Representation of
**OS EXPLORER
MAP OL 17, 1:25,000**

Route profile

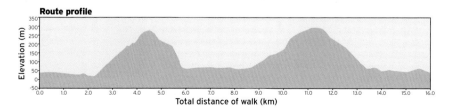

Elevation (m) — Total distance of walk (km)

fingerpost. Turn R here to begin the descent to the lake, but at the point 5mins later where the path drops more steeply, look for a little sidepath running R to a bluff – our featured viewpoint of the day (at SH613489), from where a wonderful panorama over Llyn Dinas is revealed.

3 Once you've reached the foot of the hill and joined the lakeside path, turn R; the route keeps close to the water's edge initially, before drifting inland a short way to skirt a large outcrop of rock. Having crested the shoulder of this and dropped back to the lake, you then skirt the edge of a small wood. Roughly 30mins after arriving at the lakeside, the track makes a right-angle turn into Llyndy Isaf farm, passing between the buildings. It then bends R to join a larger tarmac road, where you turn L to reach the A498. Cross to the far side of the main road, and head R a short way to Caffi Gwynant (see review below).

4 Just beyond the café, a sign on the L flags the start of the Watkins Path. This climbs through old oak woods above the river, emerging after 10mins from the trees as it climbs around the bottom of a hillock into the Cwm Llan valley. The sound of waterfalls swells as the path approaches a disused incline (an old mine tramway that used to transport ore from mines further up the mountain).

5 Immediately before the Watkins Path crosses the incline, keep your eyes peeled for a smaller path branching off to the L – the start of a National Trust waymarked route leading to Craflwyn Hall. The path is clear and easy to follow throughout, with little black arrows on metal plaques pointing the way. It climbs at an easy gradient, crossing a drystone wall via a ladder stile to enter a secluded high grazing area known as Bylchau Terfyn. Continuing uphill, a second wall stile is scaled, shortly after which the path reaches its high point of 315m/1033ft, from where it descends sharply to a collection of old mine workings.

6 Keep to the main mine track as it winds downhill through the ruins alongside a stream. A short way beyond the point where the track crosses this stream, the NT waymarks route you R, over the stream again and past a ruined mine cottage. Our path, however, keeps to the main track, which shortly after drops through a series of sharp switchbacks. At the next junction (SH607496), where the main track turns L to Hafod-y-Porth farm, keep R, walking above a drystone wall overlooking a hidden valley that's dominated by the wooded top of **Dinas Emrys**. An NT waymarker reached soon after indicates the route L to the fort – a recommended diversion.

7 Stick to the main path and you'll end up after 5mins at the Afon-y-Cwm. Cross the river and follow it upstream a short way, past a beautiful waterfall. Thereafter, the path curves L around the boundary of Craflwyn Hall, runs through a gap in the wall, then drops down through a wood to a field with a walled garden in the corner.

8 Cross the field to reach the lane running along the

ABOVE: Waterfall in the woods near Craflwyn Hall

side of the converted stables of Craflwyn Hall, then walk around to the front of the building. Follow the driveway down to the gate; cross the main road, and pick up the path starting immediately opposite, which turns L up the riverside to reach a small bridge below the **Sygun Copper Mine**. Having crossed the bridge, the tarmac road swings R, then L past the entrance to a driveway. Immediately after passing through a gap in a drystone wall, look for a footpath turning R, along the wall. This skirts Ty-Hen cottage, then drifts L to rejoin the lane, which runs for 1km/0.62miles past a campsite to the outskirts of Beddgelert. After 15mins or so, the lane veers R to cross a bridge, but you should keep heading straight on through a gate on to the rocky path running along the riverbank. This will take you back to the centre of the village.

Getting There

Beddgelert is served by two bus routes: the 95 Caernarfon–Waunfawr Sherpa and 97 between Portmeirion and Porthmadog. Timetables may be viewed online at &www. traveline-cymru.org.uk
&0781 200 2233

Visitor Information

Beddgelert TIC
Canolsant Hebog
&01766 890615

Eating & Drinking

Caffi Gwynant
Bethania
&01766 890855
&www.cwmnigwynant.co.uk.
The perfect pitstop midway

through our route. Close to the start of the Watkins' Path, it serves delicious, freshly cooked meals, snacks, cakes and Fairtrade coffees and teas in a funkily converted chapel, complete with pews and a covered terrace.

Cwellyn Arms

Rhyd Ddu, 6.5km/4 miles north of Beddgelert on the A4085.
&01766 890321
&www.snowdoninn.co.uk
Voted "Best Pub in Snowdonia" by the Campaign for Real Ale (CAMRA), the Cwellyn is a walkers' favourite, with a tempting range of cask bitters, home-cooked bar meals or more sophisticated specials, served next to a crackling log fire in the winter months.

Sleeping

Llyn Gwynant Campsite
5km/3miles northeast of Nantgwynant, LL55 4NW
&www.gwynant.com
One of the most perfectly situated camping spaces in the UK, at the peaceful north end of the Llyn Gwynant lake – as featured in the movie *Tomb Raider II*. Tents only, and they have bunkhouse barns for groups.

Bryn Dinas Bunkhouse

Nantgwynant LL55 4LH
&01766 890646
&www.bryndinasbunkhouse.co.uk.
Bunkhouse beds in timber cabins; the site is on the A498 between the two lakes, 3km/2miles out of Beddgelert, and well placed for walks in and around the valley.

YHA Bryn Gwynant

6.5km/4miles east of Beddgelert

on the A498, LL55 4NP
&0845 371 9108
&www.yha.org.uk
Large hostel set in forty acres of wooded grounds with superb views over Llyn Gwynant to Snowdon. Only 20mins' walk off our route.

More Info

&www.beddgelerttourism. com. Concise introduction to the village and its amenities.

&www.whr.co.uk. Official site of the Welsh Highland Railway.

&www.metoffice.gov.uk/loutdoor/mountainsafety/snowdonia.html. Detailed forecast for the Snowdon massif and surrounding area, with predictions of freezing levels, cloud base, wind speeds at altitude and other useful pointers for walkers.

&www.southsnowdonia-mountain-rescue.org.uk. Homepage of south Snowdonia's search & rescue team.

A Guide to Ancient and Historic Wales: Gwynedd by Frances Lynch (Cadw). A useful gazetteer of the region's most important monuments, including Dinas Emrys and other Dark Age forts.

More Walks

Collins Rambler's Guide: North Wales by Richard Sale (Collins/Ramblers). Thirty walks of various distances and levels of difficulty, exploring the main mountain groups of Snowdonia National Park, among them some of those around Nantgwynant and Beddgelert.

Around the Ramparts

Mynydd y Dref

The Tibetans have a saying that "horses make a perfect landscape more beautiful". In Snowdonia, castles could be said to fulfill the same function. Plenty of places in the world have mountains rising from the seashore, but where else can you admire coastal peaks towering behind massive medieval fortresses?

The great bastions dotted along the north Welsh shoreline date from Edward I's wars against Llewelyn ap Gruffydd in the late thirteenth century. To keep the rebellious Welsh under control, Edward commissioned his master castle-builder, the Frenchman, James St George, to throw "an Iron Ring" of fortifications around North Wales – the most splendid of them overlooking the mouth of the River Conwy.

Although somewhat upstaged by the three bridges since built across the estuary, the castle still strikes an imposing profile, especially when viewed from the hills above the town, from where it forms the centrepiece of a magnificent panorama stretching from the Great Orme promontory behind Llandudno to the Carneddau range

inland. On a clear day, you can even make out Merseyside and the distant Isle of Man.

Apart from holding some of Europe's most splendid medieval architecture, Conwy also offers a unique walking experience. It's the only walled town in Britain to have preserved its original ramparts. Dipping and rising to the high ground above the market square, the walls provide some great vantage points over the tightly packed gardens and slate-roofed houses of the old town to the castle, lording it over the quayside and tidal river flats below.

A walk around Conwy's ramparts makes the perfect preamble to this superb sixteen-kilometre/ten-mile trek through the hills behind the town. Taking its cue from the long-distance "North Wales Path", our route will lead you from the castle to the faded Victorian resort of Penmaenmawr, via an impressive Iron Age hillfort, a Neolithic droveway flanked by stone rows and tombs, and a "panoramic walk" cut around the sides of an extinct volcano.

The real highpoint of the day, however, comes in the form of a lonely stone circle

At a glance

Where Conwy to Penamenmawr, North Wales.
Why Conwy castle and town walls; Neolithic and Iron Age monuments; The Jubilee Panoramic Walk
When October: Conwy's mussel-centered food festival takes place annually on the third weekend.
Downsides The A55 coastal dual carriageway is audible at some stages of the walk.
Start/Finish Conwy Castle Visitors' Centre (SH783775)/ Penmaenmawr (SH713762).
Duration 5hrs.
Distance 16.5km/10miles.
Terrain Mostly waymarked, clear paths crossing upland pasture, with a brief section along a tarmac lane. Includes several strenuous ascents and descents.

on the ridge above Penmaenmawr. Nestled in a saucer of wild moorland, the so-called "Druid's Circle" stands in striking counterpoint to the expressway scything along the coastal strip below it, which you'll use to return to Conwy after one final, steep descent. From the end point of the walk, frequent bus services travel eastwards along the dual-carriageway, allowing this exploration of Conwy's coastal hinterland to be completed as a linear route, rather than a more limiting circuit.

Numerous options for cutting the route short offer themselves along the way, the most obvious of them from the end of the Jubilee Panoramic Walk. At the pillared entranceway to the Walk, instead of continuing up to the Druid's Circle you can head down Mountain Lane and straight back to the finishing point at

On your way

For many centuries, the Conwy River served as Wales' northeastern border – a troubled frontier that successfully repulsed both Romans and Normans. Not until 1282, when Edward I descended with a massive army, was an English monarch able to establish a secure foothold on the far bank.

Flanked by eight barrel-shaped towers, **CONWY CASTLE** was, and remains, the most handsome of the chain of fortresses erected by the Plantagenet king in Wales. Among the architectural wonders of its era, it was built in only four years, and provided protection for a self-contained garrison town, or bastide. Welshman were allowed to enter it during the daytime, but not to trade.

The original medieval grid plan survives little altered, enclosing picturesque streets of half-timbered inns, shops, cobbled lanes and cafés, and a church that originally served the Cistercian monastery founded here by Llewelyn the Great in 1199. But what makes Conwy unique in Britain are its ramparts. Nowhere else in the country will you find such extensive, well preserved **MEDIEVAL WALLS**. Punctuated with twenty-one towers and three double gateways, the battlements run for nearly 1300 metres (1400 yards) – in places at impressive gradients.

One of the advantages of viewing the castle from its ramparts is that it blocks out the three unsightly bridges across the Conwy River. The first of the trio – a narrow suspension bridge sporting mock-medieval turrets – appeared in 1826 as part of Thomas Telford's Chester–Holyhead road. Next, in 1849, came Robert Stephenson's tubular, wrought-iron railway bridge, which is still in use. And finally, to its north, stands the modern concrete road bridge, built in 1958. Contrary to appearances, the latter isn't the main route across the river: traffic on the A55 trunk route plunges beneath the water via a tunnel.

Our route into the hills follows a much older path – an ancient upland trackway

The Welsh Cliff Mystery

The steep-sided headland on the eastern side of Penmaenmawr, known as Penmaen Bach, was for a time in 1909 the focus of national attention when an empty car was found discarded on the road winding around it. Gossip started to circulate after the vehicle's owner, a flamboyant socialite named Violet Charlesworth, could not be traced. Following fruitless searches of the rocks beneath, reporters poured in to cover what became dubbed as "the Welsh Cliff Mystery".

Violet, it soon transpired, had disappeared leaving a pile of debts, mostly to male admirers from whom the beautiful heiress had borrowed large sums to fund her decadent lifestyle. Inevitably, suspicions were soon being raised that she may have staged her own demise. Then came the bombshell that Violet was in fact not an heiress at all, but an ordinary girl from Derby who'd been living a double life as a conwoman.

Due to all the press coverage her "disappearance" had received, it wasn't long before the 25-year-old was tracked down – to a rented room in Moffat, southern Scotland, where she was arrested and later sentenced to three years of hard labour.

It seems Violet never recovered from the ordeal of imprisonment. Only a few years after being released, her crumpled body was found at the foot of Beachy Head in East Sussex. Her memory lives on at Penmaenmawr, however, immortalized in the name of the bend in the road where her car had apparently crashed, since dubbed "Violet's Leap".

that once connected the mouth of the Conwy with the Afon Ddu valley in the west. After a steady ascent over bracken, heather and bilberry-covered slopes, it skirts the rock-studded ridge of **CONWY MOUNTAIN**, or **MYNYDD Y DREF**. Remnants of an Iron Age fort called **CAER SEION** spill from a summit plateau encircled by the vestiges of walls and ditches. More than sixty hut circles are discernible amid the rock debris. Their Neolithic inhabitants would have enjoyed much the same view as you see today, which in clear weather extends as far as the Cumbrian Fells.

Wayposts of the **NORTH WALES PATH** lead walkers downhill from Caer Seion to the **SYCHNANT PASS**, via a former toll road which horse-drawn traffic used when the beach route was covered by the tide. As you contour around the hillside beyond, a bird's-eye-view opens up over the secluded Gyrach Valley, dubbed by Victorian holidaymakers as the "Fairy Glen" because of its magical woods and waterfalls.

A phalanx of defunct volcanoes dominates this stretch of the walk, plunging sheer to the coast. Hidden in the heather halfway up the most prominent of them, **FOEL LÛS** ("Bilberry Hill"), is the once famous **JUBILEE PANORAMIC WALK**, a leisure path cut from the hillside in 1888 to mark Queen Victoria's Golden Jubilee. Traditionally entered through the pair of stone pillars on the southwest side of Foel Lûs, it proved an instant hit with visitors, though isn't particularly well frequented today considering the fine views.

An outcrop of rock a hundred metres below the Jubilee Panoramic Walk is known locally as the "Trwyn-yr-wylfa", or "Weeping Point". The name harks back to a disaster in the sixth century AD, when a tidal wave is believed to have swept over a township at a site now a mile or two off

shore. Having swum to safety, the survivors scrambled up the rock, then wept as they watched their homes and fields disappearing under the waves. The catastrophe gave rise to local legends telling of a palace called "Llys Helyg", the seat of an evil prince who tortured and murdered his subjects in bloodthirsty orgies. The tsunami was the prince's come-uppance, destroying his castle, which in the popular imagination has become a kind of Welsh Atlantis.

A large, rectangular stone building was once sighted by amateur archeologists in the waters of Conwy Bay, lending some credence to the old stories. During very low tides, stumps of ancient trees sometimes emerge from the shallows, accompanied – or so some fisherman insist – by the tolling of an invisible bell.

From the western flank of Foel Lûs, towards the end of the Jubilee Panoramic Walk, you get a fine view across the valley to the scarred slopes of Penmaen Mawr, the "Great Stone Head" from which the town below derives its name. Old postcards show it once had a pointed summit, but this was long ago dynamited flat by quarrying, spilling vast avalanches of spoil down the hillside below.

The hill has been the focus of a quarrying industry for at least five thousand years. Around 3000BC, chunks of a fine-grained igneous rock known as "augite granophyl" were being dug out of Craiglywd, the eastern flank of Penmaen Mawr, and polished into fine quality axe heads for export. Peak production seems to have coincided with the spread of agriculture, when Britain's forest cover was being cleared to create cultivable land.

The axes would have been traded along precisely the same path our route follows after looping around Panoramic Walk. Next to the prehistoric artery, the presence of

numerous stone monuments testify to the wealth the trade must have brought.

The most impressive of them is the **MAENI HIRION**, or "Long Stones", circle. Sited alongside a major crossroads in the ancient trackway, it is also misleadingly known as the **"DRUID'S CIRCLE"**, even though the ring of thirty monoliths predated the emergence of Celtic Druidism by at least a few millennia. Excavations inside the enclosure revealed the cremated bones of a twelve-year-old boy buried next to a small bronze knife.

Maeni Hirion marks the final turning point in our trail, which from here drops steeply downhill to its conclusion at **PENMAENMAWR**. The seafront, with its promenade and broad sands sliced by lines of old wooden groynes, has been horribly disfigured since the A55 trunk road was upgraded to a dual-carriageway in 1991. Nowadays, the quarry town and former resort exudes the feel of somewhere that's seen better days – which indeed it has.

In the mid-nineteenth century, "Pen" ranked among the most desirable retreats on the Welsh coast. Gladstone and his family holidayed here a dozen times or more, inspiring waves of well-heeled tourists from across the country to follow in their wake. That they were able to do so was due largely to the construction of the North Wales Coast Railway, built in the 1850s along a route devised by Messers Stevenson and Telford. After the smoggy, industrial cities of Victorian Britain, the dazzling blue bay and backdrop of wooded valleys, mountains and cliffs that greeted new arrivals in Penmaenmawr must have seemed breathtakingly exotic.

ABOVE: Conwy Castle from the highest point on the medieval walls

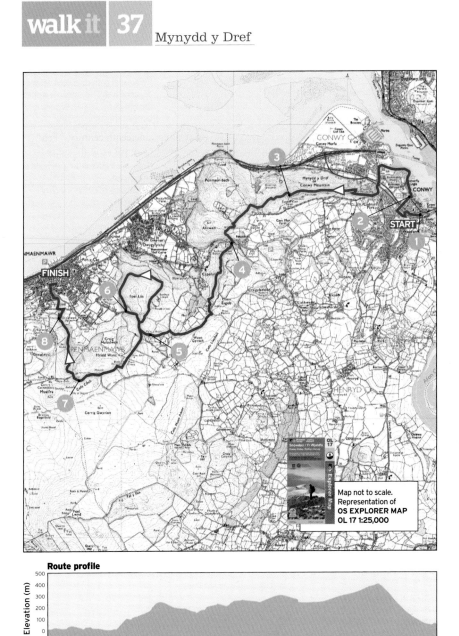

CONWY

Mynydd y Dref
Conwy Mountain

START

FINISH

PENMAENMAWR

Map not to scale.
Representation of
**OS EXPLORER MAP
OL 17 1:25,000**

Route profile

Elevation (m)

Total distance of walk (km)

1 Leave **Conwy Castle**/TIC via the door on its upper level and bear L towards the far corner of the car park outside, where you'll see the start of the first, short section of **medieval walls**. Once you've walked as far as you can, a staircase deposits you back at street level inside one of the medieval gateways.

Bear L on to Rosehill Street and keep heading around the bend on the main road for a couple of minutes until you reach a turning next to the HSBC bank. Head L here down Rosemary Lane. Cross the railway bridge, and turn R immediately after it down a little alleyway leading to the start of steps on to the train platform. Walk to the end of the platform to the exit at the far end, then head L to reach the start of the second, longer segment of town walls. This leads you around three sides of the medieval ramparts, ending up at their far northern corner.

When you reach the end of the rampart walk, turn R at the bottom of the steps onto Berry St. Go under the arch and then immediately R down Lower Gate St, then bear L where the lane forks to pick up the tarmac path along the riverfront. A green **North Wales Path** (NWP) sign on your R points the way.

2 The NWP runs past the marina, and along the bottom of Bodlondeb Wood, bending W after 10mins to skirt Aberconwy School; ignore the footbridge here. Eventually, it reaches a road (Morfa Drive) which you turn L onto, past the front entrance to the school. Keep heading down the road until you arrive at the busier Bangor Rd, which you cross to reach the footbridge over the railway at the end of the lane visible directly ahead (use the pelican crossing to your R).

Once over the bridge, keep to the path continuing from the bottom of the steps, but bear R uphill when it meets Mountain Rd. After a short climb, look for a track rising R in front of a row of white terraced houses to a wooden stile. This leads to the start of the path up **Conwy Mountain (Mynydd y Dref)**.

You can follow the well worn NWP along the south flank of the hill, or cut R up a side track to reach the ridge. A choice of trails presents itself when you get to the crest: keep to the one closest to the ridgeline, which will take you after 10-15mins to the Iron Age hillfort of **Caer Seion** - the day's featured viewpoint.

3 A clear path drops downhill from the W end of the fort, but things get a little more complicated once you're on level ground, where a tangle of moorland trails takes over. Keep following the NWP waymarks, which will lead you through a gap between a pair of low hillocks, then L down to a metal gate and cattle grid, where the path meets an unsurfaced farm track. Turn L here to follow the track as it loops downhill and around the foot of some crags to **Sychnant Pass**.

4 Cross Sychnant Pass Rd. But instead of following the NWP through the gateway directly ahead into the nature reserve, as indicated by a footpath sign, take the smaller path running R below a drystone wall. This contours around the hillside for 20mins or so to a tiny hill farm at SH745759, approached via a rising track flanked by stone walls. A short way beyond the farm you rejoin the NWP, arriving from the L through a grassy pass.

Keep heading R (SW) along the NWP from the pass until you reach the point where it starts to peel L away from the stone wall, at a junction near a telegraph pole marked by a waypost (SH744756). Bear R here along the wall. The path grows progressively boggier as it yields ground, arriving after 10-15mins at the Afon Gyrach stream, which you cross via stepping stones (at SH739754). Clamber up the far bank and over the ladder stile ahead, then up the R side of the field beyond to a metal gate. Having climbed over this, rather than head sharp L along the wall, bear diagonally L up the rise, on the far side of which you'll find Ty'n-y-ffrith farm.

5 Beyond the farm buildings, an unsurfaced track swings R to the pass dividing **Foel Lûs** and Craig Hafodwen. Having joined another track arriving from the L, look for a turning immediately on your R, marked by a low stone post with a red "viewpoint" symbol (if you reach a plinth and bench on your L you've gone too far). This winds around the flank of Foel Lûs to Ffrid-y-foel farm.

When the track bends sharply R down the side of the wall towards the farm, keep heading straight on. A short descent from here brings you to the start of the **Jubilee Panoramic Walk**, which leads off to the L.

6 A pair of stone pillars mark the end of the Walk. On reaching them, bear L up the hill to regain the NWP and pass crossed earlier. Only this time, take the route marked with a cross symbol leading R along the side of a stone wall to Bryn Derwydd.

Having passed the house, the path veers R through a gate, then L beyond another wall onto a broader track. Keep on this for 10mins, heading towards the ridge until you reach a fork (at SH725748), where you should bear L on to a narrow path cutting uphill to **Maeni Hirion ("Druid's Circle")**.

7 Several other interesting Neolithic sites lie a short way SW of the stone circle, but to continue our walk, drop down the steep slope below the monument to rejoin the main track/NWP, turning L onto it to reach the corner of a large drystone wall. Follow this wall downhill a short way as far as an iron kissing gate, from where an obvious path continues down the valley all the way to **Graiglwyd** Farm.

8 Bear R to skirt around the farm buildings when you reach them. From the far side of the farm, a track runs down to a road. Turn L when you reach the tarmac, then R very soon after through a gate beneath a tree. The path drops straight down the field towards a ruin in the corner in an old hedgerow; pass through a gate (to the L of the hedge continuing downhill) and follow the track down to the bottom of the field and upper limits of **Penmaenmawr**. Once on Helyg Rd, the first residential cul de sac you reach in the estate, bear L, then R at the

end of it on to Cwm Rd. This runs downhill to a junction; head straight on to Gilfach Rd, which soon after reaches Penmaenmawr's main street, Bangor Rd. A final R turn here will take you to the bus stop for Conwy (on the L, north side of the street).

Getting There
Arriva trains run a good service between Penmaenmawr and Conwy. Conwy is also a regular stop on the North Wales Coast Railway.

Visitor Information
Conwy TIC
Castle Buildings
☎ 01492 592248
✎ www.visitconwy.org.uk

Eating & Drinking
Conwy is famous for its fresh mussels, harvested at the mouth of the estuary through the winter. The best place to buy them is direct from Trevor Jones' purifying plant down on the quayside, at the foot of the castle.

Bistro Conwy
Chapel Street, Conwy
☎ 01492 596326
Homey little Welsh restaurant tucked away next to the medieval walls. It's a tiny place, hard to find, and pricy for the town, but serves the best food for miles – mostly locally sourced meat, game and vegetables. The atmosphere's relaxed and service courteous. Book well ahead.

Sleeping
YHA Conwy
Larkhill, Sychnant Pass Rd, LL32 8AJ.
☎ 0845 371 9732

✎ www.yha.org.uk
Large, very well equipped hostel at the top of the town, closed for a major refit when we were visiting, but due to re-open in May 2009.

Gwynfryn
4 York Place, Off Lancaster Square, Conwy, LL32 8AB
☎ 01492 576733
✎ www.gwynfrynbandb.co.uk
Award-winning luxury B&B in the heart of Conwy, with views of the castle and river from its fancily furnished rooms.

Bryn Guest House
Sychnant Pass Road, Conwy, LL32 8NS.
☎ 01492 592449
✎ www.bryn.org.uk
Overshadowed by the medieval walls, this pleasant B&B is set in its own spacious garden at the top of the town. It's especially recommended for veggies, and boasts superb views of the ramparts.

More Info
✎ www.penmaenmawr.com.
The village website is worth a browse for its pages on local history, which include a write up on the Jubilee Panoramic Walk.
✎ www.castlewales.com/conwy.
Masses of historical background on Conwy Castle and related sites in Wales.
✎ www.cadw.wales.gov.uk. Current opening times and admission charges for the castle.

More Walks
Collins Rambler's Guide: North Wales by Richard Sale (Collins/Ramblers). Thirty walks over a range of distances and levels of difficulty, exploring the main mountain groups of Snowdonia.

A "Cliff of Savage Fells"

High Cup Nick

'There where the Eden leisures through
Its sandstone valley, is my view
Of green and civil life that dwells
Below a cliff of savage fells …'
From *New Year Letter*, W H Auden (1940)

The most dramatic of the Pennine watershed is without doubt its northwestern flank, where the high fells tumble abruptly into the lush checkerboard of the Eden Valley. A phalanx of low, conical hills – known locally as "pikes" – stand proud of this mighty scarp edge, gazing like sentries across the vale to the peaks of the Lake District. Writing from exile in New York during World War II, a homesick WH Auden described this forgotten corner of northern England as, "one of the sacred places of the earth." And if your first glimpse of it is happens to be through the mists swirling around the head of High Cup Gill, you'll soon understand why.

A great chasm of dolerite gouged from of the fellside above Appleby-in-Westmorland, High Cup Gill forms the western extremity of the Great Whin Sill layer of igneous rock running northeast

from here to the Farne Islands. Viewed from the stream trickling over its head – a vantage point known as "High Cup Nick" – the valley's smooth, grassy, scree-streaked walls sweep in spectacular fashion to a fringe of blue-grey crags. On those rare days when the mist has lifted, you can look straight down the silver stream meandering across its floor and out across the rolling farmland beyond to survey the entire range of Lakeland summits – one of the most arresting views the North has to offer.

For walkers following the Pennine Way between Cross Fell and Teesdale, High Cup Gill comes as the scenic highlight of a superb day's trek over some of the Pennine's highest moorland. Our route follows its well worn track uphill from Dufton, one of a string of pretty red-sandstone villages nestled at the foot of the escarpment, to the famous viewpoint at the top of the gill. From there, it runs around the opposite, eastern rim of the valley, descending down a moorland spur to regain road level, from where a leisurely amble over pasture land takes you back to the Pennine Way just above Dufton.

At a glance

Where High Cup Nick, Dufton, near Appleby-in-Westmorland, Cumbria.
Why Striking geological formations; Cumbria's only winery; outstanding village pub.
When Early June, to coincide with

the famous Romany horse fair at nearby Appleby.
Downsides Public transport patchy.
Start/Finish Dufton village green (NY689251), 6km/3.7miles north of Appleby-in-Westmorland.

Duration 4hrs 30mins.
Distance 16km/10miles.
Terrain Farm tracks and moorland paths, some of them faint, uneven and boggy in places, with a final leg across pasture.
Maps OS Explorer OL19.

On your way

The striking vertical crags encrusting the rim of **HIGH CUP GILL** were formed 295 million years ago, when plate movements in the earth squeezed volcanic lava into gaps between giant seams of limestone. On cooling, the magma crystallized into blue-grey dolerite which, because it's more resistant to erosion than limestone, held firm long after the rock around it had dissolved away. The result is a belt of distinctive geological formations known as the Great Whin Sill – an intrusion at its thickest here at High Cup Gill, where it lies 70 metres deep.

The rock of the Great Whin Sill only serves to underline Cumbria's historic role as a buffer zone between Scotland and England. When the Romans decided to erect a barrier to bar the Scots from their empire in the first century AD, it was the rugged northern limits of the Sill they reinforced with Hadrian's Wall. On this northwest perimeter of the Pennines, however, their roads and forts were erected primarily to defend valuable lead and silver mines. Clay tablets found at Vindolanda near Housesteads Fort also record that this area served as a important source of meat, wood, milk and beer for the soldiers, as well as axe heads and even chariot parts.

With the end of the Pax Romana, the old antipathies between Scots and English erupted again, making the Eden Valley a troubled, lawless region whose inhabitants lived in constant fear of cattle raids and pillage. Though they frequently found themselves in the crossfire, the Cumbrians also enjoyed a fearsome reputation as warriors: it is said the local dialect has one hundred different words for "striking a blow".

Violence from another quarter plagued the early Christian era of the seventh and eighth centuries, when Norse war parties repeatedly wrought havoc here. In 875AD, Bishop Eardulf, Abbot Andred and seven of their monks from the monastery in Lindisfarne carried the sacred relics of St Cuthbert into the Eden Valley to escape a Viking raid. But when they got there they found Westmorland under attack too, and instead fled northeast into the Pennines – quite possibly via High Cup Gill – in the direction of Durham cathedral, where the remains were eventually interred.

More destruction was to be visited on the region under the Normans. In revenge for the rebellion of Gospatric, Earl of Northumberland, William the Conqueror ordered his infamous "Harrying of the North", a devastating assault that forced the local population into the fells. A long guerilla war ensued as the Cumbrians mounted retaliatory strikes on Norman supply lines, disappearing afterwards up hidden valleys such as High Cup Gill, where any Frenchmen foolish enough to follow them would get swallowed by the mist and bogs.

Apart from turmoil, one constant in this area's past – at least since it was introduced by the Danes a thousand or so years ago – has been sheep farming. Lush green pastures, overlooked by miles of immaculate drystone walls and barns, still lap the base of the Pennine scarp edge north of Appleby.

In the course of walking our route, you'll also see plenty of evidence of mining activity, most of it carried out in the eighteenth and nineteenth centuries, when the pits exploited by the Romans were being revived by the Quaker-owned London Lead Company. Houses, schools and chapels were provided for the workforce in the villages at the foot of the fells before the lead industry collapsed in the 1870s.

Small-scale mining for barytes (used in the manufacture of paint) recently resumed in the valley north of High Cup Gill, but in terms of economic importance tourism eclipses both mining and sheep farming in the North Pennines region. JMW Turner, who passed through with his sketch book in 1816, did much to publicize its charms to a wider world, painting **HIGH CUP NICK** and other local landmarks to dramatic effect.

The majority of visitors to this side of the fells these days follow in the footsteps of Turner, arriving from the heights of Cross Fell via the Pennine Way for a night in Dufton, where the Stag Inn is the focal point of a picturesque green, little changed since the lead boom of the nineteenth century. WH Auden once described Dufton as, "the loveliest village in England" – a judgement with which few emerging on a pleasant summer's evening from the Stag would disagree.

ABOVE: Stone barn at Harthwaite, a legacy of the Eden Valley's ancient wool trade

High Cup Nick

1 From the village green in Dufton, head down the Appleby road, past the post office-shop and car park on your R. After Brow Farm, the lane drops into a little dip, where a footpath sign for the Pennine Way points L up a surfaced farm track, marked with an MOD range flagpole.

2 Turn L here and follow the track through the trees and out towards Bow Hall. Just after the farm, the tarmac is succeeded by a rougher quarryman's track. This continues steadily up Dod Hill, bending to R and growing progressively more broken and muddy as it rises across open fell land.

3 At NY722250 you arrive at a sheepfold, which you can either walk through via a stile, or skirt to the L via a hand gate. Either way, follow the little dry combe beyond it past the entrance to an old mine to the crest above, where the first in a long chain of cairns guides you around the shoulder of Peeping Hill in the direction of Narrow Gate.

4 Once beyond Strands Beck, where it branches briefly in two, the path levels off for the easy walk NE across springy turf to the head of the valley. Keep R, following the edge of the crags to reach our featured viewpoint of **High Cup Nick**, where the stream plunges into the chasm.
If time and weather allow, it's worth making a detour NNE for 0.7 miles/1.1km, following stone marker posts across High Cup Plain to the footbridge over Maize Beck. The path crosses some very unusual limestone pavements to reach an impressive mini canyon cut by the beck into the rock at this point. Bear in mind, however, that this area can present a serious navigational challenge in poor visibility. Return to High Cup Nick by the same route.

5 Cross the stream at the head of the gill and follow the Pennine Way up a slight incline

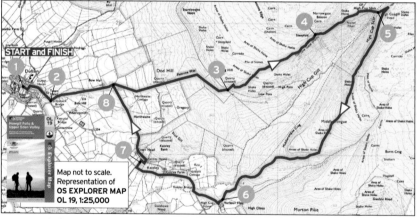

Route profile

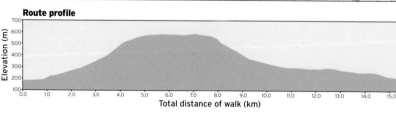

for about 50m to the second stone marker, where it intersects a fainter, narrower path. Turn R onto this and continue parallel with the edge of the cliff past two waymark posts to a stone wall at NY742253. Once over the ladder stile, you begin a sustained decent over the bracken-covered slope of Middle Tongue, following a well-worn quad-bike track. Keep to the main track as it drops downhill, then bears slightly L around the base of Middle Tongue, with the valley of Trundale Gill to the L. Eventually, the trail swings R and meets a broader track which fords a stream just before a gate. Continue to Harbour Flatt Farm, now visible ahead.

6 At the farm, do not enter the yard but instead turn R to cross a pasture toward a stand of tall trees with a stream beyond. Bear R around a small hillock with the stream on your R. A finger-post can be seen across the field. Cross the stile to join a narrow road. Turn R and walk up the road for 10 minutes until you see a finger-post signed "Bow Hall". Walk up the lane toward Keisley House (aka "Midtown Farm").

7 The actual right of way here, marked on OS maps as heading diagonally L across the field to Town Head, has been wrongly signposted by the council. Plans are afoot to construct new signs and stiles, routing you the correct way over the high wall next to Town Head's barn – should these be in place by the time you read this, then use them. In the meantime, continue around the bend towards the farmyard. Just before the house, you'll

see another post flagging a L turn. Take this, and continue to a waymarked gate a few yards in front, leading through an intake wall. Turn L behind the wall, then follow the well-worn and clearly waymarked path through a number of gates back to the lane at Bow Hall.

8 Turn L when you rejoin the track (at NY704251) and retrace your steps, following the Pennine Way down the hill past Bow Hall and back to Dufton village.

Getting There
Regular bus services run to Appleby-in-Westmorland, 4miles south; the town is also on the Settle–Carlisle railway, with connections to the West Coast Mainline at Penrith. Taxis are on hand for the short onward leg to Dufton. Try JVR on ☎017683 52382.

Visitor Information
TIC Appleby-in-Westmorland
Moot Hall, Boroughgate, Appleby-in-Westmorland
☎01768 351177
www.applebytown.org.uk

Eating & Drinking
The Post Office in Dufton stocks essential supplies of food and drink for walkers, but little else.

The Stag Inn
Dufton
☎01768 3516080
www.thestagdufton.co.uk
The location of this tiny, old-fashioned pub on the village green couldn't be more perfect, and the Blacksheep ales and home-cooked meals are all you dream they'll be on your way back down the hill. Get there early for a table.

Sleeping
Brow Farm, Dufton, CA16 6DF
☎01768 352865
www.browfarm.com
Comfortable, inexpensive B&B in a converted mid-eighteenth century barn made of local red sandstone, 5mins from the pub in Dufton. They also offer a couple of self-contained cottages for rent.

Dufton Youth Hostel
Dufton, CA16 6DB
☎0845 371 9734
www.yha.org.uk
Large, red-sandstone house in the village centre, with a couple of double rooms as well as larger dorms. The hostel manager's a mine of info on local geology.

Grandie Caravan and Campsite Mrs E M Howe, Edenstone
Dufton
CA16 6DB
☎01768 351573
Small, peaceful site just east of the village green, with sixteen static caravans and ample tent pitches overlooking Dufton Ghyll woods. Popular mainly with Pennine Way walkers.

More Info
www.visitcumbria.com/pen/highcupnick.htm. Some great pics of the mighty trough through the seasons.

www.dufton.org.uk. Heaps of background on the village, with links to its businesses.

More Walks

Walks in the Penrith Area by Graham Allan (Penrith Ramblers). A selection of thirty walks to celebrate the 25th Anniversary of the Penrith Ramblers group.

A Hill with Attitude

Fleetwith Pike

The English Lake District is justly famous for the interplay between its mountains and water – a relationship that reaches a mesmerizing climax at Buttermere. At less than two miles long, this is far from the largest lake in the region, but it couldn't have been more perfectly formed to complement the high fells surrounding it. Superb views are guaranteed from any of the adjacent mountains, improving steadily as you gain altitude. There is, however, one perspective on Buttermere that's truly in a class of its own.

Overlooking the southwestern end of the lake is what looks, when seen from the water's edge, a rather squat, pyramidal fell, noticeably stumpier than its neighbours, but possessing heaps of what the Americans would call "attitude" (that's with a "t", not an "l"). In late summer when the heather's in bloom and the enfolding summits trail shreds of mist, Fleetwith Pike has a truly commanding presence about it.

Apart from its position slap in the centre of one of Lakeland's most scenic enclaves, the main reason Fleetwith qualifies as a great viewpoint is the abruptness with which its northwest ridge – known ominously as "the

Edge" – rises from the waterside. And it's this airy, broken line which our route follows to the top. You don't have to wait long to see why. After barely ten minutes of strenuous climbing, a superb vista unfolds of wavering ridges, cliffs, corries and summits, centered on a string of lakes that draw your eye down the valley to the blue line of the sea, with the distant mountains of Dumfries and Galloway fringing the horizon.

Although less satisfyingly symmetrical than those from Fleetwith Pike, the great views continue as our route progresses south and west towards Hay Stacks, Wainwright's favourite fell and another magnificent vantage point over the valley. From its craggy crest you also gain a wonderful panorama of Ennerdale and its presiding giants Great Gable, Kirk Fell and Pillar. Throw in a scattering of delightful high tarns and the possibility of extending the itinerary along the lake and you've a recipe for a classic hill day.

In spite of its relative isolation from the Lakes' most frequented honeypots, the valley is well served by public transport, with a dependable bus link running between Keswick and Cockermouth.

At a glance

Where Fleetwith Pike, Buttermere, 21km/13miles southwest of Keswick, Lake District.
Why Honister slate quarry; Hidden mountain lakes; Alfred Wainwright's favourite fell, Hay Stacks.
When Mid-May, to coincide with the Keswick Mountain Festival.
Downsides This corner of the Lake District is notoriously wet – come well prepared.
Start/Finish Gatesgarth Farm car park (NY195150).
Duration 3hrs 30mins.
Distance 9km/5.5miles.

Terrain Mostly rough and rocky mountain paths, with some easy scrambling and stream crossings. Route finding is relatively straightforward in good weather, though potentially tricky with poor visibility.
Maps: OS Explorer OL4.

On your way

Although it looks wedge-shaped from Buttermere, **FLEETWITH PIKE** is actually the spur of a larger, more rounded fell dividing the Gatesgarthdale and Warnscale valleys. Steep crags crenellate two of its sides, while to the east the hill shelves at a more gentle gradient to the Honister Pass, headquarters of the slate quarry whose satellite workings pockmark the high ground in this area.

Slate quarrying is thought to have been started at Honister by the Romans, but was carried out on a small scale until the building boom of the industrial revolution caused a surge in demand for roofing materials. Extraction peaked after the Buttermere Green Slate Company, formed in 1879, built long tramways, or "inclines", to transport finished rock down the mountain.

Like their counterparts in North Wales, the Honister quarrymen trekked long distances to work each Monday morning, living on site during the week and returning to their families on Saturday afternoons. The conditions in which they lived, worked and slept were appalling. Disease was rife and life expectancy less than fifty years for most of the nineteenth century.

The steady decline in the slate industry saw the quarry close in 1987, but the site recently re-opened – partly as a functioning quarry, and partly as a visitor attraction offering mine tours. One of its sidelines is a Via Ferrata route that cuts, by means of fixed cables and metal ladders, across the vertiginous **HONISTER CRAG** below Fleetwith Pike's north ridge – an approach to the summit recommended only for those with a good head for heights.

The inspiration for the Via Ferrata was the recent rediscovery of a crumbling nineteenth-century incline which, amazingly, sliced across the middle of the 1000-foot

crag; it was used to reach the seam of high-quality green slate that erupts from the hilltop. Access to the tramway was from the quarry hub at the pass, Honister Hause, from where tracks ran along the so-called "Monkey Shelf" to cross a succession of terrifying gullies and buttresses with names like "Bull Gill" and "Ash Crag". Three winding drums were used to haul the bogies of slate up and down the cliff, in places crossing dizzying voids on lengths of timber.

It looks insane by the standards of modern engineering, but the Honister Incline ranked among the nineteenth-century slate industry's most impressive technological achievements. The line, however, was only in use for thirty years. Howling gales and landslips on Fleetwith Pike (one of the wettest places in Britain with an average rainfall of around 2.5m/100 inches per year) played havoc with the installations and made maintenance very expensive. Rockfalls would regularly sweep away sections of the track and during icy conditions the whole route became inaccessible. Eventually, a new, less weather-vulnerable incline had to be constructed on the south side of the hill.

This second tramway is the one followed

Bathroom with a View

The entrepreneurial owners of Honister Quarry were behind a headline-grabbing stunt in 2007 when, to support Cumbria Tourism's £3-million "Wilderness Refined" campaign, they set up a bath tub on top of Fleetwith Pike, complete with hat stand and bottle of champagne. In freezing winter temperatures, a model was then cajoled into stripping off for a dip, and sipping bubbly while a helicopter buzzed overhead to film the event. You can watch footage of the bizarre episode on the quarry company's website, ✐ www.honister-slate-mine.co.uk.

ABOVE: Herwick lamb on Hay Stacks

by our route to reach the lower of Honister's working quarries, above **WARNSCALE BECK**. Once across the stream, the rumble of digger trucks gives way to the trickle of open water as you enter a tract of rumpled, rocky moorland dotted with little lakes.

The largest of these, **BLACKBECK TARN**, nestles in a hollow against a backdrop formed by the high summits of Great Gable and Kirk Fell to the south. Its smaller neighbour, **INNOMINATE TARN**, was a favourite haunt of the guide-book writer Alfred Wainwright. The Grumpy Old Fellwalker asked for his ashes to be scattered here – a wish his wife, Betty, fulfilled two months after his death in 1991. Some suggested the tarn should be re-named in his honour, but Innominate it remains.

Describing the path that winds west from the lake to the nearby summit of **HAY STACKS**, Wainwright famously quipped that "if you should get a bit of grit in your boot... treat it with respect. It might be me!". The precise spot where his ashes were dispersed has always been kept a secret, so this is a piece of advice worth heeding.

By the time you've scrambled to the top of the hill, you'll appreciate why the craggy top of Hay Stacks was where the legendary fells man wished to be his final resting place. Set at a right angle to the main crest, the summit ridge is marked at either end by cairns – the northern one is generally considered to be the higher of the pair. Both yield wonderful views. Peaks rise on all sides, with High Crag dominating to the northwest.

"A shaggy terrier in the company of foxhounds," was how "AW" saw the hill, which he came to regard as the loveliest in Lakeland. "For beauty, variety and interesting detail, for sheer fascination and unique individuality, the summit area of Hay Stacks is supreme. This is in fact the best fell of all."

Before tackling the scrambly drop down to **SCARTH GAP** for the descent back to Buttermere, make a short detour into the heather south of the summit crags for a peek into Ennerdale, one of the Lakes' most remote valleys. The only building visible for miles is the white-washed croft of Black Sail Youth Hostel, used by walkers as a base camp for explorations of the mighty wall of mountains ringing the head of the valley, culminating in the bell top of Great Gable.

CHECKED BY
✔ **West Cumbria Ramblers**

1 Leaving the Gatesgarth Farm car park, turn L up the Honister Pass road (B5289), passing Gatesgarth Cottage on your R, immediately after which you'll see a footpath sign pointing R towards the base of **Fleetwith Pike**'s NW ridge. Overlooked by a white crucifix commemorating a woman who fell to her death after tripping over her walking pole here in 1887, the path zigzags steeply up, with the views back over Buttermere growing more spectacular at every step.

Having surmounted the initial obstacle of Low Raven Crag, the trail levels off briefly before getting stuck into the rocky spine of Fleetwith Edge. Simple hand holds may occasionally be needed during the rest of the ascent, but the steepest crags can always be avoided. After 45-50mins of relentless gradient, you arrive at the lumpy topped summit of the hill, marked by a cairn.

2 Keep heading past the cairn on the same clear path, which winds E over humps of heather, past the heads of gulleys slicing down mighty **Honister Crag** to your L, then skirting a succession of little tarns. After the last of these, at around NY212141, the trail begins to drift R, away from the ridge, towards the open-cast slate quarry below. Pick your way across the top of the mine workings, and turn L when you reach the unsurfaced road lined by huge slate standing stones.

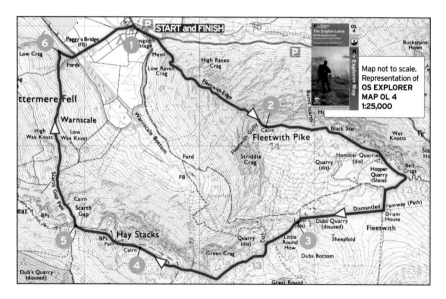

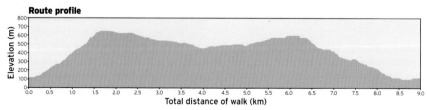

Route profile

Walk along this for a minute or so, then head R (S) down a faint fell track that drops down to a disused incline. Turn R on to this old tramway, which runs in a dead straight line down to a second quarry site, where you'll see the bothy, **Dub's Hut** (see 'Sleeping').

3 Drop down to **Warnscale Beck**, now visible below, from which a clear path rises on the opposite side. Follow this onwards as it climbs through the rocks ahead, past a prominent junction at NY205130, where you should keep R, then through a saddle pass and down the other side to pretty **Blackbeck Tarn**. The famous **Innominate Tarn**, where Wainwright's ashes are scattered, lies another 5mins' walk further along a rising, rocky trail. The route from here is impossible to lose as it wriggles W through the crags to the summit of **Hay Stacks**.

4 Small cairns flag the two main paths tumbling off the top off Hay Stacks. Whichever you opt for, hand holds will be required on some of the trickier, steeper sections, as the crags descend in steps to Scarth Gap.

5 Turn R when you reach the large cairn marking the pass that divides Hay Stacks from Seat, and follow the well worn trail as it drops at an easy gradient through the little col known as **Scarth Gap**, passing a collapsed wall before fording a beck. Great views across Warnscale Bottom to Fleetwith Pike accompany this sustained descent down the side of the valley, which eases as only slightly it approaches the valley floor, now dominated by the lakeshore.

6 On reaching the path junction at NY188148, take the route cutting sharply back to your R, which drops along the side of a little plantation to a gate through a drystone wall. From there it crosses the footbridge spanning Warnsdale Beck, and runs in a straight line over level ground back to Gatesgarthdale Beck, the farm and adjacent car park.

Getting There
The Honister Rambler, Stagecoach Service 77/77A (www.stagecoachbus.com) runs eight times daily (May–Oct only) past our start point from Penrith, Whitehaven, St Bees, Cockermouth and Keswick. The nearest railhead is Whitehaven, 25 miles/40km west, but you're better off taking a train to Windermere or Penrith, and then the bus to Keswick to connect with the Honister Rambler. For timetable information, contact Traveline 0871 200 2233, www.traveline.org.uk.

Visitor Information
Cockermouth TIC
Town Hall, Crockermouth
01900 822634
www.cockermouth.org.uk

Eating & Drinking
Both the Fish Hotel and Bridge Hotel in Buttermere village serve quality bar food and more fancy restaurant meals, as well as real ales, and tea, coffee and cakes during the afternoon. Alternatively, try the Croft House Café, which rustles up tasty filled rolls and other light snacks. And don't, whatever you do, leave without sampling Skye Farm's delicious ice cream, made with milk from its own herd of Ayrshire cows, which you can see grazing in the surrounding fields.

Sleeping
Dalegarth Guest House
Hassness Estate, Buttermere, CA13 9XA
01768 770233
www.dalegarthguesthouse.co.uk
Less than a mile from the start of our route, Dalegarth is well situated option run by Ramblers Holidays. Good-value accommodation is offered in the Swiss-chalet-style guest house on the lakeside, and there's a nice little site on the water's edge for campers.

Honister Hause Youth Hostel
Seatoller, Keswick, CA12 5XN
0845 371 9522
www.yha.org.uk
Comfy 26-bed hostel housed in a former quarry workers' building set at the bleak summit of Honister Pass.

Buttermere Youth Hostel
Buttermere, CA13 9XA
0845 371 9508
A less atmospheric option than Honister Hause, and slightly further from our route, but close to the pubs.

Skye Farm
Buttermere, CA13 9XA
01768 770222
No-frills farm campsite, in a perfect lakeside setting only a short stumble from the village centre. It's an exhilarating spot to camp, though be warned that you have to lug all your gear across a footbridge to reach the field. No alcohol or camper vans allowed. They also offer inexpensive B&B in the farmhouse. Open year-round.

Gatesgarth Farm Campsite
2 miles southeast of Buttermere village, Grid ref: NY195150
01768 770256

Because it's beyond range of the pubs, this site tends to get less busy than those further up the lakeshore, but it's right at the start of our route, on the grassy floodplain next to the water – and the views are to-die-for.

Dub's Hut
Book through the Honister Slate Mining Company
Grid ref: NY209134
📞017687 77230
Tiny, ultra basic stone bothy set amid the bleak surroundings of the mine's spoil heaps, but bang on our route. Give the mine a ring to check it's not block-booked.

 More Info
✎www.buttermere-lorton. com. Comprehensive portal for the area, featuring links to visitor-oriented businesses.

✎www.visitcumbria.com/cm/ buttermere.htm. Includes a nice little introduction to Buttermere and environs, with lots of inspiring photos.

✎www.honister-slate-mine.co.uk. The slate quarry's characteristically quirky site.

✎www.metoffice.gov.uk/ loutdoor/mountainsafety/ lakedistrict.html. The most accurate and detailed weather predictions for walkers: you're given estimates on visibility, cloud base heights, freezing levels and windspeed at different altitudes.

More Walks
Collins Ramblers Guide: The Lake District by John Gillham & Ron Turnbull (Collins/Ramblers). Thirty detailed routes in some of Britain's most spectacular landscapes, ranging from a short 7km/4.5mile route around Hampsfell, to a 21km/13miler in the Langdale Pikes.

Walks in South Lakeland by Kendal Ramblers (Ramblers). Eighteen walks of different lengths – from 6.5km/4miles to 24km/15miles. Most are low level but some are on the higher fells.

Walks in South Lakeland Book 2 by Kendal Ramblers (Ramblers). Eighteen new walks developed by Kendal Ramblers.

ABOVE: The Borrowdale tops from Fleetwith Pike

The Golden Road

Mynydd Preseli

If hills were ranked according to the distance you can see from them, Mynydd Preseli in Pembrokeshire would make it into Britain's top twenty – quite a feat for a diminutive moorland ridge that barely breaks the 500m contour. But the Preselis, as anyone who has walked among them will tell you, are very special. From the outcrops of volcanic bluestone dotted along their spine, you can see all the way across Cardigan Bay to the summits of Snowdonia and the Lleyn peninsula, and southwards over the Channel to Dartmoor and Bodmin in Cornwall. On a really clear day, it's even possible to pick out Mullagh Clevaun in the Wicklow Hills – 105miles/169km across the Irish Sea.

To the ancient Britons, this 360-degree panorama must have been a source of great awe, roving as it did across their entire known world. No wonder they seemed to have invested the ridge with great ritual significance. Dozens of standing stones, dolmens, alignments, burial mounds and cairns dot the hillsides hereabouts – one of the greatest concentration of prehistoric remains in Europe. The only region of Britain boasting more is Salisbury Plain, whose inhabitants deemed the rock of the Preselis

so important that they dragged and floated huge lumps of it across the country to build the great circle at Stonehenge.

Quite how and why our Neolithic ancestors performed this miraculous feat remains the great enigma of British prehistory. But the aura of it lends a vivid undercurrent to any walk along the Preseli ridge. And who knows, maybe the old bluestones really do hold healing powers, as some of the New Age settlers who've congregated in the area since the 1960s insist. Hunker down out of the wind in one of the Preseli "carns", with wild ponies grazing on the heather-covered hillsides below, and a gigantic vista of sea and distant mountains unfolding at your feet, and you'll feel the magic start to work.

Thanks to the recent introduction of a special walkers' bus – the Green Dragon – it is now possible to complete the traverse of the Mynydd Preseli crest without having to leave a car at either end. Just be sure to save the walk for a clear day. And if you want to believe your own eyes, come armed with a topograph (downloadable from ✐www.viewfinderpanoramas.org) and a pair of binoculars to help identify those unfeasibly far-off landmarks.

At a glance

Where Mynydd Preseli, Crymych, 20km/12miles southeast of Newport, Pembrokeshire.
Why Spectacular Iron Age hillfort and other prehistoric remains; red kites, coughs and ravens.
When May-Sept for the Green

Dragon walkers' bus.
Start/Finish Crymych (SN183339)/Bwlch Gwnynt car park. (SN075322).
Distance 16km/10miles.
Duration 5-6hrs.
Terrain Clear, but frequently

boggy and muddy paths over undulating moorland and rocky outcrops. Navigation could present some challenges in poor visibility, though escape routes to lower ground are numerous.
Maps OS Explorer OL35.

Carn Menyn and the Golden Road from Foeldrygarn

On your way

A simple, east-to-west traverse of the Preseli crest, our route follows the course of an ancient trackway known as the **GOLDEN ROAD**. For 5000 years or more this rutted upland path served as the main artery linking Wessex with Ireland. Trade goods, notably dolerite axe heads carved nearby, would have passed along it. And probably songs and stories too, such as those immortalized in the *Mabinogi*, a compendium of ancient Celtic myths and legends first set down in the fourteenth century, but including some stories thought to pre-date the arrival of Christianity by a thousand years or more.

It's tempting to imagine that tales from the Mabinogi – or distant versions of them – would have enlivened dark evenings around the hearths of the Iron Age hillforts crowning several of Mynydd Preseli's peaks. **FOELDRYGARN,** just above the village of **CRYMYCH** where our walk begins, is the most impressive of these. Two protective walls of loose stones girdle the hilltop citadel, where the remains of more than two hundred hut circles pockmark the ground. From its centre rise the three enormous cairns from which the fort derives its name. The view from their sunken tops is magnificent, but to fully appreciate the scale and striking form of the fortress itself you'll have to charter a light aircraft, or scour the internet for photos by someone who has already (see "More Info").

The volcanic rock of Foeldrygarn is thought to have provided five of the major monoliths at Stonehenge. However, the bulk of the sacred stones originated at nearby **CARN MENYN**, the chaos of blue-grey pinnacles erupting from the bracken slopes a short way southwest of the hillfort.

Sir Herbert Thomas, researching in 1923 for the Geological Survey, was the first to suggest that the spotty dolerite used to build the core of the great circle on Salisbury Plain must have come from this exact outcrop. His theory has since been contested by proponents of a rival hypothesis – that the rock was carried to Wiltshire by glaciers – but this has been discounted by modern studies. Somehow, around 4500 years ago, the four-tonne bluestones were dragged south to the banks of the Cleddau estuary, floated down to Milford Haven and around the Bristol Channel to the Avon, then hauled overland to the Wylie River, floated again, and pulled – or pushed – the last miles to the top of Salisbury Plain – a journey of 400km/250miles (involving 40km/25miles of overland portage).

One piece in the puzzle of how our Neolithic forebears managed this was solved recently: the giant stones probably didn't need to be quarried. At Carn Menyn, the dolerite has been cracked by frost into tall pillars, which would have been relatively easy to break off. Examples of cup art – round hollows carved within circles – have also been discovered here, showing that people venerated these rocks at precisely the same time Stonehenge was being built. Moreover, dolmen (or "cromlech") sites such as the one at nearby Pentre Ifan prove Neolithic

ABOVE: The Tafarn Sinc, Rosebush

ABOVE: Sunrise over the Rhinnogs — the expansive view north from the Preseli crest

engineers were definitely capable of manhandling huge chunks of rock.

In medieval times, the stone circles and other prehistoric remnants littering the moors crossed by the Golden Road were seen as relics from the era of King Arthur and his Knights. Two sites just west of Carn Menyn – the tor of **CARN ARTHUR** and bluestone oval of twelve menhirs known as **BEDD ARTHUR** – were believed to have marked the burial site of the mythical king himself, whose exploits are recounted at length in the *Mabinogi*.

One of Arthur's many missions impossible – undertaken to secure for his young kinsman, Cwlhwch, the right to marry his beloved Olwen, a giant's daughter – was to steal a comb and shears from the head of the magical wild boar, Twrch Trywth. Quite why a fierce porker with secret powers should have carried such hair-cutting tools the *Mabinogi* doesn't make clear, but Arthur and his knights are said to have chased the creature from the coast into the hills, eventually running him to ground at **FOEL ERYR** (the "Eagles' Mountain"), the westernmost of the Preselis' summits. A fight ensued in which a number of Arthur's men were slain before Twrch Trywth turned tail.

Capped by a Bronze Age cairn and national park lookout plinth, Foel Eryr provides the ultimate viewpoint in the range – although it's not the highest peak (that honour goes to nearby **FOEL CWMCERWYN**, 68m/223ft taller). Extending for a radius of more than two hundred miles from Snowdon to Cornwall, and west to County Wicklow in Ireland, the wonderful panorama is a fitting culmination for a walk across one of Britain's truly epic landscapes.

walk it | 40

Mynydd Preseli

CHECKED BY
✔ **Cardigan & District Ramblers**

1 Head south from the centre of **Crymych**, past the garage (on your R) and school (on your L), and take the first turning R at the bottom of the hill – a long, straight lane leading to Blaebanon cottage. At the T-junction, turn L past Llainbanal farm and continue for 5mins until you reach a broad entrance to a field and bridleway on your L.

2 A footpath sign on the opposite side of the road marks the start of a muddy farm track; follow this for a couple of minutes until it reaches a junction with another track arriving from the L. Ahead you'll see a national park gate leading on to open moorland. Go through this and

bear R towards the summit of **Foeldrygarn**, improvising a route across the lumpy water courses until a clear path up the hillside is reached.

3 From the top of the fort, an obvious breach on the south side of the encircling ramparts leads to the start of the onward route, which winds downhill to a boggy saddle, and then up the other side to join the main **Golden Road** bridleway (at SN157329). Turn R on to the bridleway and continue west for around 10mins until a path peels L towards through the heather to **Carn Menyn**.

4 Once you've finished exploring Carn Menyn, pick up the path that skirts the westernmost outcrop of rocks and then drops to the head of

the Rhestr Gerrig stream. It contours L around the top of the valley to rejoin the main path (at SN140328). A ten- to fifteen-minute ascent up the hillside rising to the west brings you to a prominent fork (at SN132327); bear L here for **Bedd Arthur** stone oval, rejoining the main trail afterwards, which runs just below nearby Carn Bica.

5 Having skirted **Carn Arthur** and crossed the shoulder of the hill, the path – marked for a while by white-topped wooden posts – descends sharply to a boggy pass, where another path crosses it from the south. Just beyond the junction, the posts veer R around hillside at a fork (at SN120324 – not marked on OS maps) – ignore this, and continue to the L up a rise to the top of

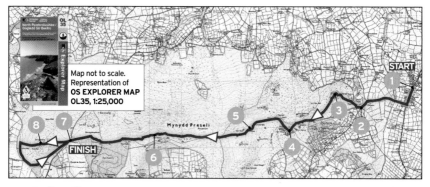

Map not to scale.
Representation of
**OS EXPLORER MAP
OL35, 1:25,000**

START

Mynydd Preseli

FINISH

Route profile

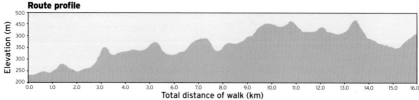

Foel Feddau (467m/1532ft), with the imposing profile of **Foel Cwmcerwyn** (the highest point in the Preselis at 536m/1758m) now looming to the southwest.

6 At Foel Feddau, a wonderful view opens up for the first time over St David's and St Bride's Bay in the far west. The path then drifts downhill to the R of the ridge, continuing over very boggy ground along the edge of a conifer plantation. By the time the trees end, Bwlch Gwnyt car park and the B4329 are clearly visible below.

7 Having got this far, be sure to press on for the final ascent of the day to **Foel Eryr** (468m/1535ft), the featured viewpoint of our route, reached via a heavily eroded path which the national park have recently reinforced with steps. A topograph on the summit, erected on top of a Bronze Age burial cairn, identifies the landmarks visible from this magnificent vantage point.

8 From the top of Foel Eryr, continue onwards in the same direction, descending steeply down a fainter trail that plunges towards the head of a valley. A waypost reached 5–10mins later flags a path junction (at SN059321) where you should turn L and contour around the base of the hill via a tangle of sheep trails to a stile over a fence, marked by another signpost. Instead of crossing the stile, continue L along the line of an ancient earthwork as far as a second fence, which this time you should climb over. From here the path ascends gradually northeast back to the car park (at stage **7**).

Getting There

The Preseli "Green Dragon" walkers' bus runs twice weekly (Tues and Sun, May–Sept), connecting Crymych with Newport, via Bwlch Gwynt car park, just below Foel Eryr. There are only two services per day in either direction, and it's advisable to book ahead, 0845 602 7008. For details of connections with other buses to and from Cardigan, Fishguard & Haverfordwest, contact Traveline Cymru on 0845 602 1386 or go to www.traveline-cymru.org.uk.
If the Green Dragon isn't running, you could always arrange for a taxi to pick you up at the end of the route: contact "Home James" on 01239 711201.

i Visitor Information

Newport TIC
2 Bank Cottages, Long St
01239 820912
www.newport-pembs.co.uk

Eating & Drinking

Tafarn Sinc
Rosebush, on the B4329 nr Maenclochog
01437 532214
www.tafarnsinc.co.uk
The highest pub in Pembrokeshire, and a recommended diversion from our route. Housed in a former GWR railway hotel, the pink-painted, corrugated iron building reminded Jan Morris of, "a ghost town saloon in Nevada." Cured hams hang above the bar, there's sawdust on the floor, and proper Preseli lamb is offered on an old-fashioned food menu, as well as home-brewed ales.

Sleeping

Penyrallt Uchaf Farm
Crymych, SA41 3RT
01239 831282

www.farmaccommodation.net/index.html
Delightful farm B&B, a couple of miles north of Crymych in the depths of the countryside. Lovely views and fluffy angora goats are additional attractions. They also have a three-bedroom holiday cottage for rent.

YHA Newport
Lower St Mary Street, Newport, 10km/6miles from the end of our route, SA42 0TS
0845 371 9543
www.yha.org.uk
Pleasant hostel in a smartly converted Victorian school, with a couple of two-bed and family rooms as well as basic dorms.

Rosebush Caravan & Camping Park
Rhoslwyn, Rosebush, SA66 7QT
01437 532206
This is the nearest campsite to our route, located 4.5km/3miles southeast of the finishing point. It's nothing to write home about, but well maintained, and within easy walking distance of Tafarn Sinc.

More Info

www.viewfinderpanoramas.org. Click on the Wales list of this site to find a fabulous free topo-panorama from the summit of Foel Cwmcerwyn – not identical to the view from Foel Eryr, but close.

www.coflein.gov.uk. The website of the Royal Commission on the Ancient and Historical Monuments of Wales features aerial photos of Foeldrygarn.

www.pcnpa.org.uk. Homepage of the Pembrokeshire Coast National Park Authority.

walk | 41

The Limestone Trinity

Malham Cove

I won't know for sure if Malhamdale is the finest place there is until I have died and seen heaven (assuming they let me at least have a glance), but until that day comes, it will certainly do.
Bill Bryson, in *Notes from a Small Island*

The Limestone Uplands of Yorkshire possess an unfair share of Britain's natural wonders, and no less than three of them fall within a two-mile radius of Malham, a pretty village of babbling streams and stone cottages on the edge of the Yorkshire Dales National Park. It was so difficult to decide which of the famous trinity of sights here – Malham Cove, Malham Tarn and Gordale Scar – provided the most beautiful view that we ended up including all three in a classic route which, over the course of 12km/7.5miles, brings you alongside gigantic white cliffs, rushing waterfalls, some outlandish rock formations and the highest lake in the country – not to mention a string of wildly contrasting vistas.

Arguably the most majestic of these extends from the rim of Malham Cove itself, a spectacular amphitheatre of escarpments from whose foot a dark river mysteriously

emerges. Back in the last Ice Age, this same river used to plunge over the top of the precipice, but when the ground thawed the water began to flow underground, leaving in its wake an elaborately ribbed "pavement" of blue-grey limestone that today forms a surreal foreground to the panorama of lush hills and dales infolding from below it.

The view from the top of Malham Cove stands as a grand finale to a circuit that's been a popular excursion since Victorian times, when its landforms inspired Turner, Ruskin and Charles Kingsley. More visitors than ever are now coming to Malham to experience these great sights, but thanks to sensitive management by the National Trust you still have to walk – and in one instance scramble – to reach the most impressive viewpoints, which has ensured these limestone treasures remain relatively undiminished by the attention lavished on them.

Having said that, Malham village itself can feel deluged on sunny Sundays. Moreover, because of its popularity, accommodation can be thin on the ground – book well ahead, and take advantage of the many other superb trails in this area.

At a glance

Where Malham, 11km/7miles northwest of Skipton, Yorkshire Dales National Park.
Why Malham Cove; Gordale Scar: a dramatic ravine with leaning sides; Janet's Foss waterfalls; Malham Tarn: Britain's highest lake.
When Early summer when the

limestone slopes are ablaze with wild flowers.
Downsides Malham village draws big crowds on weekends and bank holidays.
Start/Finish National Park Visitor Centre, Malham (SD900626).
Duration 3hrs 30mins-4hrs.

Distance 12km/7.5miles.
Terrain Well made paths through-out, some crossing steep, rocky ground that can get slippery in wet weather, plus one very short scramble which involves some hand holds.
Maps OS Explorer OL2.

On your way

The defining feature of the landscape lining the south and west perimeters of the Yorkshire Dales National Park is the so-called **CRAVEN FAULT** – a geological faultline dividing the park's limestone uplands from the gentler pastures below. Formed 330 million years ago, when the area lay beneath a tropical ocean sprinkled with coral islets, its bedrock of carboniferous limestone was lifted up by earth movements and gradually eroded by millennia of rainfall and glacial action.

Limestone is unique among the hard rocks of Britain for being soluble. The carbon dioxide absorbed by rain as it falls through the air renders it slightly acidic, and thus able to dissolve the alkaline stone as it percolates downwards, forming cracks that over time widen into passages and caves.

As a consequence, the stepped plateau to the north of Malham is honeycombed by invisible channels which allow water to drain rapidly away. Walk on a wet day up Gordale Beck, the stream followed by the early stages of our route, and you'll gain a vivid sense of the volume of water pouring from the high ground.

The beck reaches a crescendo at **JANET'S FOSS**, where it plunges over an outcrop into a deep pool ringed by mossy boulders and trees. "Foss" derives, like its namesake "force", from the Norse word for "waterfall"; "Janet" is a Fairy Queen of local folk lore, suggesting this magical glade has been popular with the area's inhabitants for many centuries.

Elderly residents of Malham still recall the time when the pool was used for an annual mass sheep dip. Stripped to the waist, shepherds would wash their flocks to encourage the growth of new wool – a spectacle around which a small festival grew up over the years. As you approach the falls through the wooded gorge below them, look out for fallen tree trunks into which people have hammered lucky pennies as offerings to the fairies who inhabitat these glades.

Janet's Foss is the perfect scene setter for the big event of the beck's course. Hidden until the last second by a bend in the surrounding cliffs, **GORDALE SCAR** comes as a complete revelation – a vertical trench bounded by 100-metre/328-feet cliffs that seem almost to meet at their tops. Through this narrow defile the stream froths down two superb waterfalls, the higher of the pair cascading over a rock arch above the first. The geological explanation is that the gorge was formed by the collapse of a massive underground cavern, but this fails to convey the gloomy magnificence of the scene, which has long fascinated visiting artists.

The Romantic poet Thomas Gray (1716–71) claimed he could only bear to stay in the Scar for a quarter of an hour at a time, and then, "not without shuddering". And after being invited here by the local landowner, Lord Ribblesdale, in 1811, James Ward declared the vista "un-paintable", before proving himself wrong

with a rendition as awe-inspiring as it was huge. His enormous canvas, measuring 3.7m x 4.3m/12ft x 14ft, now hangs in the Tate where it is regarded as the apotheosis of the so-called "Regency-Gigantism" school of Romantic landscape painting.

Art history, however, is decidedly far from most peoples' minds as they tackle the outcrop of water-worn limestone, or tufa, blocking onward progress up the Scar. Seven or eight moves are all that's required to carry you above the obstacle, but these are enough to deter many walkers. The reward for the little scramble is a superb view back down the gorge and access to the radically different landscape above.

The source of Gordale Beck lies a couple of miles further north, amid the hills enfolding another of the national park's hidden gems, **MALHAM TARN**. Originally formed by glacial meltwater, the lake – the highest in Britain – presents a serene spectacle against its backdrop of moorland ridges. The eastern shore is dominated by the stately façade of Malham House, an elegant aristocratic bolthole that formerly belonged to Lord Ribblesdale. The mansion which nowadays serves as a field centre run by the National Trust.

It was here Rev Charles Kingsley stayed with his friend, and then owner of Malham Tarn House, Walter Morrison in 1858 – a

The Invisible River

Until recently, it was assumed that Malham Tarn was the source of the beck flowing from the base of the Malham Cove, a couple of miles further south. Our route passes the precise spot where the stream dives underground – marked on OS maps as the "Water Sinks" (at SD894657). However, dye tests have revealed that the lake's outflow feeds a quite different river – one that re-surfaces not at the cove but south of Malham village at Aire Head, source of the River Aire. The exact course of the stream between its disappearance and reappearance at Aire Springs remains a mystery, hinting at the existence of an as yet undiscovered cave system of massive proportions.

ABOVE: Gordale Beck reaches a crescendo at Janet's Foss

sojourn that would furnish the author with much of the raw material for his popular fairy-tale, *The Water-Babies* (1863). One memorable scene in the book recounts the ten-year-old hero, Tom, encountering a talking caddis fly, one of several rare insects that continue to flourish in the tarn, along with various species of seldom glimpsed molluscs, brown trout and pike.

The gradual growth in size of the passages through the limestone beds below mean that even during times of heavy flooding, run-off from the surrounding hills is easily absorbed, though on at least one occasion in the nineteenth century the falls flowed again, drawing crowds of admirers.

Lining the top of the 80-metre/262-feet escarpments, the clints (blocks) and grykes (fissures) of the old river bed have created a unique micro-habitat for rare flowering plants and ferns. Though if you do rummage around in search of them, do so with great caution: some of the clefts are deep, and slippery in wet weather. Access to the vantage point on the far western side of the cliff rim is restricted, but you still get a good look at the scale of the escarpments from a spot just off the path, next to the perimeter fence. The nests of peregrine falcons can sometimes be spotted from here, and it's a good place to watch the local climbers in action.

A long flight of steps leads from the opposite side of the cove back to river level via the Pennine Way, winding up at the best spot of all from which to take in the cliffs and the river flowing silently from the dark cave mouth at their foot. Walking back to the village, look out for the remnants of early-Medieval field strips sculpting the hillsides to your right.

ABOVE: The limestone slopes around Malham Cove are ablaze with wild flowers in early summer

walk it 41 Malham Cove

1 Turn L out of the National Park Visitors' Centre onto the main road through the village, past the Methodist Chapel on your L. Opposite the River House Hotel you'll see an old smithy, behind which a stone clapper bridge crosses to the far bank of Malham Beck. Once over this, turn R and follow the Pennine Way downstream. After passing through two swing gates, you reach a kissing gate where you should turn L off the Pennine Way in the direction of "Janet's Foss", as indicated.

The path winds along the side of Gordale Beck and a wall for 10mins, passing a couple of handsome old stone barns, and a concrete bridge to the R which you should ignore. Another gate leads into the National Trust-owned **Janet's Foss** woodland,

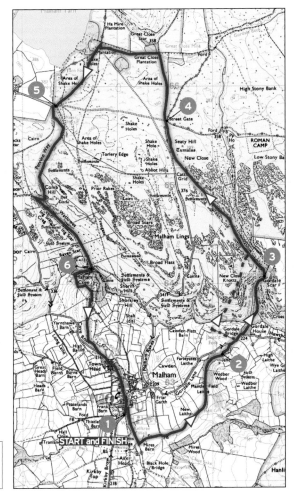

Map not to scale.
Representation of
**OS EXPLORER MAP
OL02, 1:25,000**

Route profile

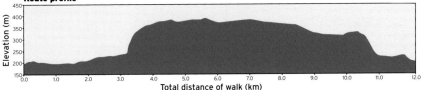

past a succession of mossy crags and fallen tree trunks on its approach to the famous waterfalls and pool.

2 The path climbs L of the falls and on across a field to meet Gordale Lane; turn R on to the tarmac and follow it for a couple of mins until you reach a bend, where a gate and footpath signposted L lead on to the campsite at the mouth of **Gordale Scar**. The ravine itself is reached via a well-made path running to the R of the stream.

3 Some walkers turn back when they reach the waterfalls, but the short scramble up the rock between the two main spouts is more straightforward than it looks from a distance, with good foot and hand-holds all the way up. That said, at times when the falls are frozen, or when the river is in spate, this section may have to be avoided. In such cases, an alternative route is easily achieved (see box opposite). Once atop the gorge, keep to the obvious path, which gradually drifts to the L of a dry valley in the direction of the Malham Tarn road. The last stretch shadows a drystone wall, funnelling you into a corner where a stile carries you over to Street Gate.

4 Continue straight ahead from here along the broken-surfaced track, heading due north, with a wall to your R. Bending away (L) from this wall, the path eventually drops downhill to arrive at a gate next to Great Close Plantation. Ignore the trail leading ahead beyond the gate and instead turn L along

the wall bounding the trees, then make for the L side of the second coppice ahead of you, ignoring the small wood on the L. Skirt the south edge of this second clump of trees until you arrive at a gravel track, where you should turn R and then L almost immediately onto the Pennine Way, as indicated by a FPS. From here you can either keep to the Pennine Way, which glances the southern tip of nearby **Malham Tarn**, or follow a broader track southwest to crest a rise from where views of the lake and house are best.

5 Both trails eventually converge on a small car park. Turn R on to the road, cross the stream and pick up the Pennine Way, which veers L through the gate just beyond stream, passing the famous Water Sinks. The next leg down Watlowes is rocky, muddy and hard going in wet weather. After 5mins or so you reach a small clearing; stay with the clear path going L, which then circles R to a stile above a steep, rocky path. This drops to the L, eventually taking you to a lower level of the valley, where it splits below some dramatic crags. Once on level ground the rest of the route to the head of Malham Cove is relatively plain sailing.

6 Turn R along the Pennine Way when you reach the rim of the Cove – our featured viewpoint – picking your way across the limestone pavement, or over the crags to its R. At the point the rocks peter out, the path plunges L through a drystone wall to start its stepped

descent back to Malham. It's worth making a short detour L from the foot of the path to admire the cliffs from below. The remaining stretch into the village runs above the beck via a good path, scaling a rise to rejoin a lane on the northern fringes of Malham; turn L on to this and follow it for 5mins past Beck Hall to the footbridge next to the shop. The National Park Visitor Centre lies a couple of minutes' walk further down the same road, past the Methodist Chapel and Buck Inn on your R.

Route Avoiding Gordale Scar

(Marked as a dotted line on our map.) Return down the path to the tarmac road. Turn R and follow the road for 40m/50yd until you reach a gateway on your R at Gordale Bridge, signposted "Malham Cove 1 mile". Go through this gate and keep to the clear path ahead, which runs up the side of a drystone wall to a second gate. Turn sharp R (NE) after the gate, making for a third gate visible on the far side of the field, just beyond a wall junction. From the other side of this gate a clear path strikes steeply R up the hillside to the crags above. Running in parallel with the drystone wall lining the cliff edge, it then goes along the top of the ravine before making a slight descent to rejoin the main Gordale Scar path at a ladder stile over a wall.

The cliffs of Malham Cove
– a rock-climbing hotspot

Getting There

Regular buses and Royal Mail post buses run during the week from Skipton, the nearest railhead. On weekends, you can also get there from Skipton and Ilkley on the Malham Tarn Shuttle bus. Timetables for these services are posted at ✐www.malhamdale.com/transport.htm.

Visitor Information

Yorkshire Dales National Park Visitors' Centre, Malham
📞 01969 652380
✐www.yorkshiredales.org

Eating & Drinking

The Lister Arms
22 The Lane, Malham
📞01729 830330
✐www.listerarms.co.uk
The best of the two pubs in the village for food, offering a predictable menu of standards, served next to a blazing log fire. Ale enthusiasts, however, may wish to nip across the road to the Buck Inn for a pint of Old Peculier. Note that the Lister doesn't take bookings: tables are allocated on a first-come-first-served basis.

Sleeping

Beck Hall
Cove Rd, Malham
📞 01729 830332
✐www.beckhallmalham.com
Reasonably priced, pleasantly furnished rooms, some with four-posters and bay windows overlooking the stream, in an eighteenth-century building. Welcoming, efficient and well set up for walkers.

The Lister Arms
(As above)
This ivy-covered, traditional pub just off the village green is a popular B&B option. Its recently refurbished rooms are all en suite and good value.

More Info

✐www.malhamdale.com. Exhaustive local info for the Malham area, with dozens of useful links.

✐www.yorkshiredales.org.uk. The national park's homepage.

✐www.yorkshire-dales.com/malham. Background on local landmarks.

✐www.nationaltrust.org.uk. Introduction to the NT's holdings around Malham Tarn and Moor.

✐www.outofoblivion.org.uk/video.asp. Computer generated video of the formation of Malham Cove.

More Walks

Collins Rambler's Guide: The Yorkshire Dales by David Leather (Collins/Ramblers). Thirty walks covering the entire length and breadth of the national park, from Wharfdale to the Upper Eden Valley. Strong historical narrative and Harvey maps, all wrapped in a handy waterproof cover.

Country Walks Around Harrogate Volume 2 West by Douglas Cossar (Ramblers West Riding Area). Twenty four enjoyable walks in Nidderdale and the Washburn Valley, between 6.5km/4miles to 13km/8miles. All with clear descriptions, sketch maps and colour photos.

Harrogate Ringway by Harrogate Ramblers (Ramblers). An easy signposted trail encircling the spa town at a radius of 3-4 miles, mostly on attractive country paths. This 33-km/21-mile route can be divided into shorter stages using public transport or linked with the Knareborough Round (below) to form a 58-km/36-mile route.

Harrogate Dalesway by Harrogate Ramblers (Ramblers). A 32-km/20-mile waymarked trail from Harrogate to Bolton Abbey with a link to the Dales Way. It leaves the town via the valley Garden and Pine Woods to traverse Haverah Park and passes a succession of reservoirs along the Washburn Valley, before climbing over the open heights of Rocking Moor into Bridgedale.

Knaresborough Round by Harrogate Ramblers (Ramblers). An easy signposted 32-km/20-mile trail passing through the Nidd Gorge and a succession of villages to the north and east of the historic town of Knaresborough. Can be divided into two stages using buses or linked with the Harrogate Ringway (above) to form a 58-km/36-mile route.

The Minster Way by Ray Wallis (East Yorkshire & Derwent Ramblers). Guide to this 80.5km/50-mile route between Beverley and York, crossing the chalk hills of the Yorkshire Wolds. Devised by the Ramblers and now fully waymarked and included on OS maps. Includes detailed route descriptions with sketch maps and colour photos. A great introduction to the peaceful countryside of East Yorkshire.

From the Horse's Tail...

Lochcraig Head

This route, set in an intriguing corner of the Southern Uplands of Scotland, combines two great views: one a wide-ranging panorama, and the other a close-up peek at a hidden waterfall. It revolves around the Tweedsmuir and Ettrick hills, dividing Selkirk and Moffat – a tract of round-topped fells separated by deep glacial valleys. Although carved up today by forestry plantations and sheep fences, the landscape remains almost as wild as it was several centuries ago, when its trails were trodden by drovers, cattle reivers and feuding clansmen. This was where Robert the Bruce fled to escape Edward II in medieval times, where William Wallace retreated to after launching raids against the English, and where the wizard Merlin is supposed to have hidden after a bloody battle near Carlisle.

You can still easily lose yourself in these lonely hills today. Having scaled their steep sides, trails fan out across rolling, empty grassland plateaux, where skylarks and curlews call under big skies. Winters here can be long and harsh, drawing white mountain hares down the valleys and freezing the burns solid for days on end.

One sight above all other entices visitors up Moffat Water, the dale slicing northeast into the hills from the Victorian spa town of Moffat. Hidden by a fold the valley side, the Grey Mare's Tail is a superb waterfall crashing 61m/200ft down a rock gulley. A precipitous footpath leads high above the road to the only spot from where the full drop can be viewed. However, a second, and still more wonderful secret awaits walkers who press on a short way up the mountain.

Screened until the last minute by a fellside strewn with glacial debris, Loch Skeen reveals itself as the source of the waterfalls, and one of the true gems of the Southern Uplands. It sits amid an unexpectedly dramatic amphitheatre – a hidden enclave hugged by sweeping crags and high, smooth, moorland ridges. One of these, Lochcraig Head, provides the perfect, front-circle vantage point from which to admire the full extent of the loch, and stands as the first summit in a fine horseshoe route culminating with an ascent of the highest peak in the Southern Uplands, White Coomb. Catch a rare clear day and you'll be treated to a view extending all the way across the Solway Firth to the Cumbrian fells.

At a glance

Where Tailburn Bridge, 16km/10miles northeast of Moffat, Dumfries & Galloway.
Why Britain's fifth biggest waterfall; secluded Loch Skeen; grouse, peregrines and mountain hares.
When October, for the Moffat

Walking Festival.
Downsides Very popular with families: avoid school holidays.
Start/Finish Tailburn Bridge visitor centre (NT186145).
Duration 4hrs 30mins.
Distance 12km/7.5miles.

Cut it Short The out-and-back route to the loch is 4km/2.5miles.
Terrain Steep paths and muddy trails, with a section around a boggy lochside. Includes some steep ascents and descents.
Map OS Explorer 330.

On your way

You'll hear the Grey Mare's Tail waterfall well before you see it. Cascading down a runnel of rock flanked by sheer, bracken-covered slopes, **TAIL BURN** plummets 61metres/200feet into a plume of spray. Some insist its name derives from Robert Burns' humorous poem *Tam O'Shanter*, but as this mock-heroic narrative was penned in 1790 and map references to it crop up from at least 1754, it seems more likely that Burns named his mare after the waterfall.

Written in a mixture of lurid English and (still more lurid) Scots, the poem recounts the story of a farmer called Carrick who, returning from market late one night, spots a fire burning inside a village kirk. He stops for a peep in the window, and is amazed to see a circle of witches, several of whom he recognizes, dancing wildly to tunes being played by the Devil on the bagpipes.

Wearing no more than skimpy night dresses, the dancers present a striking spectacle and Carrick, unable to contain himself, blurts out "weel done, Cutty-sark!" – a call of encouragement which might, in modern parlance, equate to something like, "Yee-haa, you in the short skirt!"

When they realize they're being spied on, the witches set off in pursuit of the farmer. He and his horse, however, speed in the direction of the nearby Doon, knowing that agents of the Devil cannot cross rivers at night. But before he quite reaches the bridge, one of the witches succeeds in grabbing the tail of his trusty mare, which falls off, lizard-like, leaving Carrick and his steed to gallop to safety.

The poem ends on a note of warning against the twin ills of liquor and fornication, uttered with the poet's tongue planted firmly in his cheek: "Whenever to drink you are inclined/Or short nightshirts

The Wild Wood

Just over the mountain from Loch Skeen, to the south-west of White Coomb, lies an extraordinary valley. Roadless and wild, with a dramatic head wall of crags, Carrifran was the site of a major archeological find in 1990, when a fell walker stumbled upon a wooden bow protruding from the peat. Carbon-dated to the early Neolithic era, it turned out to be six thousand years old. The discovery sparked off a spate of scientific investigations into the valley and its prehistoric ecosystem, which, in common with the rest of the Southern Uplands, has over

the centuries been devastated by over-grazing. Core samples of peat around the spot where the bow was found revealed that at the time the weapon was in use, the land would have been carpeted with dense forest of alder, ash, cherry and elm. Higher up, hazel, oak and thorn would have given way to birch and rowan, while willow scrub and juniper bushes would have colonized the high plateaux areas – a far cry indeed from the bare grassland of today. The revelation inspired a group of enthusiasts to form the "Carrifran Wildwood" project, whose aim was to re-afforest

the valley with native species of trees and plants. By 2000, the trust had raised sufficient funds to purchase the land, and it initiated a large-scale re-planting scheme: 453,000 native saplings now thrive on the estate, and more are in the pipeline. In the decades to come, the Carrifran Valley will be returned to a forest wilderness hosting dozens of indigenous species of birds, animals and insects long-disappeared from the Southern Uplands.

You can find out more about the Carrifran Wildwood project at ✎www.carrifran.org.uk.

ABOVE: The Grey Mare's Tail falls

run in your mind/Think! You may buy the joys too dear/Remember Tam O'Shanter's mare" (translated).

In his younger days, Burns was a regular visitor to the Moffat area. Many local inns boast of having hosted him for a drunken night; the Black Bull in Moffat itself even claims the bard etched a romantic verse on one of its windows.

Two other famous writers associated these hills are Sir Walter Scott, who lived a day's ride away near Melrose, and the Gothic novelist James Hogg, aka "The Ettrick Shepherd", whose work Scott enthusiastically promoted in Edinburgh, and who hailed from a village over the mountain south of the falls. The pair used to meet up in the famous Tibbie Shiels Inn, on the shores of nearby St Mary's Loch, a few miles up the road from the **GREY MARE'S TAIL**.

The pass separating Moffat Water from St Mary's Loch – a misty, desolate col named Dob's Linn – was one of several hereabouts crossed and re-crossed in the late 1520s by King James V of Scotland. Fuelled by vengeful anger fermented over two years of incarceration at the hands of the Earl of Douglas, he and his force of 1200 men rampaged around the Southern Uplands and

Borders subduing cattle thieves, marauders, bandits, rebellious clan chiefs and anyone rumoured to support church reform.

In his 1803 poem *Lament of the Border Widow*, Scott depicts the cruelty with which the King hunted down his adversaries, and the bitterness the pogrom inspired among the local population. It tells the story of Perys Cockburne, a freebooter from the shores of St Mary's Loch hanged by James V from his own doorway, while his wife hid by a waterfall so as not to hear his cries.

It is known that many such persecuted covenanters found refuge on the shores of **LOCH SKEEN**. Completely invisible from the floor of the valley, the lake forms a perfect mountain sanctuary. The only routes into it were, and remain, the steep path around the head of the Grey Mare's Tail, or over the top of the surrounding high fells.

Today part of a 2800-acre estate owned by the Natural Trust for Scotland, the lake, and approaches to it, form part of an important nature reserve noted, in particular, for its stock of rare arctic and sub-arctic plants. Squelching around the pale-yellow bogs of sphagnum moss and banks of coarse purple heather spread around the lakeside, you may also be lucky enough to catch a glimpse of a mountain hare or black grouse. Sightings of redpoll, reed bunting, grasshopper warbler and siskin have also been recorded, while down at the rangers' hut at **TAILBURN BRIDGE**, a live CCTV link allows visitors to monitor comings and goings from a peregrines' nest, perched high on the cliffs above.

The greatest rarity of all at Loch Skeen, though, is the humble vendace (*Coregonus albula*) – a kind of herring introduced here in the 1990s from Bassenwaithe in the Lake District, where they've since became extinct. The only other place in Britain supporting a viable population is Derwent Water.

walk it 42 Lochcraig Head

1 The visitor centre at **Tailburn Bridge** has car parks on both sides of the stream. You can start at either. From the one below the rangers' information hut, follow the surfaced trail up the burn and across the footbridge to the circular enclosure marking the start of the path up the true R (NE) flank of the valley. Alternatively, from the car park on the Giant's Grave side, head past the prehistoric earth mound towards the footbridge and round enclosure, where the climb starts. Steep from the outset, a neatly

made path slices across the eastern flank of the hanging valley to a viewpoint overlooking the **Grey Mare's Tail** falls. As you ascend, look out for feral goats grazing on steep slopes high above the stream. The gradient eases as the route approaches the burn higher up, which it follows NE to the bottom edge of the loch.

2 Views of the surrounding crags open gradually as you ascend, but for your first glimpse of **Loch Skeen** itself you'll have to wait until you're almost next to it. From the rocks where **Tail Burn** flows out of the lake, follow a faint, intermittent path to your R, which

winds across the boggy, undulating eastern lakeshore. After a 30-40-min slog, you'll reach a prominent tributary stream flowing from the R at the NE corner of the loch: follow its course uphill (to your R) over brakes of heather and saturated ground to meet a wall (known locally as a "drystane dyke") at NT173169.

3 This same wall, which marks the boundary of the National Trust for Scotland's estate, will shepherd you around the entire high portion of our route, providing a dependable navigation aid which you'll be glad of if the weather closes in. Turn L (uphill) when you get to it, and stick to the obvious path as it scales a steepening grassy slope for a stiff ascent to the rounded top of **Lochcraig Head** (800m/2624ft).
The path arcs L as it approaches a wall-junction marking the meeting point of three counties (the true summit lies a short way further N and isn't worth the trouble to

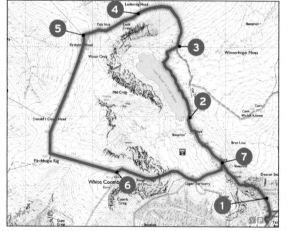

Map not to scale.
Representation of
**OS EXPLORER MAP
330, 1:25,000**

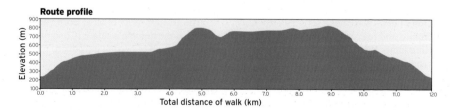

Route profile

reach). The views, however, aren't as impressive as they are from a point further S, closer to the edge of the Head – though take great care when exploring this dangerous ground as it steepens quite suddenly, ending in a sheer drop.

4 From Lochcraig Head, continue W along the wall, which drops down to the marshy pass of Talla Nick before climbing up Firthybrig Head (766m/2513ft).

5 Turn L at the wall junction here and carry on SSW to crest Firthhope Rig, where another L bend and a junction in the wall leads you ESE to the highest point of the day, White Coomb (821m/2693ft). Peak tickers will want to make the short detour SE, over the partly collapsed wall and new fence across a heath to the summit proper, marked by a cairn which sits on a low mound believed to date from Bronze Age (it is one of a pair: the other is visible on the horizon some 100m to the SW). The view from here extends to the Eildons, Cheviots and Lakeland.

6 Keeping close to the old wall, the path off White Coomb starts gently enough, but grows increasing steep as it drops through the rocks of Rough Craigs, where the wall peters out and you might need to use your hands once or twice on some slippery rocky footsteps. Having cleared this awkward outcrop, the remaining stretch to Tail Burn via a good path is much easier going.

7 Walk L upstream a short way when you reach the burn to find an simpler crossing point, then clamber up the far bank to regain

the main path down the valley. Turn R onto it, and return via the same route followed for the ascent, in reverse; take great care if it's wet.

Getting There
Houston's minibus, which used to run past Tail Bridge en route between Moffat and Selkirk, was recently axed by the local council, but may be resurrected in future; check by phone on ☎01576 203874. Otherwise, your only option would be to jump in a taxi.

Visitor Information
NTS Ranger Tail Bridge
☎01683 222714

Moffat TIC
Churchgate. ☎01683 220620
✎www.visitdumfriesandgalloway. co.uk

Eating & Drinking
The Buccleuch Arms Hotel
High St, Moffat
A handy option if you're staying in Moffat, this old-fashioned market-square inn serves the best steak in town, in addition to carefully prepared bar meals and a more adventurous a la carte menu. Book in advance as it gets packed out, especially on weekends.

The Glen Café
St Mary's Loch
☎01750 42241
✎www.glencafe.co.uk
Don't be put off by the basic appearance of this roadside hut on the shores of St Mary's Loch. The cooking's as superb as the location, whether a Big Breakfast of blackheart sausage, crunchy filled baguette at lunchtime, or evening meal of locally sourced beef in whisky sauce. They also serve fair-

trade teas and coffees, along with home-baked cakes, which you can enjoy indoors next to a roaring fire, or out on picnic tables, while ospreys swoop over the lake. A real gem.

Tibbie Shiels Inn
St Mary's Loch, Selkirkshire
☎01750 42231
✎www.tibbieshielsinn.com
Historic inn situated on the little isthmus dividing St Mary's Loch from Loch of the Lowes. Frequented by the likes of Sir Walter Scott, James Hogg, RL Stevenson and Gladstone, it's seen better days, but the location is perfect. Basic pub grub is served in the bar, and they also do afternoon teas. Book well ahead in summer, when the place gets packed out with walkers following the Southern Uplands Way.

Sleeping
Tibbie Shiels Inn
St Mary's Loch, Selkirkshire, TD7 5LH
☎01750 42231
✎www.tibbieshielsinn.com
Simple B&B rooms (all ensuite and centrally heated) on the lochside. The rooms are nothing special, but the rates are low for the area and the waterside location undeniably romantic – perfect for couples and walkers happy with basic amenities. Campers can pitch tents in the garden of the inn.

More Info
✎www.mwis.org.uk. Detailed mountain weather forecasts.
✎www.visitmoffat.co.uk. Tourist site for Moffat, the nearest town.
✎www.robertburns.org.uk/Assets/ Poems_Songs/tamoshanter.htm. The original text of Burns' *Tam O'Shanter*, alongside an excellent English translation.

On the Black Hills
Capel-y-ffin

"One of the emotional centres of my life," is how Bruce Chatwin described the Vale of Ewyas, a remote Shangri-La buried deep in the Black Mountains, the easternmost massif of the Brecon Beacons National Park. The fugitive author of *The Songlines*, whose novel *On the Black Hill* was set here, was merely one in a long line of writers, artists, hermits and monks who have sought refuge in this hidden corner of Wales.

Squeezed against the border with England, the head of the valley, in particular, holds an undeniably special atmosphere. Once in the fold of its steep, bracken-covered sides, the rest of the world can seem oddly distant. No mines or quarries mar the sheep pastures and ancient hedgerows spread across its floor. Only the medieval ruins of Llanthony Priory, built on the site of a church founded by St David in the sixth century, suggest the place was ever anything more than it is today: a profoundly beautiful, but largely forgotten sanctuary.

That this is the prettiest of all Welsh valleys few would deny. But to fully appreciate why, you have to follow one of the old pony trails zigzagging up its flanks through the ferns to the round-topped, heather-covered moorland plateaux beyond. Looking down the Vale, the exquisite symmetry of its glaciated sides is fully revealed, along with the drama of the valley's setting. When clouds swirl about their ridges, as they do most days, and great beams of sunlight sweep across the fields, the Black Mountains embracing Ewyas certainly live up to their name.

It's hard to think of another walk in Wales that combines two such wildly contrasting atmospheres as this. Following old drove tracks for most of its course, our route climbs from the sheltered floor of the valley at Capel-y-ffin to the windswept, bleak hilltop marking the English border to the east. Having reached Offa's Dyke Path, you've a choice between carrying on via the ridge, or a more strenuous foray down into the Olchon Valley – another forgotten mountain cul de sac.

At a glance

Where Capel-y-ffin, 24km/ 15miles north of Abergavenny in the Vale of Ewyas, Monmouthshire.
Why Atmospheric chapels and medieval farmsteads; wild mountain ponies; possible sidetrip to the ruins of twelfth-century Llanthony Priory.
When Early spring, for the new lambs and larks.

Downsides Traffic on the narrow road through the vale on summer weekends; no public transport.
Start/Finish Capel-y-ffin (SO265314).
Duration 4hrs 30mins–5hrs. 6hrs-7hrs with the Olchon Valley variant.
Distance 16km/10miles. 20km/12.5miles with the Olchon

Valley variant.
Terrain Mostly well used mountain paths, often muddy and boggy, but with some paved sections, and sustained ascents and descents. The sections along the valley bottoms may be very wet and involve walking along flooded paths and streams after rain.
Maps OS Explorer OL13.

On your way

Welsh place names tend to delight in the self-evident, and **CAPEL-Y-FFIN** – "Chapel at the End" – is no exception. Dotted around the confluence of the Nant Bwlch and Afon Honddu streams, the hamlet stands as at the head of the Vale of Ewyas, walled in by steep, glaciated hillsides. Beyond it, the patchwork of pasture carpeting the valley floor forks into a perfect wishbone, rising rapidly to meet the great escarpment of the Black Mountains.

Judging by the age of the yews ranged around its cemetery, the village was probably considered sacred centuries before the **CHURCH OF ST MARY**, the older of its pair of chapels, was erected in 1762. Only 8m/25ft long internally, the building can barely accommodate a congregation of twenty – although most people who pause here these days tend to do so for solitary contemplation. "I lift up mine eyes to the hills from whence cometh my salvation," proclaims the inscription on the window pane behind the altar, its letters barely distinguishable from the backdrop of rain-swept ridges and sky.

In Victorian times, the church's distinctive wooden belfry reminded diarist Francis Kilvert of "an owl". Kilvert, a penniless young clergyman from Hay-on-Wye, had travelled here to visit a monastery newly established just up the lane. "Llanthony Tertia" was the brainchild of missionary-preacher Joseph Leycester Lyne (1837–1908), aka "Father Ignatius."

Lyne's project was part of a lifelong, but ultimately doomed, attempt to reintroduce monasticism to the Anglican church. For a couple of decades, despite opposition from the clergy and a chronic lack of funds, it flourished. A following of black-robed, Benedictine-style monks grew up, and pilgrims poured in from across the world.

The regime, however, was tough even by Benedictine standards. Comforts in this dank corner of the Welsh mountains were in short supply. And daily ritual life was harsh to the point of perversity: it is said the brothers and novices even used to take turns to be led by halter through the cloister, begging for bread while the rest of the community spat on them.

Such privations seemed to be sustainable only as long as Lyne himself was there to provide the drive, and when he died in 1908, the Order soon floundered. Thereafter, the decaying house and adjacent chapel were acquired by the Catholic sculptor and typeface designer Eric Gill and his family, who founded a kind of Utopian colony where residents could, "bathe naked, all together in the mountain pools . . . and smell the smell of a world untouched by men of business".

The desire for peace and quiet in which to pursue his art may not, however, have been Gill's only reason for choosing this remote location. It seems he also felt compelled to have sex with every female that came within his orbit, including his daughters, sisters and pet dog – a predilection that can have done little to endear him to the locals, who on at least one occasion blocked off the family's water supply in an attempt to remove them.

The Vision

A lone statue of a Madonna next to the lane leading to the old monastery at Capel-y-ffin marks the spot where, in 1880, local choir boys witnessed visions of a woman in flowing robes, surrounded by a halo of bright light. As the monastery established by Father Ignatius was Anglican, these divine apparitions – which were widely interpreted as being of the Virgin Mary – did not make Capel-y-ffin a Welsh Lourdes, though they are commemorated each year by a small pilgrimage.

ABOVE: Joseph Lyne's former monastery and church of Llanthony Tertia, Capel-y-ffin

Like their predecessors, the Gills found the remoteness that attracted them to Capel-y-ffin in the first place hard to sustain. After only four years, the family fled to a retreat closer to London in the Chilterns, leaving Fr Ignatius' church to decay.

The conflicting needs for isolation and community are framing themes of Bruce Chatwin's 1982 novel, *On the Black Hill*, which is set in the Vale of Ewyas. Adapted for the big screen by director Andrew Grieve in 1987, the book centres on the twin brothers, Lewis and Benjamin Jones, whose lives were led almost entirely within the confines of a hill farm called "the Vision". Chatwin based his portrait on a farm of the same name, which still stands on the fringes of Capel-y-ffin. He was a regular visitor to the Vale since the age of fifteen, and towards the end of his life often came here to write.

The opening sequence of the movie roves at bird's-eye level over the mountains rising immediately behind the Vision's barns, where **OFFA'S DYKE PATH** snakes along the England–Wales border. Flagstones airlifted into place by helicopter to prevent erosion of the fragile peat hags nowadays pave this popular long-distance route, which follows the 172-mile line of earthworks erected by the Saxon King of Mercia in the Dark Ages to mark the extent of his territory – a kind of low-budget "Great Wall".

Having reached it you can either veer northwest along the stone pavement, or else continue northeast, over the brow of the hill, to enter the beautiful **OLCHON VALLEY**. A forgotten enclave of derelict pink-stone farmsteads and ancient fields, the Olchon is worked by shepherds who pasture their flocks on the eponymous Black Hill of Chatwin's novel – a 640-metre razorback ridge which locals insist resembles a recumbent cat. If you're lucky, you'll get to see them gathering up the sheep on horseback – one of the great spectacles of the Welsh borders.

ABOVE: Welsh mountain ponies grazing wild in the Vale of Ewyas

HAY BLUFF, highpoint of the magnificent scarp shelving into the greener pastures of mid Wales, brings Offa's Dyke ridge to an abrupt, and spectacular, end. A superb view ranging from the Cotswolds, Malverns and Shropshire Hills to distant Cadair Idris extends from the trigpoint, from where, on an exceptionally clear day, you can even pick out the top of Snowdon, 129km/ 80miles to the north. Even in the depths of winter, the skies here tend to be filled with parascenders and gliders taking advantage of the famous updrafts.

Windblown **GOSPEL PASS**, below the Bluff, marks the low point in the Black Mountain scarp. Populated by wild ponies and scraggy sheep, the col is thought to have taken its name from a meeting that was convened here in 1188 by the Archbishop of Canterbury, who'd come to assert his authority over the Welsh church and drum up support for the Third Crusade. Accompanying him was the chronicler Geraldus Cambrensis, a writer whose account of the journey survives in his book, *Itinerarium Cambriae* ("Itinerary of Wales"). "About an arrow-shot broad, encircled on all sides by lofty mountains," was his description of the Vale of Ewyas, now revealed in all its glory below the pass.

Cambrensis reserved his highest praise for Llanthony Priory, midway down the Vale, hidden in a fold of the valley below Capel-y-ffin. One of the finest Norman-Gothic buildings of its era, it was originally founded by William de Laci, a knight who'd renounced violence and taken holy vows here in 1118, close to the spot where St David dedicated a small chapel to St John the Baptist centuries earlier.

Having been badly damaged in Owain Glyndwr's rebellion in the early 1400s, when the Welsh mounted an insurrection against their English overlords, the building sustained further abuse during the Reformation. By the eighteenth century, seekers of the "picturesque" were travelling here to admire what had become a charismatic ruin, among them the poet Walter Savage Landor. A contemporary of Wordsworth, Landor owned the Priory and its estate for a time. JMW Turner was one of his more illustrious visitors, producing in the course of his sojourn what John Ruskin later described as, "the most perfect painting of running water in existence." The famous watercolour of the priory now resides in a museum in Indianapolis, USA.

Though all but a few fragments of its tracery windows have collapsed, Llanthony survives largely as it did at the time of Turner's visit, its crumbling arches and walls seeming to rejoice at the proximity of the mountains. For Cambrensis, and those who have followed in his footsteps over 800 years, it remains a place, "truly fitting for contemplation... a happy and delightful spot."

1 Facing the **Church of St Mary's**, go through the metal gate to your R and follow the track down to the stream. Cross the footbridge and continue past the Victorian Baptist Chapel on your L, passing through a five-bar gate to reach Blaenau Farm. The footpath runs between the barn and farmhouse, then around the back of the latter, through a second five-bar gate and onwards at a more level gradient up a wide stream bed.

After crossing a brook, you arrive at a waypost with a yellow arrow: follow this to the L of the hedgerow ahead, then over another couple of fields to arrive at a stone stile where the path drops steeply into a stream gulley. Beyond it, a wider track funnels you towards Ty'r-onen farm, then via tarmac to the Vision farmstead.

2 Just before you reach the Vision's driveway, look for a stile next to a metal gate on your L (marked "To the hill/**Offa's Dyke**"). Above it, wooden steps lead to second stile; follow the path uphill until you see a waypost pointing R through a gap in the hedge. Having skirted along the bottom edge of the field beyond, the trail then swings L to begin a steep climb through the woods.

Turn R when you reach the stile and open moorland at the top, then keep to the clear path as it zigzags uphill through the bracken via series of four sharp switchbacks.

A pair of stone markers stand at the final hairpin turn, from where our path arcs across the steep hillside above the Nant Vision

Map not to scale.
Representation of
**OS EXPLORER
MAP OL13
1:25,000**

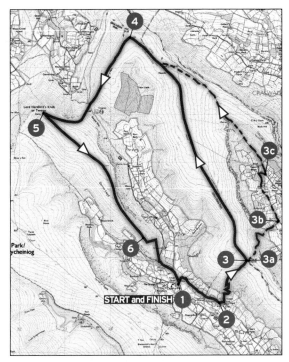

Route profile

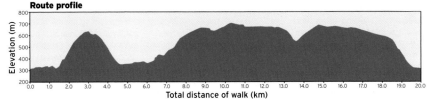

stream gulley. Be sure not to be tempted L, up what at one point looks like the main path but isn't; keep instead on a steady, straight traverse above the gulley. After crossing the stream this eventually brings you out on the paved Offa's Dyke Path at its intersection with the Olchon Valley track.

3 Readers intending to descend into the Olchon Valley should refer at this point to the "Olchon Valley Variant" box below. If you're heading along the shorter route straight to Hay Bluff, turn L on to Offa's Dyke Path, and keep to the flagstones all the way, bearing L at the only junction passed (at SO251361), which is marked with a National Trust waystone.

The Olchon Valley Variant
This extension into the Olchon Valley only adds 4km/2.5miles to the standard route, but it can feel like a lot more because of the additional 580m of ascent and descent. Even so, it's well worth the effort.

3a The start of an old drove track descending from Offa's Dyke ridge into the Olchon Valley is marked by a small cairn and inscribed waystone. If you can't see these at the point you join the flagstones of Offa's Dyke Path, then you've probably been drawn up one of the pony trails that drift left above Nant Vision, emerging too far NW – in which case, turn R onto Offa's Dyke and walk a short way downhill until the trail levels off, where you should easily spot the stone marker and cairns. From the crosspaths at SO2703109, the drove track falls NE down the flank of the valley,

bending sharply R after 10mins. Ignore the path running straight on at the bend, and continue instead down the main track as far as a waypost (at SO273325), 3 or 4mins further on. This flags the path to the valley floor, which you'll reach after crossing two metal gates.

3b Once at the lane, turn L and follow the tarmac NW. After half a mile, the road bends sharply R to cross the river. Just beyond the bridge, head L along the drove track signposted "Public Bridleway".

3c This well-worn track will take you out on to open moorland and all the way up the head of the valley – one of the finest miles of footpath in the Welsh Mountains. A small cairn marks the spot where another path arrives from the R (from the Black Hill). From here, the trail curves gently below the ridge to meet the Offa's Dyke Path at SO251361, where we rejoin the standard route. Note that this latter stretch of bridleway – from the valley head to the junction – is incorrectly drawn on OS maps; refer to our version.

4 A long, straight stretch of paving stones takes you to the trigpoint at the top of **Hay Bluff** (677m/2221ft). Turn L here and follow the boggy path running along the level top of the scarp edge, which drops more steeply as it descends Ffynnon y Parc to reach the Gospel Pass. Cross the road and pick up the heavily eroded path continuing uphill from the col. This drifts R along the rim of the scarp to arrive at Lord Hereford's Knob (or Twmpa) - another superb

viewpoint overlooking the Wye.

5 The onward route SE from Twmpa along the top of the moorland ridge is level and simple to follow. Turn L from the trigpoint, and follow the obvious trail SE via a succession of cairns to a slight summit at SO238339, from where you begin the day's last descent, down a spur known as Darren Lwyd. Keep L for the best views over the valley.

6 The finest panorama of the route is from the spot where Darren Lwyd steepens dramatically above Capel-y-ffin, marked by an unusual rectangular cairn. From here, the path falls very steeply downhill, veering L, then sharply R to avoid the sheerest section of the slope.

When you intersect another path towards the bottom, head straight across it until you reach a fence and large alder tree, where you turn L onto a track following a stream bed downhill through a stand of trees. This brings you out at a gate leading to a pair of stone cottages; continue along the path between them, then through the swing gate into a field. In the bottom L corner of the field you'll find a stile opening onto the lane where a R turn will take you back to **Capel-y-ffin.**

Getting There
Capel-y-ffin, indeed the entire Vale of Ewyas, lies beyond the reach of southeast Wales' patchy public transport. You can get to Llanfihangel Crucorney (15.2k/9.5miles southwest) by bus from Abergavenny, but will have to arrange an onward taxi from there. Alternatively, travel

to Capel-y-ffin via Hay-on-Wye (13.7km/8.5miles north). Taxis can be arranged through the Hay-on-Wye/Abergavenny TICs (see below).

(see below)

ℹ Visitor Information

Abergavenny TIC
Swan Meadow, Monmouth Road
Abergavenny
☎ 01873 857588

Hay-on-Wye TIB
Oxford Rd
☎ 01497 820144

✕ Eating & Drinking

Llanthony Priory Hotel
Llanthony, NP7 7NN
☎ 01873 890487
✎ www.llanthonyprioryhotel.co.uk
You have to walk through the ruins of the priory to reach this atmospheric inn. A spiral stone staircase leads up a tower to four basic rooms. Downstairs, the old abbot's cellar accommodates a refreshingly downbeat pub where simple meals and decent ales are served under whitewashed stone arches.

Half Moon Inn
Llanthony, NP7 7NN
☎ 01873 890611
✎ www.halfmoon-llanthony.co.uk
The village's other pub has less character than the one in the Priory, but it's generally livelier, attracting locals as well as walkers. The rooms are simple but adequate, and the hot meals – served in a bar with boot-friendly flagstone floors – copious and good value.

Sleeping

Castle Farm
Capel-y-ffin
☎ 07973 837820
✎ www.capel-y-ffin.co.uk
Pretty self-catering cottage and adjacent five-bedroom farmhouse (a former youth hostel), for rent by the day or week, only a stone's throw from the start of our walk.

📖 More Info

✎ metoffice.gov.uk/loutdoor/mountainsafety/brecon.html. Detailed weather forecast for the Brecon Beacons, featuring

ABOVE: Llanthony Priory, built on the site of a church founded by St David in the sixth century

projected visibility, cloud base, wind speeds, freezing level and lots more useful info for walkers.

✎ www.brecon-beacons.com. Online guidebook to the national park: the most comprehensive site for walkers in the Brecon Beacons National Park.

✎ www.offas-dyke.co.uk. Support pages for the long-distance path tracking the Dark Ages rampart, with handy links to associated businesses and services.

✎ cistercian-way.newport.ac.uk/. Dedicated to a long-distance path linking up all of Wales' Cistercian abbeys, this site features in-depth histories of Capel-y-ffin and Llanthony.

✎ anglicanhistory.org/bios/kindly/ignatius.html. Biography of Joseph Leycester Lynne, aka "Father Ignatius".

walk | 44

DERBYSHIRE

Kiera's Clifftop

Stanage Edge

Seen from the floor the Derwent Valley, Stanage Edge can seem like a strange Stone Age fortress suspended in the clouds, its rock walls crumbling into a huge, curved buttress of bracken and heath. The mightiest of the Peak District's gritstone escarpments, the crag near the Derbyshire–Sheffield border has long been an icon of the region. When the makers of the 2005 movie, *Pride & Prejudice*, wanted a suitably epic location for Kiera Knightley (as Elizabeth Bennet) to gaze across, it was here they chose. And with good reason. The cliffs themselves aren't huge by British standards, reaching only 30m/100ft. But they sweep northwest in an exhilarating, 5-km/3-mile arc with a view matched by few places in the country.

From the lip of the precipice you take in a panorama ranging from the gentle uplands of the White Peak in the south, across the amphitheatre of summits enfolding the Hope Valley, to a shadowy expanse of windswept moors in the northwest, with names redolent of upland Britain at its most damp and desolate: Moscar, Derwent, Strines, Ughill, Brogging Moss and Kinder Scout.

Beginning on the floor of the valley at

Grindleford, our route climbs up to Stanage via the magical broadleaved wood of Padley Gorge. An Iron Age hillfort and boulder mountain await at the head of the Burbage Valley by way of appetizers before the main course of the escarpment itself. From its highest point, High Neb, you'll drop down almost to river level again at Hathersage, via a traverse of delightful Derbyshire farmland. But the fun isn't over yet. To regain Grindleford, there's one last climb into the heather and ferns, then a drop along the course of an old millstone quarry, swathed in luminous silver birch forest.

This isn't a walk for fainthearts. Though rarely steep, it's long, with a sustained initial ascent and no pubs or cafés along the way. But the rewards more than repay the effort. You'll gain a vivid taste not only of the Peak District's wildly contrasting landscapes, but also the ways in which it has been exploited over the centuries – for protection against invaders, as a source of timber and stone, and as somewhere to escape city life. And if you get back in time, a pint of tea and slice of home-baked fruit cake awaits at the famous Grindleford Station Café.

At a glance

Where Stanage Edge, 17km/11miles east of Sheffield, the Peak District.
Why The Dark Peak's most spectacular gritstone edge; ancient oak and birch forest; famous film locations; Little

John's grave.
When Late autumn, when the moorland colours are most vivid.
Downsides You have to carry a day's food and drink with you.
Start/Finish Grindleford Railway Station (SK250788).

Duration 6-7hrs.
Distance 20km/12.5miles.
Terrain Clear footpaths through woodland, across moors and pasture; generally dry, though with some moderate ascents.
Maps OS Explorer OL1 & OL24.

On your way

The engineering achievement that first rendered the Peak District accessible to Sheffield's oxygen-starved Victorians was the Totley Tunnel, on the edge of Grindleford in the Derwent Valley. At 5.7km/3.5miles in length, it's the longest tunnel running under land in the country. Navvies toiled for four years to excavate it, living and working in appalling conditions. Constant flooding and lack of air took their toll, as did the outbreaks of diseases that swept through the shanties at either end where the diggers slept cheek-by-jowl, often twenty to a cottage. But when it opened in 1893, the new rail route transformed the fortunes of the valley as people spilled from the industrial suburbs over the mountain to hike, picnic and build spacious new homes along the line.

At the tunnel mouth, the legendary **GRINDLEFORD STATION** café serves as the gateway to the Peak for this generation of walkers and climbers. Little changed in decades, it occupies the old station waiting room, with cream-painted, tongue-and-groove walls plastered in rhyming notices warning the parents of unruly tots, "human fireguards" and anyone impertinent enough to request mushrooms to stay away. The café's eccentric owner died in 2007, but his famous "0% fat-free" fry-ups and pint mugs of tea are still lapped up by devotees.

Grindleford Station sits next to Burbage Brook, whose peaty and frothing waters tumble through a series of waterfalls, providing a cheerful soundtrack as you climb the old stone-paved track through the woods above. Known as Padley Gorge, this is one of the last surviving tracts of a type of oak and birch forest once common on the fringes of the Peak District, but which has now largely vanished, the rest having been destroyed to produce charcoal for the iron industry in the eighteenth and nineteenth centuries. Part of the National Trust's Longshaw Estate (former hunting reserve of the Duke of Rutland), **PADLEY GORGE** is now protected as a nature reserve, renowned among bird watchers as the nesting site of pied flycatchers.

The forest also provides a fragrant approach for walkers to the high moors. Our route follows the course of the stream to its headwaters on Burbage Moor, overshadowed by the sinister bulk of **CARL WARK** – an Iron Age hillfort surrounded on three sides by gritstone cliffs, and on the other by an L-shaped wall of boulders. Little is known about the citadel or its original inhabitants, the first mention of whom is in Roman records of the Brigantine uprising in 72AD.

HIGGER TOR a still more impressive boulder hill looming out of the peat bog to the north, may also have been used as a fort at one time, though its name, derived from the old Celtic word for "holy hill", suggests ritual associations now long forgotten.

A spur of the old Sheffield turnpike road separates Higger Tor from the southern battlements of **STANAGE EDGE**. Keep to the stepped path wriggling though the rocks and you'll emerge close to the trigpoint that flags the finest view of the walk – if not the entire Peak District. From here, the Edge faces straight up the Hope Valley to Mam Tor and Great Ridge, with the escarpment itself tapering northwest in a grand arc.

The path along the level top of Stanage rocks offers some of the most inspiring walking in Britain. Yet considerably more people come here to climb. The BMC guidebook to the area lists no less than 1300 routes, from "moderate" to "E8". Many reputations have been forged on these crags since the likes of Joe Brown and Don Whillans pioneered leads up the most famous formations. For sheer grit, though, none compare with the marathon, 3000-metre/9850-ft Girdle Traverse completed by Ron Fawcett in 1992 – still the longest unbroken rock route in the UK.

The jangling of harnesses recedes as you progress northwards, beyond the remnants of a paved quarrymens' track and the **LONG CAUSEWAY**, a Roman road that formerly ran, via this gap in the Edge, between Navio (Brough) and Doncaster. From here onwards, you're on land belonging to the Moscar Estate, whose owner periodically asserts his rights to close it (see box overpage).

HIGH NEB (458m/1502ft), the ridge's highpoint, was once the site of a lonely millstone quarry. In the bracken next to the path lie dozens of stone rings, left where they were carved more than a century ago. Until the bottom was knocked out of the market by the invention of cheaper, safer

carborundum (silicon carbide) in 1890, millstones from here were exported all over the world to grind grain, pulp timber and edge cutlery. Laboriously hand-cut, they were fitted in pairs onto wooden axles and rolled down to Sheffield for shipment.

From Stanage, our route drops downhill too, passing en route the beautifully restored Elizabethan manor house of **NORTH LEES HALL**, former seat of the Eyre family. Charlotte Brontë, who visited this area in 1845, was captivated by the building and used it as a model for the Rochesters' home, Thornfield, in *Jane Eyre* (Mrs Rochester, fans of the novel may recall, plunged to her death from a three-storey tower very much like the one here).

BELOW: North Lees Hall – the Elizabethan manor house that captivated Charlotte Brontë

ABOVE: Millstone, Bolehill - discarded where it was carved after the collapse of the quarrying industry

trusty lieutenant, but when exhumed in the nineteenth century, the remains included what onlookers called "a giant thighbone".

Two medieval, typically Peak farmhouses – **TOOTHILL** and **MITCHELL FIELD** – are passed as our trail approaches its final climb of the day, to the head of the massive former quarry complex at **BOWILL**. Over a period of seven years in the early 1900s, 1.25 million tons of the hardest-grade gritstone were extracted from this "super quarry" to build the Gothic-style Derwent and Howden dams (where the Dambuster 617 squadron trained with Barnes Wallis' bouncing bombs in 1943). Over four hundred men and their families worked the site, living in a shanty village of tin huts erected on a series of giant terraces above Padley. Gifted to the National Trust after World War II, the land now supports a serene plantation of silver birches, teeming with woodpeckers and colonies of red ants.

At the time, Charlotte was staying with friends in a vicarage at the nearby town of **HATHERSAGE**. History doesn't recall whether she was shown the **GRAVE OF LITTLE JOHN**, hidden under a yew tree in the cemetery of **ST MICHAEL AND ALL SAINTS CHURCH**. No historical proof actually connects the site with Robin Hood's

The birch trees spill down the old terraces to the upper fringes of **PADLEY VILLAGE**, where the only intact remains of a medieval manor is an ancient stone-walled chapel dedicated to three Catholic priests hung, drawn and quartered in the pogroms of the Tudor period. Grindleford Station lies a short walk across the bridge.

Access to High Neb

The well-used path running along the top of Stanage Edge's northern end - from Long Causeway, past High Neb and on to the main road at Moscar Lodge - crosses private moor-land run as a grouse-shooting reserve. Owned by an old family of Sheffield snuff makers, it was technically off-limits to walkers until the CRoW Act of 2000 secured open access. However, you might find the path closed during the spring nesting season. But fear not: in practice, even though gamekeepers erect signs suggesting otherwise at stiles and gates, walkers and climbers may use the high path, as long as they don't venture into the moor itself and disturb his birds, and provided they do no take dogs along. Full details of access rights in this area are available via the Natural England website, ✎ www.open-access.gov.uk.

walk it | 44
Stanage Edge

CHECKED BY:
Sheffield Ramblers

1 From **Grindleford Station**, cross the bridge over the brook into **Padley** village. Following the lane through the hamlet, look for a public footpath signpost on your R indicating the trail to the "Longshaw Estate via Padley Gorge"; 5mins later a gate is reached leading onto NT land. An old stone track winds uphill from this point through the forest, emerging after 20mins or so onto open moorland. Ignore the first footbridge (signposted to "Longshaw Estate") on your R, and instead keep the brook to your R as far as a second footbridge. Cross and follow the path up through a coppice to a fork where the path bends R. Continue straight ahead to a gate onto the main road (A6187) at Burbage Bridge.

2 Cross the road; turn L across the bridge, then R over a

stile immediately after onto the footpath running along the edge of the brook. After 5-10mins, this meets a larger path, which you follow L (north) to **Carl Wark** hillfort, now visible ahead. Scale the fort and cross from E to W,

dropping down the far side to join the path to **Higger Tor**. On the far side of the latter, take the trail that plunges directly to the road. Cross this via a stile and from the opposite side keep straight ahead to reach a small layby, from

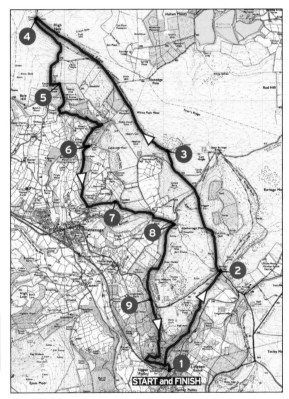

START and FINISH

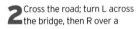
Map not to scale. Representation of **OS EXPLORER MAP OL 1 and OL 24, 1:25,000**

Route profile

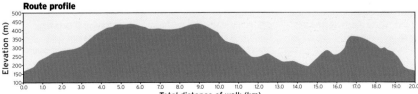

Elevation (m)

Total distance of walk (km)

where the path heads straight for the trigpoint on **Stanage Edge**.

3 Once on the Edge, it's plain sailing for the next few miles. A well-worn path follows the rocks NW to the **Long Causeway**, shortly beyond which you cross a stile onto access land. **High Neb**, reached 30mins later, is marked by a trigpoint, which you pass, keeping on the well worn path until cairns are reached at SK225856.

4 Here, a small breach in the Edge falls L to the main public right of way running below the rocks. The gap, however, easy to miss. Care should be taken; look for a small cairn. Follow the path below the cliffs L until a prominent fork is reached at SK229852, where you should bear R, dropping downhill to rejoin the Long Causeway. At the track, turn R and follow it around the side of Dennis Knoll plantation to the road, where you should turn L and then R after the cattle grid, as indicated by a waymarker.

5 From here, the well signed path runs along a wall then bends R towards Green's House. Turn L through the former farm and follow the driveway straight ahead between the buildings on to fields. Dropping down to a coppice, you cross a stream and then climb a short rise to reach **North Lees Hall**, with the shell of a ruined chapel to your R. Follow the track past the front of North Lees, and downhill via surfaced driveway to the road, where you should turn L.

6 Just past the entrance to the campsite, a waymarker indicates the onward route from the opposite side of the road, to your R. This takes you past Cowclose Farm and on across a fenced pasture towards **St Michael and All Saints Church**, on the edge of **Hathersage**. Having crossed a small stream below the church, the path then climbs to reach a lane. Turn R to visit the site of **Little John's grave** in the cemetery, or L to continue our route.

7 After 5mins of steady ascent up the lane, look for the path forking R to **Toothill** Farm. At the top of the fields, skirt the farm buildings and cross the yard, from where a track contours R around the head of the valley to join the road. Turn L onto the road and follow it for 4mins, looking for a waymarked footpath on the opposite (E) side. This drops sharply to the floor of the combe and climbs up the other side to **Mitchell Field** (another converted farm). The next bit's tricky: instead of following the main waymarked footpath around back of buildings at Mitchell Field, you should turn L off the track through an opening into a field opposite the top of the long converted barn. Keep climbing straight up the field and cross the road. The path resumes directly opposite.

8 At the junction soon after, turn R and follow the track down across open moorland in the direction of Over Owler Tor, bearing R at a fork to reach the quarries and woods below. From here, a choice of paths

winds down through the old Lawrencefield Quarry workings (labeled "Millstone Edge" on OS Explorer maps). For simplicity's sake, keep to the lowest one following the fence along the edge of the woods, which will bring you out on the main A6187 directly opposite:

9 the start of the onward path through **Bolehill Quarry** and the silver birch woods above **Padley**. Follow the main path, which after 5-10mins begins to drop through a series of overgrown terraces. Keep R when you reach the first houses in the village, following the wall around until it meets a lane, where you turn L for Padley Chapel and Grindleford, reached shortly after.

Getting There
Regular trains call at Grindleford Station on the trans-Pennine line between Sheffield and Manchester. On Sundays and bank holidays in summer, the national park also lays on a hail-and-ride minibus for walkers from Sheffield (service 284), which stops at the car parks below Stanage Edge, and at Hathersage. Call ☏0871 200 2233.

Visitor Information
Castleton VIC
Buxton Rd, Castleton
☏01629 816572
✎www.peakdistrict.org

Eating & Drinking
Grindleford Café
Station Approach, Grindleford Railway Station
☏01433 631011
✎www.rigsville.org.uk/breakfast
A Peak institution, and still going

strong despite the recent demise of its famously obstreperous owner. Serves the best greasy-spoon grub for miles, along with pints of tea.

Sleeping
Hathersage YHA
Castleton Road, Hathersage, S32 1EH
📞0845 371 9021
🖱www.yha.org.uk
Set in a converted Victorian town house on the edge of the village, with mostly six-bed dorms. No self catering.

Canon Croft
Canonfields, Hathersage, S32 1AG
📞01433 650055
🖱www.cannoncroftbedand breakfast.co.uk
Outstanding B&B in a beautiful setting, a train stop (or lovely riverside walk) away from the start of our route in neighbouring Hathersage.

The Plough Inn
Leadmill Bridge, Hathersage, S32 1BA
📞01433 650319
🖱www.theploughinn-hathersage.co.uk
Smart rooms and fine dining (at fair prices) in a sixteenth-century inn set amid nine acres of gardens.

North Lees Campsite
Birley Lane, Hathersage, S33 1BR
📞01433 650838
Secluded, tents-only campsite managed by the national park, a twenty-minute walk north of Hathersage near North Lees Hall.

More Info
🖱www.cressbrook.co.uk.
Contains a wealth of information about the Peak District.
🖱www.peakdistrict.org.
The National Park's predictably sober website.
🖱www.nationaltrust.org.uk.
The Trust owns the Longshaw Estate, which laps the bottom of Stanage Edge.

More Walks
Collins Rambler's Guide: Peak District by Roly Smith (Collins/Ramblers). Thirty walks exploring the main northern moors of the Peak District National Park.

Freedom to Roam Guide: Peak District Eastern Moors and the South by Roly Smith (Frances Lincoln/Ramblers). Compact guide with OS 1:25,000 scale maps featuring twelve walks celebrating new access land in Britain's first national park.

Freedom to Roam Guide: Peak District Northern and Western Moors by Roly Smith (Frances Lincoln/Ramblers). Compact guide with OS 1:25,000 scale maps featuring twelve walks in the northern and western regions of the Peak District.

Freedom to Roam Guide: The Pennine Divide by Andrew Bibby (Frances Lincoln/Ramblers). Twelve walks (with 1:25k maps) in the beautiful but often overlooked stretch of the Pennines between Manchester and Yorkshire.

Explore and Discover: Around Fox House by Peter Machin (*Ramblers South Yorks & NE Derbyshire Area*). A pack of themed leaflets covering the archeology, geology, landscape, history and culture of the Peak District around the historic Fox House Inn, near Sheffield.

Five Walks Around Oldham (Oldham Ramblers). Five simple walks of between 8km/5miles and 14.5km/9miles around Oldham.

The Heron Way by Dave Ward (Doncaster Ramblers). Guide to the 48-km/30-mile linear walk linking Doncaster's north and south bus corridor.

Car-Free Stanage

The fabulous views from Stanage Edge, combined with ease of road access from nearby Sheffield, ensures that the car parks below the cliffs see more than their fair share of traffic – which does little to enhance the natural beauty of the area. Efforts are being made by the national park to reduce the number of vehicles by scaling up public transport, but until the park's 284 Sunday minibus service is extended to weekdays, Grindleford Station provides the only dependable, week-long and environmentally friendly approach to the moors. Walkers resentful of the extra couple of miles this requires can reward themselves with a pile of scrumptious chips at Station Café, located at the end of our walk in Grindleford.

Medicine Mountain

Mynydd Ddu

The Black Mountain – "Mynydd Ddu" in Welsh – is the most westerly of the quartet of massifs comprising the Brecon Beacons National Park – and the wildest. Seen from the north, it could be a Highland Munro, its wedge-shaped summits and escarpments of striated sandstone towering above folds of empty moorland, sheep pasture and deep, wooded valleys. To the south, the peaks are even more steadfastly protected by a tract of bleak limestone upland, riddled with peat bogs and swallow holes into which men have been known to disappear without trace.

As the source of the Usk and Tawe Rivers, the mountain has always occupied a special place in Welsh literature and folklore. Yet today, despite lying only a little over twenty miles as the crow flies from Swansea and the M4 corridor, relatively few boots tramp along the ancient paths of Mynydd Ddu – which is all the more surprising when you're up close and realize what an astonishing land form it is. For sheer drama, the ridge path zigzagging between the summits of Bannau Sir Gaer in the west and Fan Brycheiniog in the east has no equal in southern Britain.

Moreover, a hidden treasure lies in wait

for anyone determined enough to penetrate this imposing wilderness on foot. At the bottom of the mountain, entirely screened from view until you're right upon them, nestles a pair of exquisite glacial lakes – Llyn y Fan Fach and Llyn y Fan Fawr. Said to be the abode of Fairy Folk, or "Tylwyth Teg", their dark, glassy waters form a serene counterpoint to the backdrop of scree and cloud-swept summits.

Looping over the ridge from west to east, our route encompasses viewpoints over both lakes, and takes in all six of the peaks behind them. The descent follows a switchback path from the lowest point in the crest, and then winds under the cliffs of Bannau Sir Gaer and around the base of the mountain to the north shore of Llyn y Fan Fach, from where it plunges back down the valley.

From start to finish, this is a glorious walk of sweeping, constantly changing vistas, but one that should be approached with some caution. Up on the ridge the weather can change dramatically with little warning. Come armed with a 1:25,000 map and compass (and GPS if you have one) – and the skills to use them should the cloud close in.

At a glance

Where Mynydd Ddu, Brecon Beacons National Park, 12km/7miles south of Llanddeussant, South Wales.
Why Views stretching from the Bristol Channel to Cader Idris; two glacial lakes; red kites and ravens.
When Early summer, when the

foxgloves, wild thyme and cotton grass are in bloom.
Downsides No public transport to the trailhead; tricky stream crossing.
Start/Finish Water Board car park at SN799238.
Distance 12km/7.5miles.

Duration 4hrs 30mins-5hrs.
Terrain Clear mountain paths over boggy ground, then across a rocky ridge, with a final descent via a gravel track. Gaiters and walking poles recommended for the stream crossing.
Maps OS Explorer OL12.

On your way

It's hard to pick out just one of the many
magnificent views to be had from the Black
Mountain's ridgetop, but the panorama over
LLYN Y FAN FACH from the western rim
of **BANNAU SIR GAER** has to be a strong
contender. From this vantage point, nearly
200m above the water, you look lengthways
over the lake, with the dark cliffs of the
escarpment rising in spectacular curves from
the shoreline. In summer, the mudslips that
gash the steepest slopes stand out almost
blood red against the vivid green of the grass
separating them, dotted with tiny white
clumps of sheep which defy the wind roaring
up the cwm to graze near vertical pasture.

Little wonder ancient stories swirl about
this magical amphitheatre like the ravens
rolling around in the thermals above it.
The best known concerns a beautiful fairy
princess who emerged from the depths of
Llyn y Fan Fach to be wooed by a handsome
shepherd boy she found grazing his flocks
on the shore. The pair married and had
three sons, the eldest of whom – Rhiwallon
– was granted magical healing powers by his
mother before, in fulfillment of a curse cast
on her marriage by her father, she was forced
to return to the underwater world.

It is at this point the old Welsh legend
becomes entangled with historical truth.

Red Kites

Approaching Mynydd Ddu through the remote valleys to the north, you're almost guaranteed to see at least a couple of red kites circling above the sheep pastures. Until recently, this area was one of the last bastions of a bird that, by the 1960s, had become almost extinct in Britain. Regarded as a threat to expanding agriculture from the sixteenth century onwards, kites were hunted as vermin by gamekeepers. Only thanks to a handful of maverick Welsh farmers, who loved the sight of these beautiful birds soaring above their land and realized they posed no risk to their lambs, did a few breeding pairs survive here.

No-one knows exactly how close the species came to completely disappearing from Britain, but in 1977, researchers established the entire population emanated from just one female. The revival of the red kite ranks among the great conservation success stories of the twentieth century. Around 600 breeding pairs now nest in Wales alone, and this corner of the country boasts the highest density in the UK.

Coloured chestnut red, with white patches under their impressive two-metre wingspan and a trademark forked tail, kites are easily distinguished from buzzards. One place you can be one-hundred percent certain of seeing them, in numbers undreamed of two decades ago, is the Red Kite Feeding Centre, next to the Cross Inn at Llandeussant, a couple of miles north of the start of our route at SN773258, where fifty birds appear at 3pm each day to be fed.

Because in medieval times the nearby village of Myddfai, five miles from the base of the mountain, was the home of an acclaimed physician also called Rhiwallon. Under the patronage of the local lord of the manor, he and his three sons – the "Physicians of Myddfai" – were renowned across Christendom as the authors of a book of medicinal recipes featuring 175 herbs that grew on the flanks of Mynydd Ddu.

The last in the illustrious line of doctors was buried in the village churchyard in 1842, but the dynasty's legacy endures. Set down on calf vellum in the late fourteenth century, a single version of the family's herbal treatise survived in the "Red Book of Hergest" (a folio of ancient Welsh songs, poems and proverbs), which the local community in Myddfai is now consulting in its attempts to grow the same medicinal herbs on a commercial scale.

The appearance of the Black Mountain has remained unchanged since the days when the Physicians gathered mallow, comfrey and whinberries on its upper tiers – and altered very little since the glaciers retreated eleven thousand years ago. Having sculpted the hillside into smooth curves, the ice fields left in their wake a moraine of rock debris impeding the flow of the Afon Swadde stream, which is how the lake originally formed. **LLYN Y FAN FACH**, by contrast, has swollen considerably thanks to the Welsh water board, who built

BELOW: Fan Brycheiniog, from the east

a dam across its outflow in the 1930s to create a reservoir to supply Llanelli.

No such encroachment has blighted the Black Mountain's other jewel, **LLYN Y FAN FAWR** – the prettier of the pair and, at 600m, the highest glacial lake in the national park. Shimmering on the east side of the massif below the horn of Fan Brycheiniog, it's most beautiful when viewed at dawn in midwinter after a fresh fall of snow, when the first rays of sun strike the summit behind, casting an ethereal reflection of red alpenglow on the freezing water.

BELOW: Sunset over the north ridge of Bannau Sir Gaer, from Llyn y Fan Fach

Cerrig Duon

The spot where the outflow from Llyn y Fan Fawr meets the River Tawe must have held ritual significance for our prehistoric ancestors. For just above the confluence they erected an oval of twenty sandstones – the Cerrig Duon circle – with an avenue of lower megaliths leading back in the direction of the lake. A solitary, human-sized sentry – Maen Mawr – stands guard to the northeast. Hardly anyone knows these stones are there, but the site, only 5mins walk off the Glyntawe-Trecastle road, ranks among the most atmospheric in the Welsh mountains.

walk it | 45

Mynydd Ddu

CHECKED BY
✔ **Dinefwr Ramblers**

1 Welsh Water has made a small, unsurfaced car park at SN799238 – a couple of hundred yards east of the "Rain Gauges" marked on OS maps. From the car park, follow the lane back towards the last farmhouse (actually part of a trout hatchery), and just

before reaching the driveway gate, turn L and head across the grass directly towards the Afon Swadde stream. From the opposite bank you'll see a clear track rising to the R. Ford the stream, and follow the path as it bends L around the hillside above and then strikes south above Garwnant gulley. The onward route, though boggy in places, is

obvious as it climbs steadily over occasional peat slips following the Brecon Beacons Way to the west ridge of **Bannau Sir Gaer**, reached after 1hr of ascent.

2 A small cairn marks the first summit, the grassy mound of Waen Lefrith (677m/2221ft), at the far northwestern edge of the escarpment. From here, a

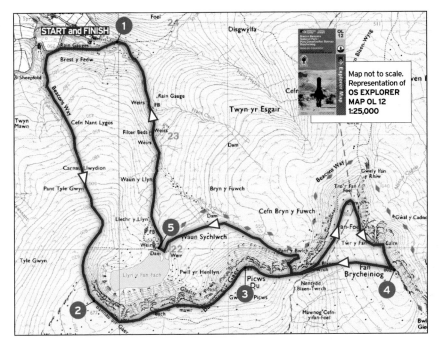

Map not to scale.
Representation of
OS EXPLORER
MAP OL 12
1:25,000

Route profile

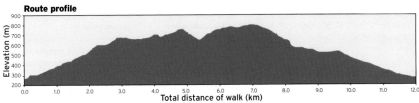

mostly dry path sticks close to the northern lip of the mountain as it rises gradually past a series of projecting spurs to **Bannau Sir Gaer** (749m/2457ft), the most dramatic of the peaks along this ridge, known in Welsh as "the Black Peak" (Picws Du).

3 A roller-coaster section ensues as you drop 100m/328ft from Bannau Sir Gaer to the lowest point in the ridge, at the head of a stream gulley known as Pant y Bwlch (SN816218), and then climb northeast to the cairn marking the top of Fan Foel (781m/2356ft). Here the path swings sharply SW, following the edge to cross the 800m contour at **Fan Brycheiniog** (802m/2631ft), where there's a trig point and drystone windshelter.

4 From Fan Brycheiniog, you can follow a rough path that cuts downhill across the spur of Fan Foel (follow a bearing off the summit of Bannau Sir Gaer if you lose it), to rejoin the main ridge path at Pant y Bwlch. Here you plunge steeply downhill to the R, along the L bank of the stream initially, on a narrow path that zigzags to the foot of the mountain (note that this stretch can be very slippery and difficult in wet, icy or snowy conditions, when crampons may be necessary). Turn L when you reach a junction at the bottom, following the path as it wriggles L around the foot of Bannau Sir Gaer, whose northwest face towers above; one section squeezes past a rock outcrop, beneath which the path i snarrow and has crumbled away in places

– cross with caution.

At SN812221, directly below the sharp nose of the summit, you reach a second fork in the path, where you bear L towards the lake (not R down the Afon Sychlwch stream). A Water Board feeder canal then ushers you SW. Cross the canal via the second of the two concrete footbridges you come to and follow it to the dam on the north side of **Llyn y Fan Fach**, where there's a grim little bothy/rescue hut.

5 Keep to the path dropping to R of hut (past the memorial to a World War II Lancaster bomber crash site) as far as its junction with main track, which falls steadily down the left bank of Afon Swadde river, past the trout hatchery, to the car park.

🚌 Getting There

The nearest you can get to the start of our route by public transport is Myddfai village, five miles north, which is served by daily Royal Mail post bus No.426/291 between Llandovery and Myrtle Hill – though it's a 90min plod through the lanes from there to Llanddeusant.

ℹ️ Visitor Information
Llandovery TIC
Heritage Centre, King's Rd
SA20 0AW
📞 01550 720693

🍴 Eating & Drinking

There are no pubs within walking distance of our route, but you'll find a broad choice of places to eat and drink in Llandovery, 12km/7miles north. Some local B&Bs also offer evening meals by prior arrangement.

🏠 Sleeping
Llanddeussant YHA
The Old Red Lion. Llanddeussant, SA19 9UL
📞 0870 770 5930
✎ www.yha.org.uk
Perfectly situated close to the trailhead, in a 200-year-old former inn overlooking the Swadde Valley.

Rhiwe Cottage
Llandgadog, Llanddeussant, SA19 9SS
📞 01865 343464
Self-catering holiday cottage with a spectacular outlook, only minutes from the start of the walk.

The Bunkhouse
Ynysmarchog Farm, Trecastle, 13km/8miles northeast of the trailhead, LD3 8UR
📞 01874 63800
✎ www.bunkhousewales.com
Cosy dorm beds in a converted Elizabethan barn with original stonework and beams.

📖 More Info
✎ www.breconbeacons.org. The National Park's offical site, featuring a handy round up of public transport routes to and around the region.

✎ www.redkites.co.uk. More on red kites in Wales.

✎ www.hiraeth.com/alan/misc/gott-nov97/myddfai.html. For the full version of the Lady of Llyn-y-Fan story.

✎ www.metoffice.gov.uk/loutdoor/mountainsafety/brecon.html. Walker-oriented forecast for the mountains, featuring freezing levels and wind speeds.

Top of the Range

Pen-y-Fan

From the time of the Hundred Years' War in the fourteenth century, successive British monarchs developed a system of early-warning fires to alert the country of imminent invasion. In South Wales, the pivotal point of this network, visible across fifteen shires, was the anvil-topped peak rising to the south of Brecon: Pen-y-Fan.

Over time, the beacon leant its name to the entire range of hills extending to either side of it. Stretching from the Herefordshire border to the hinterland of Carmarthen, the "Brecon Beacons" actually comprise four separate massifs, distinguished by their angular, northwest-facing scarps of Old Red Sandstone. At 886m/2906ft, Pen-y-Fan is the loftiest of the line – and the highest summit in Britain south of Snowdon.

Lying within easy reach of the Welsh valleys and the Cardiff-Newport conurbation, the mountain serves as a much loved escape for around 120,000 town and city dwellers each year, the majority of whom start their ascent from the Storey Arms car park on the A470, at the pass where the road crosses the

Beacons' watershed. This heavily eroded approach, however, holds less interest than others tackling Pen-y-Fan from the north.

On the Brecon side, five bare, grassy ridges taper in parallel from the main summit ridge, spreading like fingers towards the Vale of Usk's fertile patchwork far below. As you gain altitude, ever more spectacular views open up of the glaciated valleys below them, and even confirmed mountaineers cannot fail to be impressed by the first glimpse of Craig Cwm Sere – the 120-metre/400-foot triangle of near-vertical strata and grass ledges crumbling beneath Pen-y-Fan's summit.

The route we've devised splices together the most dramatic views the massif has to offer, in a linear walk starting either in Brecon or, if you jump in a taxi, the foot of the mountain itself. It's long and physically challenging day's walk. But in good weather, when the cloud base is well clear of the summits, assures a close encounter with a line of peaks possessing a much wilder, higher feel than their vital statistics might suggest.

At a glance

Where Pen-y-Fan, Brecon Beacons National Park, nr Brecon, 67km/42 miles north of Cardiff.
Why Views over the Vale of Usk to mid-Wales to Shropshire, and south across the Bristol channel to Exmoor; spectacular high-mountain terrain.
When First weekend in August, for the Brecon jazz festival.

Downsides The summit draws big crowds of walkers on summer weekends.
Start/Finish Bulwark, Brecon (SO045286) or lane end at Cwmcynwyn (SO038237)/Libanus, 4miles/6km south of Brecon on the A470 (SO995260).
Duration 5hrs or 6hrs 30mins.
Distance 16.5km/11miles or 12km/

7.5miles (from Cwmcynwyn).
Terrain Mostly clearpaths over grassy mountainsides, with some short, steep and rocky sections below the summits requiring an easy scramble. The walk in from Brecon follows mostly unsurfaced tracks, pasture, and some sections of quiet lanes.
Maps OS Explorer OL12.

Cribyn and the Bryn Teg
ridge from the summit of
Pen-y-Fan

On your way

The distinctive appearance of the Brecon Beacon range, with its text-book scarp-and-dip-slope profiles and table-top summits, derives from the durability of Old Red Sandstone. Formed three hundred million years ago when the area lay under a huge marine estuary, this pinkish rock was created after mud and sand from the seabed was compressed and forced upwards, to be sliced and molded by glaciers.

Few landscapes in Britain exemplify more vividly the action of glacial ice than do the four cwms, or cirques, that scallop the northwest flanks of **PEN-Y-FAN**. As they retreated, the ice fields scooped massive bowls from the mountainsides, revealing cross-sections of their geological fillings – the trademark strata that bands the Beacons' exposed crags. The hardest rocks of all, known as "plateau beds", rest on the topmost layers, which is why the summits tend to be flat. More resistant to erosion, the plateaux have remained largely intact while the slopes below them are gashed by landslips and run-off gullies.

The combination of dramatic, smooth-sided valleys and steep dividing ridges on the north side of the Pen-y-Fan massif makes for superb walking. **BRYN TEG** – "Beautiful Hill" – is the most elegant of these spurs, not least because it scythes

straight up the mountain to meet the knife-edge, northwest ridge of **CRIBYN** (795m/2608ft). Walkers approaching this pyramid for the first time are sometimes intimidated by its culminating step, but the path ascends it easily via a natural rock staircase that's not nearly as exposed as it looks from a distance.

From the top of Cribyn, the magnificent view south over the heads of the Welsh Valleys to the distant Bristol Channel is revealed for the first time. But it's the northwest face of Pen-y-Fan – formidable **CRAIG CWM SERE** – which tends to steal the show at this stage, as you drop to the pass dividing the two peaks.

The cliff was the scene of a tragedy in World War II, when a spitfire pilot crashed into a gulley only 25m/80ft below the ridgetop. The wreckage wasn't found for almost nine months, making it the longest missing plane to have disappeared over land in the entire war. With a pair of binoculars, you can pick out fragments of the aircraft at the bottom of Cwm Sere's main gulley.

Old maps mark a trig point on the summit plateau of Pen-y-Fan itself. But this was dismantled recently by archeologists excavating the Early Bronze Age cairn below it, in which pots of human ashes were discovered dating from 2200–1400BC. Semi-nomadic herdsmen once

The "Fan Dance"

Military selection tests don't come much tougher than the one undertaken by would-be recruits to the SAS (based 34miles north of Brecon at Credenhill Camp), the cen-trepiece of which is a gruelling 24-km/15-mile out-and-back yomp over the Pen-y-Fan massif carrying a 35lb backpack. For any soldiers able to complete the so-called "Fan Dance" in less than four hours, a still-more agonizing ordeal awaits in the form of the "Long Drag", covering a 64-km/40-mile route with a back-breaking 55lb sack over the same ground.

The Tommy Jones Tragedy

Pen-y-Fan's fickle weather has inflicted many losses over the years – none of them more poignant than that of five-year-old Tommy Jones, a farmer's son from the Rhondda Valley who perished on the mountain in 1900. Tommy had become separated from his father and cousin while walking from Brecon to his grandparents' farm at the bottom of Cwm Llwch on a summer's evening. Quite how this happened remains a mystery, as do the circumstances that led to his eventual death, high on the ridge just shy of the summit of Corn Du.

For 29 days following the disappearance, rescuers scoured the valley for traces of the boy. In the end it was a gardener's wife from north of Brecon who located his body slumped in the bracken, after its whereabouts had been revealed to her in a dream. The obelisk erected on the spot stands as a memorial both to the extraordinary stamina of the lad – who, already tired and hungry after a long walk from Brecon, somehow managed to climb two miles up 1300ft of mountain in the dark – as well as to the treacherous nature of Pen-y-Fan itself, a hill deserving of more respect than its benign appearance sometimes suggests.

hunted, farmed and grazed their flocks on these uplands, thanks to a climate that was much drier and milder than today's. However, as the weather turned colder, and the effects of overgrazing reduced the soil to impoverished peat bog, the beaker folk retreated to lower ground, leaving their tumuli behind on the mountain summits.

Another ancient cairn crowns Pen-y-Fan's sister peak, **CORN DU** – the "Black Horn" – reached via a graceful saddle overlooking Cwm Llwch and its tiny glacial lake. Before dropping off the ridge to begin its descent into the valley, our path skirts the memorial to Tommy Jones, the five-year-old who lost his life at this desolate spot in 1900 (see box above). Tommy's grandparents lived in the first farm you come to on the valley floor – and a more splendid site for a house it is hard to imagine. Enfolded on all sides by huge amphitheatre of grassy mountains, the cottage seems to inhabit its own separate world.

RIGHT: The obelisk marking the spot where little Tommy Jones' body was found in 1900

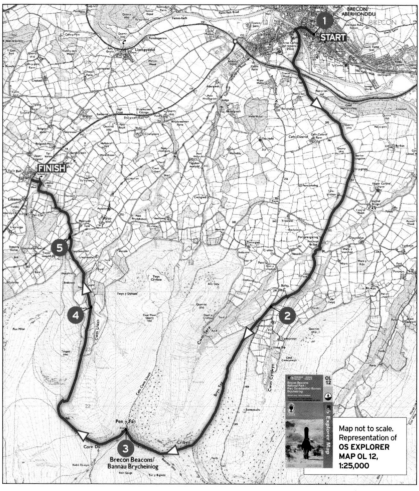

Map not to scale.
Representation of
**OS EXPLORER
MAP OL 12,
1:25,000**

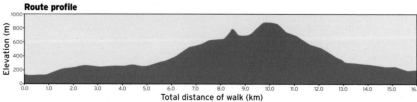

Route profile

It's a good ninety-minute, mostly uphill plod, from the centre of Brecon to Cwmcynwyn, where the country lanes yield to open mountainside. Given an early enough start, and sufficient fitness, you could cover the full distance on foot, using the first stage of the route description below. But be warned that this makes for a long, hard day, and that you might prefer to jump in a taxi from Brecon Market square. Cabbies charge around £6-7 for the 6-km/3.5-mile trip to Cwmcynwyn. Whichever way you begin the route, be sure to check timings for the bus from Libanus at the other end (see "Getting There").

1 From the Bulwark in the centre of Brecon town, walk down Ship St and across the bridge over the Usk. Turn L at the far side onto Dinas Rd, past a pay-and-display car park on your L, and keep going until the lane forks. Bear R here through a wrought-iron gate marked "Private Drive Footpath Only", and continue for 5mins down this track along the side of Christ College playing fields. Where the lane starts to bend sharply L, head straight on through a pair of stone gate posts, turning L on to a tarmac lane that rises steeply uphill.

Follow this lane across the bridge over the bypass to begin a steady, steep climb. After 5mins, the lane swings sharply R to Pen-y-Lan farm; do not follow the tarmac, but instead continue straight ahead on an old, unsurfaced quarry track. The gradient eases as you crest the hill 15mins later, from where

you'll be rewarded with your first glimpse of Pen-y-Fan and Cribyn. After a short descent, follow the lane ahead past Tir-y-groes cottage, ignoring the waymarked path to your L here. Keep dropping down the lane until it makes a 90-degree bend at Tyle-brithos. Just after the bend, a stile on your R, marked with a finger-post hidden in the hedge, leads to a path skirting a barbed wire fence. Follow this to a second stile, then keep to the R field border, crossing a few more stiles to reach a metal gate and final stile where you rejoin the lane.

Cross the lane junction to head straight on, over the stream and up a rise past Pontbrengarreg farm. Bearing L at the fork just beyond the farm, you should cross a stone bridge and turn R immediately after it.

After the five-bar gate, the lane turns into a rough, stony track. Keep walking up this, past Tir-ciw farm and the S-bend just beyond the midway point. After 15-20mins yo'' reach a gate where the path joins the lane end at Cwncynwyn.

2 Having reached the head of the lane, follow the tree-lined track up the hill (remains of the old Roman road over the Beacons). At the gate onto access land, instead of keeping to the track cutting along the L border of the field, follow the clear trail rising up through the bracken to your R up the ridgeline of **Bryn Teg**. After a steady but strenuous climb, the path gains the spine of the hill, levelling off momentarily before steepening on its approach to Cribyn (795m/2608ft), whose summit is reached by means of a step requiring simple hand holds.

From **Cribyn**, descend R down the ridge to a saddle pass, from where a heavily eroded trail strikes up the lip of **Craig Cwm Sere** to the summit of **Pen-y-Fan** (886m/2907ft).

3 Head SW off the summit plateau, keeping to the path on the very edge of the ridge falling to your R. This drops to a second saddle, then rises briefly to reach the top of **Corn Du** (873m/2864ft).

Getting onto the Craig Cwm Llwch ridge from here can be tricky if the mist has closed in: look for a notch in the edge of the summit plateau of Corn Du, only 50m/150ft SW of the cairn, from where the path descends steeply to the ridge. In poor visibility, it's easy to be drawn SW along the much more obvious, paved route running down to Bwlch Duwynt.

After the steep initial descent along the Cwm Llwch ridge, ignore the path peeling off at the 760m contour, and continue instead downhill past the Tommy Jones memorial on your L.

From the obelisk, keep to the path closest to the cliff edge as it swings north around the head of Cwm Llwch, and then bears R above the lake. At SN999220, you'll reach a prominent fork. Take the L branch to follow a well worn route that runs all the way down the valley to Cwm Llwch Farm.

4 Cross the stile to the L of the farm, and follow the path as it skirts the buildings to join a broad track. This winds alongside the Nant Cwm Llwch stream a short way to Login (look for a modern barn through the trees on your R), where it crosses a tributary stream by means of a footbridge.

Continue on the main track for a couple of minutes, but bear L when you reach a fork, up a short rise to a field with a small wood on your L. Keep heading along the L edge of the field, over a stile and down to a pair of cottages, which the footpath skirts to the R, as indicated.

A stile in the bottom of the next field (a little to the R of its bottom L corner) leads to another small field and, after a couple of mins, to a second group of cottages (marked "Clwydwaunhir" on OS maps), which you pass through the middle of via a track, turning R to pass through a gate and onwards down the driveway.

5 The driveway arrives soon after at a tarmac lane, where you turn R, then immediately L. Follow the winding lane N, bearing L at the fork soon after, then L again when you've dropped down to Libanus Mill to cross the river over an old stone bridge. The main A470 and bus stop lies a couple of mins further down the lane at Libanus village, where buses stop for Brecon.

Getting There
Brecon is well connected to the rest of Wales by bus. The end of the walk at Libanus on the A470 is served by regular services travelling between Merthyr and Brecon (for timetable information, go to ✎www. traveline-cymru.org.uk, or phone ✆0781 200 2233). Libanus is also a stop for the walker-friendly Beacons Buses (Sundays in summer only; timetables at ✎www.breconbeacons.org).

ℹ️ Visitor Information
National Park Visitor Centre (Mountain Centre)
Libanus (at SN977262), 6.4km/ 4miles SW of Brecon
✆01874 623366
✎www.breconbeacons.org

Brecon TIC
Market Car Park
✆01874 622485

🍴 Eating & Drinking
The Tai'r Bull Inn at the end of route (see "Sleeping" below) is just the place to get a quick pint in before jumping on the bus. It also serves meals made with local produce including game, mountain lamb, pork and beef. The National Park Visitor Centre (Mountain Centre), near Libanus, (see above), has a popular cafeteria serving freshly cooked, inexpensive meals, which you can take out on to a terrace for a panoramic view of Pen-y-Fan.

🛏️ Sleeping
Penstar Bunkhouse & Cottage
Libanus, nr Brecon, LD3 8NE
✆01874 622702
✎www.penstarbunkhouse andcottage.co.uk
Perfectly placed bunkhouse and self-catering cottage in a former farm, only 5mins off our route.

Llwyn y Celyn YHA
3miles south of Libanus, nr Brecon, LD3 8NH
✆0870 770 5936
✎www.yha.org.uk
On the western side of the mountain, just below the A470 – a walkers' favourite that's perfectly situated for explorations of the mid and eastern Beacons.

Tai'r Bull Inn
Libanus, LD3 8AL
✆01874 625859
✎www.freewebs.com/tairbullinn
Basic, en-suite rooms on the first floor of a roadside pub, with views across the main road to the hills.

📖 More Info
✎wwwviewfinder panoramas.org. Print off a free, colour-coded panorama showing all the landmarks visible from the summit.
✎www.metoffice.gov.uk/loutdoor/ mountainsafety/brecon.html. Detailed, walker-oriented forecast for the mountains.
✎www.brecon-beacons.com. This enthusiast's site is a bit homespun, but packed with useful information.
✎www.breconbeacons.org. The national park's main site, featuring a handy round up of public transport routes.
✎www.breconbeaconsparksociety. org. Walks programmes and special events in the Beacons.

🚶 More Walks
Amazing Place: Walks Within the Cwmcarn Forest by Maggie Thomas (Islwyn Ramblers). Pack of thirteen laminated cards featuring walks of between 7.2km and 14.5km (4.5 and 9miles) exploring the little-known but beautiful Cwmcarn Forest, near Caerphilly.

Walks You Will Enjoy by East Radnor Ramblers (Ramblers). Eighteen walks on pocket-sized, laminated cards. The route are between 4.5 and 9miles in length, focussing on Radnorshire, Herefordshire and mid-Wales.

walk | 47

ARGYLL & BUTE

The Butter Mountain

Ben Ime

Barely an hour north of the Clyde, the Arrochar Alps have served as a playground for Glaswegians starved of green spaces and fresh air since the great depression of the 1930s. Unemployed shipbuilders, with plenty of time to kill but not much money, used to hitch-hike or cycle up the banks of Loch Lomond to walk, climb and sleep rough in the wilderness of craggy mountains dividing the head of Loch Long and Loch Fyne.

Today the hills, named after the village that stands as their principal gateway, are as popular as ever, thanks in no small part to the extraordinary, triple-peaked form of the Cobbler (Ben Arthur; 881m/2890ft), whose gnarled summit crags see processions of trekkers and runners (and their intrepid pet dogs) year round. Lacking the same aggressive profile, its neighbours, by contrast, tend to attract far less attention – and feel much wilder as a result.

For a really vivid taste of how rugged this area can be, you won't do better than an ascent of Ben Ime (1011m/3317ft) – the wedge-shaped "Butter Mountain" rising to the north of the Cobbler. As the

highest peak in the range, this Munro affords a view of exceptional character: to the north and west you can gaze across a seemingly endless spread of mountains and sea, ranging from Ben Nevis in the central Highlands to Mull, the Paps of Jura and Goat Fell on the Isle of Arran, while to the south and east are the Pentlands and fells of Ettrick. The real show-stealer, though, is the view back over the mountain's east ridge to the silvery expanse of Loch Katrine, snaking towards the horizon, with the unmistakable pyramid of Ben Lomond standing guard to the south.

A straightforward out-and-back walk, the route follows well frequented, purpose-built paths for most of its length, with the final pull to the top over soggier ground where you might need to refer to your compass or GPS should cloud close in. Involving 2000 metres/6562 feet of ascent and descent, the route is, however, a physically challenging one over high ground where weather changes can be sudden and dramatic at any time of year. So don't attempt it without the proper equipment and navigation skills.

At a glance

Where Ben Ime, near Arrochar, 68km/42miles northwest of Glasgow.
Why Magnificent views of the southern and central Highlands; a close encounter with Ben Arthur ("the Cobbler"); access via the West Highland Railway.

When In winter, with a covering of snow – though you'll need the necessary mountaineering skills and equipment for ice conditions.
Downsides The approach path gets busy on weekends.
Start/Finish Forestry Commission Car Park, Succoth

(NN294048), 1km around the loch head from Arrochar.
Duration 5hrs.
Distance 16.2km/9.4miles.
Terrain Forest tracks, made paths and fainter trails over high, open mountains.
Maps OS Explorer 364.

The view east from the summit of
Ben Ime, with the distant pyramid
of Ben Lomond on the horizon

On your way

BEN IME is the culminating peak in a group of mountains clustered around the top of Loch Long (literally "Straight Loch"). Their name, the Arrochar Alps, derives from that of the village draped around the loch's northeastern shore, which in turn is thought to be a corruption of the Gaellic "ard tir", "high ground".

"Savage hills, swept by savage rains, peopled by savage sheep, tended by savage people," is how Rabbie Burns characterized this wild corner of the southern Highlands, the traditional territory of the MacFarlanes, notorious brigands and cattle thieves. Their original seat stood at nearby Inveruglas, but after its castle was razed to the ground by Cromwell's army the clan moved to the more easily defensible isthmus separating Loch Lomond from Loch Long.

The ground they settled was known as Tarbert, from the Gaellic "tairbeirt", meaning "boat drag" – a reference to the ancient trackway of greased logs over which local fishermen used to haul their boats between the lochs. This same laborious route was crossed by an armada of Viking longboats in 1263, after the Norse king Haakon Haakonson sent a fleet to consolidate his occupation of Scotland's northwest coast. Having traversed the isthmus with sixty ships, the invaders pressed south down Loch Lomond and on to loot Stirling, before being defeated in the Battle of Largs in north Ayrshire.

MacFarlane clansmen slain while trying to halt the invaders at Tarbet were interred in a burial ground nearby, along with the bodies of some of their Viking adversaries. Later incorporated into the graveyard of Tarbet's Ballyhennan Church, the enclosure still contains the ancient memorial stones, though the church how

houses a restaurant and heritage centre.

A water-borne invasion of a less menacing nature sailed up Loch Long in the mid-nineteenth century, in the form of the first pleasure steamers from Glasgow. Daytrippers used to alight in **ARROCHAR** at a small pier, whose remains still protrude from the water in front of the village.

Most of the hotels and little B&Bs ranged along the roadside opposite the jetty, however, date from the later advent of the West Highland Railway, laid along the east bank of Loch Long from Glasgow between 1887 and 1894. Around five thousand navvies were drafted in to build the line. Crammed into five separate camps, the workers, who were mostly from Ireland, Poland and the impoverished far north of Scotland, endured terrible conditions. Fatalities were all too common: over the seven years of the project, 37 men died, some of them while still in their teens.

They were laid to rest in a plot next to the MacFarlane graveyard at Ballyhennan Church in Tarbet. Quite why they were refused burial inside the main enclosure remains a matter of debate, but a memorial has since been erected to their sacrifice on the roadside nearby.

The new train line brought prosperity to Arrochar, stimulating the construction of a string of rather grand houses and hotels along the loch. The comfort of a cosy waterside B&B, however, lay well beyond the pockets of the rough, tough contingent who began to colonize the nearby hills in the early 1930s. Laid off following the closure of the Clydebank's shipyards, many working-class men took to exploring this spectacular terrain in the decade before the war, climbing the crags by day and dossing in caves or hollows under boulders ("howfs") by night.

Once such camp centered on the

NARNAIN BOULDERS, at the head of the Coire a'Bhalachain, the high valley separating the **COBBLER** from **BEN NARNAIN**. This is where members of working-class mountaineering clubs, such as the "Creagh Dhu" and "Cobbler Club", used to congregate and bivouac between forays into the crags.

The appearance in these mountains of Glasgow's lower orders was a revolution in the conservative Highlands, whose hill country had up until then been the exclusive preserve of wealthy sportsmen. As the historian Ken Wilson once remarked: "[it] was rather as if a group of east enders had suddenly decided to take up grouse shooting or polo."

An evocative account of the times features in the autobiography of Glasgow-born author and broadcaster, Alastair Charles Borthwick (1913–2003). *Always A Little Further* recounts with great relish the expoits of the "gangrels of all sorts" Borthwick encountered while a young reporter writing on the local outdoor scene for the *Glasgow Evening Herald*.

In common with many of the characters he described, Borthwick's mountain days were temporarily curtailed by the outbreak of World War II, during which he saw active service in North Africa and Europe. Navigation skills learned in the hills around Arrochar were to come in useful during the Allies' assault on the Netherlands after D-Day. Borthwick garnered considerable praise after steering six hundred men under cover of darkness one-and-a-half miles behind German lines, "dead reckoning" his position using only a compass and an unreliable map.

Meanwhile, back in Arrochar, Loch Long had become the country's leading testing site for submarine torpedoes. By the end of the war, more than twelve-thousand shells – 48 per day – had been fired down the loch. The navy kept the installation going until 1987, by which time innovations in torpedo design necessitated deeper waters for testing.

Arrochar had originally been chosen for the dubious honour of hosting an under-water firing range because of its proximity to the Faslane naval base, 18km/11miles south down the loch – nowadays the home of Britain's nuclear Trident submarine fleet. Bitterly opposed by the SNP and many Labour politicians in Scotland, Faslane is also the site of a long-established peace camp, where protesters routinely attempt to disrupt the transport of nuclear warheads by road.

The hurly burly of Faslane's disarmament campaign feels a million miles away when you're on the summit of Ben Ime, enjoying a bird's eye view over hundreds of miles of serene mountains and lochs. To the north, the giants of Lochaber are ranged around the unmistakable form of Ben Nevis. The furthest point of land you can theoretically see from the top is Sawel, in the Sperrin mountains of County Londonderry – 194km/121miles southwest.

Visible in the same direction, though closer to home at the foot of the mountain, is the grey line of the famous "Rest and Be Thankful" road, known affectionately to Scottish mountain lovers as simply "the Rest". Running northwest from Loch Long and up Glen Croe to Loch Fyne, the route was originally carved out in the 1740s, in the wake of the Jacobite Uprising, to enable the swift movement of militia from Argyll, whose Duke was loyal to the Hanoverian crown. A stone seat erected by the 24th Regiment, who did most of the spade work, bears the legend "Rest And Be Thankful" – whence the road, and its modern counterpart's name.

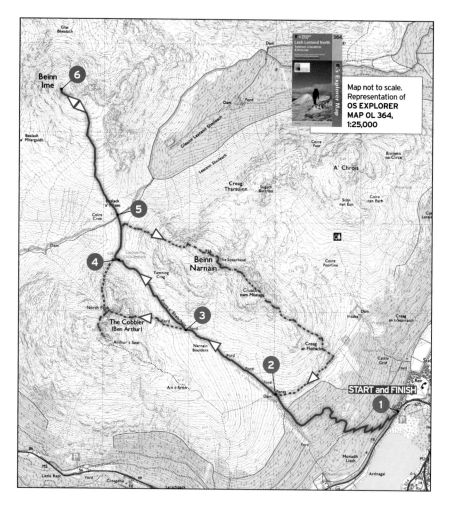

Route profile

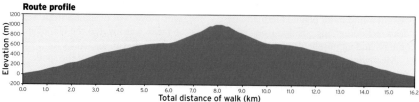

1 From the Forestry Commission car park and bus stop on the A83 at Succoth, just around the head of the loch from **Arrochar**, cross the road and continue a short way L. A gate, marked by a carved fox on your R, flags the start of a broad track heading R into recently cleared spruce forest. Climbing via a series of easy switchbacks, it arrives after 5-10mins at a bench next to a broader, motorable track, where you should turn L, and then R immediately after. The view back over Loch Long to Ben Lomond improves rapidly as you begin to tackle steeper, wooded ground lining the banks of the Allt a' Bhalachain. This long slog is where much of the day's work is done. It eventually brings you out at a small dam, from where the Cobbler's three peaks are revealed for the first time.

2 The gradient eases here, as the path climbs above the rushing burn. The next landmark along the trail are the Narnain Boulders, where climbers used to bivouac in the 1930s.

3 Having passed the boulders, and a small lochan soon after on your R, bear R at the prominent fork in the trail (a L turn here would take you up the southeast side of the Cobbler), keeping to the main path as it follows the stream bank. This eventually arrives at the pass dividing the **Cobbler** and **Ben Narnain**, where a second fork marks the start (to the L) of

the climb up the former's steep northeast flank.

4 Head straight at this second fork, shortly beyond which the path swings decisively R, rising slightly, then contouring north towards the foot of **Ben Ime**, now visible directly ahead. The trail grows muddier as it approaches the Bealach a' Mhaim. Take a well-earned break at the stile over the fence along the pass, to steel yourself for a long ascent of more than 350m/1148ft.

5 Ben Ime seems a sheer and rocky mountain from most angles, but this route up is benign enough - albeit fairly strenuous, and boggy at times, especially lower down the mountain. Affording great views back to the Cobbler, the path is easy to follow most of way, though it does peter out in places. Just keep heading towards the rocks above and you'll eventually reach the grassy incline leading to the summit, marked by a trig point and wind shelter.

6 Return by the same route. In poor visibility, be sure to take a compass bearing before starting your descent or you might end up following the much rockier and more challenging NE ridge off the mountain.

Route Extensions:
The Cobbler and Ben Narnain
Given an early enough start, and plenty of stamina, it's perfectly possible to tie ascents of either - or both - the Cobbler and Ben Narnain into this route. If you intend to bag Ben Narnain on the outward leg, turn R at the

dam at NN280051, and contour NE until a fork is reached, from where a steep path strikes L up the rocky NW ridge to the summit. After the trigpoint, this then descends to the Bealach a' Mhaim and the start of our route up Ben Ime.

For the Cobbler, we recommend an ascent via the NE ridge - the stepped path's much easier to climb than descend. It breaks up a little towards the top, as you reach the ridge at a point between the mountain's north and central peaks. Turn R to explore the higher central summit, whose top is gained via a notoriously tricky scramble, and descend back to the pass afterwards. You can then have a crack at the north summit, before dropping back to the pass one more time. A cairn marks the start of the rough descent down the southeast ridge, which will take you down to rejoin the main path along the valley floor. Full route descriptions for these ascents are featured in most walking guides to the region (see More Walks), and online at ✎www.walkhighlands.co.uk.

Getting There
Arrochar can be reached from Glasgow via the West Highland Railway; the station stands 2km west of Loch Long, midway between the village and Tarbet. Scottish CityLink bus service 915 also runs there.

i **Visitor Information**
Ben Lomond Heritage Centre
Ballyhennan Church, Tarbet
☎01301 702393
✎www.thebenlomond.com

Eating & Drinking
Greenbank Restaurant
Main St, Arrochar
☎0131 702305
Down-to-earth cooking at down-to-earth prices, served in a tiny roadside restaurant with views across the water to the mountains. This is the only commenable place in the village to eat, and it's open year round. Cards accepted.

Sleeping
Rowantreebank
Main St, Arrochar, G83 7AA
☎0131 702318
✐www.rowantreebank.co.uk
One of a string of budget places lined up along the main road through the village, Dave and Angie Heckle's cosy little B&B is a popular option with walkers.

The rooms are on the small side, but impeccably clean, and have hot showers in their little en suite bathrooms. Those on the top floor boast lake views through dormer windows.

More Info
Always A Little Further by Alastair Charles Borthwick. The perfect companion to a stay in this area, recounting the life and times of the mavericks who blazed the first climbing and hiking routes up the Arrochar Alps.

✐www.mwis.org.uk. Detailed weather forecast for the southern Highlands, aimed primarily at walkers.
✐www.arrocharheritage.com. Written by local people, this is a

great site for anyone interested in the region's history.
✐www.walkhighlands.co.uk/lochlomond/the-cobbler.shtml. Recommended route description for the ascent of Ben Arthur (the Cobbler).
✐www.viewfinderpanoramas.org. Download your free summit topograph for Ben Ime, identifying every landform theoretically visible from the top.

More Walks
Collins Rambler's Guide: Ben Nevis & Glen Coe by Chris Townsend (Collins/Ramblers). The perfect introduction to the West Highlands. Thirty walks, ranging in length from 4km2.5miles to 20km/12miles, exploring the sea lochs, narrow glens and rugged mountains.

ABOVE: Ben Nanain and the Cobbler (Ben Arthur), from the south flank of Ben Ime

The Great Herdsman

Buachaille Etive Mòr

For pure grandeur, no mountains on the British mainland can hold a candle to those of the central Highlands of Scotland. And the valley that best typifies the region's distinctive splendour is without doubt Glen Coe. Among hill walkers and climbers alike, the peaks and ridges that tower on both sides of this deep trench in Lochaber are as legendary as their names are hard for Sassenachs (the Highlanders' nickname for the English) to pronounce. Each year, tongue-twisting "Aonach Eagach", "Sgorr nam Fiannaidh", "Stob Coire Sgreamhach" entice tens of thousands of intrepid souls into some of Europe's most untamed wilderness.

One peak, however, stands out from the crowd. Approaching from the desolate wastes of Rannoch Moor to the southwest, travellers through the ages have stopped to gape in awe at the giant pyramid guarding the entrance to Glen Coe: Buachaille Etive Mòr, "the Great Herdsman of Etive", known to mountain lovers across the country as simply "the Big Buachaille".

With near vertical granite crags rising from a sea of rumpled heather, bog and bracken, it's a view that has adorned countless calendars and postcards. No other peak in Scotland, not even Ben Nevis itself, is so instantly recognizable.

Yet there are many who would argue this iconic vista owes its popularity to the fact it can be seen from the comfort of the road, and that only by ascending the peak itself can you really get a sense of just how spectacular and other-worldly the mountainous fringe of Rannoch Moor really is. An eight-kilometre/five-mile-long ridge, rising and falling between 800 and 1000 metres (2600 and 3250 feet), forms the Buachaille's boney spine. To follow it is to embark on a non-stop big-dipper ride of stupendous views, encompassing a huge sweep of high mountains.

The only catch is that there is, quite simply, no easy way up the Buachaille. The classic ascent we outline weighs in well below a full-blown scramble, and in settled weather presents no technical challenges. But it involves an initial steep climb and an equally sharp descent off the other end, with plenty of ups and downs in between.

At a glance

Where Glen Coe, southeast of Fort William.
Why Superb views of Scotland's most rugged region; state-of-the-art visitor centre; the legendary Clachaig Inn.
When Late spring–early autumn, when the mountains are free of ice.

Downsides This is serious high-mountain terrain, with all the risks that implies (see "Winter Warning" box on page 362).
Start/Finish Altnafeadh, on the A86 (NN221563).
Duration 5-6 hrs.
Distance 14.5km/9miles.
Cut it Short You can skip the

stretch between Stob Coire Altrium and Stob na Bròige, heading straight down Core Altrium, which will save you 2.5km/1.5 miles.
Terrain Rough paths, heavily eroded in places, over often steep, high and exposed ground.
Maps OS Explorer 384.

Stob Dearg, highest point on the Buachaille Etive
Mòr ridge, with the Blackwater Reservoir to left

On your way

The mountains around Glen Coe owe their rugged appearance to a series of cataclysmic eruptions 420 million years ago, when a series of five huge volcanoes spewed lava across the landscape. Once empty, the magma chambers below the earth's surface could not support the weight pressing down on them and collapsed to form huge craters, some 8km/5miles across. These were then eroded by millennia of ice, wind and rain into the deep, glaciated glens and shattered granite cliffs that characterize the region today.

The wild terrain of the glen was the traditional homeland of the MacDonald clan, one of whose ancestors had been granted it by Robert the Bruce as a reward for support at the Battle of Bannockburn. But in 1493, James IV abolished the Lordship of the Isles, which effectively relegated the MacDonalds to the status of tenants under the Campbells of Glenorchy and Argyll.

This sparked off a bitter enmity between the two clans which, over the centuries, spiralled from cattle raids into mass murders. It is also generally held to be the root cause of the massacre of 1692, for which Glen Coe has since been notorious. Thirty-eight MacDonalds were killed one fiercely cold February morning by a contingent of government troops, led by Captain Robert Campbell. Their crime was ostensibly refusing to swear an oath of allegiance to King William III. In fact, the MacDonalds had intended to swear the oath, but had missed the January 1st deadline for it by five days after travelling to the wrong location.

On finally receiving the order to "fall upon the Rebells . . . and putt all to the sword under [the age of] seventy", Campbell's men set about their work with grizzly ineptitude. Maimed and terrified, hundreds of clansmen and women fled

The "Unna Principles"

Glen Coe might have a trunk road running right down the middle of it, but the mountains flanking the valley are some of the most unspoilt in Britain - and considerably wilder than many of much greater height in the Alps. You won't find painted waymarks or finger posts on these ridges, let alone summit cafés, cable-cars or ski lifts. We have the Scottish Mountaineering Club (the SMC) to thank for that, and more particularly its former president, Percy Unna. In the 1930s, Unna spearheaded a successful campaign to raise funds to purchase the

Dalness Forest estate, which encompassed Glen Coe and its neighbouring valleys. When the land was finally bought it was placed in the care of the National Trust for Scotland (NTS), though only on condition that certain obligations were respected.

Unna was adamant that future generations should find these mountains just as wild as they were in his day, and insisted in a now famous handover letter to the NTS that no improvements should be made to paths or mechanical forms of transport introduced; that

there were to be no signs, wayposts or bothies; and certainly no funicular railways and mountain-top restaurants such as those that had marred the high mountains of continental Europe.

These stipulations, which became known as the "Unna Principles", continue to shape management policy throughout the Highlands today, and explain the Scots' widespread dislike of cairns and waymarks - in fact, anything that renders the hills easier to climb. Which is why you'll need sharp navigation skills to venture into them.

through a ferocious blizzard into the mountains, where many more than were officially declared dead must have perished of exposure.

Memories of the atrocity have lingered a long time in this region, less perhaps because of the deed itself – these were, after all, violent times – but for the manner of its doing. The troops responsible for the actual killing were billeted with the same MacDonald families they would later slaughter – a heinous breach of Highland hospitality codes for which the perpetrators have never been forgiven.

Contrary to the common perception of events, however, only a small number of the soldiers involved were actually Campbells, and the massacre was less the culmination of an old clan feud than part of a wider government plan to wipe out the Highland way of life. Campbell's superior, the Secretary of State for Scotland, Sir John Dalrymple, had wanted to make an example of one of the clans and the MacDonalds seemed the softest option: they lacked a castle and, because of their widespread unpopularity, were unlikely to receive support from more powerful neighbours.

The subjugation of Highland culture accelerated greatly after Culloden and the Jacobite Uprising of 1745. This was when General Wade built the old military road up the glen and out across **RANNOCH MOOR**, to enable troops to be deployed quickly in rebel areas. A triangular plateau of sodden land dotted with tiny lochs and streams, Rannoch Moor had for centuries presented a formidable obstacle to travellers in the Highlands. The routes across it were frequently buried by snow in winter and obscured for weeks on end by drizzle and fog the rest of the year.

In Wade's day, the first sign of civilization for soldiers marching across the moor were the barracks facing the great pyramid of Buachaille Etive Mòr, at the junction of Glen Coe and Glen Etive. Originally dating from the seventeenth century, the building was later converted to an inn, the King's House Hotel, which still stands today just off the road – a much loved haven for climbers and walkers over the decades.

It also served as a watering hole for the army of navvies who, in the first decade of the twentieth century, excavated the Blackwater Reservoir, a couple of hours'

BELOW: Icicles above Lairig Gartain, with Buachaille Etive Bearg in the background

48 Buachaille Etive Mòr

Winter warning

The Buachaille, and the views from its summits, are certainly prettiest after a dusting of snow. But winter conditions bring with them significant risks. The head wall of Coire na Tulaich, in particular, can be lethal in freezing weather – a fact underlined in January 2009, when three seasoned, well-equipped mountaineers were swept to their deaths by an avalanche. We advise walkers, therefore, only to attempt this route in safe, settled weather, between late spring and early autumn, when the mountain is completely free of ice and snow. Do not venture up the Buachaille in winter under any circumstances without an ice axe, crampons, specialist cold-weather clothing, an avalanche rescue alarm and the skills to use such kit.

walk across the mountain to the north of the hotel. The men would steel themselves for the slog up the so-called "Devil's Staircase" (a stepped track now a famous landmark on the West Highland Way) with a jar at the King's House. Quite a few of them, however, never made it to work, perishing en route after collapsing drunk in the snow.

Their bodies, along with those of the other men who did not survive long enough to see the completion of the reservoir, were interred in a tiny cemetery next to the dam at its far end. By the time the project was completed, it contained a total of 22 graves, one of them marked simply with the date and the legend, "Unknown".

Built to supply electricity for the aluminum smelting works in Kinlochleven, Blackwater was the last great engineering scheme in Britain excavated by hand. Life for those involved was, by all accounts, unremittingly harsh. Crammed into a freezing, muddy shanty encampment high up the mountain, many succumbed to disease, malnutrition and exhaustion.

The Irish author Patrick McGee, who worked on the site, gives a chilling account of the conditions in his autobiography *Children of the Dead End* (1914). Hard drinking, gambling and fighting were the order of the day in a camp which, like a scene from the Wild West, was peopled by characters with names like "Moleskin Joe"

and "Two-Shift Mulholland".

The lot of the five thousand labourers who built the West Highland Railway across Rannoch Moor only a few years before can't have been much better. The longest stretch of line ever laid at one time, the West Highland Railway took seven years to complete, and this section across the moor posed more problems to its engineers than the whole of the rest of the line put together. To cross the huge bogs, some lengths had to be set on floating causeways made of brushwood and turf, or run across viaducts.

By the time the line opened in 1894, the old Sassenach suspicions about the Highlands had largely become history. Queen Victoria had made the region fashionable as a holiday destination, and the new railway provided easy access to it for the burgeoning population of Glasgow.

Some of the most ardent explorers of this northwest frontier were the members of the Scottish Mountaineering Club, which formed in 1889, a couple of decades before the completion of the West Highland Railway, when Glencoe's wilderness was still waiting to be discovered. Among the club's founders was Sir Hugh Munro (1856–1919), a keen climber and hill walker who compiled a list of all the Scottish mountains over 3000ft (914m). In all, Munro identified 236 tops, but the list has since swollen to 284. Two of them feature in our route.

1 A well-worn path drops from the Altnafeadh car park on the A86 (at NN221563) to cross the River Coupall via a footbridge. Continue past the Lagangarbh Mountain Rescue cottage, bearing R at a fork reached soon after, which takes you to the bottom of the Coire na Tulaich – a formidable sight from this angle.

A rocky path, recently paved in places by the NTS to forestall erosion, climbs to the R of the stream (ie along its true-left bank). Easy at first, the gradient steepens as you gain height. Progress slows towards the headwall of the corrie, where loose scree makes for hard going. The final stretch, following a rock staircase that's very steep in places, involves one or two simple hand holds. You may find it easier to follow a route further to your R, which switches L higher up as it approaches the ridgetop.

2 Once clear of the corrie, head along the path veering L up the slabby W ridge of Stob Dearg ("Red Peak"; 1022m/3353ft), the highest point on our route, reached after a succession of false summits. If it's not too windy, continue a short way beyond the summit cairn to a famous viewpoint above the so-called "Crowberry Tower",

one of the Buachaille's classic rock climbs, from where a magnificent panorama over **Rannoch Moor** is revealed. Keep your feet firmly planted, though: it's a long way down from here (700m/2296ft, to be precise).

When you've finished admiring the view, return via the same path to point 2 at the top of Coire na Tulaich, then press on over a broad, fairly level saddle-back ridge to a small plateau marked with a cairn,

where the path swings SW. A steeper climb of around 100m/328ft takes you to the second summit of the day, Stob na Doire ("Peak of the Copse"; 1011m/3316ft), our featured viewpoint, chosen because it not only affords a wonderful view over Rannoch Moor, but also back along the graceful arching ridge to Stob Dearg.

3 If you find yourself in cloud, check your compass here

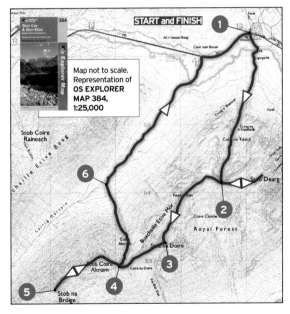

Map not to scale.
Representation of
**OS EXPLORER
MAP 384,
1:25,000**

Route profile

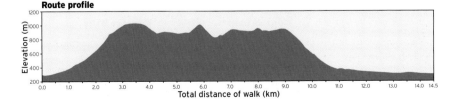

to ensure you head down the correct, SW ridge off Stob na Doire – a sharp, rocky descent leading to a col at the head of Coire Altrium. Carry on up the ridge beyond the col a short way, where a cairn flags the start of the path down the corrie.

4 This all-important location just beyond the low point in the ridge is where you'll return to later to begin your final descent off the mountain, but for the time being, press on NE to the next summit on the Buachaille, Stob Coire Altrium ("Sanctuary Corrie Peak"; 941m/3087ft). From there, a wonderfully airy ridge walk over mostly even ground takes you to the massif's final peak, Stob na Bròige ("Peak of the Shoes"; 956m/3136ft) – another great viewpoint overlooking Glen Etive to the S, and out across the tops of **Glen Coe** to the west coast.

5 From Stob na Bròige, return to Stob Coire Altrium and down its SW shoulder to the cairn passed earlier (at **4**). Turn L here to follow the most straightforward route off the ridge, following a steep line down Coire Altrium. The ground isn't as sheer as the head of Coire na Tulaich, but the descent requires concentration, particularly midway down (at around the 600m/1968ft contour), where you cross a rocky bluff. After heavy rain, when this whole corner can get flooded, or in winter, when the waterfalls remain iced up for weeks on end, you may well have to improvise a route L of the main path.

6 Once at the bottom of Lairig Gartain, cross the Coupall and climb up its far bank to join a very squelchy path that'll take you 2.5km/1.5miles NW across undulating peat hags to the main road; turn R when you reach the layby. As there isn't a walkway along the A82, it's a good idea to keep to the heather just to the R of it – the traffic can be heavy and travels fast along this stretch. The car park at Altnafeadh lies 1km further up the road on your R.

Getting There
Buses en route between Glasgow and Fort William stop at the King's House Hotel. Timetable information for all services is available through Traveline Scotland ℡0871 200 2233, ✎www.travelinescotland.com.

Visitor Information
NTS Visitor Centre
Glen Coe, PH49 4LA
℡0844 493 2222
✎www.glencoe-nts.org.uk/Visitor-Centre-g.asp

Eating & Drinking
The Clachaig Inn
Glen Coe, PH49 4HX
℡01855 811252
✎www.clachaig.com
The Clachaig Inn is an institution among hill walkers, and deservedly so. The only pub in the Glen, it looks straight across the valley to the formidable north face of Bidean nam Bian, and inside holds three cosy bars serving a great range of real ales, single malts and meals. Check their website for forthcoming live-music sessions.

Sleeping
The Clachaig Inn
Glen Coe, PH49 4HX
℡01855 811252

✎www.clachaig.com
The Clachaig also offers a choice of rooms, all en suite, smartly furnished, reasonably priced and perfectly placed for walks in and around the Glen.

King's House Hotel
Glen Coe, PH49 4HY
℡01855 851259
✎www.kingy.com
Shabbier and less commercial than the Clachaig Inn, the King's House hasn't been refurbished for years, though it's still an option worth considering, primarily for its location bang opposite the Buachaille, close to the start of our route. Not all the rooms have en suite bathrooms and toilets. Campers can erect tents for free next to the hotel.

More Info
✎www.mwis.org.uk. Detailed weather forecast for the mountains of the central Highlands, aimed primarily at walkers.

✎www.glencoe-nts.org.uk/Visitor-Centre-g.asp. Presents a great roundup of the Glen's history, geology and wildlife, as well as introducing facilities in the swanky, £3-million NTS Visitor Centre.

✎www.undiscoveredscotland.co.uk. A dependable site dedicated to promoting Scotland's less known corners, with a packed page on the Glen and environs.

More Walks
Collins Rambler's Guide: Ben Nevis & Glen Coe by Chris Townsend (Collins/Ramblers). Thirty walks, from 4km/2.5miles to 20km/12miles, exploring lochs, glens and mountains.

walk 49

CUMBRIA

A Lakeland Shangri-La

Yewbarrow

Wasdale, in the far-flung southwestern corner of the Lake District, is a place of superlatives: home of England's highest mountain, its deepest lake, smallest church and (believe it or not) biggest liar. Following a national vote on the subject for a recent ITV series, the valley also boasts "Britain's Favourite View". Accompanying film footage focused on the vistas to be had from the single-track road running up the dale via the edge of Wast Water, with its dramatic ring of pyramidal summits. But as any self-respecting local fell walker will tell you, this panorama – superb though it undoubtedly is – is a pale shadow of what can be seen from the high ridges above.

No photograph can prepare you for view over Wasdale Head. Seen from the hillsides to the west, the great mountains across the valley, dusted in snow for much of the winter, rise like stern-faced giants from the walled pastures below. They are cut with vast gashes of scree – at their most expansive on the southern side of Wast Water, from where they sweep in a near-vertical wall to Whin Rigg and Illgill Head.

At 978m/3208ft, Scafell Pike is the king of the castle hereabouts, the highest point in the land and a peak whose appearance more

than lives up to its status. Gouged by arrow-straight stream gullies, its slopes rise in spectacular lines to a crown of jagged crags, often swathed in cloud. It's a scene with no equal in the Lake District, and one that's best admired from a relatively little known fell on the opposite side of Wasdale Head. Yewbarrow's diminutive stature ensures it's often overlooked by peak baggers, but the hill's exceptionally steep sides allow some astonishing viewpoints.

A short, sharp approach to the summit can be made in less than an hour from Overbeck Bridge, at the northern end of Wast Water, half an hour's walk from the Wasdale Head Inn. However, it's worth setting aside a whole day to follow the classic route around the crest of the hidden valley to the north – Mosedale – approaching Yewbarrow through its upper defences of Stirrup Crag.

Dubbed the "Mosedale Horseshoe", this ranks among the very finest hill days Britain has to offer, and one that'll redefine your picture of the Lake District if you've never ventured beyond the central honeypots. Wild, austere and remote, Wasdale is as far away from the fluffy bunnies of Beatrix Potter as it's possible to imagine.

At a glance

Where Wasdale Head, 16km/10miles southwest of Keswick, the Lake District.
Why Iconic Lakeland views over England's highest mountain, Scafell Pike; Britain's deepest lake; the Wasdale Head Inn.

When May: during the annual Keswick Mountain Festival.
Downsides Accommodation limited during busy periods; public transport infrequent.
Start/Finish Wasdale Head Inn (NY187087), Wasdale Head.

Duration 5hrs 30mins-7hrs.
Distance 17km/10.6miles.
Terrain Mostly rocky paths over exposed ridges, requiring fluency with map and compass, and, ideally, GPS.
Maps OS Explorer OL4 and OL6.

The view over Wasdale Head to Scafell
and Scafell Pike from Yewbarrow

On your way

Protected on three sides by the behemoths of Kirk Fell, Great Gable, Lingmell and Scafell Pike, and on the fourth by the lake, **WASDALE HEAD** is a mountain sanctuary with a unique atmosphere. Its physical remoteness has screened this spectacular cul de sac from the scourges of mass tourism. But it didn't deter the Danes, who ravaged the area a thousand or more years ago. Vestiges of Scandinavian words survive in many of the place names and in the local dialect. The village church of St Olaf's, dedicated to a Norse chieftain who converted to Christianity, even incorporates the timbers of a Viking longboat in its roof beams. Surrounded by yew trees, the chapel is said to be the smallest in England.

A still more pervasive legacy of the Nordic presence is the sheep that graze the surrounding high fells. Herdwicks (from the Norse for "sheep pasture", *herdvyk*) are the hardiest of breeds, exceptionally well adapted to the harsh conditions in which they winter, foraging wild in the snow and sleet. Because they mature slowly and yield coarse wool, farming them would no longer be viable without subsidies from the EU and National Trust. But without them the landscape of Wasdale, with its close cropped grass and countless miles of drystone walls, would look very different.

The valley came close to losing its flocks during the foot and mouth crisis of 2001. Herdwicks are what farmers describe as "heafted" – that is, they keep close to familiar pastures throughout their lives, with knowledge of the land passed from ewe to lamb. So when the disease wiped out 25% of Wasdale's sheep, new animals bought as replacements kept wandering over dangerous crags and getting lost.

In April and May, the ewes are returned "inbye" – to the fields on the valley floor – to have their lambs and be clipped. The complex jigsaw of walled farmland where they're kept is a defining feature of the village.

Another is the profile of the **WASDALE HEAD INN**, an institution here since the 1870s, when it became the birthplace of British climbing. After a hearty breakfast, intrepid fellsmen would set off to explore the surrounding crags dressed in tweeds and hobnail boots. The tombstones of some of those who never returned lie in the graveyard of St Olaf's.

As well as a formidable selection of real ales, the inn also claims to be the residence of the world's biggest liar – an assertion that,

The High-Level Traverse

Regarded by generations of Lakeland aficionados as one of the finest miles of footpath in the region, the so-called High-Level Traverse makes an exhilarating alternative approach to Pillar – though one that should be embarked upon with caution. It starts gently enough, contouring around the mountainside to "Robinson's Cairn", a memorial to a local climber who, before his death in 1907, used to jog here and back from his home in Lorton (ten miles away) for a day's rock sport. Once beyond the cairn, however, the path has a radical shift of mood as it first drops across a scree field, then climbs up the other side to begin the so-called "Shamrock Traverse" above the mighty crags buttressing the mountain's northern flank. From a ledge looking down on Pillar Rock, an awesome formation comprising the two towers of Pisgah and High Man, the remaining leg to the summit involves a short but strenuous scramble up a gully.

by definition, should be viewed with some skepticism. It refers to a competition held every November in a pub down the valley, and which is almost always won either by the landlord of the Wasdale Head Inn or of his staff (although the stand-up comic Sue Perkins triumphed a few years back).

The idea of the event (from which "politicians and lawyers" are resolutely excluded) is that participants have five minutes in which to tell the most convincing fibs they can; extra marks seem to be given for ludicrous ones. A recent winner, for example, tried to convince incredulous onlookers that the Lake District had not been formed by glacial action but by eels and moles, and that a new Ministry of Underwater Fisheries and Food ("MUFF") was monitoring aquatic life in Wast Water. Entering into the spirit of the competition, Wasdale Head's village website cited an attendance figure of 50,000.

ABOVE: Looking down Wast Water from the south summit of Yewbarrow

CHECKED BY
☑ **West Cumbria Ramblers**

1 Walk through the gates of the **Wasdale Head Inn**, and bear L in front of the Barn Door outdoor gear shop, passing the entrance to Ritson's Bar on your L. The path turns R through a gate and runs behind the buildings to cross a stile – ignore the trail running over the pretty stone-arched footbridge to your L and keep following the beck upstream with the wall to your R, bearing L at a fork soon after. At the top of the rise, you pass through a gate (not the gate to its L) and follow the path along the wall to another gate.

From here, Mosedale is unveiled in all its glory, with an equally spectacular view back over Yewbarrow's Stirrup Crag, and the scree spilling from Dore Head. The onward path is clearly visible as it first dips to ford a couple of streams, then bends gently R, passing through another gate and across a rushing beck to begin its zigzagging ascent of Gatherstone Head. Once on top of this rise the gradient eases as the path approaches Black Sail Pass.

2 A line of rusty iron boundary posts runs L (NW) from the cairn at the pass – a useful navigation aid should the weather close in – towards the balcony

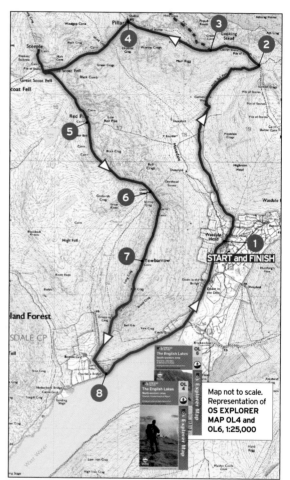

Map not to scale.
Representation of
**OS EXPLORER
MAP OL4 and
OL6, 1:25,000**

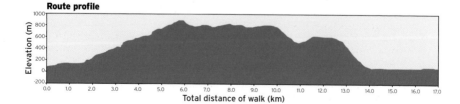

Route profile

(Route profile graph: Elevation (m) from -200 to 1000 on vertical axis; Total distance of walk (km) from 0.0 to 17.0 on horizontal axis)

of Looking Stead (worth the detour R for fine views over Ennerdale). Keep climbing over this high shoulder until the ground suddenly steepens.

3 Heading R from a pronounced step in the ridge (at NY184117) is the famous alternative route up Pillar via the so-called High-Level Traverse (see box), its start marked by a cairn. The main path heading L, meanwhile, scales the steep ridgeline ahead, skirting a series of impressive gullies as it approaches the domed top of Pillar (892m/2926ft).

4 Head SW from the trig point on the summit of Pillar to begin a short, steep and rocky descent to aptly named Wind Gap. From here, a correspondingly stiff climb up the opposite side leads after 20mins or so to the undulating summit plateau of Black Crag (828m/2726ft). The path peters out a little as it crosses this top, but grows clearer on the far side, where a narrow band of pasture falls between crags to a junction at NY162115.

Those with sufficient time and energy should consider the detour to Scoat Fell (841m/2759ft), which begins at the path heading off to the R here, then winds up the ridge to follow a wall all the way to the summit cairn. Having got that far, be sure to press on to Steeple (819m/2687ft), the wedge-shaped peak just to the N, only a short walk away. Return by the same route to the top of Scoat Fell, heading SE beyond the summit wall to pick up the main Mosedale horseshoe path again, which from the junction below Black Crag

bends south to start the climb up Red Pike (826m/2709ft). You can make the ascent of Red Pike by sticking close to the spine of the ridge, or by following a lower, easier path to the R.

5 After the breezy amble from the seat cairn on top of Red Pike to the mountain's rocky south summit (801m/2628ft; at NY165101), a long, knee-crunching descent ensues as you drop SE to Dore Head. This saddle below Red Pike, beneath the dark folds of Stirrup Crag, is where you have to decide whether to make one final push over the top of Yewbarrow – our featured viewpoint – or to go for the softer option of a descent down Over Beck.

6 The latter involves a straightforward plod on a moorland path to the south of the stream. The former can seem a more forbidding prospect, but on closer inspection turns out to be a short "grade 1" scramble, weaving its way up Stirrup Crag by means of a steep, stony path followed by a squeeze up a hidden gully. You'll need to use your hands most of the way, but there are plenty of good food and hand holds.

7 Once on top of Yewbarrow, an amazing panorama unfolds, which only grows more spectacular as you progress along the peaty ridge to the summit cairn, from where almost the full length of Wast Water is revealed, along with the Scafell massif on the opposite side of the valley.

The descent, which follows a distinct path to the R of the crag on the southern tip of Yewbarrow known as the Great Door, wriggles

down the gully of Dropping Crag, where you'll need to use your hands again. As well as being steep, the path is heavily eroded, loose in places and occasionally indistinct: anyone not confident descending unstable scree will be better off retracing their steps or missing out Yewbarrow altogether. Soon, however, the ground grows less precipitous, and the path merges with the gentler one skirting the southern side of Over Beck for last leg down to Overbeck Bridge. After the path junction, cross the wall via the ladder stile, then follow the fencing downhill, bearing L at the bottom, as indicated by a footpath sign, to climb over one last stile. From there, the path follows a narrow wood above the beck to a car park on the roadside.

8 Turn L on to the tarmac, and follow the road for 3.2km/2miles back to **Wasdale Head** - a walk that's a lot less dull than it might sound, thanks to the glorious scenery.

🚌 Getting There
The nearest railhead is at Drigg, 13km/8miles southwest. Taxi buses operate from Seascale and Gosforth to Wasdale Head on Thursdays, Saturdays and Sundays; book before 6pm on the day prior to your journey by telephoning ☎019467 25308. Timetables can be viewed at ✎www.cumbria.gov. uk/elibrary

i Visitor Information
The Gosforth Pottery in nearby Gosforth holds a Lake District National Park information point.
☎019467 25296.

ABOVE: The old packhorse bridge near the Wasdale Head Inn

Eating & Drinking
Ritson's Bar
Wasdale Head Inn
(See below)
If all you want after a hard day on the fells is a hot meal and a proper pint in a bar with oodles of old-fashioned Lakeland charm, look no further than the public bar in the Wasdale Head Inn – though be warned that its food is overpriced and the service not always smiling. Try their cracking house beers, brewed on the premises.

Sleeping
The Wasdale Head Inn
Wasdale Head, CA20 1EX
019467 26229
www.wasdaleheadinn.co.uk
The world-famous inn at the top of the valley sits at a plum spot, in the heart of the high fells. Prices reflect its near monopoly, but the en suite rooms, most of which lie on the first floor and enjoy fine views, are comfortable enough. They also offer a suite for families, and some self-catering options.

Burnthwaite Farm
Wasdale Head, CA20 1EX
019467 26242
www.burnthwaitefarm.co.uk
B&B with simple, spacious rooms (showers and toilets are shared) on a working sheep farm, 5mins' walk from the pub down a rocky lane. You also get the run of a lounge with an open fire. A sound and welcoming budget option.

National Trust Campsite
Wasdale Head, CA20 1EX
019467 26064
www.nationaltrust.org.uk
This has to be one of the most fabulous campsites in the world, thanks to its setting near the head of the lake; and they even have electric hook ups these days. Open year round, but with reduced facilities Nov–Easter.

More Info
www.wasdaleweb.co.uk.
Handy links to all the businesses in the area, including B&Bs and self-catering accommodation.

www.herdwick-sheep.com.
Everything you ever wanted to know about Herdwicks.

www.wasdale-mountain-rescue.org.uk. This lot are on standby to save your bacon: respect!

www.lake-district.gov.uk. The national park's site.

More Walks
Collins Ramblers Guide: The Lake District by John Gillham & Ron Turnbull (Collins/Ramblers). Thirty detailed routes, ranging from a short 7km/4.5mile route around Hampsfell, to a 21km/13miler in the Langdale Pikes.

Walks in South Lakeland (Kendal Ramblers). Eighteen walks ranging in length from 6.5km/4miles to 24km/15miles. Most are low-level, but some are on the higher fells.

Walks in South Lakeland Book 2 (Kendal Ramblers). Eighteen new walks, as described above.

A Peek into the Cauldron

Sgùrr na Stri

It is ironic that the Black Cuillin of Skye are often referred to as "hills". Ironic, because this is one of the few ranges in Britain which most continental Europeans would recognize as proper mountains. Jagged, bare and dark brown in colour, the peaks form a dragon's-back ridge which, despite being only one fifth the height of Mont Blanc, more closely resembles an Alpine massif than any other in this country. The Cuillin's isolated position, tucked away on the least accessible corner of "the Isle of Mists", explains why their distinctive profile is not better known. Because it's entirely surrounded by wilderness, the range is difficult to view close up.

You get a wonderful glimpse of it side-on from Elgol, to the south. But for an unimpeded view of the full amphitheatre, with all twelve of its Munros on display, you have to walk for several hours down one of the wildest, most rugged glens in Scotland, and then climb a little hill few Scottish mountain enthusiasts would even be able to name.

At 494m/1620ft, Sgùrr na Stri may be a wimp among giants, but its view can kick metaphorical sand in the face of any of its loftier cousins nearby. It offers, quite simply, one of Scotland's – indeed, Britain's – most spectacular panoramas.

There are two reasons why. Firstly, like a child who's squeezed through the grown-ups legs to get to the ring side, the hill occupies a prime position facing the "open end" of the Cuillin cauldron, with nothing rising between it and the famous pinnacles.

The second is that from the summit of Sgùrr na Stri you gain an exclusive, bird's eye peek at the jewel in the range's crown: Loch Coruisk. Walled in on three sides by soaring cliffs and corries, this exquisite glacial lake forms the centerpiece of a perfect mountain sanctuary – completely wild and pristine, save for a lone cottage on its shore. Excursion boats run across Loch Scavaig from Elgol to within a stone's throw of this Hebridean Shangri-La. But only Sgùrr na Stri surveys the entire length of the lake, and takes in its awesome backdrop, along with a sprinkling of islands out to sea, in one rolling vista.

The hilltop lies a long trudge away from the nearest roadhead. But nobody who's ever done the walk on a clear day returns feeling short-changed: catch a window in the weather, when the Cuillin's tops are revealed in all their glory, and you'll be rewarded with what many regard as Britain's ultimate view.

At a glance

Where Sligachan, 14km/9miles south of Portree, Isle of Skye.
Why Black Cuillin and Loch Coruisk; spectacular walk in, passing Glamaig and Marsco; a historic mountaineers' inn.
When You stand your best chance of clear weather in May.
Downsides The Cuillin's tops are rarely clear of cloud.
Start/Finish Sligachan Hotel (NG486298), Sligachan.
Duration 7-9hrs.
Distance 23km/14.3miles.
Terrain Mostly clear, rocky paths, with straightforward stream crossings and a final ascent over rough, pathless hillside for which navigational skills are required in poor visibility.
Maps OS Explorer 411.

On your way

Opinion is divided over the origins of the name "Cuillin". While some historians suggest it recalls a great warrior chief of Scottish legend, Cuchullin, others claim it derives from the Gaelic word "holly" – *cuilionn* – a reference to the range's prickly main ridge. Another plausible explanation is that the word has its roots in *kjølen*, old Norse for "high mountain".

Whatever the source of its name, there's no doubt of the origins of the massif's shark's-tooth-shaped summits: a volcanic rock called gabbro. Dark red, grey-brown or black depending on the light, gabbro is not only extremely hard, but also grippy, even when wet, which accounts for the popularity of the Cuillin among scramblers and climbers.

Boasting some of the toughest routes in Britain, the range is primarily famous for the great traverse of its central ridge. Hundreds complete this formidable

walkbritain

Great Views

The Ramblers' top 50 walking routes to Britain's finest views

Foreword by BBC Coast presenter Mark Horton

ramblers

walkbritain

First edition: *Great Views*, published April 2009
ISBN: 978-1-906494-04-9

Published by the Ramblers
020 7339 8500
www.ramblers.org.uk

A CIP catalogue record for this book is available from
the British Library.

Distributed by Frances Lincoln
www.franceslincoln.com

Mapping produced by Global Mapping Limited
www.globalmapping.uk.com

Designed by
River Publishing
www.riverltd.co.uk
Printed and bound in Italy by Imago

This product includes mapping data licensed from
Ordnance Survey® with the permission of the
Controller of Her Majesty's Stationery Office.
©Crown Copyright 2009. All rights reserved. Licence
number: 100033886.

Going for a walk and exploring the countryside on a
day out is a great and cost-effective way of exercising.
Ordnance Survey is delighted to be working in
partnership with the Ramblers to help make it easier to
get outdoors and get active.

The Ramblers' Association is a registered charity in
England & Wales (no: 1093577), a registered charity in
Scotland (no: SC039799), and a company limited by
guarantee registered in England and Wales (company
registration no: 4458492).
Registered office: 2nd Floor, Camelford House, 87-90
Albert Embankment, London SE1 7TW.

challenge each year, taking an average of ten to fourteen hours to cover the full course. In May 2008, however, a 27-year-old student from Edinburgh named Es Tressider managed it in a record-breaking three hours and seventeen minutes – then hitch-hiked home afterwards.

Since the birth of climbing as a sport in the late nineteenth century, the traditional watering hole for visiting crag hoppers has been the **SLIGACHAN HOTEL**, at the head of Loch Sligachan (pronounced "Sli-ga-han", "Lake of the Small Shells"), where our route begins. A small museum inside gathers photographs, old newspaper clippings and other documents relating to the earliest ascents of the area's Munros, made by gentlemen climbers in tweed suits and hobnail boots.

The Sligachan Hotel looks across the head of the glen to Sgùrr nan Gillean (964m/3162ft), the mostly northerly of the range's big tops. On the opposite side of the valley, the view is dominated by **GLAMAIG**

(775m/2542ft), northernmost outlyer of the so-called "Red Cuillin" range. This shapely peak was the scene of another record-breaking feat in 1889, when a Nepali Gurkha soldier named Harkabir Tharpa ran from the bar of the hotel to the summit and back in a breathless 55 minutes – barefoot. A race is held each year in July to commemorate the achievement.

From the foot of Glamaig, the path along the floor of Glen Sligachan winds south across countless sidestreams and glacial debris. The scenery grows a notch more spectacular once you're beneath the distinctive pyramid of **MWSCO**, opposite which awesome **HARTA CORRIE** curves into the main Cuillin massif to the west.

A large boulder on the floor of the corrie, known as "the Bloody Stone", recalls that this side valley was in past centuries the scene of several violent encounters between the MacDonald and MacLeod clans. The goriest of all their battles, however, took place on the far side of the ridge above Harta – the equally desolate Coire na Creiche, "Corrie of Spoils".

This is where, in 1601, a decades-old feud between the two rival clans reached its climax. A clue to the catalyst of the struggle lies in its name – the "War of the One-Eyed Woman". Local legend holds that the woman in question was the daughter of a MacLeod chief who'd married one of the MacDonalds' sons. It was traditional in those days to observe a cooling-off period of one year after a wedding – a custom known as "hand-fasting" – during which the marriage could be terminated by either partner. In this instance, it seems the groom tired of his new wife after she'd lost an eye in an accident, and then failed to bear him a child. So before the trial year was up, the MacDonalds decided to return her to her father's house, putting her on a one-eyed horse, led by a one-eyed man and dog.

Such a cruel insult could only have been intended to rub salt in old wounds, which is exactly what happened. A terrible clan war erupted that culminated with a mass slaughter at Coire na Creiche, after which there were virtually no clansmen left on Skye to wield a broadsword.

Violence, loss and lament are implicit in many of the Gaelic place names in this wild corner of Skye. "**SGÙRR NA STRI**" itself means "Peak of Strife" – most likely a throwback to the tragedy of the mid-nineteenth century, when crofters at the hill's base, in the hamlet of Camasunary, were "cleared" by the local landlord. They fled to the tiny islet of Soay, just across Loch Scavaig, where more than one hundred refugees scraped a living.

Evacuated in the early 1950s, Soay was where author Gavin Maxwell (of *Ring of Bright Water* fame) later set up a factory to

process shark oil. The misguided initiative, which floundered after only a few years and all but wiped out Loch Scavaig's population of basking sharks, is described in the book *Harpoon at a Venture*.

The dominant feature of the view from the top of Sgùrr na Stri, however, is less the islands of the Inner Hebrides – Soay, Muck, Eigg, Canna and Rum – spread across the Minch to the southwest, than the Black Cuillin, and in particular, Loch Coruisk unfolding to the west. Few outsiders knew of this beautiful lake's existence until Sir Walter Scott, who'd accompanied a party of lighthouse servicemen on a tour, set eyes on it in 1814. But the experience inspired a now famous description in his last epic poem, *Lord of the Isles*, where Robert the Bruce and his men take refuge in the awesome corrie behind the lake.

"For all is rocks at random thrown/Black Waves, bare crags, and banks of stone," wrote Scott. His picture of Loch Coruisk was exaggeratedly stark, but it enticed JMW Turner, and a string of other painters in his wake, to travel to Skye to see it, and their images put this extraordinary landscape on the nineteenth-century tourism map.

Apart from the addition of a tiny white mountain rescue hut (a memorial to two young climbers who died in Glen Coe in 1953) nothing has changed at Loch Coruisk since Scott first came here. That said, the lake does attract boat-loads of visitors from Elgol these days – though high up in the eagle's lair of Sgùrr na Stri, with the isles stretching across the sea into the distance, you'll be blissfully oblivious of their presence.

BELOW: Sgùrr na Stri (right) rising from the green floodplain of Camasunary

1 Cross the old packhorse bridge in front of the **Sligachan Hotel**, with **Glamaig** towering ahead, and bear R through the gate along the path signposted "Elgol & Loch Coruisk". Bear R at a fork after the next gate, as indicated: this takes you onto the pitched path running south all the way down the glen. It becomes progressively rougher and rockier, with numerous small stream crossings and boggy patches to negotiate – but is easy to follow throughout.

2 Three kilometres or so into the walk you reach a major tributary stream, the Allt na Meassaroch, flowing from the L, which you ford via stepping stones. From here on the path rises gently over saturated ground around the foot of **Marsco**, giving a great view up **Harta Corrie** across the valley. Growing a little drier underfoot, it then bends slightly to the L as

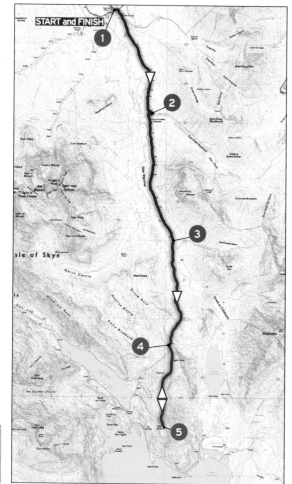

Map not to scale.
Representation of
**OS EXPLORER
MAP 411, 1:25,000**

Route profile

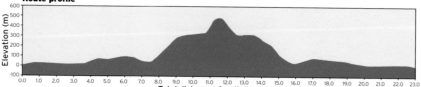

it crests an almost imperceptible watershed. Just after the path begins to drop, look out for a prominent fork, marked with a cairn.

3 Bear R at this fork, which crosses another large stream, then skirts the river. Dominating the valley at this point is the massive bulk of Blàbheinn's west face. After a boggy section, the path starts to rise up the R (W) side of the valley via a stony, badly-eroded path. The summit visible ahead is not, alas, that of Sgùrr na Stri, but Sgùrr Hain (418m/1371ft), whose north ridge you eventually crest after a strenuous 40-min climb from the valley floor.

4 The view of the Cuillin from the pass, marked with cairns, is formidable, taking in all of the range's major summits, and the bottom end of Loch Coruisk. Make a detour to the R for even better vistas down to the loch. When you're done at the pass, bear L at the fork ahead (the path branching R would take you down to sea level), and follow the clear and mostly level, but boggy, path around Sgùrr Hain.
This path gets gradually rougher and wetter as it approaches the bottom of the **Sgùrr na Stri**'s north ridge. With the summit firmly in your sights, strike L up the ridge, improvising a route over lumpy patches of grass and rock. This section can be hard going.
The final stretch to the top takes you over a huge, inclined slab, which can be easily avoided if desired by following the green slope to its R. Either way, you shouldn't have to tackle any real scrambling to reach the summit.

5 Return by the same route. The descent is straightforward from the pass north of Sgùrr Hain onwards (stages **4**-**1**), but in poor visibility, the first leg, from the summit to the pass (**5**-**4**), can require careful navigation. Descend too far, and you'll miss the path contouring north around the hill.

Getting There
Any of the buses running from the mainland to Portree will drop you at the Sligachan Hotel.

Visitor Information
Portree TIC
Bayfield House, Portree, IV51 9EL
☎ 01478 612137

Eating & Drinking
There's only one place to refuel and bed down within reach of our route. Thankfully, the Sligachan Inn (below.) has most needs covered, whether you're camping or splashing out on a hotel room.

Sleeping
The Sligachan Inn
Sligachan, Isle of Skye, IV47 8SW
☎ 01478 650204
✐ www.sligachan.co.uk
The famous nineteenth-century hotel at the top of the glen holds 21 en suite rooms, most of them with great views across to Glamaig and Sgùrr nan Gillean. On the ground floor is a smart restaurant and a couple of bars serving beer from the inn's own micro-brewery. They also have a self-catering lodge, a basic bunkhouse, and even run a seasonal campsite across the road.

More Info
✐ www.mwis.org.uk. Daily weather bulletins for the mountains of the northwest Highlands.

✐ www.es-on-ice.co.uk/article/show/5. The full story of Ed Tressider's record-breaking run over the bristly Skye Ridge.

✐ www.bellajane.co.uk & ✐ mistyisleboattrips.co.uk. Home pages of the two riival boat operators running excursions to Loch Coruisk from Elgol.

More Walks
✐ www.walkhighlands.co.uk/skye. Dependable route descriptions for fine walks at all levels on Skye, including a few in and around Sligachan and the Cuillin, backed up with downloadable maps, photos and GPS waypoints.

Collins Rambler's Guide: Isle of Skye by Chris Townsend (Collins/Ramblers). Thirty walks over a range of distances and levels of difficulty exploring the full gamut of mountain and marine landscapes on Skye. Featured is the famous shoreline walk to Camasunary from Elgol, passing the notorious "Bad Step" below Sgùrr na Stri.

ABOVE: The Black Cuillin from Elgol

Index

Index

JOIN US

If you've enjoyed reading this guide, why not sign up to the Ramblers? Members receive **walkbritain**'s Great Views completely free. Also by joining the Ramblers you'll be supporting the work of Britain's biggest charity for walkers. Our campaigns' work across town and countryside, protecting Britain's ancient network of public paths and championing access to wild and beautiful places. We're also one of Britain's key organizations promoting walking for health and wellbeing.

Our historic campaigns have led to the introduction of national parks and the GB-wide mapping of footpaths. Today we're as busy as ever standing up for the rights of everyone who walks. Please visit our website for more information about our campaigns: www.ramblers.org.uk

ramblers
at the heart of walking